CRIMINALIZING THE CASBAHS

A volume in the series

Police/Worlds: Studies in Security, Crime, and Governance
Edited by Kevin Karpiak, Sameena Mulla, William Garriott, and Ilana Feldman

A list of titles in this series is available at cornellpress.cornell.edu.

CRIMINALIZING THE CASBAHS

Policing North Africans in
Marseille and Algiers,
1918–1954

Danielle Beaujon

CORNELL UNIVERSITY PRESS   ITHACA AND LONDON

Copyright © 2025 by Cornell University

All rights reserved. Except for brief quotations in a review, this book, or parts thereof, must not be reproduced in any form without permission in writing from the publisher. For information, address Cornell University Press, Sage House, 512 East State Street, Ithaca, New York 14850. Visit our website at cornellpress.cornell.edu.

First published 2025 by Cornell University Press

Library of Congress Cataloging-in-Publication Data

Names: Beaujon, Danielle, 1993- author.
Title: Criminalizing the Casbahs : policing North Africans in Marseille and Algiers, 1918-1954 / Danielle Beaujon.
Description: Ithaca : Cornell University Press, 2025. | Series: Police/Worlds: studies in security, crime, and governance | Includes bibliographical references and index.
Identifiers: LCCN 2024049165 (print) | LCCN 2024049166 (ebook) | ISBN 9781501781476 (hardcover) | ISBN 9781501781483 (paperback) | ISBN 9781501781490 (ebook) | ISBN 9781501781506 (pdf)
Subjects: LCSH: Racism in law enforcement—France—Marseille—History—20th century. | Racism in law enforcement—Algeria—Algiers—History—20th century. | Police brutality—France—Marseille—History—20th century. | Police brutality—Algeria—Algiers—History—20th century. | North Africans—France—Marseille—Social conditions. | North Africans—Algeria—Algiers—Social conditions.
Classification: LCC HV8204 .B45 2025 (print) | LCC HV8204 (ebook) | DDC 364.1/30944912—dc23/eng/20241220
LC record available at https://lccn.loc.gov/2024049165
LC ebook record available at https://lccn.loc.gov/2024049166

*To my Mother, who introduced me to her love
of France and words.
To my Father, who taught me to ask questions.*

Contents

Acknowledgments	ix
List of Abbreviations	xi
A Note on Terminology	xii
Introduction	1
1. Controlling Mediterranean Movement	17
2. Locating Dangerous Algerians	48
3. Policing an Empire at War	74
4. Mapping the Enemy Within	101
5. A New Police for a New Republic	128
6. Policing Politics at the End of Empire	155
Epilogue	180
Notes	189
Bibliography	229
Index	241

Acknowledgments

Though my name is on the cover, this book would not have been possible without a much larger community. I began this research in graduate school at New York University, and the people I met there shaped my project from an amorphous interest into a reality. In this, I am grateful to the faculty in the History department, the Institute of French Studies, and most particularly my committee members: Edward Berenson, Frederick Cooper, and Robyn D'Avignon. I am also grateful to Jim House, whose work inspired my interest and whose insightful suggestions pushed me in new directions. Over the years, several scholars generously took time to discuss my work with me, including Natalya Benkhaled-Vince, Emmanuel Blanchard, Melissa Byrnes, Joshua Cole, Claire Eldridge, Samuel Kalman, Chris Millington, Kenneth Mouré, Clifford Rosenberg, Emmanuelle Saada, and Sylvie Thénault. Most of all, I owe my profound gratitude to my PhD advisor Herrick Chapman, who has seen and shaped this project at every iteration. Thank you for teaching me how to be a historian.

This book is also indebted to a myriad of institutions that provided material support and technical expertise. My research was sponsored by the American Institute for Maghrib Studies Short-Term Research Fellowship, the Robert Holmes Research Award for African Scholarship, the Michel Beaujour Doctoral Research Fellowship, the Remarque Institute-École Normale Supérieure Doctoral Fellowship, and the Mellon Pre-Dissertation Grant. Funding from the US Department of Education Foreign Language and Area Studies Fellowship allowed me to develop my knowledge of Arabic. The writing of this book was also supported by the Institute for Research on Race and Public Policy at the University of Illinois Chicago and by an Institute for Advanced Studies Aix-Marseille University (Iméra) Fellowship.

I am grateful for the feedback that portions of this book received through the Centre d'Études Maghrébines en Algérie (CEMA) in Oran, the University of Chicago's Transnational Approaches to Modern Europe workshop, Stanford University's French Culture workshop, the University of Illinois Chicago's Global Middle East Studies working group, and the Reading, Researching and Writing the French Empire workshop. I am also appreciative of the archivists and librarians who helped me, particularly at the Archives Nationales d'Outre-Mer, the Archives Départementales des Bouches-du-Rhône, and the Bibliothèque Nationale de l'Algérie. Some material in chapters 4 and 5 has been previously published as "The Algerian Enemies Within: Policing the Black Market in Marseille and Algiers, 1939–1950" in *French Historical Studies* vol. 47, no. 1 (2024): 289–318.

At Cornell University Press, I am grateful to my editors—Jim Lance and Bethany Wasik. I also want to thank my series editor, Kevin Karpaik, for believing in this book and offering guidance. Several scholars gave me invaluable feedback on the completed manuscript, including my anonymous reviewer, Jennifer Boittin, Herrick Chapman, Julian Go, Minayo Nasiali, and Sandrine Sanos (of Les Plumes Rouges). Jill Petty provided editorial advice and, as important, confidence in my writing. Tim Stallmann created the excellent maps for this book.

I could not have finished this book without the support of my friends and colleagues, including my friends outside academic circles who reminded me that there was more to life than this book. My work was informed by exchanges with scholars in the GROC collective, especially Vincent Bollenot and Aliénor Cadiot. Greg Valdespino shared conversations about colonial urbanism and curated the joy of the French Empire virtual workshop with me. Special thanks to Brooke Durham, for traveling through France and Algeria with me and designing conference panels so we can catch up. To Hilary Handin, Emily Shuman, and the MacDougal Street History Workshop, including Mohamed Abdou, Kimberly Cheng, Danny Cumming, Marek Eby, June Hawkins, Briana Royster, Sarah Sklaw, Michael Salgarolo, Brittney Lewer, and Emma Young, for reading seemingly endless chapter drafts and championing me when academia got hard. In many ways, you feel like coauthors. Sarah Griswold and Jess Pearson provided mentorship and kindness—the best of the IFS is evident in you both.

At the University of Illinois Chicago, I am grateful to my Bridge to Faculty cohort, the Global Middle East Studies Cluster, and my Criminology, Law, & Justice and History colleagues, especially Dean Adams, Liat Ben-Moshe, Jessica Bird, Andy Clarno, Xiomara Cornejo, Zack Cuyler, Lisa Frohmann, Alana Gunn, Susila Gurusami, Clare Kim, Rahim Kurwa, Bill McCarty, Ellen McClure, Ashley Muchow, Nadine Naber, Nicole Nguyen, Ivón Padilla-Rodríguez, Naomi Paik, Justin Phan, Kareem Rabie, Beth Richie, Atef Said, Dave Stovall, Julian Thompson, Torin White, and Zeina Zaatari. Thank you all for welcoming me into your communities and working tirelessly for a better world. I found structure, solidarity, and friendship in my writing group with Yasmine Espert. My thanks to Ash Stephens for offering sage advice, sharing an office, and sending excellent GIFs.

Finally, nothing in my life, scholarly or personal, would be possible without the love of my family. My sister, Christie, provided comfort and distraction and always knew the right thing to say. My parents, Patty and George Beaujon, believed in me, encouraged me, and pushed me to be curious. This book is dedicated to them.

Abbreviations

AMA	Association des Musulmans Algériens
BAMNA	Bureau des Affaires Musulmanes Nord-Africaines
BNA	Brigade Nord-Africaine
CIE	Centre d'Information et d'Études
CAI	Service de Contrôle et d'Assistance en France des Indigènes des Colonies
ENA	Étoile Nord-Africaine
FLN	Front de Libération Nationale
HCM	Haut Comité Méditerranéen
MOI	Office de la Main-d'œuvre Indigène
MTLD	Mouvement pour le Triomphe des Libertés Démocratiques
PPA	Parti du Peuple Algérien
RG	Renseignements Généraux
SAA	Service des Affaires Algériennes
SAINA	Service des Affaires Indigènes Nord-Africaines
SLNA	Service des Liaisons Nord-Africaines
UDMA	Union Démocratique du Manifeste Algérien

A Note on Terminology

I use *Algerian* to refer to what French administrators would have called *indigènes* or *Français Musulmans d'Algérie*. Although *Algerian* flattens ethnic, linguistic, religious, and class divisions, I use it to distinguish Algerians from French and European settler populations, whom I refer to as *European*. Algerian Jews had also lived in Algeria for centuries, but in police parlance, *indigène* meant the nominally Muslim population, and my use of *Algerian* refers to this same group. I also use *North African*, particularly when discussing Marseille, to include the small numbers of Moroccan and Tunisian migrants also present in the city.

I intentionally leave the word *indigène* untranslated in quotes, as the offensive colonial term has no obvious English translation. *Indigène* was both a legal category defined by the *indigénat* code and a derogatory racial marker, used to refer to the population I call *Algerian*.

All archival material used in this book is freely available to the public, per French and Algerian laws. However, given the sensitive nature of many stories, I protect the anonymity of those accused of misconduct in police records by using only their first name and last initial. Police officers, elected officials, political activists, journalists, and other historical figures, however, are given full biographic information when available.

CRIMINALIZING THE CASBAHS

FIGURE 1. Map of the Mediterranean. Map by Tim Stallmann.

Introduction

On an April afternoon in 1953, Saïd sat in a Marseille police station, staring at his hands. That morning, as he moved through the line to board a boat taking him from Marseille to Algiers, he had declared the three hunting rifles in his baggage to customs officers.[1] Saïd had saved up in Paris to buy them, intending to give two to his brothers as gifts. Hunting rifles, he explained with bemusement to the officer, for hunting. Saïd had been confused when the officer promptly confiscated his guns, had been unaware that it was a criminal offense to transport them to Algeria without special authorization from the colonial government. The resulting debacle had led here, to a cold bench in a Marseille police station. Eventually, another officer came to give him the news. He would be fined five thousand francs. And was lucky to have not been jailed, too, the officer admonished. Saïd, angry, annoyed, without guns, and now facing a fine he could ill afford, had officially missed his boat to Algiers.[2]

Saïd's life, as recorded in a police file, looked similar to the trajectory of many other Algerians. He traveled back and forth between France and Algeria cyclically during the early twentieth century, routinely passing through the Mediterranean ports of Marseille and Algiers. I stumbled upon the story of Saïd's attempt to "smuggle" guns, as the police labeled it, in a bundle of miscellaneous police records. I saw Saïd's name only once in the archives, in this report from 1953, but his journey mirrors the lives of the thousands of North African migrants who shuttled between Marseille and Algiers between 1918 and 1954. As Saïd moved through metropole and colony, other encounters with the police would have been unavoidable. When Saïd came to Marseille for the first time in 1942, he would have been pulled toward the North African neighborhood centered around Rue des Chapeliers, a vibrant if chaotic artery that nestled in the tangle of streets between Marseille's central Vieux-Port and Gare St. Charles, the main train station. As Saïd wandered Rue des Chapeliers, he might have been one of the hundreds of North Africans stopped by police in weekly, sometimes daily descents in the area. For example, one police report documented a typical "raid" on Rue des Chapeliers, blithely noting that officers had questioned 270 men and taken 59 to the station for "review."[3] Among this nameless list may have been Saïd, stopped on his way to a hotel for the night or while wandering in search of a meal, a friend, or a way to pass his time.

In Algiers, too, the police would have been unavoidable for Saïd. When the German occupiers deported him from Paris to Algiers during World War II, Saïd might have headed toward the Casbah, where many fellow Kabyles settled in the city.[4] The Casbah rose from the port of Algiers in whitewashed layers, a densely packed enclave of North African architecture and community in the expansive French colonial city. As Saïd stopped to sip a coffee in one of Casbah's many *cafés maures*, he might have seen a police officer lean over the counter, whispering to the café owner. If he strolled in a market, prayed at a mosque, or stopped to listen to a street performer, he would have felt the keen eyes of the police.[5]

In everyday encounters between police officers and North Africans like Saïd—encounters documented in thousands of pages of police reports, and others that left no archival trace—a complicated familiarity developed. Police officers could be called upon by North Africans to serve their needs or arbitrate disagreements. But the police were also a vector of abuse, discrimination, and even death. Although confrontations between police and North Africans occurred throughout the city, the story of policing North Africans was concentrated in specific urban sites, namely the Casbah in Algiers and Rue des Chapeliers in Marseille. By identifying and criminalizing "North African" spaces, the police learned where to concentrate their efforts of repression. The colonial police were ineffective, hampered by language barriers, staff shortages, and corruption. Despite these inadequacies, police maintained an undeniable power over the lives of North African colonial subjects. Overtime, police officers slowly laid claim to an increasingly large role in governing the social relations, private spaces, and daily lives of North Africans. This growth in the mandate of police power was neither inevitable nor universal. The police in Marseille and Algiers became ever more present in the lives of North Africans because of the way police discourses and practices linked race and space, painting North Africans as inevitable criminals and North African spaces as zones of danger and disloyalty.

This book traces the evolution of racialized policing in Marseille and Algiers from the end of World War I in 1918 to the dawn of the Algerian War of Independence in 1954. While Marseille and Algiers had functioned as connected commercial ports since antiquity, in the wake of World War I, new patterns of Algerian migration brought them even closer together. As thousands of Algerians entered the metropole, discourses of Algerian criminality circulated between metropole and colony, and a repressive Mediterranean system of policing Algerians emerged. Although colonial police forces had both criminalized and controlled Algerians in the past, increased trans-Mediterranean mobility introduced new imperatives to the policing of Algerians. Police practices rooted fears of Algerian criminality in urban space, targeting the "Casbahs" of Marseille and Algiers. The chaos of World War II then prompted the police to imagine Algerians as potential enemies of the French state and Algerian neighborhoods as hotbeds of "anti-French" action, even as competing visions of the French state itself emerged. The layering of race and space remained central to policing in the "color-blind" republican order of the postwar, particularly when it came to policing Algerian nationalism. The Algerian War of Independence fundamentally altered the relationship of police and North Africans, as the French military coopted policemen as frontline soldiers in the battle against nationalism. Yet the extremes seen during the Algerian War were only possible because of the systematic racialized policing of Algerians prior to its advent.

A French Mediterranean

The connection between Marseille and Algiers predated the French Empire, extending back to the two cities' shared Phoenician origins. Both Marseille and Algiers served as key ports in the Roman Empire, and from the medieval era to the eighteenth century, merchants reaped profits from the trade that flowed between them. Liaisons fostered by familial ties, population influxes, and seaborne commerce created an interconnected Mediterranean world, with Algiers and Marseille positioned as nodes in a web of connections that stretched from Lebanon to Portugal. Scholars, government officials, and residents of the two cities have long understood Marseille and Algiers as twinned cities, mirroring each other across the Mediterranean.[6] While the broader French Empire influenced this trans-Mediterranean world, this book is rooted in two specific cities. By treating Marseille and Algiers in parallel, we can see how patterns of policing shifted or held across a metropolitan/colonial divide.

Marseille and Algiers offer a unique perspective on the history of policing North Africans because of their prominence in the chain of migration between France and its empire. In other urban centers of North African immigration, such as Paris or Lyon, similar patterns of targeted policing existed, but in Marseille and

Algiers, the ports and patterns of cyclical migration colored police concerns.[7] In other ways, however, Marseille and Algiers offer useful contrasts. Marseille was a French city, where North Africans formed only a small minority.[8] Algiers was a colonial capital, ruled by a special legal regime that built racial difference into every level of governance. By connecting these two Mediterranean ports, I explore the networks through which racialized discourses and police practices circulated, while also pointing to the importance of local politics and individual relationships for our understanding of colonial policing.

In the nineteenth century, colonialism increased the pace of trans-Mediterranean movement. Following a trumped-up diplomatic dispute with the Ottoman ruler of Algiers, France invaded the city in 1830. This first invasion spiraled into decades of violent conquest. In 1848, the newly established French Second Republic formally incorporated Algeria as three *départements*. With this shift, the French established civil governance in Algiers to replace military rule and declared Algeria an integral part of France, as French as Paris and the département of the Seine. The French government quickly launched campaigns to populate Algeria with French and European immigrants. It encouraged settler immigration by offering land incentives, programs only possible because of the expropriation of land from Algerian families and religious communities.[9] Thousands of European families heeded the colonial government's call, although few remained in the countryside. Instead, immigrants from France, Italy, Spain, and Malta flowed into Algerian cities, including Algiers, creating a mixed, multilingual populace.[10] This stream of settlers, sometimes called *colons* or *pieds-noirs*, meant Algiers had a European majority throughout most of the early twentieth century.[11] As a *commune de plein exercise*, the structures of governance in Algiers in many ways functioned juridically and administratively like a metropolitan French city.[12] Algeria was a centerpiece of the French Empire, unique in the size of its settler population, the scale of investment, its juridical status, and its proximity to metropolitan France. All these factors gave Algeria and Algerians an outsized role in the French colonial imaginary.

French Algeria was a distinctly settler colonial venture, with racialized difference built into local legal codes. In 1870, the French government promulgated the Crémieux Decree, naturalizing all Algerian Jews. Then in 1889, the government implemented a mass naturalization of European colons, meaning that by the interwar period most Europeans in Algeria were French citizens.[13] As this naturalization policy makes evident, French racial hierarchies treated all Europeans as assimilable, building an idea of shared European whiteness distinct from "Arab" Algerians.[14] In contrast, only a tiny minority of Indigenous Muslim Algerians received French citizenship.[15] Based on supposed deference to local customs, the French established a distinct legal code, the *indigénat*, for Muslim Algerians in 1881.[16] The indigénat code allowed Algerians to follow Islamic law in matters of marriage, divorce, and inheritance, but it also criminalized actions such as possessing a gun or publicly critiquing the French state, curtailed freedoms of assembly and speech, and permitted tactics of repression such as collective punishment and administrative internment.[17] The indigénat created the legal categories of "French" and "*indigène*," racialized classifications used in both official and informal language. The category of indigène collapsed the linguistic and ethnic diversity of Algerians into a single racialized group, also labeled in French bureaucratic and literary texts as "Arab" or "North African." By legislating and legitimizing racial difference, the indigénat gave the police of Algiers additional tools of coercion that did not exist for their metropolitan counterparts.

In Marseille, a different, but no less racialized, system of control emerged. In the early twentieth century, populations began to flow toward the metropolitan shores of the French Mediterranean. During World War I, the French government brought thousands of Algerians to France to operate the factories left barren by wartime mobilization. A new law opened freedom of circulation for Algerians in 1914, and many embarked for France, lured by the promise of steady employment and higher wages.[18] More than 250,000 Algerians also arrived as soldiers.[19] When the war finally ended in 1918, the Third Republic sent the soldiers home, but complicated logistics made the process painfully slow. While awaiting their return, many Algerian veterans found themselves stuck in Marseille.[20] For some, this first passage to France sparked an enduring pattern of migration, one that almost invariably flowed through Marseille. The stream of colonial migrants arriving from all over the French Empire led some to dub Marseille the "capital of the colonies."[21] Although Paris attracted the highest number of North African migrants, by 1937, Marseille counted between fifteen thousand and twenty thousand North African residents.[22] Like elsewhere in the metropole, police officers and public administrators could not rely on the colonial legal regime of the indigénat to repress Algerian migrants. Instead, a system of racial control operated through specialized police brigades, targeted aid bureaus, and complicated immigration laws.

Movement across the Mediterranean was constant and cyclical. Populations arrived, unloaded, worked, settled, returned, again and again. The constant mobility of Algerians within and between Marseille and Algiers created a trans-Mediterranean lived experience, bringing the two cities together in the minds of migrants and public officials alike. Like the historical actors I trace, this book moves back and forth across the Mediterranean. Though I scaffold changes in geography, the disorientation of constant movement remains, mimicking to a small degree the dislocation at the heart of Algerians' circular experience in this Franco-Mediterranean world.

Guardians of the Imperial Peace

French control over the movement and immobility of North African populations in both Marseille and Algiers relied fundamentally on the police. After the departmentalization of Algeria in 1848, the French colonial government set up a civil police force modeled on the existing French system. By the mid-nineteenth century, the French police consisted of three major branches. The military-controlled *gendarmerie* served as the criminal police of rural areas and patrolled the empire's networks of roads. Two civil police divisions also coexisted—the *Sûreté* and the municipal police. The Sûreté supervised border control and immigration and housed France's notorious political police. The municipal police dealt with administrative matters, and contained specialized units that policed prostitution and vice, monitored public venues, inspected hotels, and performed a myriad of other functions.[23] All three branches could, depending on the circumstances, be involved in criminal policing. Even police officers at times expressed confusion about the complicated bureaucratic structure, and tensions periodically arose from rivalries between units.[24] In addition to police, specialized administrative bureaus also monitored North Africans, with bureaucrats culling information in service of policing aims.

In both Marseille and Algiers, local leaders converted the municipal police to a nationalized *police d'état* in the early twentieth century. The difference between a municipal and national police force lay in financing and administration, as actual police duties remained largely unchanged. Municipal police received funding from the city and reported to the mayor, while police d'état received national subsidies and reported directly to the regional authority, the prefect. Marseille's municipal police underwent *étatisation* in 1908, following long-standing concerns about insufficient funding. Two decades later, Algiers considered the same shift. Algiers had grown from 180,000 residents in 1914 to more than 230,000 in 1920. Despite the growth, the police had not expanded, and supporters hoped that nationalization would increase funding.[25] Politicians in Algiers looked to Marseille to counsel them, writing to the mayor of Marseille to ask his advice on nationalization.[26] Ultimately the Algiers Municipal Council voted to form a police d'état in 1930. As the police in Marseille and Algiers navigated an economic depression, another world war, and rumbles of anticolonialism in the coming decades, they would continue to look to each other, especially for matters concerning the mobile North African population.

Repression had been at the heart of the French police from its very origins. The police began as an undemocratic institution in service to an authoritarian monarchy, and in *ancien régime* Caribbean colonies, police supported slave society and upheld the *Code Noir*.[27] Scholarship, however, typically focuses on the evolution of the French police from a tool of despotism into a modern force intended to protect citizens and enforce the rule of law.[28] Under the Third Republic, officials described police officers as neutral arbiters of public safety, and the institution gained a mostly positive public reputation.[29] Yet this same republican police was also noted for its violent suppression of the "dangerous" urban working class.[30] The French police hounded political dissidents, too, targeting anarchists in the nineteenth century, Communists in the early twentieth century, and the Resistance under Vichy.[31]

In nineteenth-century Marseille, southern European immigrants, especially Italians, had been the object of negative stereotypes and assertive policing. Ultimately, however, historians argue that Marseille integrated these communities into the hodgepodge of the port. Despite xenophobic prejudices, Italians never faced the targeted brigades and bureaus used to control North Africans.[32] For Europeans, the experience of policing in Marseille followed the pattern scholars have traced more broadly in France—an increasingly professionalized police reserved violence primarily for certain categories of criminals or political activists.

In Algiers, European settlers (correctly) understood the Algiers police as an institution that worked for them.[33] Statistics produced by the Algiers police divided crime data into "indigène" and "European" criminals, revealing the primacy of racialized colonial categories for police understanding of crime.[34] These statistics consistently demonstrated an overrepresentation of "indigène" criminals. This overrepresentation indicates, I argue, not higher levels of North African criminality but rather a more invasive police presence in North African communities.

As scholars have documented, Europeans could experience police violence, and leftist political activists, in particular, frequently criticized the French police for their harsh tactics.[35] Ultimately, however, this book demonstrates that race and colonialism shaped police relationships with North Africans in distinct ways. In both Marseille and Algiers, the main priority of police officials was to make North Africans legible. The police constantly sought to name, categorize, and register North Africans. As with all projects of legibility, this required a "typification" of North Africans that reflected the simplified identities that had meaning to the state, and thus to the police, rather than the true range of North Africans' experiences and backgrounds.[36]

For North Africans, it was not always politics or personal action that led to encounters with police. Rather, the police of Marseille and Algiers inscribed criminal identities onto Algerians, particularly those whose transient existence threatened colonial norms.[37] As migration increased during the interwar years, police officers began to describe Algerian men as inherently dangerous, a stereotype that seeped into daily police practices. This racialized control made the policing of Algerians different from policing political groups. How, for example, could you be an "apolitical" Algerian when the police deemed cafés maures to be a space of political resistance and Arabic theater to be a risk to French power? This is not to discount the real political agency of Algerians, whose resistance to French colonialism is evident throughout police records. But rather than Algerians being persecuted for political affiliation, police practice made the fact of being born Algerian a political identity, one Algerians had little ability to claim or deny. It was this messy "political" policing, the ill-defined categories that rested on race rather than ideological beliefs, that distinguished the policing of Algerians.[38]

Colonial police forces, in Algeria and elsewhere, played an important role in creating and maintaining imperial dominance. Colonial policing developed without accountability to local populations, and the dangerous overlap of police power and colonial-capitalist interests generated pervasive violence.[39] Yet despite a growing field studying colonial policing, few researchers have examined policing in Algeria.[40] This book builds on a small but rich scholarship on policing North Africans in twentieth-century Paris, a telling case study but also an exceptional one.[41] The history of policing North Africans outside of the uniquely dense and resourced surveillance apparatus of the capital has not yet been written. I also shift the periodization of many studies of policing North Africans, focusing on the decades *before* the Algerian War of Independence. Shifting focus in this way reveals the origins of discriminatory police practices during the Algerian War and makes clear the dysfunction and oppression of colonial policing in cities beyond Paris.

Dual Mediterranean case studies also reveal the tangled, transnational network of colonial policing. Historians have argued that the military experience of colonial conquest and decolonization seeped back into metropolitan policing, weakening citizens' civil liberties.[42] This network of transfer existed in Marseille and Algiers, but without the rigid distinctions of colonial "experimentation" and metropolitan "return." Instead, exchange between Algeria and France was constant and multidirectional. The stereotypes and preoccupations that circulated in Algiers made their way to Marseille, and the advice and best practices of police in Marseille trickled back to Algiers. Police officers themselves exchanged information, circulating techniques and prejudices among colleagues. Framing policing through a Mediterranean lens allows us to see that the "colonial situation" was perhaps not so singular, and that similar practices could and did exist in the metropole.

The police are an institution of oppression, and this was undeniably many North Africans' understanding of the police. At times, however, North Africans also made demands on the police, calling on officers to arbitrate conflicts or protect their person and property. This was a conscious decision. Police officers were often the most recognizable representative of the state in the lives of colonized populations, and in calling on them, North Africans made use of the limited resources available to them. The decision to turn to the police was also motivated by the way that French colonialism eroded other forms of social regulation. In Marseille, colonial wage migration created a largely young, male North African community. Cut off from elders, religious institutions, and kin networks, North African migrants perhaps came to the police because they had few other places to turn. Algiers, too, underwent social shifts under colonialism, including intentional French efforts to undermine the authority of religious leaders and educators. Faced with weakened traditional institutions, some Algerians turned, more or less willingly, to the French police.

Violent, Intimate Policing

The defining function of the police is violence. When citizens call the police, they are calling on individuals endowed with the state's monopoly on violence.[43] Micol Seigel pushes this logic to argue that police are not just vectors of violence—they are the embodiment of state violence, or "violence workers."[44] Police officers in Marseille and Algiers were undoubtedly violence workers. This violence occurred in physical assaults on North Africans' bodies, but also in the symbolic violence of misspelled names, racial slurs, and the informal "*tu*."[45] Insisting on the ubiquity of violence, however, can obscure how police officers used violence in unequal and discriminatory ways. Police violence must be understood as a purposeful strategy of social control, deployed in recognizable patterns to subdue those considered enemies of the state or of societal norms.[46]

Violence is also racialized. The disproportionate use of force against racialized minority groups persists because the brutality serves the economic and social interests of the (white) majority.[47] This racialized use of violence, and of policing, was certainly true in Marseille and Algiers. In studies of the United States, scholars frame police brutality as a legacy of racialized slavery and a deep history of anti-Blackness.[48] This, however, cannot explain violence toward Algerians, defined in French colonial hierarchies as racially distinct from "Black Africans" and never subjected to the historical horror of the Atlantic slave trade. Instead, I examine the development of police violence in a colonial context and in cosmopolitan Mediterranean ports where visual markers of race remained fluid.

While the police might always have "legitimate" recourse to violence on behalf of the state, in colonial situations this violence expanded to new heights.[49] Histories of colonial violence tend to focus on conquest or decolonization, when violence was excused by conditions of war.[50] I present a different picture. Police violence was constant and, often, racially motivated in both Marseille and Algiers. But between 1918 and 1954, violence had constraints. Anticolonial movements kept up a steady stream of dissent, but until the mid-1950s, many French administrators and politicians believed that the ties between France and Algeria would be unending, if not unchanging. The way that the police treated Algerians in this period, then, illuminates the complexity of colonial policing before what Emmanuel Blanchard calls the "blank check" for violence that emerged during decolonization.[51] As long as France asked Algerians to believe the myth that Algeria was France, the police were bound, in principle if not in practice, to uphold a republican ideal of egalitarian justice. Violence necessarily operated differently in this context than during war.

If the police were violence workers, they were also something else. The policing of North Africans in Marseille and Algiers was an intimate practice. Historians of colonialism and feminism have shown how empires created and managed hierarchies of difference through the control of marriage, family, sex, and the home.[52] In intimate moments, bodies acquire meaning and individuals bump into the concepts of race and gender being erected around them. The intimate is laden with relationships of power, including struggles over the power to regulate behavior, emotion, production (labor), and reproduction (sex). But for all the focus on regulation and control, policing itself rarely features in scholarship on intimacy and empire.[53]

But there is intimacy, too, in policing, an intimacy rooted in space. Scholars of empire often define intimacy as sex or romantic love, but as I relate it to policing, intimacy evokes a broader spectrum of relationships. I define the intimate as the close, the familiar, the private, the personal, the communal. North Africans living in Marseille and Algiers were constantly, inescapably surrounded by the colonial state. When I speak of intimate policing, I refer to the moments when police raided the cafés where North Africans gathered to eat and talk, when they stopped and searched men and women making their way home from work, when they interrupted prayer meetings, plays, or protests. There was intimacy when police interceded in disputes between family members, conflicts between lovers, disagreements rooted in betrayal, affection, and lies. The intimacy of policing was walking into the police station where you knew you would find the same officer that you hated (or tolerated) at the same front desk. It was walking along your street in the Casbah and seeing officers pacing their route, inevitable, unavoidable. Intimacy was inflected by gender. The exclusively male police officers adopted a self-consciously paternalistic attitude toward North Africans. Police interventions into the daily lives of Algerian men in Marseille looked different than their confrontations with Algerian women in Algiers. Despite these gendered differences, police were everywhere for North Africans, the most visible, familiar, and inescapable presence of the state. Standing in the closeness of policing, the intimacy of daily exchange, gives us insight into the discretion within colonial policing and reveals the deeply personal nature of police work.[54]

This daily, intimate, violent policing stands in contrast to what popular portrayals emphasize as the true job of the police—catching criminals.[55] While TV shows and detective novels imagine policing to be about crime, police more frequently asserted control over ordinary tasks of household management, bureaucratic necessities, and the right to one's own labor. Officers inserted themselves into the most mundane and private moments of North African life in pursuit of an often-imaginary enemy. In this sense, I try to show in Marseille and Algiers what Ilana Feldman has called "deep and wide" police presence, meaning not only the large scope of police intervention but also their personal connection to local populations.[56] In their surveillance of North Africans, police officers regulated not just crime, but bodies, not just laws, but lives.

Racializing the Casbahs

Drawing on quotidian examples of this intimate surveillance, I argue that the racialized policing of North Africans in Marseille and Algiers built not just on visual codes of race but also on how police practice mapped ideas of race onto the space of the city. In both Algiers and Marseille, it was not only French and Algerian populations that lived side by side. As Mediterranean ports, Marseille and Algiers existed in a broader web of migration and trade. Commercial ships and individual travelers came from Spain, Greece, Turkey, Egypt, Morocco, Italy, and beyond, creating an oceanic network of exchange. Both cities were Mediterranean melting pots. Marseille, for example, was a favorite stop for African American GIs and a center of immigration from other colonies, including French West Africa and Indochina.[57] The cosmopolitanism of port life had implications for policing. The police in both cities dealt with a transient, seaborne population of sailors and workers who shifted from city to city and country to country following the currents and their luck. The turnover inherent in port life made both these cities notoriously difficult to control. The policing of North Africans at times overlapped with the surveillance of other colonial populations, particularly during sporadic conflicts with the West African soldiers stationed in both cities.

Yet policing North Africans was also distinct. Police in both Marseille and Algiers formed ideas of "North African" criminality that distinguished them from other populations. Police officers and government officials frequently described North Africans as a race, insisting that the morals and "mentality" of the "Arab race" made them particularly criminal, infantile, or inferior. The focus on race, then, is not my presentist invention but reflects the language and worldviews of these historical actors. Ideas of race, however, could be difficult to pin down in Mediterranean cities. Centuries of immigration, intermarriage, and shifting imperial borders within the Mediterranean region made physical definitions of race hazier than the "Black-white" divide often analyzed in American policing.[58] "Seeing race" was a dubious endeavor in Marseille and Algiers, and so police officers in both cities instead inscribed race through language, dress, and, I argue, space.

Police officials and beat officers defined Algerian criminality by mapping it onto particular neighborhoods and streets. In some studies of French policing, space is a neutral category, at most defined by class or crime rates.[59] But space is not neutral. As Henri Lefebvre reminds us, space is socially constructed, "a set of relations and forms."[60] Landscape cannot be divorced from geographies of oppression, from dynamics of class, gender, and race. Police and North Africans understood space through a series of social relationships determined by colonial discourses and realities of inequality and criminality.[61] When we think about the state's role in producing race and space, the focus often turns to the work of urban planners, politicians, or jurists.[62] Historians of empire point to how bureaucrats in the French and British empires used public health codes, zoning laws, and pass systems to create racial segregation.[63] But neither Marseille nor Algiers had such an obvious or legally ordained system of spatial segregation. Nonetheless, Algerians remained concentrated in specific areas of both cities, for reasons of convenience, necessity, choice, and discrimination. If the police did not create North African enclaves, however, they did police their boundaries, deciding where and how North Africans could inhabit the city. Police decisions about where to operate raids, where to set up their networks of surveillance, and how to divide the city for patrols reflected their "commonsense" understandings of who lived where.[64] In doing so, police helped produce the ideas of danger that haunted North African neighborhoods.

In police work, bodies and space define each other. In North American contexts, this can be seen in the way officers assign "risk" to spaces understood as spaces of Blackness. In my own dual case study, I trace an entanglement between police and North Africans rooted not in Blackness and risk but in colonial discourse and racialized criminality.[65] In Marseille and Algiers, urban space was imbued with racial categorizations. Influenced by stereotypes that filled the pages of academic studies, popular newspapers, and official government reports, the police of Marseille and Algiers came to understand North Africans as a particularly criminal population. These ideas were reinforced by their targeted policing of North Africans, with North African criminality a self-fulfilling prophecy resulting from the endless sweeps of North African neighborhoods. Officers linked imagined criminality to the "Casbahs," simultaneously "coding" North Africans and North African space in a mutually reinforcing narrative of crime and danger.[66]

Police officers did not themselves create the colonial stereotypes, nor the urban segregation, but officers' beliefs about North African criminality had tangible implications for how they policed North African spaces. The French police denied racial discrimination, instead describing targeted strategies in terms of space. Space and race became intertwined, a convenient tool for police to label and identify racialized identities in a fluid Mediterranean context. Teasing apart the interwoven history of race and urban geography, this book unravels that denial by showing how discrimination operated on a daily level. The everyday, intimate, and violent policing of North Africans demonstrates how institutional racism was built and normalized in France and its empire.

The Everyday Policing of North Africans

While researching this book, I spent months in archives in France and Algeria poring over pieces of paper written by French officials, concerned citizens, and, most of all, police officers. These records were first stored by police departments as their own functional archive and then preserved by the collection practices of the French state. The documents were carefully culled for a utilitarian purpose, filed to aid police in future investigations. Police reports provide tantalizingly rich descriptions of life in Marseille and Algiers.[67] Unlike most dry, bureaucratic sources, investigation notes and witness testimonies offered shimmers of personality and intrigue in the archive. But I know there is risk in these records. Police officers present their accounts as objective observations, verbatim recordings of what they saw and did. But these reports are not impartial. They tell the story the police wanted to be preserved, leaving historians guessing at what is truth, what is fiction, and what is unsaid.

To counteract this inherent bias, I deliberately complicate and question police records. I use dissident sources, particularly the Algerian press, to highlight the strategies Algerians developed to resist police intervention. I propose a critical reimagining of police documents, engaging with events as they were recorded by officers but also suggesting alternative interpretations that foreground the violences left unspoken. Through thick descriptions of ordinary incidents and reading "against" the archive, I weave a history of policing that explores multiple versions of the past, a method not of historical fiction, but historical curiosity.[68] The approach draws on Black feminist historians of the Atlantic slave trade such as Saidiya Hartman, who grapples with the scarcity of historical records by deploying "critical fabulation," a speculative narration that uses storytelling to redress historical omissions.[69] In my archives, I was faced not with a dearth of sources but a seemingly endless trove of paper, sheets that present a carefully constructed vision of history. Instead of invention, my method focuses on questioning what the archives tell me, insisting on the multiple possibilities that exist within narrowly narrated state records. I investigate motivation, emotion, and consequences, even as my sources remain stubbornly silent on these points. I do not always know how the story ended, but I offer the reader interpretations, questions, and my own confrontations with the unknowable nature of some histories.

In this methodology, I foreground everyday policing, incidents when neighbors "called the cops," times when Algerians came to the police for help, standard rounds of police surveillance, unremarkable crimes, and ubiquitous moments of violence. When I explore scandalous events, I do so with the intent of showing how these headline-grabbing outliers fit into broader trends and daily patterns.[70] While the political choices of Algerians are evident throughout, I choose not to emphasize the policing of Algerian nationalism, except in my final chapter. The police orchestrated a fierce repression of Algerian nationalism, and other historians have fruitfully explored this topic, particularly in the context of the Algerian War of Independence.[71] Instead, my focus on everyday policing reveals a more complicated picture of policing, one in which violence is omnipresent but Algerians and the police are not always antagonists. The daily policing of Algerians contributes to the exploration of the "world of contact" in colonial Algeria, allowing for an understanding of social relations that does not take decolonization as a foregone conclusion.[72]

Looking at an everyday, rather than institutional, history of policing also makes clear the very real power of individual officers to enact or ignore the law. "The police" were individuals often in conflict with one another, with those they policed, and with the government that ostensibly controlled them. In the lives of North Africans, "the police" could also be office bureaucrats, administrative staff, and aid workers who used proximity as a tool of surveillance. In examining two local, on-the-ground histories of colonial policing, I underscore the importance of discretion. Police officers developed relationships with those they policed, relationships that North Africans leveraged to their advantage when possible and that police officers used to glean intelligence. Officers had the ability to decide the limits of their own actions, and these decisions had real impacts on North Africans' lives.

In seeking out the everyday, I prioritize street-level anecdotes over high-level policy. The chapters of this book move through a series of ordinary events, individual stories of encounters between police and North Africans. I dwell on these stories because it is through these quotidian moments, these unremarkable confrontations, that we can see patterns being formed. The collection of anecdotes reveals how police officers understood their jobs, how North Africans understood the police, and the myriad of ways that race and space and violence and resilience colored daily life in Marseille and Algiers

As France went through pivotal moments of political and social change between 1918 and 1954, policing adapted to meet the needs of the moment. Yet throughout this transformation, the intimate policing of race and space operated in recognizable ways. It is the local dynamics of both continuity and change that the six chapters of this book explore. Chapter 1 begins with the end of World War I, when Algerian soldiers brought to France for the war effort started an enduring pattern of circular migration, both legal and illicit, between Algiers and Marseille. Police feared the mobility of North Africans, building a Mediterranean network of surveillance to track them. Newspapers, government reports, and ethnographic studies from Marseille and Algiers produced strikingly similar narratives of the supposedly inherent criminality of North Africans. Chapter 2 follows these stereotypes into the 1930s, when they sparked the creation of specialized police units in Marseille and targeted criminal laws in Algiers. The complex quotidian relationship of North Africans and police became increasingly defined by space—the "Casbahs" that the police identified as North African.

Chapters 3 and 4 turn to World War II, looking at how this pivotal moment of political and cultural upheaval altered colonial policing. As the economic pressures of war mounted, the police redoubled their efforts to control North African movement, labor, and social life, becoming arbiters in contentious debates over private life and public space. Marseille and Algiers stood on opposite sides of the war effort following the Allied conquest of Algiers in 1942. Despite different political goals, however, police in both cities were united in their wary treatment of North Africans, fretting over German influence and painting North Africans as "anti-French." In chapter 4, I examine how police homogenized the North African community along racial lines, denying their ability to be part of the "true" French nation. The Casbahs of Marseille and Algiers became coded not just as the space of an "Other" but also as the center of the black market and a hiding place for enemies of France.

In 1945, France sought to start anew, resuscitating an ideal of the egalitarian republic after the racism and antisemitism of Vichy. In chapter 5, I begin with this moment of optimism and reform, when both French officials and Algerian activists tried to imagine a new relationship for France and Algeria. Changes in public discourse, however, proved insufficient to change police practice. By eliding race and space in naming and designing new brigades or strategies, the police altered the public representation of their work without dismantling discriminatory practices. The final chapter examines the police response to the rising tide of Algerian nationalism. The policing of nationalism spilled beyond the realm of party politics into matters of religion, culture, and daily life. The imaginaries of criminal enclaves and enemy Algerians produced in previous decades now merged with political fears, as the police began to treat all Algerians as potential nationalists.

Through interlocking stories of two cities, this book offers a critical history of how policing and ideas of race evolved together. It illustrates the development of practices of racial violence and shows how ideas of difference shaped daily realities, marked physical environments, and scarred human bodies. This history of policing North Africans is connected to the present. The questions of race, space, and police violence explored here continue to resonate in France. They are visible, to give just one tragic example, in the police shooting of Nahel Merzouk, a seventeen-year-old of North African descent, in the suburbs of Paris in the summer of 2023. Killed by police after being stopped for a routine traffic violation, Nahel's death launched protests throughout France. The role of police in society is not an idle question, then, but the center of an ongoing, urgent, global debate.

When we speak of policing, scholars and policymakers alike tend to treat the police as an immutable, centralized body, in unquestioning service to the state. The impact of structures of racial oppression is undeniable, and in Algiers and Marseille, the police responded to cultural forces they did not create. Yet it is too neat to assume that policing can be fully understood through state imperatives. This top-down analysis ignores the role of the police, both as individual officers and as an institution, in creating and shifting racial hierarchies. National directives defined the limits of policing, but individual officers, in their daily interactions with ordinary people, are the ones who made policing a reality. Police officers in Algiers and Marseille, like police officers elsewhere, manipulated a system designed to empower them, deciding what was and was not political, who was and was not criminal. They failed, over and over, to understand the North Africans they sought to control, displaying a cultural incompetency that exemplified the dysfunction of the colonial state. The boundary between public and private, personal and political, blurred in the practices of the colonial police. This expansion of police control was only possible because the police came to understand North Africans as a threat to be controlled, rather than a population to be protected.

1
CONTROLLING MEDITERRANEAN MOVEMENT

A misty haze covered the bow of the boat, a hint of salt lingered on the breeze. As the sun slowly burned away the moisture of dawn, the passengers standing on the deck looked out at a seemingly endless span of crisp, blue water. The boat cut through the waves, carrying the travelers between Marseille and Algiers, as boats had for centuries. Visitors to Algiers described the stunning arcade of whitewashed buildings that greeted them as they approached the city. From the deck, they could spot the Casbah, its traditional Algerian architecture distinct from the more recent French construction. In Marseille, an arriving voyager might have been forgiven a twinge of apprehension as the sprawling, grey city appeared on the horizon. Though an ancient port, Marseille exuded the chaos of an industrial city, extending haphazardly in all directions. The boats that traversed the Mediterranean, and the people on board, connected Marseille and Algiers, twinned metropolises of France's Mediterranean Empire. Algiers and Marseille anchored a connected Franco-Mediterranean world, one stitched together by a shared history of commerce, migration, and colonialism.

Policing in Marseille and Algiers was also linked. Police tracked the constant migration between these two cities, convinced that the movement of North Africans posed an inherent threat to colonial order. As North Africans traveled between France and Algeria, so too did discourses of "Arab" criminality, stereotypes that the police helped to circulate and cement. In the interwar period, the police sought to control North Africans by defining the spaces of North African life in Marseille and Algiers. They mapped ideas of North Africans' dangerous difference onto streets, stores, and homes. Police engineered a pervasive, unavoidable presence in spaces of North African daily life, bringing officers into an uneasy intimacy with the North African community.

The history of policing North Africans in the Franco-Mediterranean world is one of enduring patterns that shifted in response to changing local and global circumstances. I begin, therefore, with a baseline, an introduction to the structures of French colonial policing and to the geographies that are as much a protagonist of this book as the police and North Africans. These spaces, the "Casbahs" of Algiers and Marseille, were physical locations but also chimeric worlds of discourses and assumptions. French government, journalistic, and pseudoscientific writings about Algerian criminality and deviant sexuality colored police views of the Casbah in Algiers and Rue des Chapeliers in Marseille, the principal North African neighborhoods of each city. In responding to stereotypes of Algerian crooks and fighting to regulate migration and mobility, the police helped to create the criminalized community they feared.

Defining the Casbahs

Marseille and Algiers were the main arteries of imperial movement, the ports through which passengers traveled to reach empire or metropole. In the nineteenth century, French government initiatives encouraged Europeans to move to Algiers. By the early twentieth century, Algerians began to migrate in large numbers to the metropole in search of jobs. In Algiers, the police struggled to control a population once considered the enemy and now seen as childlike recipients of French civilization. Across the sea in Marseille, the police watched warily as Algerian immigrants began to settle into the fabric of their city. As exchanges of goods and people knit Marseille and Algiers together, French observers began to identify specific areas of the two port cities as "North African." The coproduced narratives of race and space in these "North African" neighborhoods would become fundamental to how police officers in both cities approached the policing of North African people.

In Algiers, this space was the Casbah. Prior to French conquest, the city of Algiers was contained within the ramparts of an Ottoman fortress, the literal *casbah* or walled fort that gave the neighborhood its name.[1] After invading Algiers in 1830, the French army reconfigured the city, renaming roads, expropriating homes, and eventually tearing down the walls of Algiers. The French military hacked through the Casbah to create thoroughfares for military training, demolishing much of downtown to create a new neighborhood dubbed the Marine Quarter.[2] Reshaping urban space was more than a matter of logistics. In remaking Algiers, the French strategically created space for European settlers, an "urbicide" that mirrored practices in other segregated colonial cities.[3] An influx of Europeans began to populate the city, and Algerian families fled to the upper reaches of the Casbah, pushed by inflated rents, expropriation, and conflict with settlers.[4] Wealthy Algerians left the city entirely, heading to suburban towns such as Kouba and Saint-Eugène.[5] As the army ripped apart Algiers, they often did not compensate the Algerian owners of requisitioned buildings, reducing families to poverty and homelessness.[6]

By 1921, Algiers had a population of 195,655. Only 47,669 were Algerian.[7] Algerians, now a minority in the growing city, became increasingly confined to the whitewashed buildings of the Casbah.[8] Laws introduced under Napoleon III's Second Empire prevented Europeans from settling in the "Muslim" Casbah. The same decree focused "beautifying" projects on European quarters, claiming that modern improvements were not conducive to an Algerian way of life.[9] The law implicitly divided Algiers into Algerian and European sectors, marking the Casbah as Algerian space and reserving new construction for the colons. Continued expropriation and rampant speculation by European investors also prevented Algerian families from living in the growing urban sprawl.[10] While the flight of wealthy Algerian families continued, rural Algerians moved into the Casbah, particularly from the mountainous Kabylia region. By 1936, nearly a third of the residents of the Casbah were Kabyle. These newcomers reconfigured Algiers's connection to the countryside and introduced a new language—Amazigh.[11] Some older *Algérois* families began to call the Casbah Tizi Ouzu, referring to the largest Kabyle city. The Casbah was also home to a small population of sub-Saharan Africans, believed to be the descendants of Ottoman servants or enslaved domestic workers.[12] As the population of the Casbah increased, impoverished Algerian families piled into what were once single-family homes. By the 1940s, families of six or seven could be found crammed into a single room.[13] Most residents of the Casbah lived in buildings that lacked the modern comforts of electric lighting or gas hookups well into the 1960s.[14]

French observers described the Casbah as sensuous, mysterious, and exotically dangerous. As American tourist Elizabeth Crouse explained, "The solid front which is presented from the water, on closer acquaintance discloses passages like burrows . . . Through the heart of the old town the torturous, tunnel-like passages are scarce wide enough for two to pass; and the streets form a maze of cul-de-sacs, where no foreigner may find his way."[15] Europeans evoked fanciful street names, smells of powerful spices, and alleys so narrow that donkeys, rather than cars, served as the primary mode of transport.[16] The Casbah sat above the port, a mass of white buildings with few exterior windows but sunny interior courtyards. With the construction of the Marine Quarter, the Casbah came to an abrupt halt at a large boulevard. The road was called Rue Randon until it

FIGURE 2. Street of Algiers. Photograph of a street in the Casbah of Algiers by Philippe Joudiou (1950). Courtesy of the Joudiou family and the Bibliothèque Nationale de France.

reached the synagogue at Place Rabbin Bloch, where it became Rue Marengo.[17] The Casbah lay semi-concealed behind this Haussmann-style boulevard, masked by the unmistakably French apartments and shops lining Rue Marengo. When I wandered the Casbah, I was struck by the ornamental fountains, cracked mosaic designs, and streets shrouded by overhanging archways. There is certainly a mazelike quality to the interlocking staircases and passages of the Casbah, but I found it more difficult than colonial observers claimed to get lost. The sheer verticality serves as a sort of guide: to leave, simply descend until you emerge onto Rue Marengo.

French colonialism restructured the social reality of the Casbah. Prior to conquest, Algiers had been governed as more than fifty neighborhood units, each with its own *qadi*, or Islamic judge, to settle disputes.[18] French rule dismantled this intricate, highly local system of social regulation. The departure of wealthy families and the arrival of rural, Amazigh migrants also shifted preexisting social networks in the neighborhood. Conquest crippled the local economy and deci-

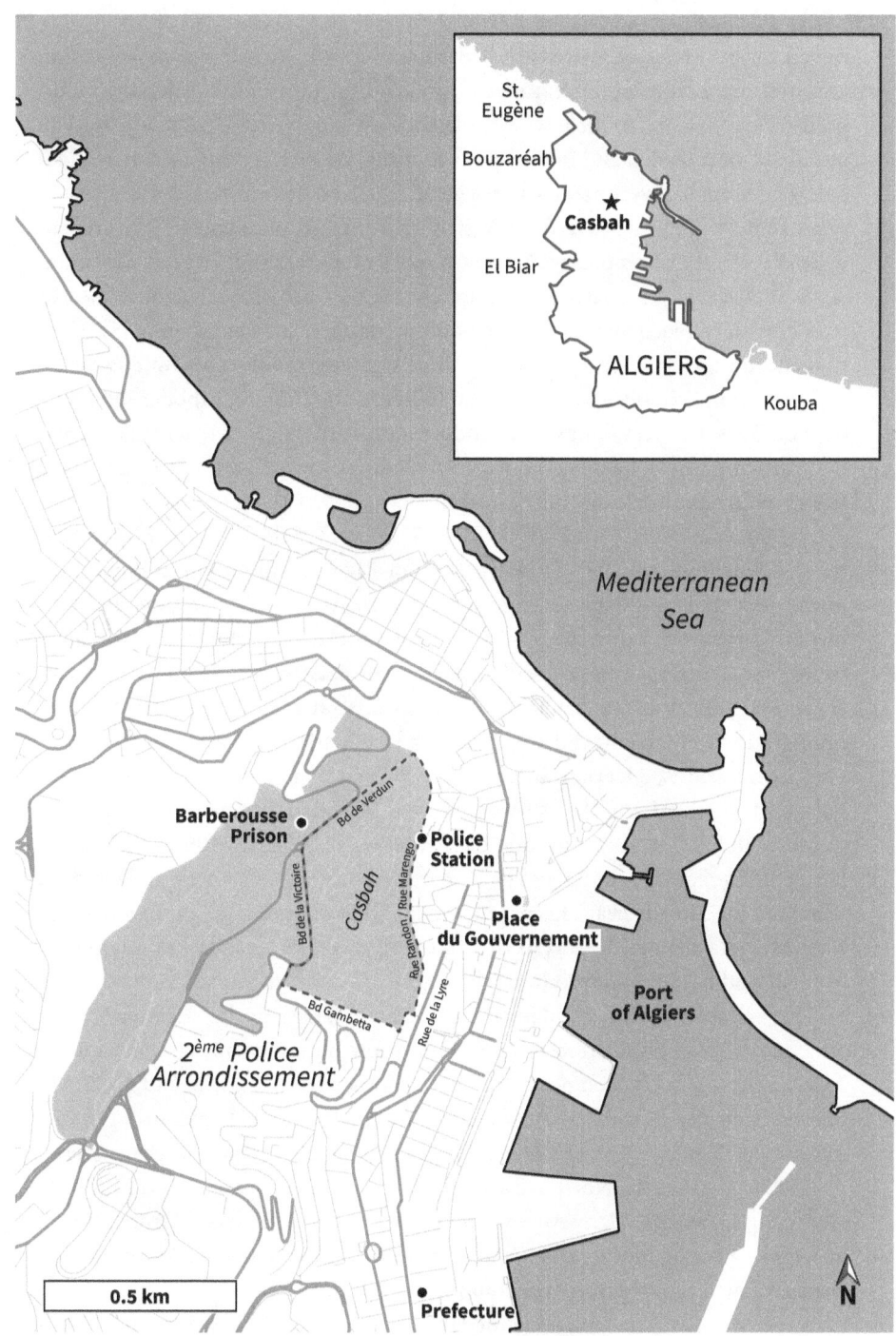

FIGURE 3. Map of Algiers. Map by Tim Stallmann.

mated the revenues of artisans.[19] Denied access to French-language education and prevented from obtaining many public-sector jobs, most Algerians found themselves relegated to the lowest-skilled, lowest-paid work. Unable to afford all but the most crowded and insalubrious housing, Algerians poured into the Casbah. The French government also relegated legalized prostitution to the Casbah, safely removing this perceived moral danger from European areas.[20] The ancient district of prestige and palaces became a space of increasingly overt poverty and population density. French colonialism rewrote the Casbah as a neighborhood of vice, creating a place that the French administration identified as uniquely Algerian and uniquely dangerous. Despite this, Algerian middle-class functionaries, merchants, and shopkeepers continued to live in the Casbah, rubbing shoulders with dockers, laborers, and street vendors. People of all genders and ages called the Casbah home. The *2ème* police commissariat surveilled this vibrant world from a police station at 26 Rue Marengo.

In Marseille, North African life looked different. Scholars have highlighted the overwhelmingly male, circular pattern of Algerian migration to France following World War I.[21] Over time, some North African shopkeepers and café owners carved out positions of relative economic stability, but the vast majority of North Africans in Marseille eked out an existence as laborers or dockers in Marseille's port, a staunchly working-class population. The heavily male immigration to Marseille did not mean that no Algerian women came to France. On rare occasions, Algerian women accompanied their husbands to the metropole, and North African Jewish women also formed an important social group in Marseille.[22] Most Algerian immigrants, however, arrived without their families, sending regular remittances back to support parents, partners, and children who remained in Algeria. This practice meant that migrants sought to maximize their meager earnings. Reporters described Algerians living in crumbling *garnis*, or furnished hotels, each room "a cell" where five or six men lived collectively.[23]

The police and press of Marseille variously referred to the Algerian, North African, or Arab population of Marseille. A few hundred immigrants came to Marseille from the French protectorates in Morocco and Tunisia, and fewer still arrived from other "Arab" countries such as Egypt, Syria, and Lebanon.[24] The vast majority of "Arabs" in Marseille were Algerian, but the slippage of terms erased distinctions within the North African population and collapsed the ethnic diversity of Algerians, too. Many Algerian migrants, for example, arrived from Kabylia and spoke Amazigh rather than Arabic.[25] Authorities in Marseille, however, consistently failed to recognize or accommodate this diversity.

As early as 1913, the police claimed that two thousand North African workers lived in Marseille, clustered in the tangle of streets between the Vieux-Port and Gare St. Charles.[26] This area, referred to in police records as "behind the Bourse" and today called Quartier Belsunce, nestled in the shadows of the Chamber of Commerce's Palais de la Bourse. The 1913 police report suggested that Algerian workers may have initially congregated behind the Bourse because of construction jobs available there following the razing of almost the entire neighborhood in the early 1900s. The report identified Rue des Chapeliers as the main hub of North African life in Marseille, with at least seven restaurants catering to North Africans located on the street. It also linked "these Algerian indigènes" to a broader criminal world, highlighting the popularity of gambling, hinting at conspiracies of arms smuggling, and describing violent fights. Police reproduced colonial stereotypes, decrying Algerians' lack of hygiene and insisting the men posed "a certain danger to the city, from both a sanitary and security point of view."[27] The police conducted frequent raids on Rue des Chapeliers and the surrounding streets, charging Algerians with crimes such as vagrancy or improper residency paperwork.[28] Reliance on these types of charges indicates police assumptions that any Algerian in Marseille must not really belong there, must be either vagrant or migrant rather than resident.

As more Algerians arrived in Marseille, Rue des Chapeliers gained a reputation as a North African space. Popular French journalist Albert Londres evoked the exoticism of the street in his portrait of Marseille published in 1927. "Do you want to see Algeria, Morocco, Tunisia? Give me your arm. I will take you to Rue des Chapeliers: here are the *gourbis*, the *bicots*, the *mouquères* . . . Here are the *sidis* coming back to the Casbah after working in the port."[29] Londres's scornful description used words taken directly from colonial Algeria. *Gourbis* denoted huts found in North Africa, and *mouquères* meant North African women, particularly sex workers. *Bicot* and *sidi*, both offensive racial slurs, reflected the colonial racism that informed French views of North Africans. Londres described a sensory experience of Rue des Chapeliers, evoking smells of sweat and Turkish coffee, and the "unhealthy" darkness of homes lit only by candle stubs. As Londres put it, you entered "Arab territory" when you stepped onto Rue des Chapeliers, the Casbah of Marseille.[30]

Although observers like Londres described Rue des Chapeliers as an "Arab" space, in fact North African migrants settling behind the Bourse joined an ethnically mixed neighborhood. Though streets like Rue des Chapeliers, Rue Bernard du Bois, and Rue des Petites Maries became indelibly linked to the North African community, in the 1920s they were home to European immigrants and French citizens too. There was also a continuous presence behind the Bourse of other colonial populations, including a small number of migrants from French West Africa.[31] This mix differed from the more rigid segregation of colonial Algiers. Petitions from shopkeepers on Rue des Chapeliers in the 1930s, for example, list Arabic and European names side by side, showing an active alignment of

FIGURE 4. Street view of central Marseille. Photograph of central Marseille (street unmarked) by Germaine Krull, 1935. The photo is from a section of a photobook on Marseille documenting immigration and was likely near Rue des Chapeliers (Germaine Krull and André Suarès, *Marseille* [Éditions d'Histoire et d'Art, 1935]). Courtesy of Estate Germaine Krull, Museum Folkwang, Essen.

different ethnic and racial groups along lines of class.[32] The neighborhood was dirty and noisy, filled with cheap restaurants, bawdy bars, and infamous brothels. Machines rattled in small-scale industrial operations nearby, the construction of new buildings in the decimated Bourse neighborhood pounded away, and crowds milled about at all hours, chatting in a slew of languages. Into this raucous world settled Marseille's North African population. As in Algiers, the 2ème police commissariat surveilled the North African neighborhood of Marseille, labeled administratively as the Bourse. The local police station sat at one end of Rue des Chapeliers in an imposing neoclassical building called La Halle Puget.[33]

The police did not invent the territorial realities of these two cities. Algerians moved into the Casbah in Algiers and behind the Bourse in Marseille because of a combination of personal preference, limited opportunity, and unofficial discrimination. We can also see the concentration of Algerians in specific urban

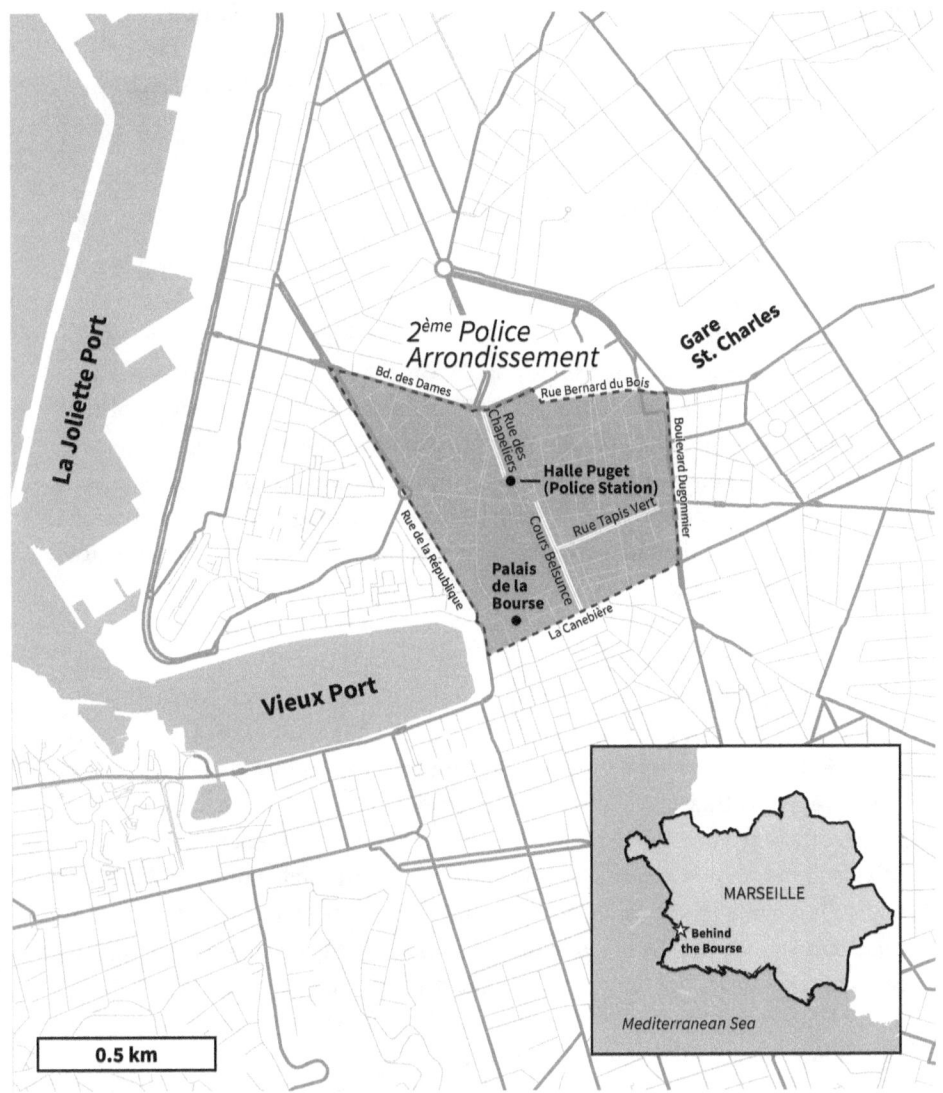

FIGURE 5. Map of Marseille. Map by Tim Stallmann.

sites as a strategic choice, a way of building solidarity in a hostile colonial world.[34] As the Mediterranean ports grew and diversified in the interwar years, Algerian families etched their lives into these two port towns. Yet the spaces that they called home would also be turned against them by the police. Officers did not devise the urban segregation of Algerian life, but the way they policed it inscribed ideas of race onto city streets and storefronts, a tool used to control Algerians.

Peopling the Colonial Police

As Algerians' movement across the Mediterranean ramped up after World War I, the French government turned to the police to control their mobility. World War I marked a watershed in French policing. Seeking to meet the security demands of a growing, and increasingly urban, population, the French government pushed through reforms after the war to gradually increase the size and scope of the police.[35] The slow increase in police personnel coincided with a longer project to "nationalize" the police of France's largest cities, including Marseille in 1908 and Algiers in 1930.[36] World War I also transformed the demographics of the French police. The losses of the war depleted the young men available to become police officers. Conversely, incentives for veterans effectively ensured that the new crop of recruits had all served in the French army. Moreover, labor shortages after the war shifted the demographics of France itself, sparking immigration surges from neighboring nations and France's imperial possessions. In both Marseille and Algiers, changes in the composition of who was living in these cities and who was serving in the police shaped the priorities and structure of local policing.

In both Marseille and Algiers, all police candidates had to be French men over the age of twenty-one but under forty. This category of "French" could prove difficult to define in Algeria. Did French nationals, the status of most Algerian men, count? Laws specifically reserved senior positions, like commissioner, for French citizens. By this logic, noncitizen Algerians counted as French enough to serve in lower ranks, but only citizens could ascend to the top of the police hierarchy.[37] The competitive exam used to hire police officers tested oral and written communication as well as knowledge of the French legal code. In Algiers, the test also examined candidates' knowledge of Algerian laws and awarded additional points to candidates with an advanced degree in Algerian law or "Muslim law and indigenous customs."[38]

The police recruitment system rewarded French markers of knowledge of Algerians, but by denying Algerians access to French education, the colonial system largely excluded those with real knowledge of the Algerian community—Algerians themselves. Often, colonial states selected so-called martial races among their colonial subjects as policemen, using these favored ethnic groups to police other colonial populations.[39] In the settler colonial project of Algeria, however, the local government instead reserved public jobs, including that of police officer, for Europeans. The police of Algiers did not keep racial statistics on their hiring practices, but one survey of the personnel of the police d'état of Algiers from 1943 reveals a telling pattern. A compilation of the names of all 888 employees of the police d'état showed that as one moved up the ranks, Algerian names became scarcer. All sixteen chief brigadiers were European, as were sixty-two of sixty-three brigadiers. Even in the entry-level "guardian of the peace" position, only 49 of 542 officers had Arabic names.[40] In total, Algerian officers represented a mere 9 percent of the department. This stands in stark contrast to colonial police forces elsewhere in the French Empire, where Indigenous officers made up the bulk of lower-level agents.[41]

The European officers reflected the immigrant melting pot of Algeria's European population, including men with French, Italian, Spanish, and Maltese origins. French officers from the metropole served alongside local recruits, possibly drawn to the colonies by a chance for upward mobility. Nearly all officers boasted a record of military service, a result of the mass drafts of World War I. Most European officers had no knowledge of Algerian languages. They were more likely to speak Italian, Spanish, or even Provençal, the dialect of southern France, than Arabic or Amazigh. Officers had to live in the commune where they worked. Forced proximity offered a chance to develop personal relationships with those they policed, but it also gave police officers an implicit power over their neighbors that they could, and did, wield in daily interactions.

French officials justified the disparity between the number of European and Algerian police officers in Algiers. In 1938, an Algerian municipal councilor complained that since the creation of the police d'état in 1930, the administration set aside fewer positions for Algerians. The municipal council unanimously voted to send a recommendation to the prefect about hiring more Algerians.[42] The prefect responded that the police considered "indigène" candidates on equal terms with French citizens. However, he claimed that they struggled to find qualified, literate Algerian candidates.[43] While the prefect's statement was undeniably accurate, he left unspoken the reason for these illiteracy rates. The inequality in education in Algeria was a result of the colonial state's destruction of traditional Arabic schools and their refusal to provide adequate funding for French schools for Algerians.[44] When the police did hire Algerians, these officers generally received lower wages and less permanent contracts than their European colleagues.[45]

Despite prioritizing European recruits, the colonial police needed Algerians to serve in crucial roles as translators and intermediaries, to access the gossip central to surveillance. These Algerian officers spoke Arabic, Amazigh, or both, as well as French, the language of internal police communication. They also brought with them connections to the Algerian community, although not always desirable ones. For example, Officer Mohamed Hamidi worked in the hygiene department of Algiers before transferring to the police in 1944, a typical trajectory.[46] Hamidi was noted by his superiors as zealous and loyal, but over the course of his career, several Algerians lodged complaints alleging that Hamidi used his power as a police officer to settle scores with individuals who had feuded with his family.[47] Police officers like Hamidi and Algerian urbanites developed complicated, intimate relationships, interacting in everyday realms that had little to do with crime. Policing, as Hamidi's story shows, was a relational endeavor, inflected by the imperatives of individual officers even as it reflected the desires of the state.

Scandal plagued the police of Algiers. Complaints in officers' personnel files noted incidents of violence or abuse, aimed particularly at Algerians. One example was Commissioner Hebert, who served in the seaside Algerian suburb of Hussein Dey in the 1920s before being transferred to Algiers in 1937. In 1921, an Algerian grocer, Aissa B., lodged a grievance saying that Hebert had beaten him during an investigation.[48] Hebert denied hitting Aissa, but the conflict became a public scandal when the Algerian newspaper *L'Ikdam* picked up the story. The prefect of Algiers convened a disciplinary council to investigate, but in the end, the committee cleared Hebert of wrongdoing. Similar accusations of racial violence followed Hebert throughout his long, and ultimately successful, career. Cases like this littered the personnel files of officers in Algiers, and these were only the accusations the police themselves chose to treat as credible. Many other stories of violence surely slipped through the archival cracks.

Across the Mediterranean, the police of Marseille deployed similar recruitment tactics. The men of the Marseille police force were often born in Marseille, deeply familiar with the urban landscape.[49] Many officers came from Italian or Spanish immigrant families, and a significant minority were originally from the French island of Corsica.[50] Men from other regions of France also joined the force, brought by personal preference or career opportunities to the south. Officers spoke a wide range of languages, with dossiers noting fluency in Spanish, Italian, German, and Provençal. Though different ethnicities and languages filled police stations, some languages were notably missing—Arabic and Amazigh.

Being a police officer provided stability, but the pay remained relatively low compared to other bureaucratic appointments. To that end, the police of Marseille tended to attract upwardly mobile artisans. Officers often worked as low-level bureaucrats, office workers, farmers, butchers, or bakers before joining the force. Few recruits had worked as industrial laborers, perhaps a reflection of the educational standard required to be a police officer. Often Catholic, typically married, and frequently fathers to large families, police officers in Marseille operated as their families' primary breadwinners in traditional patriarchal fashion. As in Algiers, candidates joined the police with a competitive exam, and all officers had to be literate. However, few men had advanced education. Even attaining a certification of primary studies, a CEP, was a noted accolade. Police training happened largely on the job, with junior officers assigned to shadow senior partners.[51] As in Algiers, almost all officers in interwar Marseille had military experience.

Although they purported to provide order and security, the Marseille police faced constant accusations of corruption. Marseille earned a reputation as a tough town, nicknamed the "Chicago" of France in reference to the gang violence of interwar Chicago.[52] The police, too, mirrored their famously crooked Chicago counterparts. Marseille's police became so synonymous with corruption that in 1938, Parisian authorities launched a comprehensive investigation of the force. One of the officers caught in this sweep was Marius Bretin. A native of Marseille, Bretin stood accused of taking bribes during a murder investigation, "disappearing" a file in exchange for a hefty fee. As evidence, the investigators pointed to Bretin's new country home and expensive car, luxuries beyond the budget of a police employee.[53] In total, the investigation brought ten officers before a disciplinary council.[54]

A few police officers in Marseille had ties to Algeria, providing the language skills and cultural familiarity the police desperately needed to monitor Algerian migration.[55] These officers often came from the Algerian Jewish population of Marseille, a community with ties to both Marseille and Algiers.[56] However, controversy tinged the careers of many Algerian Jewish police officers, including Salomon Benichou. Benichou was born in Algiers, eventually migrating to Marseille and joining the police in 1908. Surprisingly, Benichou's personnel file noted that he understood Provençal but never mentioned Arabic, although he likely spoke at least some.[57] By 1922, Benichou had accumulated a staggering twenty infractions, reprimanded for everything from insubordination to public drunkenness. The police fired Benichou in 1928 without a pension, labeling him an untrustworthy drunk.[58] While Benichou's termination resulted from his documented misconduct, it perhaps reflected, too, antisemitic attitudes on the rise in interwar France.

A range of motivations drove police officers to join the force in Marseille and Algiers. For some, joining the police simply meant obtaining a secure, middle-class job. Others saw themselves as fulfilling a fundamental social role, protecting citizens from criminals. Left adrift after the war, former soldiers might have valued the discipline and civic duty of a career in policing. Some may also have been attracted to the warrior masculinity associated with the profession. The European officers who served in Marseille and Algiers came from different perspectives and backgrounds, many from immigrant communities. Would an officer who grew up speaking Italian feel more loyalty to his linguistic community than an abstract idea of the French Empire? Or perhaps officers with tenuous ties to French citizenship might have supported a narrow framing of national belonging, a way of asserting their own French identity.

The exam to become a police officer included a dictation, often on the theme of the police. In one such exercise, a potential officer had to transcribe a description of the police. The dictation defined the police as "working in the general interest with benevolence, conciliation, persuasion, and, if needed, the use of force."[59] As an institution, then, the police saw themselves as guarding the greater good, a protective role nonetheless underpinned by violence. In my research, I found no diaries or letters, no accounts of police officers explaining their own motivations. I have no first-person sources to understand what "colonial order" meant to a beat cop in Marseille or how their interpretation differed from a colleague in Algiers. Instead, I understand police ideology through practice. The reports, arrest records, and correspondence in the state archives tell us what police *did*. The internalized goals of police action are less central to this project than the way policing was experienced, how police actions shaped the possibilities of movement, of labor, of love, and of life for North Africans in the French Mediterranean.

Speaking "Algerian"

Though the police of Marseille and Algiers tried to recruit officers who could speak Arabic and Amazigh, communication remained a constant problem. European empires claimed to exert absolute sovereignty over colonial territories, but imperial power always depended on intermediaries, local actors who served as representatives of the distant colonial state.[60] In Marseille and Algiers, French authorities were omnipresent. Instead of rural emissaries, the police needed urban intermediaries whose language skills and personal proximity to Algerian social life offered access to a "closed" community. The police needed men who could communicate with North Africans in Arabic and Amazigh, who could sit in a café maure and not stand out, who could live among the transient North Africans in Marseille and in the established Algerian enclave of the Casbah.[61] These men—and they were invariably men—served as translators not just of language but of "customs" and "morals."[62]

The police of Algiers employed an important minority of Algerian police officers, but Marseille struggled to staff its force with any officers who could speak Arabic or Amazigh. Officers who understood the Algerian Arabic dialect, *darija*, as opposed to formal, classical Arabic, proved particularly elusive.[63] A report from 1916 by the prosecutor of Marseille to the central police commissioner commented on these linguistic difficulties. The prosecutor described the growing North African community of Marseille as shut off to outsiders. Densely packed into tiny, shared rooms and constantly moving, Algerians proved hard to track. Because police agents did not speak Arabic, they found it impossible to gather information for their investigations, he said.[64] Moreover, the police lacked understanding of Algerians' "very special mentality."[65] The letter drips with colonial prejudice, but it also attests to a real problem in police attempts to serve and surveil North Africans in Marseille—a pervasive language barrier. The struggle of translation was obvious in the police reports I read in both Marseille and Algiers. A single case file might contain several different names for the same accused North African criminal or victim, varying in spelling across departments or between reporting officers.

In Marseille, problems of language hampered the control of immigration. In November 1937, the divisional commissioner of the port of Marseille, Sallet, requested two auxiliary North African agents.[66] Justifying his demand, Sallet noted that no one in Marseille's port police spoke Arabic. Sallet's plan, however, was to no avail. Though the local government was sympathetic, no one wanted to provide the funds.[67] By the end of the 1930s, estimates put the number of North Africans in Marseille at around twenty thousand. Although North Africans made up a significant immigrant community in Marseille, they paled in comparison to the volume of Italian immigrants, for example.[68] Despite the relatively small number of Algerians, officials like Sallet fixated on the potential danger of this colonial population. Local and regional governments shared Sallet's fear but refused to prioritize funding for officers familiar with North African languages. North Africans arriving by boat undertook the process of immigration without official help translating forms or answering questions. Instead, immigrants relied on each other, with Algerians and other Arabic speakers offering translation services to new arrivals for a price.

In Algiers, too, the police struggled with communication. The Algiers police hired more Algerian employees than the police force of Marseille ever could. Even some European officers born in Algeria spoke Arabic, although their fluency proved questionable.[69] Still, if more police officers in Algiers spoke Amazigh and Arabic, this did not solve all issues of translation. Police services made conflicting demands on the time and skills of the Algerian agents who spoke local languages. A minority of the overall force, Algerian officers simply could not provide all the services needed. In August 1939, for example, police officials decided that an officer needed to surveil a baptism in Tagarins, a hilly neighborhood just above downtown Algiers. Even labeling the event as a "baptism" betrays miscommunication. Muslims do not practice baptism, and this ceremony was probably a circumcision. By framing Islamic practices in Catholic vocabulary, the police made Algerian practices legible to themselves but ignored the complexity of Algerian culture. Apparently strapped for personnel, the police sent *Garde champêtre* Georges Mezergues to watch the "baptism."[70] Leaders wanted Mezergues to observe two well-known political figures, the nationalist Ferhat Abbas and the religious-social leader Cheikh El Okbi, who were slated to speak. However, Mezergues's presence at this event proved essentially useless. His report stated, "Not understanding the Arabic language, we could not say what was said in the two speeches."[71] It seems an almost comically inept error to send an officer who spoke no Arabic to observe a Muslim religious event where speeches would certainly be in Arabic. The image of a police officer attending this circumcision, clueless about the speeches and lacking even a coherent understanding of the event itself, reveals much about the difference between the aspirations and the realities of colonial policing.

Other complaints about miscommunication with the police in Algiers seem to suggest, in contrast, a willful "misunderstanding" by Algerians. In a Municipal Council meeting in 1931, Algerian municipal councilors raised complaints about police violence toward Algerian street vendors. One European councilor suggested that the solution would be to decrease pressure on officers by increasing their overall numbers. An Algerian councilor retorted sarcastically, "In summary, in order to make the brutalities stop, the number of agents must be increased?"[72] As the debate continued, European Municipal Councilor M. Dominique sought to find a middle ground. He said officers needed to arm themselves with patience and described an incident he had witnessed personally, in which a police officer had intervened to stop a vendor breaking the law. However, the peddler "did not fully understand" the reprimands of the officers, and the misunderstanding turned a simple ticket into a complicated affair.[73] Although Dominique read this as miscommunication, we might interpret it differently. Did the vendor not understand the officer? Or did he not *want* to understand him? In moments of miscommunication, Algerians could also use the language barrier to insist on the validity of their own actions. By refusing to understand French, the street vendor in this story also refused to accept French control of his movement and livelihood.

Speaking "Algerian," a skill of linguistic ability but also cultural competency, was coveted in both Algiers and Marseille. Algiers employed more Algerian officers, but the systematic favoring of Europeans in hiring meant that these Algerian officers remained a minority. The Algerian police recruited according to the same standards as the metropole. Speaking a foreign language added points, but equal weight was given to German and Arabic, English and Amazigh. If the Third Republic positioned its police force as a neutral service that protected all civilians, the constant miscommunication, misspelling, and misunderstanding challenged this vision when it came to Algerians. Moments of incomprehension show the complicated reality of policing a multicultural city but also betray the mechanics of empire. By insisting on the primacy of French in policing both Marseille and Algiers, the police prioritized imperial power over local accountability. French authorities again and again identified language as an imperative tool for their control of North Africans, yet failed to invest in it.

"Knights of the Knife"

When the police of Marseille and Algiers discussed Algerians, they described a slew of dangerous, supposedly inherent, traits. Ideas of Algerian criminality built upon an established academic discipline of criminology. French criminology can be traced back to the French Revolution, but most scholars see the nineteenth century as its true advent.[74] Nineteenth-century criminologists explained criminal behavior as a hereditary trait, diverging from previous social or individual explanations of crime. Criminology built on theories of evolution, as well as ideas of eugenics and fears of the degeneration of the "French race" in the late Third Republic.[75] But when experts discussed French criminals, they treated criminality as a characteristic of specific families, passed between parent and child. With Algerians, concepts of criminality overlapped with developing narratives of race and imperial conquest. French ideas of Algerian criminality therefore applied to an entire "race," rather than family lines.

Insidious stereotypes about Algerian criminals gained traction in part because of the pseudoscientific evidence marshaled to support the claim. The "Algiers school" of psychiatry insisted on the innate psychological deficiencies of North African men, describing them as primitive, unstable, and naturally criminal.[76] The precursor of this school of thought is visible in Adolphe Kocher's 1884 text, *On Arab Criminality*. Originally from Lyon, Kocher compiled his observations while working as a doctor at the Civil Hospital of Mustapha in Algiers. In his book, Kocher featured typical, gendered stereotypes of Algerians, describing Algerian men as nomadic, lazy, and despotic and Algerian women as the perpetual victims of domineering men.[77] Kocher admitted that statistics showed non-French Europeans in fact committed the most crimes in Algeria but insisted, nonetheless, on the uniquely criminal nature of Algerians. As his text described, "The Arab is essentially a thief because of habit, because of temperament and sometimes, because of need."[78] Kocher described Algerians as violent, motivated by primitive urges of greed, jealousy, and vengeance. Although presenting himself as an objective scientist, Kocher sought to prove stereotypes he clearly already believed. Describing the low rate of infanticide among Algerian families, for example, Kocher asserted that, "This fact confirms what we have already said countless times, that the vast majority of crimes rest, in Algeria, unknown to justice."[79] Faced with evidence that contradicted his racist certainties, Kocher reimagined this as a point in his favor by evoking supposedly unreported crimes.

Kocher was not the first to propagate these stereotypes, nor was his text necessarily influential. Rather, the book exemplifies a variety of similar sources that built a collective knowledge among French observers, and the French police, of the Algerian criminal.[80] The racialized and criminalized stereotypes of Algerians appeared ubiquitously in administrators' discussion of Algerian immigration, they peppered police reports on Algerians in metropole and colony, they seeped into news articles on everyday crime. Without ever reading an ethnographic work on Algerian criminality, French police officers could hardly have escaped exposure to the criminalizing stereotypes that work such as Kocher's promoted. Nor was this type of essentialization new to the French colonial project. The racialization of North African criminals borrowed from discursive strategies previously used to negate the humanity of enslaved Africans in the seventeenth- and eighteenth-century French Empire.[81]

Similar portrayals of Algerian criminality also appeared in the headlines of dramatic *faits divers* articles in both Marseille and Algiers. These newspaper stories provided short, gory accounts of crime, giving readers a horrifying but scintillating glimpse into the underbelly of modern life.[82] Historians have argued that metropolitan faits divers articles reflected class dynamics, particularly in their negative portrayal of the working class.[83] In Algiers, however, race proved the relevant category, as papers supplied a steady stream of tales about Algerian "knights of the knife."[84] The faits divers featured a disproportionate number of stories about Algerian, as opposed to European, criminals.[85] Algiers newspapers often noted the location of bloody crimes, adding to the dangerous mystique of places like the Casbah. Reports ascribed Algerian violence to jealousy or pride, and theft became routinely associated with Algerians. The details of these thefts, however, are revealing. Laundry was stolen from a line, a lamb chop was slipped out of a butcher shop window, a man was arrested for stealing an umbrella or a bar of soap. If French reporters called theft inherent to the Algerian "temperament," we could also see stealing a piece of meat or a bar of soap as evidence of the abject poverty created by French colonial exploitation.

In Marseille, the appearance of North Africans in the local faits divers coincided with the increase in Algerian immigration after World War I. Headlines like "A drama of jealousy in Mende: An Algerian kills his wife with blows from an axe and a knife" delivered a narrative of violent jealousy and hypermasculinity.[86] Marseille papers described Algerian criminality as omnipresent, as in one article titled,

"The Arabs Again."[87] Faits divers stories spoke of North Africans as jealous lovers, wily thieves, cold-hearted scammers, and violent thugs but suggested that North African violence was directed internally, labeling conflicts as "between Arabs." Both the *Petit Provençal* and *Petit Marseillais*, the two major local newspapers of Marseille, also reported the most sensational crimes from Algeria. The reproduction of colonial criminality offered readers in Marseille a glimpse into the "exotic" world of Algerian crime, reinforcing negative stereotypes of Algerians.

The ideas of Algerian criminality circulating in newspapers and ethnographic studies had a real impact on police practice. In 1914, the governor general of Algeria sent a special delegate, Ahmed Saïd Mehdi, from Algiers to survey the conditions of Algerian laborers in Marseille.[88] To get a sense of the desires of the Algerians living and working in Marseille, Mehdi visited the bars and cafés on Rue des Chapeliers. The primary complaint among Marseille's Algerian residents was that the police treated Algerians not as ordinary residents but like the "*apaches*" (bandits) of Algeria. The men complained that the police "brutalize them without reason and always rule against them."[89] Evoking faits divers reports of banditry in Algeria, these workers claimed the police saw all Algerians as little more than outlaws, a tangible effect of imagined Algerian criminality.

At times, Europeans deployed the prevalent ideas of Algerian criminality to deflect police suspicion. In 1918, the police accused Marcel B. of setting fire to a forest near Marseille. Marcel insisted that an "Arab" had set the fire and then fled. Based on his tip, the police went off in search of the mysterious "Arab." The officers did in fact find an Algerian worker nearby, but he had only entered the region after the first in the series of fires had occurred, eliminating him as a suspect. The police eventually concluded that there could be no doubt that Marcel himself set the fires and blamed the "Arab" to redirect suspicion.[90] Marcel's red herring ultimately failed to distract the police, but officers diligently spent weeks searching for the mysterious "Arab," ignoring the obvious suspect in front of them. Stereotypes had real power.

In both Marseille and Algiers, locating North African criminals was equal parts the creation of an imaginary of "typical" crimes and motivations and physically mapping spaces of North African life. The police came to superimpose these two imaginaries, mutually reinforcing ideas of spatial distinction and danger. The police looked upon the North African community in both Marseille and Algiers with suspicion, a distrust focused specifically on Algerian men and rooted in a belief about their uncontrolled violence. The boogeyman of the "dangerous Algerian" shaded the physical gathering spaces of North Africans in the eyes of the police, haunting the narrow streets of the Casbah and the crowds behind the Bourse in Marseille. The urban divisions and racial segregation present in both cities deepened over the course of the twentieth century.[91] Police understanding of the North African neighborhoods of Marseille and Algiers, both their physical geography and their supposed criminality, laid the foundations for racialized policing based on space. In these cosmopolitan ports, the police struggled to phenotypically distinguish between Greek, Armenian, Italian, Spanish, French, and North African populations that poured in from across the Mediterranean basin. Spatial modes of discrimination addressed messy visual constructions of race in multiethnic ports, giving police officers a way of "mapping" North Africans.

Dangerous Masculinity

The recurrent newspaper stories about North African criminality discussed scandals of theft and horrific examples of violence, but there was also a specifically gendered idea of North African vice. In his 1884 tome, for example, Kocher linked Algerian criminality to the practice of polygamy.[92] According to Kocher, jealousy motivated most Algerian violent crime. He blamed jealousy on the "shameful commerce" of marriage in Algeria and asserted that polygamy was connected to a broader spectrum of sexual deviance, including "sodomy."[93] In accusing Algerians of nonnormative sexual practices, Kocher issued a blanket condemnation of Algerian morality. He linked homosexuality and polygamy to cruelty, describing Algerian men as insatiable and thus prone to sexual violence. The French obsession with polygamy was largely misplaced. According to the colonial government's own statistics, only 6.4 percent of Algerians lived in polygamous households in 1911, and this percentage decreased over time.[94] Still, fantasies of sexual difference stoked French fears of Algerians. In Algiers, French observers described the Casbah as a decadent, vice-ridden space, establishing state-sanctioned brothels that clashed with the desires of many Algerian families. In Marseille, fears of North African sexuality tinged police reports on the relationships between North African men and local European women.

In Algiers, French observers routinely described the Casbah as a wonderland of sexual pleasure. In part, this portrayal derived from French imaginaries of "harems" of Algerian women in polygamous marriages, seen as subservient to male desires. In French author Lucienne Favre's "insider view" of the Casbah, she describes the neighborhood as the Montmartre of Algiers, linking it to the notorious red-light district of Paris.[95] Rues Bologhine, Barberousse, and Kataroudjil, at the top of the Casbah, housed dozens of state-regulated brothels that employed mostly Algerian women.[96] French writers frequently painted prostitution as an innate vice of the Casbah. Sex work certainly existed in the Casbah prior to colonial rule, but French writers ignored how colonial policies and urban planning had been responsible for labeling the Casbah as the center of prostitution in colonial Algiers.

Residents of the Casbah frequently complained about the undistinguished mix of brothels and family residences. Lucienne Favre alleged that Algerian fathers would place signs over their doors reading "Honest Home" in broken French, to warn away tourists seeking sex.[97] Algerian representatives in the Municipal Council of Algiers repeatedly emphasized the dangers that the concentration of brothels posed. In 1919, with World War I just concluded, they blamed the rising insecurity experienced by the Algerian population on increased prostitution during the war.[98] Drunk, rowdy Europeans trekked through the Casbah, getting into fights and offering tempting targets to pickpockets. French soldiers from metropole and colony housed in nearby barracks stumbled through the red-light district of the Casbah on their days off, venting pent-up aggression on each other and locals. The Casbah even became a popular destination for sex tourism for European travelers.[99] The supposed availability of exoticized Algerian women drew a continuous, unruly crowd of European revelers.

Despite Lucienne Favre's comparison, the Casbah was not Montmartre. Colonial segregation cordoned the vast majority of Algerian residents into the Casbah, including connected political elites, relatively wealthy merchants, middle-class civil servants, and working-class laborers. Descriptions of the Casbah evoked women shrouded in their *haik*, a white veil that covered the face and draped to the ground. Children gamboled about, running errands, hawking newspapers, or playing games. The Casbah was not just a space of vice; it was also home to thousands of "respectable" Muslim families. It was European visions of sexual deviance that made the Casbah into a dangerous space of male desire. The police were called upon to regulate the uneasy mix of vice and respectability in the Casbah. In the debates about the dangers of prostitution in the Casbah, Algerian political representatives often demanded an increased police presence.[100] Residents wanted the police to protect them from misplaced European desire, separating families from the sexual commerce encouraged by French colonial authorities.

In Marseille, the French imagined a different sort of dangerous masculinity, one that focused on the "insatiable" desires of Arab men. French immigration policy made it difficult for Algerian women to come to the metropole alongside their partners, and few women made the journey.[101] The neighborhood surrounding Rue des Chapeliers featured a cosmopolitan immigrant community, and interethnic marriage was a simple fact of life. In contrast, interracial marriages in colonial Algiers remained exceedingly rare.[102] The romantic relationships that developed between Algerian men and European women were a cause for concern among Marseille's police force. In carefully tracking Algerian relationships with European women, the police could at times insert themselves as paternalistic caretakers, defending white women from "dangerous" Algerian men.[103] By labeling relationships between Algerian men and European women as deviant, the police imposed an idea of racial separation between Europeans and Algerians, even as their physical proximity within the central neighborhoods of Marseille lent itself to exchange.

The most detailed information on these mixed couples comes from the 1940s, when wartime practices of archival preservation led to richer collections. Although the sources come from the 1940s, many of the relationships they describe began in the interwar period. A police report from 1940 suggested that four thousand Algerians lived in Marseille but emphasized that the fluid and often undocumented nature of the North African diaspora made statistics little more than an educated guess. Among this group, sixty North Africans had contracted legal marriages to Frenchwomen, and the police suggested that two hundred or more lived in "*concubinage*" with French or European women in Marseille.[104] The document does not describe how the police arrived at the number of informal "concubine" relationships, which could mean anything from a casual girlfriend to a common-law wife. Perhaps they obtained a list from the owners of the furnished hotels where Algerian workers lived, or from the records of local aid groups. Regardless, the police identified relationships between European women and Algerian men as requiring observation.

Franco-Algerian couples faced scrutiny and disdain from police observers. In 1942, the *Renseignements Généraux* (RG) of Marseille ordered their "special service for North African Affairs" to conduct a survey of North African families.[105] This brigade identified and interviewed thirty-six families, carefully listed by last name and address.[106] Among the thirty-six families, the police found several Algerians married to French or European immigrant women. Their opinion of these couples was far from complimentary. Rather than elevating Algerian men, these mixed marriages, the police report said, "reduced" European women to the standards of their Algerian husbands. Police reports often emphasized the deviance of women associated with Algerians, labeling them as prostitutes or dupes tricked into a life of debauchery. If police disparaged mixed relationships, some Algerian men described their partnerships as evidence of their assimilation into French society. To them, their relationship with a French woman served as the embodiment of their attachment to France.[107]

Discrimination against mixed couples could also come from family members, with the police acting as middlemen. In these cases, police intervened in sexual relationships but also, more broadly, in intimate family conflicts. A Frenchwoman wrote to the police of Marseille in 1941, asking them to search for her seventeen-year-old sister, Yvonne K. The police discovered Yvonne in Marseille, living "maritally" with one Belkacem H. for almost eight months. When the police communicated this information to Yvonne's sister however, she declared that she was no longer interested in Yvonne's fate. The police then arrested young Yvonne for "vagabondage of a minor," as she was underage and living apart from her family.[108] The charge of vagrancy contradicts the fixed nature of the life the police had discovered. Yvonne was hardly homeless or panhandling. She shared an apartment and a life with her boyfriend in Marseille. The police relied on the tools they had at their disposal to remove this white woman from what they considered to be a morally reprehensible situation. Yvonne's sister cared enough to initiate a police search, but immediately ostracized her sibling when the police revealed she was living with a North African, even though this rejection had criminal penalties for Yvonne. Though an atypical case, this family drama suggests the social consequences faced by Franco-Algerian couples.

In other cases, however, the police were called upon to act as arbiters in disputes between Franco-Algerian couples. One example comes from the story of a European woman, Pauline B., who wrote a letter to the prosecutor of Marseille describing her regrets about getting involved with "a mister of Algerian origins." After meeting him in 1938, she had let him move into her apartment. Shortly thereafter, however, he lost his job and started drinking "bad wine" and mistreating her. He even fraudulently filed for unemployment in her name. Finally, Pauline had enough and left her "friend," departing to find work in the Hautes-Alpes. She informed the police that she left her boyfriend's belongings with a neighbor, then changed the keys and locked her apartment. She later heard through neighbors that her lover had kicked in the door and reinstalled himself in the apartment. Pauline begged the police to recover her furniture, to prevent her ex from selling it off.[109]

The police dutifully intervened but encountered a very different story of the relationship when they spoke to Pauline's "friend," Chérif K. Chérif painted a rosier picture of their love, saying that they had been living together for four years. He admitted that he lost his job but claimed that when employed, he gave his whole salary to Pauline, whom he considered his wife. He alleged that although the apartment was in her name, they had used his income to pay for it and he had always considered the apartment theirs. Pauline lied when she left, according to Chérif, saying she was going to care for her sick mother and would soon return. Chérif indeed produced a letter to this effect from Pauline, which she had signed "your wife [ta femme]."[110] Pauline did change the locks, but Chérif simply called a locksmith, assuming she would eventually return. Chérif denied mistreating Pauline and claimed the furnishings had been purchased with his earnings, although again in Pauline's name. Chérif mournfully told the police that he now realized Pauline had taken advantage of him, buying things in her name knowing that he could not read and therefore would not realize. Every bit the rejected lover, Chérif called Pauline flighty and said she left him because she was bored.[111]

Presented with two radically different narratives, the police hedged their bets. They did not evict Chérif from the apartment but neither did they characterize Pauline's accusations as false. The prosecutor had a copy of the investigation sent to Pauline, but no legal action was taken. Although a story without a clear ending, Chérif and Pauline reveal the facility with which Algerian men and European women created relationships in Marseille. Pauline's landlord and neighbors testified to the police that they thought Chérif and Pauline were married and spoke of Chérif with seeming respect. Pauline knew how to appeal to the French authorities. She told the police she had only lived with Chérif in their apartment for a few months, omitting the four years of cohabitation Chérif claimed. She presented herself as swindled, wooed by Chérif only to find herself at the mercy of an unemployed, drunk, and violent Algerian man. Chérif, too, played into French stereotypes. He claimed he could not read and had no idea that Pauline purchased the furnishings in her own name. Why then would Pauline have written him a letter explaining her departure? Why not pass the message to him verbally through a neighbor instead?

In an ugly story of love gone sour, neither party seems to be entirely truthful. The police had to sort out who was lying, who was the victim, and how to respond. Although all domestic disputes presented similar challenges, no matter the origins of the partners, cases involving Algerian men and French women unfolded within an extra layer of prejudice about Algerian "morals" and the European women romantically involved with them. The investigation of Pauline's letter reflected diligent police work but also ingrained biases. The evidence the police gathered seemed to indicate that Pauline had lied, but the officers did not exonerate Chérif, a decision well within in their power. Instead, they tacitly supported Pauline, framing themselves as protecting her from the wiles a "dangerous" Algerian man.

It was not just relationships with European women that worried the French police. French observers also highlighted the supposedly deviant sexual appetites of Arab men.[112] In everything from scientific publications on Algerian criminality to popular press outlets, French authors accused Algerian men of homosexuality, stigmatized by French society at the time. French discussions of Algerian sexuality treated homosexuality as an extension of Arab men's hyperdeveloped sexual appetite. Overstimulated by their multiple subservient wives, this racist logic went, North African men sought more exotic pleasures. In policing, suspicions of Algerian homosexuality reinforced police assumptions about Algerians as nonnormative and non-French, a danger to European communities.

Frequent reports in Algiers referred to the arrest of Algerians for charges of indecency related to homosexual sex or soliciting. Files also detailed horrific accusations of rape, almost invariably listing Algerian men as the aggressors and young men as the victims. These rape cases are difficult for a historian of colonial violence to assess. The suffering of assault survivors is clear. Yet there also seems to be a too-simple link between sexual assault and Algerian sexuality that mirrors the tirades of ethnographers like Kocher. In one case, for example, European parents came to the police to report that they suspected their son, Jean-Pierre, of stealing from them.[113] When the police brought Jean-Pierre in for questioning, he claimed that he had stolen the money to pay off an Algerian youth who had threatened him. As the case evolved, Jean-Pierre eventually claimed that this same Algerian youth, a sixteen-year-old named Mohamed, had raped him. The police investigation wound through a tangle of claims and accusations, eventually resulting in the arrest of four Algerians aged thirteen to twenty for rape or complicity. The four arrests were based largely on the "confession" of a thirteen-year-old accused accomplice, held and questioned without parents or a legal advisors present. As if by magic, the investigation into Jean-Pierre's alleged theft disappeared. Although the archives are opaque, it seems possible that Jean-Pierre invented the rape accusation to distract from the charges leveled against him by his parents. If that was the case, it worked. Preexisting tropes of Algerians' deviant sexuality disposed the police to understand Jean-Pierre as the victim and Mohamed as the menace.

Assumptions of Algerian homosexuality similarly played into the policing of North African spaces in Marseille. Frequent notes list Algerians arrested on the quays, near the train stations, or in other public spaces for "attacks against modesty [*attentat à la pudeur*]," a vague charge that could be used to prosecute anything from public nudity, to soliciting, to homosexual encounters, to sexual assault. The police, conditioned by the discourses around them and their own arrest records, accepted the idea of Algerians as a homosexual threat. In January 1941, Giovanni G., a sixteen-year-old Italian immigrant and apprentice baker, informed the police that he had been passing by Porte d'Aix, a triumphal arch known as a gathering spot for North Africans, when an "Arab" attacked him and dragged him into a nearby building.[114] Giovanni claimed this man sexually assaulted him, threatened to kill him if he screamed, and stole his wallet. Miraculously, Giovanni managed to get away. The police investigated and identified a potential Algerian suspect named Benaissa (also spelled Bouaissa), who admitted to knowing Giovanni but denied taking his wallet or assaulting him.

As the investigation continued, Giovanni's story began to fall apart. He had lied about where the crime took place, and several witnesses had seen him trying to go into Benaissa's room in a worker's hostel. By all accounts, Benaissa and Giovanni appeared friendly. When the police confronted Giovanni about his inaccuracies, the baker abruptly changed his story. Originally interviewed at 2 a.m., by 4 p.m. the next day, Giovanni said that the attack took place on Cours Belsunce. He claimed that Benaissa asked him for a match and after giving it to him, the "Arab" invited him into his lodging across the street for a coffee. The owner would not allow them in, despite Benaissa lying and saying Giovanni was his brother. Although not successful, the lie indicates that a sort of "passing" might have been possible in Marseille, with an Algerian visually indistinguishable from an Italian. However, Giovanni maintained that once away from the concierge, Benaissa attacked him, forcing him to take off his shoes and drop his pants. Giovanni managed to get away but, in the process, lost his wallet. Nearly every element of his original statement changed in this second interview, from the location, to the context, to his relationship to Benaissa. The only part that Giovanni kept consistent was the accusation that Benaissa had attempted to sexually assault him and then had stolen his wallet.

The second police interview revealed another key detail. The first police report had been established not because Giovanni went to the police but because the police found *him*. Two police agents had stopped Giovanni as he wandered the neighborhood near the port and asked him for his ID. It was at this moment that Giovanni "spontaneously," and conveniently, declared his wallet had been stolen. He told the officers that he thought the wallet had been taken by "an Arab." The police gave chase to the man Giovanni pointed out but had been unable to catch him, leading to the more in-depth interview with Giovanni and the investigation into Benaissa.[115] Given the constant shifts in Giovanni's story and the witness support for Benaissa, it seems likely that Giovanni lied. Perhaps illegally in France, Giovanni invented a story for the police when asked to present ID papers he did not have. Yet, incredibly, the police believed him. They not only chased after the man he pointed out on the street but also delegated several agents to investigate Giovanni's ever-shifting accusations. The police even searched Benaissa's house for the missing wallet and then, despite finding nothing, put him in jail.[116]

The influence of colonial stereotypes in police practice is obvious in this case. Giovanni knew that pointing a finger at a North African migrant would exonerate him. An Algerian accused of sexual perversion toward a young man fit police expectations. Even when Giovanni's story clashed with witness testimony and Benaissa's account, the police continued to favor Giovanni's version, attempting to corral evidence to support Giovanni rather than investigating the accusations themselves. Giovanni walked away a free man, while Benaissa sat in jail, waiting to prove his innocence instead of the state being forced to prove his guilt. Benaissa's fate rested in the hands of the individual officers working this case, who decided which story to believe. Choosing the account of a young European over that of an Algerian, the Marseille police recreated colonial hierarchies of truth in the metropole.

Asked to settle domestic disputes and regulate sex in both metropole and colony, the police navigated clashes in cultural codes and love stories gone wrong. In some ways, policing intimate conflicts looked the same for mixed-race couples in Marseille as it would have for any other couple. Policing prostitution in the Casbah, too, operated similarly to regulating brothels in Paris or Marseille. But the police also acted with discourses of Algerian deviance in mind, stepping in to uphold French norms of sexuality, family, and race. Police views of the Casbah as a place of sexual vice led to a "boys will be boys" approach to patrolling public thoroughfares. Police beliefs about dangerous Algerian sexuality in Marseille influenced their reaction to cases where Europeans called on them for protection. Stories of policing sexuality and love also show how Algerians and Europeans manipulated the narratives they knew the police believed, playing on police bias for their own self-interest.

Policing Mobility

These negative stereotypes of Algerian criminality and sexual danger emerged alongside a marked increase in Algerian migration between Marseille and Algiers after World War I, a mobility closely tracked by the police. In Marseille, police focused on the port and the continuous flow of immigrants from Algeria. The wave of migration, however, also brought a swell of Algerians from the countryside to Algiers, the main port of exit. In 1913, the French government eliminated the travel permit previously required for Algerians to come to France, encouraging Algerian immigration to man wartime industries.[117] The freedom of movement would not last long. By 1924, the French government required Algerians going to France to have a work contract.[118] Four years later, another decree required Algerians to obtain a special photo ID, a prepaid boat ticket, a deposit of 125 francs for return passage, an additional 150 francs "nest egg" (*pécule*) for unspecified expenses, a certificate of health, and their criminal record.[119] Additional *circulaires*, or internal government memorandums, from 1926 forbid entry to Algerians with "a criminal conviction or a conviction for rape, provoking soldiers to disobedience, and attacks on public order."[120] This odd mix of crimes reveals French preoccupations. The list suggests deviant sexuality, highlighting rape convictions. Yet it also places this violent crime on equal standing with misdeeds aimed at the

French state, like provoking soldiers or disturbing "public order." These restrictions on mobility took on newfound importance in the 1930s, as French xenophobia toward foreign workers mounted during the global economic depression.[121]

Not everyone needed this long list of documents. Algerians who served in the French administration, like municipal councilors or *caïds*—rural Muslim administrators or neo-tribal chiefs—could travel freely.[122] Although police in Marseille tended to collapse all "North Africans" into the same category, there were also significant differences for Moroccan and Tunisian immigrants. France declared protectorates in Tunisia and Morocco in 1881 and 1912, respectively. Neither Moroccans nor Tunisians could travel freely to France and immigrated in much lower numbers. Moreover, none of the immigration rules applied to European Algerians, who had total freedom of movement as French citizens. Ultimately, the enforcement of various regimes of immigration depended on the interpretations of individual police officers and customs officials, a power granted essentially by default.

As Algerians moved back and forth across the Mediterranean in greater numbers, Marseille and Algiers played a crucial role. French officials reported in 1938 that Marseille had become "the central point of transit between Algeria and France," with nearly forty thousand North Africans passing through the city.[123] Other cities routinely sent Algerians awaiting repatriation to Marseille, where the burden of housing and feeding these men fell on local budgets.[124] The police of Algiers, too, fretted over the movement of Algerians. Although the police of Marseille regulated and recorded the arrival of North Africans in Marseille, they proved lax in their control of Algerians going "home," to the consternation of the Algiers police. As Commissioner Sallet of Marseille admitted, the police on his side of the Mediterranean only checked the papers of "foreigners" on boats bound for Algeria.[125] While not French citizens, North Africans, or anyone who could pass for North African, could enter Algeria without restriction.

The fear of Algerian movement blossomed into a panic over illegal immigration in the 1920s. In 1925, the commissioner of the port police in Marseille reported to the prefect that his service had recently stopped twenty-six Algerians who had arrived from Algiers without proper paperwork. According to the migrants, they had managed to evade the rules in Algiers with the help of another Algerian, whom they had paid two hundred francs each.[126] The commissioner filed several more reports in 1925 on the problem of "clandestine" Algerian immigration. In one such letter, the commissioner discussed the arrival of two Egyptians, three Moroccans, and three Algerians on a boat from Algiers. The commissioner noted, "All these foreigners had embarked illegally to come to France."[127] The language is telling. If Egyptians, and perhaps even Moroccans, could be considered foreigners, Algerians had no nationality other than French.

This casual reference to Algerian "foreigners" belies the elaborate veil of Frenchness cast over colonial Algeria.

Scandals of illegal immigration tended to highlight networks of trafficking between Marseille and Algiers. In 1927, for example, the port police of Marseille received an anonymous tip warning them that a group of Moroccans had reached France with the help of a ring of smugglers. The police tracked down seven of these "clandestine" Moroccan workers, all of whom lacked work contracts. The Moroccans claimed that they had gone to a police station in Marseille and paid twenty francs each for their IDs. The Marseille police suspected that the men had obtained the IDs through an illegal immigration scheme that involved the negligence, or complicity, of one of their own officers.[128] Following a tip to check the cafés on Rue des Chapeliers, they eventually tracked down Commissioner Francisi. Francisi had handled more than two hundred immigration cases and had given out IDs to both Italian and Moroccan immigrants without requiring the proper dossier. His fraud, or perhaps carelessness, allowed workers to obtain false IDs. Francisi received administrative sanctions but ultimately kept his job.[129]

The "Francisi affair" was about more than the misconduct of a lone French police officer. In interviews, the Moroccan migrants testified to the participation of Moïse B., also called "the Jew" or "Marius" in police investigation notes, and a restaurateur named Abderahmane.[130] Although members of different religious communities, both Abderahmane and Moïse came from Algeria, settling in Marseille and opening small businesses. The Moroccan interviewees described the two men as Francisi's accomplices, but Francisi framed things differently. Francisi said that Moïse had worked with the police for ten years as an interpreter, helping process Armenian refugees who fled to Marseille during World War I. Francisi also noted that the primary witness against the trio was another North African, Ali. Francisi pointed out that Ali owned a restaurant that competed with Abderahmane's café, a clear conflict of interest.[131] The record is inconclusive on whether Francisi's errors were dishonesty or inattention, but the incident demonstrates the power of individual officers to make ground-level decisions with life-changing consequences for North Africans. It was Francisi's personal relationships with his collaborators and, through them, with the North African community that were at the crux of this affair. Moreover, the relationship between Francisi and his "accomplices" highlights the role of informal urban intermediaries in the shifting regimes of immigration control.

To stem the tide of immigration, both legal and illicit, the police of Marseille and Algiers had to work together. If there were moments of collaboration, there was also conflict. In 1929, the commissioner of the special police in Marseille wrote to the prefect of the Bouches-du-Rhône about twenty-five Algerians who had arrived from Algiers. The men lacked the required documents, including IDs and work contracts. The police sent all twenty-five men back to Algiers the same day, sparking a trans-Mediterranean feud. The prefect of Algiers complained to his Bouches-du-Rhône counterpart that the Marseille police had mistreated the Algerians as they waited to return. The police commissioner in Marseille, meanwhile, denied any wrongdoing and blamed the problem on Algiers. If the Algiers police properly vetted immigrants before departure, he insisted, there would be no need for controversial expulsions.[132] Although working within a common immigration regime, the two police departments feuded over who ultimately bore responsibility for controlling Algerians' movement.

Officers carefully tracked the arrival and departures of Algerians in both Marseille and Algiers because they believed that the trans-Mediterranean mobility of Algerian populations posed a threat. This threat came not so much from the actions of Algerians themselves but from the fears and assumptions that the police heaped upon them. Police interpretations fed on strains of racialized thought in national discourses on colonialism, ethnographic works on crime, and salacious reports in the press. Officers understood Algerians with the biases of their social world, including the ingrained prejudices of colonial Algiers and the xenophobia of interwar Marseille. By interpreting Algerians as uniformly criminal, the police could treat each crime as proof that they were right to be afraid. Police reports emphasized the anonymity of Algerians. The fear of nameless, untraceable immigrants might seem obvious in Marseille, but it was also a problem in Algiers, where police officials described the indistinguishable masses of the Casbah. On both sides of the Mediterranean, the police understood Algerian immigration as a connected story, a problem and a pattern that linked Algiers and Marseille.

Immigration law presents perhaps the most obvious example of the fallacies of the departmentalization of Algeria. The French government may have claimed that Algeria was France, but no one was under the illusion that this was true. When police sent Algerians back to Algeria or prevented them from boarding a ship for Marseille, they enforced the boundaries of imperial belonging. Immigration laws shifted over the interwar period, but the police's central administrative role, and individual interpretive power, remained constant.

Migration locked Marseille and Algiers in a connected history, tied by police surveillance but also by individual Algerians and their families. In Algiers, immigration was a story of departure and eventual, hopefully triumphant, return. The Algiers police, some of them Algerian themselves, cultivated relationships with the residents of the Casbah, building networks of surveillance. In Marseille, by contrast, the police struggled to regulate the North Africans who arrived in their city. The demographics of the police department, peopled mostly with locals, left the force worried about their ability to engage with North Africans. In both cities, the police remained convinced that Algerians presented a unique threat to

French communities. Police officers responded to Algerian mobility by identifying fixed North African spaces within their cities, a spatial understanding of a racialized colonial identity. As police patrolled the "Casbahs" of Marseille and Algiers, they linked racialized ideas of Algerian criminality to the places where Algerians lived. Despite significant local differences and moments of tension, the continuous communication between Marseille and Algiers generated similarities in "colonial" policing across metropole and colony. Officials' fear of North Africans and the imagined risk of their mobility changed policing in the 1930s, prompting new laws and brigades that explicitly targeted North Africans.

2
LOCATING DANGEROUS ALGERIANS

In a 1937 exposé, French reporter René Janon mused, "Nowhere resembles a street in the Casbah of Algiers quite like Rue des Chapeliers."[1] Janon, a resident of Algiers and a reporter for the local *Écho d'Alger* newspaper, had been sent to Marseille to write a multipart series on the city's Algerian diaspora.[2] In his articles, Janon illustrated what he called the "colonization of the metropole" by the twenty thousand Algerians in Marseille. Highlighting the link between Algiers and Marseille, Janon described the colorful markets on Rue des Chapeliers, marveling that visitors would think they were walking on Algiers's Rue Randon. Janon also hinted at illicit activity on Rue des Chapeliers, evoking the "resellers anxious to unload . . . the proceeds of more or less recent robberies."[3] Janon painted Algerian urban space in Marseille as a mysterious criminal underworld and, parroting colonial stereotypes, portrayed Algerians themselves as naive, easily manipulated, and prone to crime.

Janon had been sent to Marseille to document the growing number of Algerians in France in the 1930s, a circulation heavily monitored by the local police. In Algiers, rural Algerians headed to the colonial capital, in search of jobs and, for some, the opportunity to go to France. The arriving migrants in Marseille and Algiers settled into existing residential patterns, blending into the two "Casbahs" Janon evoked. These Casbahs existed as a tangle of ideas as much as physical spaces. A series of ever-present media tropes, seen in Janon's article, followed Algerians as they moved between Marseille and Algiers. Newspaper articles, ethnographic studies, and official reports repeated the dangers of the Casbah and the characteristics of the "Algerian criminal," an invariably male figure. Algerians were thieves. Algerians were violent. Algerians were jealous lovers. Algerians were opportunists. Algerians were irrationally proud. Operating within this web of stereotypes about deviant masculinity and morality, French officials in both metropole and colony argued that they had to contend with a specific criminality among Algerians. Algerian migration to Marseille and Algiers increased just as economic depression hit Europe in the 1930s. As job competition became fierce, French workers turned their hostility toward foreigners, including Algerians.[4] In a context of increasing immigration and economic difficulty, police in both metropole and colony closely surveilled Algerians.

If the police of Marseille and Algiers shared concerns, they responded to fears of the "Algerian criminal" with different models of control. In Marseille, national authorities sponsored the creation of specialized police and aid services designed to target North Africans, singling them out as a dangerous population and blurring the distinction between surveillance and service. In Algiers, in contrast, police units supplemented their authority with new laws that created legal justifications for expansive police power. Despite differing approaches, the police of Marseille and Algiers deployed similar practices in their everyday interactions with North Africans. Police officers combing through the Casbah and patrolling Rue des Chapeliers developed intimate connections with the people they policed, paradoxical relationships of animosity and dependence. Policing expanded to include not just uniformed officers but bureaucrats gathering intel or, in Marseille, an aid service that became a one-stop shop for all interactions between North Africans and the state.[5]

As France faced the political challenges of anticolonialism, the growing popularity of fascism, and a global economic crisis, the police in Marseille and Algiers sought to control the movement of North Africans and the way they used space. Police intervention in North African life stretched beyond crime. Officers inserted themselves into social life, religious practice, and the private sanctum of the home. Police officers were also called upon by North Africans, asked to mediate disputes or solve personal problems. In both Marseille and Algiers, the police developed simultaneous but contradictory roles as enforcers of a discriminatory colonial order and mediators solicited by both North Africans and Europeans to uphold conflicting ideas of justice. As police officers navigated this intermediary role, their interventions relied fundamentally on an understanding of "North African" spaces of the city, defining acceptable behavior within racialized urban zones. The intimate policing of daily life in the Casbahs was built on violence and racialized ideas of crime, but defining these neighborhoods as North African could also, at times, allow North Africans to assert control over urban space.

Colonial Codes in Algiers

The Algiers police had tracked "criminal Algerians" for decades, but developments in the 1930s provoked changes that solidified a new system of control. Armed revolts had periodically challenged French rule throughout the nineteenth century, but after World War I, Algerian resistance moved from the battleground to the ballot box. The interwar period saw the birth of Algerian nationalist political parties, inspired by nationalist movements in Europe and the Middle East.[6] In 1926, Messali Hadj founded the Étoile Nord-Africaine (ENA) in Paris, calling for an end to the indigénat code and for sweeping colonial reforms. Though the government disbanded the ENA in 1937, Hadj and his allies reconstituted it as the Parti du Peuple Algérien (PPA) just months later. In interwar Algiers, Cheik Abdelhamid Ben Badis formed the Association des Oulémas Musulmans Algériens (*'Ulamā*), preaching a return to traditional Islamic values and a rejection of French cultural influence. Ferhat Abbas, another rising political star in interwar Algeria, advocated for assimilation for Algerian elites. French officials reacted fearfully to the emerging formal structure of Algerian nationalism, monitoring meetings and tracking political leaders.

Then, in 1934, violent antisemitic attacks in Constantine shook colonial authorities. Sparked by tensions between Constantine's Muslim and Jewish populations, a disagreement between neighbors escalated into bloody riots. Though French administrators at the time interpreted the incident as evidence of Muslim Algerians' deep-seated antisemitism, historian Joshua Cole has suggested a more complicated history of political provocation.[7] In the wake of the riot, Governor General of Algeria Georges Le Beau created the Centre d'Information et d'Études (CIE) to survey the movements and attitudes of the Algerian population. Le Beau charged the CIE with collecting information, asserting that the Constantine murders had spiraled out of control because officials lacked knowledge.[8] The CIE worked closely with police services throughout Algeria, operating as a collective archive by gathering and redirecting data from a variety of government services.[9] CIE employees were bureaucrats, not police officers, but the archival trail of the organization shows a constant exchange of information between the CIE and police. CIE notes often listed police reports as the source of their intelligence, and conversely, the CIE forwarded updates on "dangerous" Algerian nationalists or worrisome rumors to local police departments.[10] The CIE operated as part of a larger policing apparatus in Algiers. The mix of administration, passive information gathering, and violent intervention forces us to reframe the scope of the colonial police. Policing involved not just officers who patrolled the streets and made arrests but also these largely anonymous bureaucrats and archivists.

The CIE was not the only administrative change spurred by the Constantine riots and nationalist organizing. On March 30, 1935, French Interior Minister Marcel Régnier promulgated a decree declaring that anyone who provoked "indigènes" or foreigners "to anti-French manifestations or to resistance against the application of the law" would be punished with lengthy prison sentences and fines between five hundred and five thousand francs.[11] Critics of the new law pointed out that the Régnier decree could be used to silence freedom of the press, as any critique of the government could now be labeled an attack on the state. Régnier responded, however, that freedom of expression worked in France because the French were an "old civilization, accustomed . . . to critical thought." In Algeria, however, "printed texts have a quasi-sacred value."[12] Algerians were simply too gullible to be allowed to interpret information for themselves, Régnier insisted. Supporters claimed that the police used their new power cautiously. One French official quipped that if "a few scabious sheep" had been charged under the new law, condemnations had been rare, proving the judiciary used the Régnier decree sparingly.[13] The Régnier decree applied only in Algeria and could be used against both Europeans and Algerians, a supposed neutrality that Régnier invoked to defend the law.[14]

In contrast, critics, among them many Algerians, interpreted the Régnier decree as an obvious tool of political repression and racial discrimination. The Algerian newspaper *La Défense* published a series of articles in 1938 critiquing the police for using the Régnier decree as an excuse to persecute Algerian political activists and saying it "peoples the prisons with militants sure of truly ridiculous accusations."[15] A 1939 article in a leftist paper, *Alger Républicain*, provides another typical critique. The article criticized the condemnation of two Communist sympathizers, one European and one Algerian, due to a misapplication of the "villainous" Régnier decree. The piece contended that anti-French manifestations needed to be defined specifically as an attack on French *propriété*, or possession of the land of Algeria. The two men, the article claimed, had done no such thing. It seethed, "If such jurisprudence is established, one must from now on not open their mouth, nor take up a pen except to say: Mr. Gendarme, you are right; Mr. Police Commissioner, beatings [*passage à tabac*] are done with Turkish or even American cigarettes."[16] This last line implies that officers burned suspects with cigarettes but is also a play on words. *Passage à tabac*, a phrase that includes the French word for tobacco (*tabac*), translates to a beating, violence used in police stations to produce confessions or at times simply for sadistic pleasure.[17]

In its analysis, the article pointed specifically to the police powers granted by the Régnier decree. The decree had been designed to repress anticolonial agitation, but in practice, it gave police officers the power to arrest individuals for any reason at all. By keeping the definition of "anti-French manifestations" loose, the police could adapt the Régnier decree to repress Algerian nationalists, striking workers, or ordinary urbanites. The *Alger Républicain* article, written from a staunchly antipolice perspective, also implied that the Régnier decree granted greater permissibility for police violence. With the Régnier decree in place, Algerians, Communists, and other dissidents, the article argued, could do nothing but accept police repression.

The law set boundaries on police power, but enforcing these laws depended on the interpretation of officers and their daily interactions with locals. On a national scale, the French police aimed to create a professional service that operated according to republican codes, a police force accountable to the people.[18] Policing, however, depended on more than just Parisian debates. As the Régnier decree shows, the Algiers police gained a broad range of discretionary and interpretive powers. Everyday operations of the police in Algiers, Marseille, and the rest of France relied on internal memos, decrees, and circulaires that codified practice on a local level.[19]

Shortly after the passage of the Régnier decree, local officials in Algiers pushed through more legal codes that built ideas of racial difference into criminal law. In 1936, the prefect of Algiers launched a campaign to outlaw *matraques* in his department. In faits divers stories of colonial crime, journalists invariably associated matraques, short wooden batons, with Algerians. In their justification of the new laws, the government of one Algiers suburb explained that it would prevent the bloody fights between "indigènes" that disrupted markets and public celebrations.[20] The language of this letter reveals the racial character of the new laws, which forbid the weapon in order to prevent violence from, and within, the Algerian community.

The mayor of Algiers, however, responded to the prefect's campaign differently. He noted that a decree from July 1902 already outlawed matraques within city limits. According to the mayor's report, the law had come at the request of "the Muslim indigène elites of Algiers" who had expressed concern over the violence that Algerians armed with matraques unleashed in the Casbah.[21] Even in this earlier iteration, French authorities viewed the matraque as an Algerian problem and tailored the law to punish possession in a way that reflected colonial stereotypes. The mayor cited Algerian notables as the driving force behind the law. Perhaps these elites genuinely feared violence in the Casbah, or perhaps they played up ideas of "insecurity" to outlaw matraques for their own reasons. Alternatively, it is possible that Algerians never made this request, and police beliefs about aggression in the Casbah really drove the 1902 law. Regardless, the letters from 1936 show the influence of local context on police practice. The prefect of Algiers requested laws against matraques, but the laws were issued on a commune-by-commune basis. Debates over the laws also show the miscommunication between services, with the prefect seemingly unaware that his plan had been implemented three decades earlier in Algiers.

The political and social changes in Algeria in the 1930s brought about changes in the relationship between police and policed. In response to growing worries about nationalist agitators in the Algerian community and the outbreak of violence in Constantine, the colonial government sought to increase police power both with an expanded legal mandate and by creating services, like the CIE, that blended administrative surveillance and police repression. The police of Algiers also leaned on the precedent of the indigénat code to create targeted criminal laws, like those outlawing matraques.[22] Through these specialized laws, the racial hierarchy of colonial society was embedded in policing, giving police in Algiers the authority to treat Algerian subjects differently than French citizens.

The Îlotier of the Casbah

The daily interactions of North Africans and police officers in the Casbah produced an intricate familiarity between police and policed. In part, this uneasy intimacy was a result of the *îlotier* style of policing. Îlotiers compare to the "beat cops" of Anglophone countries, officers assigned to daily patrols of specific areas or *îlots*. The everyday relationships between police and Algerians in Algiers reflected the mix of service and surveillance, paternalistic aid and brutal force, embodied by the colonial police. Racialized stereotypes of Algerian criminality colored police understanding of the Casbah, yet officers also relied on more personal relationships with Algerians to comprehend and surveil this space.

The majority of Algerians in Algiers lived in the Casbah, crowding the old city to the point that French authorities described the population density as a public health risk.[23] Algerians lamented the miserable, dangerous conditions of the neighborhood. Algerian Municipal Councilor Messaoud Boukroufa publicly blamed the insecurity in the Casbah on a lack of investment by the colonial government and called the Casbah a breeding ground for disease and homelessness.[24] In part, the insecurity officials like Boukroufa described came from the conflicting ways that French colonial powers had defined the neighborhood, relegating both "respectable" Algerian families and the cities' lucrative brothels to the Casbah.[25] Faced with violence and vice, some Algerians saw the police as the answer. In 1935, Algerian Municipal Councilor Abderrahmane Boukerdenna demanded the fusion of the police posts on Rue d'Anfreville and Rue de la Bombe in the Casbah to create a larger station that could more effectively keep residents safe.[26] The police, Boukerdenna implied, should not just control Algerians but be held accountable for their safety, too. Police officials, however, said they lacked the funds to increase the police presence, and accusations of rampant crime in the Casbah continued to appear in municipal council reports.[27]

Despite the scarcity of officers, European observers insisted that Algerians in the Casbah turned willingly to local police, not just to report crimes but for all manner of social and economic disputes. In her Orientalizing book *Tout l'inconnu de la Casbah d'Alger*, popular French author Lucienne Favre purported to share an "authentic" look at life in the Casbah. In her description, Favre singled out the Rue Marengo police station. At first glance, she warned, the station on Rue Marengo might appear like any other. It was not. Residents of the Casbah seeking "practiced arbiters" streamed to the station at all hours, day and night, looking to settle disputes with landlords, fights with in-laws, conflicts with neighbors, and more. She called the station "a sort of improvised courtroom where the most subtly oriental comedies or the most curiously burlesque cases play out."[28] Mimicking an Algerian accent, Favre asserted that Algerians treated the "*coumissaire*" of Rue Marengo like a god. Her description of the station also highlighted the presence of police interpreters, who deployed Herculean patience to deal with the "*casbatique*" cases and the cacophony of petitioners speaking over each other in different dialects.[29] Although she spent portions of her life in Algeria, Favre did not live in the Casbah, and her book presents an inherently outsider view. Still, her description hints at the way Algerians mediated conflicts with each other through the police or used the police, at times, as a genuine resource.

Archival gaps prevent a full reconstruction of the work of the police station nestled on 26 Rue Marengo, elsewhere referred to as the station on Rue Randon.[30] The daily reports, police blotters, and personnel records did not survive. The police post itself was abandoned after the colonial period, and there is no longer a commissariat on Rue Marengo, now named Rue Abderrahmane Arbadji. Still, although the daily records are not available, reports generated by the commissioner of that area, the 2ème arrondissement, give a sense of intimacy. Police officers working in the Casbah described their close, personal knowledge of those they policed. For example, in 1934, the commissioner of the 2ème wrote a report on the relationships between Jews and Muslims in his precinct, following the Constantine riots. The commissioner referenced his views of the two communities, saying that the conflicts that arose between Muslims and Jews at the edge of the Casbah were not religious conflicts but mundane personal disagreements. Indeed, he alleged that if there was a "racist" movement growing in the Casbah, it was not antisemitism but rather anti-French attitudes.[31] French administrators believed that the Constantine riots had taken them by surprise because of a lack of familiarity with Constantine's "indigène" population. The commissioner of the 2ème emphasized that the police of the Casbah already had precisely this sort of local intel.

Evidence of the relationship between the îlotiers and residents of the Casbah is also found in scattered individual police reports. In the early 1940s, an Agent Akli filed many of the police reports emanating from the Casbah.[32] Akli took it upon himself to police matters big and small in the Casbah, a neighborhood he may have lived in. Akli's reports contained everything from official investigations to incidents that he seems to have stumbled upon. In one such case, Akli recounted how he intervened to stop a riot after *tirailleurs sénégalais* invaded the home of an Algerian woman. Tirailleurs sénégalais were West African soldiers recruited to serve in the French colonial army, and their presence in barracks at the edge of the Casbah prompted recurrent conflicts with local Algerians.[33] Officers like Akli found themselves mediating between the two colonial populations, balancing conflicting needs. In this instance, Akli credited himself with "taking care of" the Algerian community and restoring calm after the West African soldiers offended local mores that labeled the home as a quasi-sacred female space.[34] Akli inserted himself in a debate about gender and privacy, staking his power on his ability to understand and subdue the crowd. In other cases, Akli highlighted the importance of his understanding of local languages, his ability to communicate but also to listen in on gossip.[35] Akli's archival trail shows the power of individual agents and their relationships with those they policed. For Algerians in the Casbah, the "face" of the police was Akli, a familiar, if perhaps not always welcome, presence. Akli's interventionist policing suggests that he thought of himself as a resource to the community, someone those in the Casbah could turn to for protection and help.

The positive relationship described by French journalists and police officials elided a more complicated picture presented by Algerians. Algerian newspaper *La Justice* cautioned against the creeping expansion of police power, citing a case in which a police commissioner intervened in a disagreement over rent.[36] This was precisely the sort of police activity that Favre and other French observers lauded as philanthropic, an example of how police resolved Algerians' quotidian problems. The paper, however, pointed out that rent did not fall under police purview and the case should have been handled by a judge. If all seemed to agree that police power expanded beyond normal limits in officers' interactions with Algerians, not everyone was convinced this was a good thing.

There is ample evidence of Algerians' anger toward police. In an article from 1934, the Algerian nationalist newspaper *La Défense* asserted, "The agents on rue Randon are fewer but too zealous" and referred to the officers as "torturers." The author claimed that the population of the Casbah "raises fear of police officers to the level of a religion."[37] The police, this article claimed, ruled the Casbah with terror and intimidation, a far cry from European portrayals of neutral arbiters or Akli's self-styling as a community leader. Other Algerian papers accused the police of systematic brutality and a culture of provocation, pointing to a recurrent pattern of abuse.[38] Articles decried the "*indigènophobic*" police, who conducted relentless raids on the Casbah in search of political agitators while ignoring the European troublemakers living in adjacent neighborhoods.[39] Even Lucienne Favre noted that some Algerians proved reluctant to cooperate with police. She claimed that the day after a crime, residents of the Casbah questioned by police would insist, "No . . . no . . . *manarf*," dialectical Algerian Arabic for "I don't know." Algerians had good reason to be wary, Favre explained. Locals knew "too well" that witnesses could find themselves accused of the crime by officers searching for an easy solution.[40]

Incidents of police violence show the truth of these critiques. In 1935, European Guardians of the Peace Duval, Octave, and Guérin were conducting a round of surveillance in the Casbah. While walking, the officers saw two "completely inebriated indigènes."[41] They alleged that the drunk men resisted arrest, hitting one of the policemen with a matraque. Claiming self-defense, the officer shot his accused attacker in the stomach. Seeing the violence, other "indigènes" gathered to support the two Algerians in their tussle with the police. Ultimately, the Algerian shot in the stomach, Attab M., died of his wounds, and the officers arrested two other Algerians for rebellion and violence against police agents. The officer who killed Attab, Duval, received no punishment. Instead, he was given extended sick leave to recover from the minor injuries he sustained in his struggle with Attab. In this story, we see how the state prioritized the police over the civilian, refusing to hold Duval accountable and blaming Attab for his own death in an unsolicited encounter with the police. The confrontation between Duval and Attab began with a question about space. Attab was accused of being visibly drunk in the Casbah but was guilty of no other crime. The police deemed his use of public space unacceptable, with tragic consequences. As much as police officers claimed to fulfill a role of solicited arbiter and ally in the Casbah, they always maintained the mandate for violence evident in this incident.

Police were integral to life in the Casbah. Throughout the 1930s, Algerian political representatives pushed for *more* police, seeing the Casbah, to use the language of today, as "overpoliced and underprotected." Algerians themselves came to the police station on Rue Marengo for any number of reasons. They arrived to report thefts or violence, they came to seek out arbitration for marital disputes or neighborly discord, they transported patients to seek medical attention. These requests for aid were genuine but also show Algerians making the most of limited options. Police officers who worked in the Casbah emphasized their own understanding of the community and, in the case of Algerian officers, the way their identity gave them unique connections with the population they policed. Officers like Agent Akli navigated a complicated role, themselves racialized subjects but also serving a system designed to uphold racial hierarchy. Despite the fragile intimacy of their intermediary position, police in the Casbah were, ultimately, representatives of a violent colonial state, a role omnipresent in the archival records.

The "Brigade Nord-Africaine" of Marseille?

In Marseille, the policing of North Africans also underwent significant changes in the 1930s. These changes emerged out of a distinct local context, resulting in structural differences from policing in Algiers. The end of World War I sparked a new wave of North African, and particularly Algerian, immigration to France.[42] As more North Africans arrived in the metropole, Parisian officials sought to create methods to control these immigrants. The strategies tested in Paris were transferred to other nodes of Algerian immigration, like Marseille, but local constraints limited the scope of these projects. The practices of policing North Africans that emerged in Marseille inscribed colonial ideas of racial difference into local policing and adapted tools of colonial control to a metropolitan context, reproducing a familiar blend of aid and surveillance.

The template for policing North Africans in metropolitan France was crafted in Paris. In November 1923, a mentally unstable Algerian stabbed and killed two women on Rue Fondary in Paris.[43] The crime fueled fears about the colonial migrants filtering into the metropole. Parisian Municipal Councilor Pierre Godin mobilized the episode as evidence of a broad trend, rather than a singular tragedy, and convinced his fellow council members of the need for a tighter surveillance of North Africans. That same year, the Paris Municipal Council created the Brigade Nord-Africaine (BNA), a police unit designed to track North Africans in Paris, and the Service des Affaires Indigènes Algériennes (SAINA), an administrative aid service for North Africans. North Africans could, and did, turn to SAINA to settle financial disputes, intercede in disagreements with landlords and employers, expedite communication with loved ones in Algeria, or search for missing family members.[44] If SAINA offered real services, however, this social aid always came packaged with the racialized surveillance of the BNA.[45] SAINA and the BNA were part of a web of bureaucracies intended to "manage" colonial subjects in the metropole, including the Service de Contrôle et d'Assistance en France des Indigènes (CAI), created in 1923 to keep tabs on the political mobilizations of the Indochinese and West African populations in the metropole. All these services sought to gather information on the "mentality" of colonial subjects, but the policing and aid mandate of SAINA and the BNA extended beyond the political focus of the CAI.[46]

Building on the success of the program in Paris, national officials pushed for similar services in other major sites of North African immigration, like Lyon.[47] Marseille, with its central role in Mediterranean immigration and large North African population, also proved a natural choice for expansion.[48] On October 30, 1928, the national government created a SAINA in Marseille.[49] A report justified the service, saying:

> Arab workers find themselves in deplorable material and moral conditions, the abandonment in which they are left leads to too frequent newspaper reports about the bloody fights that occur between them. Many of these workers are the prey of swindlers, their compatriots from Algerian cities, who come to Marseille not to find work but uniquely to exploit honest, hard-working laborers.[50]

Marseille's SAINA would, the report asserted, protect European locals from Algerian aggression and guard Algerians from exploitation by the criminal element lurking within their own community. From the beginning, Marseille's SAINA served a police role, seeking to repress the supposedly inherent criminality of North African migrants.

Marseille's SAINA drew inspiration from administrative services in Algeria, including in its staffing. In 1927, for example, as officials began to plan Marseille's SAINA, the minister of the interior offered to detach an administrator from a *commune mixte* in Algeria to serve as the chief.[51] This functionary, the note said, would be up to date on Algerian administration and speak both Arabic and "Kabyle."[52] The first head of Marseille's SAINA was a colonial official—Stéphanopoli Jean Zannettacci, a retired administrator from an Algerian commune mixte.[53] Colonial administrators were given broad, unilateral power over local Algerians, including the right to sanction without trial, issue collective fines, and put individuals under surveillance or in administrative internment.[54] Algerians often accused administrators of abusing these powers. Zannettacci's "knowledge" of Algerians, therefore, came from experience as an authoritarian arm of the colonial state. Like other colonial surveillance services, SAINA officials valorized their "imperial capital" to justify the existence of their bureau and highlight the role they could play in managing colonial migrants.[55]

Budget difficulties, however, stymied the lofty ambitions of officials in Marseille.[56] In 1931, SAINA's full-time staff included just four people—the chief, a secretary, a stenographer, and a "*chaouch*."[57] Though the service had received applications from qualified North Africans, the staff comprised three Europeans and one Moroccan, the chaouch.[58] Zannettacci had colonial experience, but the other European employees of SAINA had no imperial ties or training, and the Moroccan chaouch had no record of experience in colonial bureaucracy. SAINA did not require or provide specialized training for its bureaucrats; the "imperial capital" they claimed developed largely on the job and through intangible interpersonal networks. This scaled-down, ad hoc organization could not carry out the same vast enterprise of surveillance and assistance undertaken by Paris's SAINA. Marseille's SAINA even had recurrent difficulties paying its employees, requesting emergency dispensations to cover salaries.[59] The lack of resources made SAINA reliant on colonial modes of control, using personal connections and clientelism as vectors of authority.

The same disconnect between ambitious goals and mediocre reality also characterized Marseille's attempt to create a police force like Paris's Brigade Nord-Africaine. In Paris, the BNA boasted a staff of thirty-four inspectors and *brigadiers*.[60] In 1931, the minister of the interior asked the police of Marseille to give Marseille's SAINA a comparatively modest one brigadier and ten agents to police North Africans. The police, however, agreed to provide only one brigadier and two guardians of the peace.[61] While planning the brigade, the prefect of the Bouches-du-Rhône suggested that a police service for North Africans could "easily recruit in Marseille a few police agents from Algeria and who speak Arabic perfectly."[62] In pencil, someone had crossed out "perfectly." Even in this initial planning phase, perfection was too lofty a goal.

According to national documents, officials had every intention of granting Marseille's SAINA an accompanying police unit. However, in 1931, Zannettacci, then head of SAINA, decided to put the officers assigned to his service "at the disposition" of the Sûreté of Marseille. The special commissioner of Marseille's Sûreté, Dhubert, wrote to the prefect to inform him that Zannettacci had given up the officers sent to control the "indigènes."[63] Dhubert expressed his confusion, saying he had received no official instructions and had no idea what he was supposed to do with these regifted officers. The brief archival reference offers no absolute proof, but it does suggest the fate of Marseille's BNA. Zannettacci apparently refused to have a police force directly connected to his services, instead sending the officers to the Sûreté, a division of the French police that included France's political police, the Renseignements Généraux (RG). In subsequent decades, the RG of Marseille consistently had a unit dedicated to surveilling North Africans. This subsection perhaps originated with Zannettacci's single-handed bureaucratic reorganization, sending officers destined to serve as SAINA's auxiliaries to work within Marseille's Sûreté. The disappearance of the "Brigade Nord-Africaine" in Marseille may therefore have been the result of a unilateral decision made by a single bureaucrat.

Although references to a BNA disappear until the late 1940s, SAINA maintained close ties with the Marseille police, including having a small contingent of officers stationed in their locale. The Marseille police attempted to provide officers to SAINA who had a connection to Algeria. The quality of these officers, however, proved dubious. In 1935, the first chief, Zannettacci, was fired, and his former secretary, Louis Poussardin, took over. Assessing the service, Poussardin unleashed a wave of complaints about SAINA's assigned police detail. He grumbled that one officer, Palmouries, was mentally worn out (*fatigué du cerveau*), while another, Atlan, had already been dismissed for "deplorable conduct" and allegedly profiting off "women of ill-repute." Referencing a colonial stereotype of animosity between Algerian Jews and Muslims, Poussardin further explained that because Atlan was Jewish, his unpleasant attitude toward the "indigènes" created "regrettable incidents."[64] Poussardin's complaints highlight the problems in finding officers in Marseille to police North Africans. Men with enough knowledge of Arabic or Amazigh to communicate with North Africans often came with colonial baggage, being themselves from European settler families or the Algerian Jewish population.[65] And yet, these rare officers, described as mediocre and unprofessional, had remarkable power over the lives of Marseille's North Africans.

The conversation about North Africans in France shifted in May 1936, when Léon Blum's leftist Popular Front government gained power. The Popular Front tackled the misery of the deepening economic depression with a variety of reforms and also turned its attention to France's colonial subjects, including proposing an expanded path toward citizenship for Algerians.[66] This citizenship reform, the Blum-Viollette law, was eventually tabled indefinitely due to virulent opposition from European settlers. Its failure soured Algerian elites on the larger promises of the Popular Front.[67] Still, the government did initiate some changes, including prompting the national Haut Comité Méditerranéen (HCM) to seriously reassess France's relationship with its North African colonies.[68]

Although the Popular Front government dissolved in 1938, the HCM continued to carry out its ethos of reform, and in 1939, the adjoint-secretary of the HCM, Fernand Vrolyk, launched an investigation into Marseille's SAINA. Vrolyk's thirty-five-page report described Marseille's SAINA as unimpressive. Vrolyk pointed out that the chief, Poussardin, barely had the minimum qualifications, having left the École des Langues Orientales Vivantes after only two years.[69] The police officers who worked at SAINA—Brigadier Palmouries and Guardians of the Peace De Vegie, Dary, and Dagonneau—were no better. Vrolyk accused Palmouries of lacking energy due to his advanced age, labeled Dagonneau as "intemperate," and noted that North Africans had filed complaints against both De Vegie and Dary. Vrolyk explained that it was these officers who actually carried out SAINA's investigations among North Africans, conducting searches, delivering convocations, and managing the logistics of repatriation. He remarked caustically that these varied duties seemed disproportionate to the number and talent of the officers.

If he dismissed the professional capacity of the police officers, Vrolyk highlighted the importance of the service's chaouch, Mohamed Ben Hadj. Ben Hadj theoretically worked as the janitor and front desk attendant, but Vrolyk explained that SAINA relied on him almost entirely for translation, as no one else had the necessary language skills. Vrolyk continued, "As for the North Africans, they never receive visits from anyone but the brigadier, the guardians of the peace, or the chaouch."[70] Mohamed Ben Hadj, along with the police officers, directly interacted with the North African community. Like Agent Akli in Algiers, it was Ben Hadj who interfaced with Algerians on behalf of SAINA, providing a service of cultural translation that no French bureaucrat could imitate.[71]

Vrolyk, like other French officials, described a "floating" population of transient Algerians that spelled danger for general security. However, he insisted that the statistics gathered by the local police demonstrated that North Africans were not disproportionately criminal.[72] Vrolyk's report also pointed out the close, if at times contentious, relationship between the Marseille police and SAINA. SAINA's cooperation was a resource for the police of Marseille, who lacked familiarity with North African language and customs. In Vrolyk's view, the problem was not the connection between police and aid but rather the mediocre qualifications of the officers. Nor did he question the necessity of specialized services. Rather, Vrolyk suggested the solution would be reform within the existing system by procuring more youthful, dynamic police officers with better training and tangible connections to North Africa.

The impetus for creating Marseille's SAINA stemmed from a two-fold fear. Officials, and many French workers, dreaded the arrival of colonial migrants, given the bleak economic outlook. Officials' concern also resulted from a popular understanding of Algerians as uncivilized and violent. The ability to act on this imaginary and dedicate a bureau to North African surveillance, however, was only possible because of the relatively small number of Algerians in Marseille. For much of the interwar period, the number of Algerians in the city hovered between eleven thousand and fifteen thousand.[73] In contrast, while Europeans comprised the majority of Algiers's roughly two hundred and fifty thousand residents in 1936, there were still more than seventy-six thousand Algerians in the city.[74] A separate brigade to police the Algerian population of Algiers would have been impractical. In Marseille, this system was embraced as the obvious, even only, solution to the "problem" of criminal Algerians. SAINA built a durable, if archivally elusive, relationship with the police, intentionally crafting a mission that embodied both surveillance and service. Although the brief interlude of reform spurred by the Popular Front triggered internal investigations into efficacy and recruitment, ultimately French critiques of SAINA did not question the necessity of this targeted service, nor its policing function.

The Faces of Policing Behind the Bourse

The brigades and bureaus developed in the 1930s to police North Africans in Marseille played an outsized role in North African immigrants' experience of the city. SAINA managed to co-opt a wide array of functions when it came to North Africans, inserting their service into North Africans' lives and leveraging this position to feed information to police. In addition to SAINA, police officers in Marseille who patrolled the neighborhoods "behind the Bourse" developed an intimate rapport of solicited aid and unwarranted repression similar to the police in Algiers. Police interactions with Algerians hinged on intermediaries with access to the "closed" North African community and the work of ostensibly nonpolice organizations like SAINA. The blending of services in Marseille might raise questions for scholars of how to define "police." But for the North Africans experiencing the surveillance, the answer was perhaps clear that there was little distinction between a beat officer and a SAINA bureaucrat.[75]

Like the station on Rue Marengo in Algiers, SAINA emphasized the myriad of requests that Algerians brought to them. Annual reports from the late 1930s tracked the thousands of cases handled by SAINA, including creating ID cards, coordinating repatriation, responding to complaints lodged by North Africans, and other "diverse affairs." As the economic depression deepened, SAINA began to focus mainly on repatriation, treating six thousand cases in 1937 alone. The service also addressed, however, 875 complaints and 977 diverse affairs that same year.[76] Poussardin insisted that the North Africans of Marseille came to the service willingly:

> The indigènes frequently come to ask for our help with the most dissimilar and the most bizarre affairs . . . For complaints, reclamations, judicial matters, to pay taxes, for social aid, the investigation and verification of Civil Status, affairs of marriage, to pronounce divorce, to certify acts of sale or purchase, recognition of debts . . . authorization to buy arms, naturalization, to demand passports and acts of Civil Status, to treat questions of inheritance, the division of goods, work accidents, payments to injured workers, to ask for permission to open cafés maures etc.[77]

The blend of services Poussardin describes included matters both personal and professional. Some of these procedures might normally have fallen to the prefecture or the police, like requests for civil status declarations or permissions to open businesses. SAINA, then, functioned as a catchall for North African interactions with the French state. Importantly, too, police officers assigned to SAINA were central to many of the functions that Poussardin said his service provided, as they were the ones going into the community to get information or follow up on investigations.

Poussardin emphasized that SAINA served not just North Africans, but all Muslims in Marseille, noting that at SAINA "we speak" Arabic, Amazigh, and Chleuh.[78] He claimed that Muslims came willingly to SAINA because they knew they would find someone who understood not just their language, but "their customs, their religion, their race, their mentality."[79] Although Poussardin intended this statement as proof of his own expertise, in fact the languages he listed were precisely those spoken by Mohamed Ben Hadj, showing the central role played by this chaouch. Poussardin also obfuscated the role of the police in translation. In one yearly report, he had requested that the police send two interpreters, one for Arabic and another for Amazigh ("Kabyle"). He also asked that the current Amazigh interpreter, a Frenchman from Kabylia, be replaced because of his "problematic character."[80] This revealing letter tells us more about police services than many police documents—namely the existence of police interpreters. Poussardin directed his ire against other services in Marseille, both civil and police, who interacted with Algerians without knowing their language and culture. He insisted, "We cannot require that a secretary at the mayor's, a gendarme, a police commissioner, or a police sergeant in the city knows Arabic, Berber, idioms of Arabo-Berber dialects, understands and speaks 'sabir,' is familiar with North African geography and possess some notions of Muslim law."[81] This, however, was exactly what SAINA *could* provide. Although he failed to acknowledge the real source of SAINA's linguistic capacities, Poussardin claimed a knowledge of Marseille's North African community that other services could not replicate. This closeness, he argued, could be used to better surveil North Africans, weaponizing relationships as a tool of colonial control.

Poussardin asserted that SAINA had deeper knowledge of North Africans than the police and would therefore be better suited to carry out surveillance. He alleged that North African "agitators" would get IDs from the Marseille police to avoid SAINA, and the police happily complied, unaware that they had been "played" by crafty nationalists. Poussardin therefore wanted all North Africans to pass through his service to get an ID card, evoking the specter of Algerian nationalism.[82] Poussardin even went so far as to ask that SAINA be granted the same authority as the police when it concerned Marseille's North African population, blurring the boundaries of policing. As he described it, SAINA's official role could be a "façade" for what would in truth function as an intelligence service, keeping tabs on activists and sowing informants within the North African community.[83] Poussardin's reforms proposed to shift the face of policing North Africans, turning office bureaucrats into law enforcement.

CHAPTER 2

Like Poussardin, journalist René Janon suggested that Algerians interacted willingly with SAINA, preferring the bureau to other services. Janon described childlike Algerians who relied on Marseille's SAINA for a broad range of services, mirroring Poussardin's list.[84] In contrast to this open relationship with SAINA, Janon said Algerians turned to the police with reluctance. Janon transcribed a conversation he had with an Algerian man who said his landlord had stolen his savings after a disagreement over rent. The Algerian man, however, noted that he had no proof that the landlord was responsible. When Janon asked if the Algerian had taken the matter to the police, the man replied that he had instead paid a "*bogato*" he met in a bar to take care of the situation. After paying this stranger, however, the Algerian never saw him again.[85] Janon called this transaction typical of Algerians in Marseille and described the "bogato" as a criminal figure who miraculously evaded police scrutiny. Rather than go to the police, the Algerian victim in this story sought out an intermediary figure within the community. Janon critiqued this method of conflict resolution, seeing it as little more than fraud, but we might instead see the avoidance of the police as a purposeful strategy. According to both Poussardin and Janon, Algerians at times eschewed the police, turning instead to SAINA and each other for alternative paths of justice.

Not all Algerians in Marseille avoided the police, however. Numerous police reports show Algerians calling on the police, demanding that the police protect their property and interests. Algerians also reached out to police mediators to settle disputes within the community. In one case from 1937, Mahfoud D. wrote a despairing letter to the prefect of Marseille, saying that he was the subject of "hatred" from other colonial subjects because they were jealous of his brother, a powerful caïd in Algeria.[86] Mahfoud insisted that he came to France to earn a living and feed his family, but bemoaned that his fellow Algerians accused him of profiting from his brother's connection. These workers had lodged a complaint with the police, accusing Mahfoud of extorting money on behalf of his brother.[87] According to the Algerians, Mahfoud had told them, "If you don't pay us, I will report you to my brother and when you return home to the *douar*, he will take his revenge."[88] The police file notes that the Algerians had first taken their complaint to SAINA, who then turned the case over to the "special commissariat," perhaps a reference to the elusive Brigade Nord-Africaine of Marseille. The police eventually arrested Mahfoud. On the note of arrest, a nameless police officer wrote in bold red letters "WHY??" As it turned out, SAINA had filed for Mahfoud's arrest before the police had completed their investigation, leading to internal confusion.[89]

The Algerian workers writing to SAINA were asking the service to step in and protect them from corruption, accusing Mahfoud of exacting the sort of bribes common in Algerian colonial administration. By arresting Mahfoud, the Marseille police took the Algerian workers seriously and even positioned themselves on the workers' side, rather than coming to the aid of the man more closely connected with the colonial state. Mahfoud was sentenced to two months in prison and a twenty-five franc fine, as well as being forced to give back the money he had extorted.[90] In this case, and in hundreds of other cases of alleged theft, petty fraud, and disagreements gone wrong, Algerians came to the police to ask for help in the same way that any French citizen of Marseille might have.

In other cases, Algerians banded together with European neighbors to request police intervention. In September 1937, for example, a letter arrived at the prefecture from a group of shopkeepers on Rue des Chapeliers, the center of North African life in Marseille. The merchants complained about the crowds that filled their street, bringing with them suspect merchandise and "dirty linens that from a HYGIENIC point of view surely have no place in the downtown center of a city like Marseille."[91] The note was signed by store owners with both Arabic and European surnames, indicating a mix of ethnic backgrounds living in this "North African" space. The letter is suggestive in multiple ways. It shows that Algerians, or at least some merchants, could see the police as allies. The message also demonstrates that the racial hierarchies that bounded colonial social relations could at times prove fluid in Marseille. In this case, class identity and shared concerns over property outweighed any racial or cultural difference between the North African and European shopkeepers.

An Officer Gelibert forwarded the petition to the police commissioner of Marseille, suggesting that Gelibert personally received the petition from the shopkeepers. Quite likely, Gelibert was the îlotier of the neighborhood, the recognizable face who reported for duty under the Grecian columns of the commissariat in Halle Puget. Gelibert defended the crowds that milled in Rue des Chapeliers. He said that the "indigènes" gathered there to talk "in an inoffensive fashion" and the police therefore rarely intervened. He admitted that at times officers found evidence of illicit sales, but said it seemed impossible to force the thousands of "Arabs" living on the street to leave.[92] Gelibert's boss agreed, saying that it would be difficult to clear the street, "encumbered by the Arabs" who lived, ate, and shopped there.[93] The shopkeepers had legitimate concerns, but the police determined they could not dictate how North Africans used Rue des Chapeliers. In identifying Rue des Chapeliers as North African, the police justified special forms of scrutiny. But racializing this space as North African could also empower ordinary North Africans, as the police felt obligated, albeit in limited ways, to respect local practices of placemaking and sociability.

Algerians at times contrasted arbitrary policing in Algeria with the supposed rule of law in the metropole. Yet evidence from Marseille shows that the relationship between police and North Africans on the other side of the Mediterranean also involved brutality. In 1921, a letter from merchants with shops behind the

Bourse complained bitterly that police would stop and harass North Africans "simply because they are Arabs."[94] A revealing case of this prejudice comes from the personnel dossier of an officer named Auguste Saurat. In 1939, Saurat went to retrieve visa forms from a print shop. When trying to pass a group of "Arabs" waiting for their visas, he saw one of them push a woman and her child.[95] Saurat reprimanded him and claimed that the "Arab" then attacked him. He was saved only by the intervention of a colleague.

According to the accused Algerian, Abdallah S., however, he had been waiting for a visa to return to Algeria when he was pushed by a "*coreligionnaire*." Abdallah said, "At this moment, a person dressed as a civilian who I did not know was a police inspector, punched me." In self-defense, Abdallah grabbed his legs and made the man fall to the ground, but Abdallah denied hitting his attacker.[96] As is often the case with police records, the truth is hard to know. Who pushed whom? Did Saurat or Abdallah attack first? Yet the incident does speak to the violence that could erupt between officers and Algerians, complicating the picture of aid that officials like Poussardin or Gelibert touted.[97] The relationship between Algerians and police officers, while at times cooperative, always existed within an imbalance of power that favored police and forgave their violence.

The police appeared in different ways in the lives of Algerians in Marseille. At times, officers served as a liaison with the French state. They helped Algerians find services, pay taxes, communicate with family members, and obtain the tedious bureaucratic permissions needed to navigate life in the French Mediterranean. Both SAINA and the local police singled out North Africans in order to control them, hiring agents who "understood" North African languages and cultures as a tool for disciplining this community. Police officers and SAINA bureaucrats could, and did, help North Africans. Yet these men also served a system ultimately designed to control North Africans and produce obedient colonial subjects.

Intimate Surveillance in the Casbahs

Although Marseille and Algiers developed two different models for controlling North Africans within their city borders, the cities' police forces shared practices and concerns. Debates over insecurity in the Casbah or fenced goods in Rue des Chapeliers suggested an ingrained link in the mind of police officials between crime and North African neighborhoods. But the police did more than just surveil criminal activity in their daily rounds. Officers stretched their power, claiming a right to control private life and ways of using urban space. This desire to regulate social relations, gender norms, and religious practice shows the intimate work of the police, a "civilizing" role that connected to broader discourses of France's imperial agenda.[98]

Policing Algerians in both metropole and colony involved the police defining who had legitimate access to public space. In February 1936, a heated debate on this topic erupted in the Municipal Council of Algiers. Municipal Councilor Aïssa Oulid brought up a law forbidding the sales of newspapers along specific streets at times of high traffic, including Rue d'Isly at the edge of the Casbah. Oulid pointed out that this law had a disproportionate impact on the young Algerians who worked as paperboys. To demonstrate the ludicrous nature of this law, Oulid compared it to a decree that had symbolically forbidden pigeons from nesting in the trees on Square Bresson. Eliciting laughter from his fellow council members, Oulid joked that in the law against the birds, policemen could hardly climb the trees to give out tickets. He concluded more somberly, "When it concerns these poor, simple boys, we arrest them, we inflict a fine on them, we prevent them from doing their job."[99]

Augustin Rozis, the right-wing mayor of Algiers, responded that he had informed the prefect of Algiers of the problems with this new law. Rozis posited that the law had not been written in "sufficiently explicit terms."[100] The lax language allowed the police to apply the law in a sense never intended by the prefect. According to Rozis, the prefect had aimed to stop the argumentative groups of newspaper hawkers who gathered on street corners and fought over political differences. The pursuit of young Algerian newspaper boys had been a police extension of a law that had originally, according to Rozis, served all interests by protecting "public order." Indeed, an Algerian municipal councilor, M. Tiar, ended the debate by saying that the mayor's promise to enforce the law in a more nuanced fashion satisfied the Algerian councilors' concerns. Tiar concluded, "Everyone is interested in maintaining order."[101] But as this incident made clear, the meaning of "order" often fell to the police. Oulid had compared forbidding young Algerians' access to the streets to a futile, absurd law outlawing pigeons, but as he emphasized, the police rendered real and even dangerous this law defining the proper use of space by Algerians.

Another key public space, in both Algiers and Marseille, was the café maure, traditional coffee shops where men gathered to eat, drink, and exchange news.[102] The owners of these cafés also played a particularly influential social role, wielding the "panoptic intelligence of the bar counter."[103] The term café maure implied a specific business license in colonial Algeria, where laws distinguished cafés maures from bars or restaurants owned by Europeans. Hundreds of cafés maures served customers in Algiers, and every year the prefecture denied dozens of requests to open a café because of the existing surplus.[104] Applications required approval from the police, who gathered intelligence on the "morality" of the potential café owners before granting permission.

In Marseille, in contrast, a café maure was simply any restaurant or bar run by a North African, or for North African clients. North Africans who hoped to open a café maure in Marseille directed their request to SAINA.[105] By 1941, Marseille boasted 120 cafés maures, all of which played a vital social role.[106] To squeeze out maximum savings, North African migrants tended to live in small, shared rooms, often lacking kitchens. North Africans turned to cafés maures for both leisure and meals, using them as a communal gathering space. When the police looked for North Africans, they tracked them in the cafés maures that dotted Rue des Chapeliers and adjacent streets.[107] North Africans even at times listed a café as their address in Marseille, much to the chagrin of the police.[108] In policing cafés maures in metropole and colony, the police tried to cultivate personal relationships with café owners, both to keep tabs on rumors and to look for criminals on the run. Police surveillance of cafés facilitated investigations, but it also pushed officers into daily patterns of North African life.

European residents "behind the Bourse" in Marseille contested the way North Africans used cafés, drawing police into a conflict over shared space. In May 1938, a group of residents on Rue Bernard du Bois wrote an angry letter to the mayor, complaining about three "Arab cafés" that played their phonographs until 3:00 a.m. The residents asked the mayor to intervene and put a stop to the music, revelry, and fights that lasted until the early hours of the morning.[109] Based on the signatures, it is evident that this letter came from European residents, and the names suggest that some of the writers were of Italian immigrant origins. The letter expressed surprise that the police, normally so "severe," had done nothing to stop the noise. In the following month, the police patrolling the neighborhood gave out no less than eight tickets for "excessive nocturnal noise" to "Arab" men.[110] In this incident, Europeans insisted that the police reprimand their North African neighbors, "educating" them on the correct way to socialize. The police responded. In this choice, officers validated Europeans' belief that the police existed to serve them, at the expense of their colonial neighbors.

In addition to debates over public space, police intervention seeped into the home. Police forcing their way into homes threated the autonomy of Algerian families and placed police officers squarely in the middle of long-standing, intimate debates over gender roles and religion. One such controversial case flared up in Algiers in July 1934, in the home of a man named Boufedji. The Algerian newspaper *La Voix du Peuple* led with the angry headline, "The Harem raped, the hijab scorned with impunity by the police scum (*la crapule policière*)."[111] According to the article, the police commissioner of the 2ème arrondissement arrived at Boufedji's house, accompanied by two European agents and "Tigrine, indigène information agent."¹¹² The writer implied that Tigrine had betrayed his fellow Algerians by informing on them to the police. When told Boufedji was not at home, the police barged in to serve Boufedji's wife with a ticket. Their decision to enter the home without warning broke Algerian gender norms, leaving the women of the household barefoot and without veils when they met the officers. Boufedji's wife and daughter protested the police invasion, and the police arrested them, sending the two women to jail for the night. Intriguingly, the article reported that the police had come to Boufedji's house in the first place because he had filed a complaint against Agent Tigrine for inappropriate conduct toward his daughter. The "Boufedji affair," as it was labeled, became a rallying cry for Algerian dissidents, referenced when the police treated Algerian women disrespectfully.¹¹³ The police invasion of the Boufedji household mattered all the more because many Algerians considered the home to be the domain of women, shielded from the intrusion of outsiders. By transgressing gendered ideas of domesticity, the police provoked the ire of the Algerian community.

In Marseille, a different idea of home emerged in police understanding, although producing the same invasive surveillance. The overwhelmingly male North African migrant community meant that "home" was no longer a feminized space. Home in Marseille instead often meant crowded boarding houses and an all-male sociability. According to reports by SAINA, furnished hotels catering to North African workers were squalid hovels, wracked with pests and lacking basic creature comforts.¹¹⁴ Reports in Marseille insisted that the precarity of this housing left many North Africans homeless, providing a ready recruitment base for the Communist party. The prefect of the Bouches-du-Rhône proposed a solution to the housing problem, one that would give the police and the French administration access to North Africans' home in the metropole. The prefect envisioned the creation of a North African *foyer*, or workers hostel. The proposed foyer included what French officials conceived of as the necessities of a North African way of life—including a *hammam* and a café maure.¹¹⁵ By 1929, the foyer had been opened in a building on Boulevard Burel, in the relative isolation of the *quartiers nord* of Marseille.¹¹⁶

Officials designed the foyer as a home, an instructional space, and a tool for surveillance. The foyer's manager, Jean-Baptiste Joseph Lallé du Chastaignier, had served as an army colonel in Algeria, giving him familiarity with the Arabic language and Algerian customs.¹¹⁷ Chastaignier's language skills would also be handy, officials strategized, for reporting the rumors he overheard to SAINA and the police. Internal reports described the foyer as "a precious center of information gathering," and suggested that police agents could be introduced to secretly spy on residents and dissuade them from joining Communist organizations.¹¹⁸ Police periodically raided the hotels where North Africans lived, but these transient spaces were not like the homes of the Casbah of Algiers, where Algerian families had lived continuously for centuries. The foyer, then, shows how police officers and officials in Marseille understood the idea of home differently and policed it differently, too.

Police officers in both cities also sought to establish their influence over the religious life of North Africans, policing the profane through an entry into sacred spaces. The very real importance of most Algerians' Islamic faith was reinforced by French discourses that insisted on the blind fanaticism of Muslim Algerians. In the eyes of the police, controlling spaces and practices of religion meant controlling the heart of Algerian society. Religion was not easily separated from politics in a colonial context. Islamic leaders used faith as a way of organizing resistance to French rule throughout French-controlled North and West Africa.[119] In Algeria, Ben Badis's 'Ulamā blended a glorification of Islamic traditions with criticisms of French culture, melding religion and politics in precisely the way the French police feared. Conversely, other religious authorities served as colonial intermediaries, interceding for the French state but also shaping religion and empire to suit their own needs.[120]

Perhaps most emblematic of the mix of political and religious power in Algiers was Cheik Tayeb El Okbi. El Okbi had been born in Algeria but spent most of his childhood in Mecca and Medina, where he studied Islamic theology. The young El Okbi launched a career in journalism, eventually making his way back to Algeria in 1920 and joining Ben Badis to cultivate a program of social uplift and religious reform. El Okbi's lectures at the Cercle du Progrès club quickly drew the attention of the police, who suspected that a nationalist ideology lurked behind his message of education and tradition.[121] A dramatic confrontation between El Okbi and the police unfolded in February 1933. Fearing the rising power of El Okbi and the 'Ulamā, the government of Algiers issued a circulaire forbidding all but "regular personnel" from speaking at mosques.[122] The Circulaire Michel, as it was known, named no names, but it was an open secret in Algiers that its intent was to prevent El Okbi from preaching.[123] Operating with Catholic structures in mind, French authorities framed imams as equivalent to priests, but this, El Okbi's supporters argued, ignored a tradition of learned speakers offering speeches during Friday prayer, even if not officially a leader at that mosque. The circulaire forbade El Okbi from speaking because he was not on the payroll of the mosque and thus not a "regular employee," pasting Catholic standards onto an Islamic context.

On February 24, Algerian protestors descended on the prefecture when they learned that El Okbi could not give his usual afternoon lecture after Friday prayers at the mosque. Although this first protest ended calmly, the next Friday, another group of Algerians again marched toward the prefecture, demanding the circulaire be overturned. The Algiers police, anticipating the protest, had organized extra police details and, controversially, called in tirailleur sénégalais troops as reinforcements.[124] Tirailleurs had passed through Algiers on the way to the metropole during World War I, and these West African soldiers had also been stationed in barracks at the edge of the Casbah during the interwar period. The animosity between tirailleurs sénégalais and Algerian civilians was at least partially rooted in French use of tirailleurs as shock troops in the policing of Algerian political movements. The racialized divisions between Algerians and West Africans were reinforced not just by colonial hierarchies that distinguished "Arab" and "Black" populations but also by government strategies that deployed one colonial population against the other.

According to the official police report, the police had defeated a movement "fomented" by El Okbi. In their own formulation, tirailleurs units "discreetly stationed" around the mosque never had to intervene, but the "excitement" of local Muslims and their calls for resistance to police intervention had created crowds at Place du Gouvernement. This spontaneous protest, the police alleged, was made up not of true Muslim faithful but rather a mix of "professional unemployed people [chômeurs professionnels]" and disgruntled workers, riled up by European Communists.[125] The police noted that they had prevented a riot by driving motorcycles through the "indigènes neighborhoods" and breaking up groups of Algerians they encountered. They arrested twenty Algerians for refusing to circulate in the square by the mosque and three more "indigènes" for "violence and rebellion" against security forces.[126] Although the police defended their actions, newspapers reported this incident as a severe overstep, focusing in particular on the alleged use of West African troops to clear the mosque.[127] Despite the protests, the prefecture held firm, refusing to overturn the circulaire and continuing to deploy police at religious gatherings.[128] In policing the mosques, the police sought to control political ideas, but in the eyes of many Algerians, they overstepped in seeming to claim the right to police religious belief.[129]

In Marseille, control over religious practice often fell to the specialized North African aid services. In Paris, the original SAINA coordinated the hadj for Algerian colonial subjects, sponsoring the visa and travel costs for a group of faithful. The Paris SAINA also was closely associated with the creation of the Paris Mosque and retained ties with the director.[130] Similar practices existed in Marseille, where the local SAINA and its successor organizations coordinated and surveilled trips to Mecca.[131] Marseille's SAINA regularly held banquets or festivals for Muslim holidays and arranged couscous distributions during Ramadan. By providing North Africans with these material resources, SAINA did more than just facilitate religious practice. The parties and food distributions sought to foster goodwill between SAINA and the North African community, which in turn increased SAINA's power of surveillance.

The French administration also tried to build and regulate religious spaces for North Africans in Marseille, although constructing a mosque proved thorny. Organizing efforts, typically spearheaded by SAINA or charitable European organizations, had difficulty locating land or scrounging together funds for a mosque.[132] At a meeting of the Marseille section of the Congrès Musulman in 1937, a protonationalist organization with local sections in Algeria and the metropole, a series of Algerian speakers vehemently objected to the creation of a mosque in Marseille. They complained that they did not want this project to result in a "fascist" mosque that spied on its congregation, like the one in Paris.[133] The archival records of SAINA and its successor organizations continued to include debates between municipal councilors, police officers, and SAINA officials over how to organize a mosque in Marseille.[134] Policing religion looked different in Marseille and Algiers. Without a mosque, the Muslim faithful of Marseille prayed and gathered in improvised spaces, including the cafés where so many other aspects of social life unfolded. Policing religion in Marseille, then, was less about penetrating religious spaces and more about using displays of state-sponsored charity to infiltrate social networks.

Tracking agitators in cafés, patrolling the perimeters of mosques, defining the use of urban space, and even asserting control over the home, police officers in Marseille and Algiers sought to control both the public and private realms of North African life.[135] Police officers in both cities identified similar spaces and practices as central to North African culture, using a racialized understanding of the city as a tool to track North Africans. Different demographics, however, meant police tactics looked distinct in each place. Like anyone else, North Africans went to the police to report crimes or seek protection. The officers stationed on Rue Marengo and the SAINA-affiliated agents who wandered Rue des Chapeliers helped North Africans figure out complicated bureaucratic procedures or settle personal disputes. At times, the police treated North Africans like any other community. Yet these benign interactions were paired with intrusive surveillance and racialized violence, undermining the paternalism of police outreach. North Africans in Marseille and Algiers needed and also resented police officers. Police and specialized services, in turn, conceived of North Africans as inherent criminals but also potential interlocutors. The police vaunted their close relationship with North Africans, insisting that this intimacy made officers better able to control them. These daily interactions in the Casbahs of Marseille and Algiers, however, were also tinged by violence, racism, and unsolicited intervention.

As police and North Africans navigated an uneasy balance of animosity and mutual reliance, the world around them began to shift. The economic and political tensions that had been building in Europe culminated in the rise of fascist governments in Spain, Italy, and Germany. Hitler's seemingly unstoppable rise to power in Germany pushed European leaders to the edge of yet another global conflict. Though French officials repeatedly sought to avoid an armed struggle, Hitler's invasion of Poland finally pushed Britain and France to declare war. France geared up for mobilization and hurtled toward political upheavals that neither the enlisted soldiers nor governing politicians could have anticipated. The dramatic changes of World War II would shift the relationship of the police and North Africans, blending existing fears of the "Algerian criminal" with new wartime anxieties.

3

POLICING AN EMPIRE AT WAR

On August 3, 1942, news broke of a tragic "accident" in the town of Zeralda. For years, Algerians living in nearby Algiers had called attention to mounting police abuses, but the Zeralda affair, as it became known, offered a stunningly blatant example. Zeralda was a beach town about thirty kilometers from Algiers, policed by its own small, local force.[1] On August 2, the police carried out a sweep of Zeralda's beach, allegedly in response to a rash of thefts. During the raid, the police rounded up a group of forty Algerian "prowlers," most unknown in Zeralda, and placed them in jail for the night. When officers opened the cell the next morning, they found that twenty-five of the men had died of asphyxiation.[2] An investigation revealed the mass suffocation occurred after a bottle of disinfectant spilled, producing noxious fumes in the locked, overcrowded, unventilated room. Official government statements carefully described "accidental deaths," portraying the tragedy as an unfortunate mistake.[3]

This narrative, however, concealed a darker truth. The commissioner of the Renseignements Généraux (RG) in Algiers collected the rumors circulating among Algerians in the days following the deaths. Chief among these rumors was the belief that the mass arrests had not been motivated by theft. According to Algerians, the mayor of Zeralda had passed a decree forbidding access to the beach for "indigènes, Jews, and dogs."[4] Internal reports circulated between the governor general of Algeria, the prefect of Algiers, and local officials in Zeralda confirmed that this decree existed and that the arrests made that fateful night in Zeralda were in connection to the new law.

The Zeralda affair unfolded at the height of World War II, a conflict that reshaped France and its empire. France entered the war it had hoped to avoid in 1939, uniting with Britain against Germany. In 1940, a powerful German offensive battered French defenses. Almost overnight, the Third Republic vanished and a new, authoritarian regime, headquartered in Vichy and led by Maréchal Pétain, emerged to take its place. Looking back after Algeria's eventual liberation from Vichy control, republican and leftist newspapers cited the Zeralda affair as an example of "fascism" at work in the French police. But what was at stake in blaming racial violence on Vichy?

In the wake of World War II, French popular culture, and for decades French historiography, treated Vichy France as a dark but temporary rupture, an authoritarian interruption in an otherwise republican trajectory.[5] Some historians have even blamed Vichy for the entrenchment of "profound racism" within Algeria's settler population or the emergence of a "police state" in Algeria.[6] Vichy's open embrace of eugenicist hierarchies did alter France's relationship to its Algerian colonial subjects, changes reflected in both police organization and practices for controlling Algerians' mobility and labor. In Marseille, police treated North Africans primarily as workers, using the wartime demands for labor to justify racial profiling and the creation of colonial transit camps. In Algiers, the divisions between Algerians and Europeans hardened as competition for scarce resources and access to public space intensified. The policing of both labor and rare goods during the war played out in intimate, daily arenas, on the streets, in the markets, and in exchanges between neighbors in the Casbahs. Most radically, the Vichy regime racialized the policing of North African Jews in metropole and colony, borrowing tools of targeted control previously used to track North African Muslims.[7] At the same time, Vichy's fragile legitimacy in the empire required police officers to negotiate power with local stakeholders.

Despite republican protests in the aftermath of the war, however, policing North Africans under Vichy was not so different from the targeted strategies of the interwar, both rooted in defining and controlling North African urban space. Arguing that the Vichy regime created racism or established an Algerian police state denies the experience of Algerians prior to the war, who might have characterized police oppression in precisely these terms. Focusing on daily policing reveals that the imperatives of wartime production and scarcity, rather than Vichy policy alone, sparked a new relationship between police and North Africans during the war.

The Administrative Chaos of War

The tensions had been mounting in Europe for years. As economic depression in the 1930s sent unemployment spiraling, fascist political parties gained popularity in France and throughout Europe. In Marseille and Algiers, the police tracked the rallies of fascist sympathizers, especially the Parti Populaire Français. In Algiers, right-wing groups had attracted growing crowds in the 1930s, gaining support from European colons and influential politicians.[8] Hitler's rise in Germany seemed unstoppable, and France braced for another war. When Germany invaded Poland in September 1939, the British and French governments declared war and launched a rapid mobilization. As it had in 1914, the French government drafted thousands of Algerian soldiers into *tirailleurs algériens* units.[9] Algerian soldiers shipping out passed through Marseille, arriving in the metropole by boat before being directed by train to the front.[10]

France's high-speed mobilization crippled the continually understaffed police forces of Marseille and Algiers. When France declared war, dozens of police officers either enlisted or were drafted into the French army. Already short on men, the police of Algiers and Marseille now found themselves policing increasingly chaotic cities with even fewer officers. In Algiers, mobilization reduced police personnel so much that the surveillance of the Casbah now had to be carried out by just two guardians of the peace.[11] Between 1939 and 1940, the police of Marseille requisitioned dozens of local men as officers, replacing those who left for the front.[12] As compared to regularly hired officers, these emergency recruits went through a less rigorous vetting process. A sporting-goods store owner, a publisher, and a taxi driver with a criminal record—these men are just a few examples of the motley group who joined the Marseille police in 1939.[13] The Algiers force, too, likely recruited haphazard replacements for deployed officers.[14]

Though France mobilized quickly, the war initially stalled, with little action on the front. Finally, the standoff of the "phony war" during the fall and winter of 1939–1940 came to an end with Germany's invasion of France in May 1940. In just a few weeks, the German army outmaneuvered French and British forces. On June 22, a stunned and shattered French government signed an armistice with Hitler, ceding a large portion of northern France, including Paris, to German occupation.[15] The World War I military hero, Philippe Pétain, led a new authoritarian government in the southern spa town of Vichy and agreed to cooperate with Hitler. France's loss threw its colonial empire into question, both in terms of internal legitimacy and international politics. Vichy political leaders believed the empire undergirded the validity of their new regime and described the colonies as necessary sources of territory, labor, and natural resources.[16] Holding onto France's imperial possessions was paramount for them.

With the armistice, Algerian soldiers who had been brought to France in 1939 now demobilized. The Vichy government carefully limited the number of colonial soldiers who could remain in France, aiming to avoid a surge of unemployed laborers.[17] The process of repatriating the rest, however, proved painfully slow and poorly organized. Sent to Marseille to await boats for Algeria, Algerian soldiers stayed in makeshift camps for months.[18] Other colonial soldiers from West Africa, Madagascar, and Indochina, unable to be repatriated, were shuttled to camps elsewhere in southern France and treated as a semimobile labor force.[19] Across the Mediterranean, the police of Algiers braced for the arrival of an estimated twenty thousand demobilized Algerian soldiers. In August 1940, the prefect of Algiers issued a circulaire, instructing police officers to be on the lookout for the influence of "extreme left" organizations that soldiers had been exposed to at the front.[20] The prefect also warned the police, however, to avoid overzealous surveillance that might provoke the ire of returning veterans. Still building a tenuous political consensus under Vichy, the prefect feared alienating Algerians with overt spying.

Armistice sowed just as much chaos within the police forces of Marseille and Algiers as mobilization had. A decree from July 1940 directed the police commissioners of France to fire all requisitioned officers. In a panic, Commissioner Gaubert of the special police of Marseille wrote to the prefect of the Bouches-du-Rhône explaining that such a measure would gut his service. Without the wartime hires, Marseille's special police would drop from ten to six commissioners and from fifty-one to twenty-five inspectors, paralyzing the service.[21] In Algiers, too, a lack of officers plagued the police for the rest of the war.[22]

The Vichy government saw the police as a key collaborator in their new political regime and won over police forces with generous funding and promises to support reforms long demanded by police personnel.[23] In April 1941, the Darlan law replaced municipal police services with a single national police, a reform police unions had demanded for decades to standardize training and benefits.[24] Between April and July 1941, Vichy issued no less than eleven laws and decrees restructuring the police.[25] The nationalization of the municipal police had little impact on Marseille and Algiers, as both cities already boasted a nationalized police d'état. Other changes had more impact, however. Vichy created new units aligned to wartime causes, like the *groupes mobiles de réserve* charged with monitoring "threats" from political dissidents and the French Resistance. The Vichy government also formed dedicated police units to track Communists and ferret out Jews.[26] These infamous brigades would be complicit in some of the most heinous crimes of World War II. The structural reforms introduced Vichy's antisemitism and authoritarianism into the very organization of the French police.

Vichy authorities never passed national legislation mandating the repression of North Africans.[27] The new government did, however, set about reorganizing the system designed to control North Africans in France. In Algiers, the Vichy police mostly appropriated existing colonial surveillance services, but Marseille experienced a more radical reorganization. Special services catering to North African immigrants, like the Service des Affaires Indigènes Nord-Africaines (SAINA), had existed in Marseille since 1928. Under Vichy, local authorities in Marseille closed SAINA, creating instead the Bureau des Affaires Musulmanes Nord-Africaines (BAMNA) in October 1943. But SAINA's entire four-person team transitioned to the new service, which even remained in the same building at 26 Rue Barbaroux.[28] This rechristened bureau dedicated the bulk of its time to creating ID cards for North Africans and gathering information from informants. The Vichy Ministry of the Interior also created the Service des Affaires Algériennes (SAA) within the prefecture of the Bouches-du-Rhône in 1941, run by the charismatic Commandant Robert Wender.[29] In part, the reorganization of SAINA sought to eliminate redundancy. An SAA report in 1941, for example, suggested it should be responsible for political surveillance of Algerians as well as coordination of social aid efforts. The report openly advised that aid could be a useful cover to "penetrate" Algerian milieus.[30] SAINA, on the other hand, would provide ID cards and repatriation services without taking on surveillance goals. This proposed division, however, proved illusory, and both the SAA and BAMNA collaborated closely with the police, a continuation of SAINA's prewar practices.

Vichy laws did target other populations, with implications for both police personnel and practice. In October 1940, the Vichy government revoked the Crémieux decree, reducing Algerian Jews to the same subject status as Algerian Muslims. A series of other restrictions followed this dramatic reversal, aimed at limiting economic participation for Jews.[31] This included a law banning Jews from holding positions within the French administration. Jewish police officers, as civil servants, lost their jobs.[32] Already plagued by administrative turmoil, the police forces of Marseille and Algiers now were deprived of essential operatives. Algerian Jews often spoke some Arabic, a skill few of their European colleagues possessed. Salomon Mamane, for example, began his career in the Sûreté of Algiers in 1919. He quickly moved up the ranks, becoming a principal inspector by 1931. Born in Algiers, Mamane spoke Arabic and had a personal knowledge of Algiers's urban landscape. Mamane's bosses consistently gave him glowing reviews, but in 1940, he lost his job. To make ends meet for his family of four, Mamane found a job as a baccarat dealer in the Casino of Algiers.[33] This story parallels the fate of dozens of officers in Marseille and Algiers, an event with personal consequences for these officers and damaging effects for the already understaffed police forces.[34]

Far from merely responding to the directives of the German occupiers, Vichy officials actively pursued their own antisemitic policies. The police of Marseille and Algiers became the enforcers of Vichy's antisemitic laws, the ones who physically went to close businesses or collect property. In Marseille, the police were responsible for tracking Jewish families and, beginning in 1942, organizing the deportation of Jewish residents to Nazi death camps.[35] In both Marseille and Algiers, policing Jews meant, in part, policing a North African population. Significant numbers of Jews had lived in Algeria for millennia, experiencing periods of both cultural florescence and religious persecution under Islamic empires.[36] North African Jews also formed an important minority of the Jewish population in Marseille, with notable immigration from Algeria since the early 1900s.[37] Vichy policing reclassified these North Africans, grouping them with other Jewish populations rather than other colonial populations.

This religious distinction had already been somewhat true in police practice, especially in Algiers where the Jewish community inhabited distinct areas of the city. There was more fluidity in Marseille, where the police and local administrators had a harder time distinguishing between Algerian Jews and Muslims. For example, the SAA's Commandant Wender reported in November 1942 that Jews had come to his services to enroll for couscous distributions meant to allow "North-African Muslim indigènes" to celebrate Ramadan. The Jewish families would produce their ration cards, on which the police had marked "North-African indigène," their legal status following the abrogation of the Crémieux decree. North African Jews hoped to blend into the Muslim community to access the supplementary grain. Wender added, "This is made even easier because they have names that sound Arabic: Bou Khoubza, Tayeb, Khalifa, etc."[38] Vichy policies changed how the police interacted with Jewish Algerians in Marseille, setting them apart as a threatening group. The couscous distribution, however, demonstrates a continued slippage, in the eyes of metropolitan bureaucrats, between different ethnic and religious communities within the larger "North African" population. In many ways, Vichy-era attempts to identify and track North African Jews built on interwar practices in Marseille that had similarly targeted "indigène" North Africans with special bureaus, ID cards, and police services. As Wender's intervention shows, the identification of North African Jews even at times relied on the same services originally intended to control the Muslim North African population.

Despite administrative reshuffling, the bulk of police officers in Marseille and Algiers remained in their positions during the transition from the Third Republic to the Vichy regime. The shifting politics of wartime collaboration, however, did lead to some personnel changes. Since 1924, Mahmoud ben Omar ben Chaouch had served as a police agent in Paris's Brigade Nord-Africaine (BNA), reaching the rank of inspector in 1931.[39] In 1941, Ben Chaouch fled to Marseille on the advice of his superiors.[40] According to his disgruntled boss in Marseille, Ben Chaouch told anyone who would listen that he had been advised to leave Paris for fear of reprisals from the German police.[41] Ben Chaouch's flight shows a tension between the German occupiers and Paris's BNA, supposedly working on the same side of an ongoing war effort. Recognizing Ben Chaouch's unique skill set, the Marseille police placed him in the local RG, where he was likely allocated to a special unit for surveilling North Africans.[42] Showing the close link between police and "aid" services, however, Ben Chaouch was quickly reassigned to the SAA.[43]

Things did not go smoothly for Ben Chaouch. By March 1942, the divisional commissioner of the Marseille RG had taken a clear dislike to him, writing a scathing review. The commissioner accused Ben Chaouch of cultivating relationships with North Africans suspected of being German propaganda agents.[44] This complaint seems paradoxical. As a member of the RG, Ben Chaouch's alleged friendships with pro-German Algerians would have produced helpful intel. Given police griping about lack of access to Algerian communities, it seems surprising for the police to interpret Ben Chaouch's suspect associations as anything but a boon. The implication that Ben Chaouch sided with German propagandists in his own political leanings also seems far-fetched, given that by all accounts he had fled Paris because of conflict with the German police.

Ben Chaouch's new commanding officer further accused him of making enemies within Marseille's North African community through "irregular" commercial dealings and demands for bribes. This charge of intermediary graft echoed allegations leveled against nearly every North African who managed to work their way into the police or social aid services of Marseille.[45] True, Ben Chaouch had the opportunity to demand bribes. North Africans had a difficult time accessing the French state, blocked by language barriers and unfamiliarity with the administration. In these circumstances, intermediaries like Ben Chaouch offered a vital channel of communication. Actively part of the Marseille police but attached to a social aid service, Ben Chaouch embodied the blending of criminal policing, political surveillance, and social "evolution" that characterized French attempts to control North Africans. The accusations against him demonstrated his superior's unease with his influential role. Ultimately, however, Marseille's police needed Ben Chaouch more than they feared him. Even in his bitter letter, the commissioner did not ask for Ben Chaouch to be fired.[46]

Mahmoud Ben Chaouch's story shows the messiness of colonial policing, particularly during the war. Vichy officials in Paris sheltered Ben Chaouch from German aggression, but at the same time, his supervisors in Marseille critiqued his conduct. Like other rare Algerian officers in Marseille, Ben Chaouch was accused of graft and intemperance. Yet his role as an urban intermediary for a police force unsure of how to communicate with the growing population of Algerians soldiers and laborers made Ben Chaouch necessary, despite his unpopularity. Discrimination against North Africans was not a Vichy invention. The charges Ben Chaouch and others faced echoed long-standing patterns evident in the personnel files of North African officers and bureaucrats, in both metropole and colony. The racist overtones of the critiques of Ben Chaouch attest to the prejudice North African officers faced, regardless of the war. What his case reveals, however, is how the complication of wartime amplified structural issues within the police.

The rapid succession of mobilization, demobilization, and sweeping reform to police organization created an environment of extremes. Although relatively few ground-level officers lost their jobs with the advent of the Vichy regime, agents found themselves working alongside new colleagues, hurriedly recruited and poorly trained. Valuable officers, sometimes some of the few to speak Arabic, lost their jobs because of Vichy's antisemitic directives. The new police organizations, including revamped aid services for North Africans in Marseille, built Vichy conceptions of racial hierarchy, antisemitism, and anti-Communism into the structure of the police.

Forced Labor and Suspect Movement in Marseille

In Marseille, Vichy changes reordered police hierarchy, but in interactions with North Africans, the new services reproduced the familiar mix of repression and aid. As the Vichy government recruited thousands of colonial subjects for wartime industries, the police came to understand North Africans as units of labor. By treating North Africans as cogs in the war machine, the police began to identify not just "North African" spaces but also spaces where North Africans did *not* belong. This racialization of space enabled practices of overt racial profiling. When the police tracked recalcitrant North African workers or raided neighborhoods to look for escaped recruits, they justified their action as meeting the needs of a country at war. Identifying North Africans narrowly as workers and broadly as possible truants empowered the police to assert control over North Africans' movement and personal choices.

In addition to the Algerians drafted as soldiers, the French government recruited thousands more North Africans as laborers, referred to as *requis* or *travailleurs coloniaux*. These men had been called to serve France not as soldiers but as factory workers, miners, porters, and agricultural laborers. The system of requis labor functioned like military recruitment in that workers could be conscripted, voluntarily sign contracts, or enlist instead of serving a prison term. The Office de la Main-d'oeuvre Indigène (MOI) oversaw the workers, rather than the military.[47] Algerian requis arrived in France via Marseille, unloading in the port before being escorted by police to trains shuttling them across France. Some Algerians received positions in Marseille, in local sugar and oil refineries, while others were sent to mines in the Gard or industrial plants in the North.[48] Shortly after defeat in 1940, the Vichy regime negotiated a deal with the occupying German forces, allowing Germany to recruit North Africans for German industries in occupied France. Reports compiled by the SAA and BAMNA record their active cooperation with the German recruitment organization, Todt. Carefully annotated ledgers document the hundreds of Algerians, Moroccans, and Tunisians funneled toward German manufacturing and building the defensive "Atlantic Wall" along the coast.[49]

Using North Africans to fuel production alleviated wartime worker shortages, but it also introduced a new pressure on police to enforce a regime of semi-free labor. Letters streamed in from all over France reporting North Africans who had left their work contracts, an act criminalized under wartime labor policy. Some suggested that German propaganda among North African workers enticed requis laborers to leave their jobs to work for Germany instead.[50] Police reports also blamed truancy on racialized ideas of the "North African mentality." The commissioner of Marseille's special police, for example, suggested that because North Africans preferred repetitive jobs, the varied work of factories put them "in a bad mood."[51] In police formulation, North Africans walked away from their assigned positions due to foreign influence or inherent laziness.

Examining the labor conditions of requis workers, however, suggests more practical reasons for leaving. Contracts for North African requis reflected minimal, if fair, wages, but the scarcity of labor during the war drove up pay for more flexible work. Demand for workers on the docks, for example, had inflated daily wages to 100–130 francs, while factory workers under requis contracts could earn only 56 francs.[52] In February 1940, the special police of Marseille tracked down a group of Algerians who had left their contracts after three weeks of work stoppages due to a lack of raw materials. The police noted that the North Africans, already living "day to day," left the factory because they had not been paid during the stoppages.[53] This remarkable case demonstrates the unfreedom built into the system of requis labor. Conscripted laborers remained tied to the factory even when work stopped. Stuck in France, living without pay and without prospects, these men nonetheless could not leave. Finding a job that would pay them constituted a breach of contract, an act for which they could be jailed. During the war, it was police officers who mediated this labor dispute. Police went to find the workers, listened to their story, and returned them (or not) to their worksite. This discretion required police officers to judge the personal lives of North Africans, weighing their reasons for fleeing. These were intimate moments, but ones with stark penalties, as officers determined whether the requis would be held in a transit camp, returned to unfree labor, or allowed to slip into the flexible job market.

Through their interactions with the requis, the police and the SAA collected a litany of accusations about the abuses Algerians experienced at their assigned posts. An Algerian named Ben Rabah, an informant for the SAA, reported that workers in Marseille who left jobs in the mines of La Grand-Combe referred to their contracts as "forced labor." The men informed Ben Rabah that their employers forbid them from going home, even when their families wrote letters pleading for their return. The workers also said the mines did not provide adequate food, nor food prepared in accordance with halal dietary rules.[54] Police in Marseille discovered other Algerians who had fled their positions in the Hautes-Alpes because they had not been provided with proper clothing for the harsh winter.[55] Still other requis complained that they had been tricked when signing contracts. Workers with specialized skills found themselves assigned to menial tasks because recruiters in Algeria had them sign agreements without arranging for an interpreter to explain the contracts.[56] Recruiters promised high salaries, clothes, and advances to send their families, but when the requis arrived in the metropole, these promises vanished into thin air. Workers complained, "But why mistreat us this way? Always because we are indigènes!"[57] In this retort, relayed to the SAA by an informant, the anonymous North African worker drew a direct line between the unfree system of requis labor and racialized inequality. Pulling Algerians from their families and making it illegal for them to leave, the requis system trapped Algerians in the metropole to serve an empire at war.

North Africans who fled job contracts filtered through Marseille, the principal port through which they could regain North Africa.[58] North Africans also came to Marseille because of the work available in local industries and on the docks. Vichy laws criminalized their movement as a breach of contract, denying North Africans control over their own labor. Although the Ministry of Labor handed out jobs, finding missing workers fell to the police.[59] Prefects and police chiefs from all over France sent letters to the Marseille police, warning them to look out for escaped North African workers. The police of Marseille already saw North Africans as a transient mass, and this influx of purported contract dodgers only increased tensions. Despite targeted surveillance, some North Africans managed to slip onto boats bound for Algeria, using the maritime link between Marseille and Algiers to evade capture.[60]

When the police did track down escaped North African requis, they often sent them to transit camps near Marseille.[61] In particular, the police directed North

Africans to Camp Lyautey, located on the border between the eighth and ninth arrondissements of Marseille.[62] The camp was seemingly named after General Lyautey, Resident-General of Morocco from 1912 to 1925, a fittingly colonial name for a camp for colonial subjects. Camp Lyautey housed a mixed group of North Africans, some arrested, some refugees, all awaiting ships bound for North Africa. A circulaire from the Minister of the Interior in 1942 directed that only "non-requis" North Africans should be taken to Camp Lyautey, with those who left work contracts forcibly returned to their assignments instead.[63] This same pamphlet, however, outlined a series of exceptional situations in which the police might direct North Africans to Camp Lyautey instead of their workplace. It fell to the local police, then, to decide what to do with North Africans who had abandoned their post. But North Africans also claimed agency. The SAA noted that some workers in Camp Lyautey declared that they "would rather have their head cut off than return to the jobs they had left."[64] Their refusal to endure the miserable conditions pressured the French state to either provide better work environments or allow them to return home.

French authorities intended Camp Lyautey as a temporary point of triage for colonial subjects on their way home, but North Africans often found themselves trapped. One Algerian man, Mohand A., told the police he had run from his work contract because the company paid him less than his metropolitan coworkers and denied him the family allocations they had promised. Mohand had left and found work on the quays of Marseille, but his boss reported him to the police. Mohand then found himself herded by police to Camp Lyautey, "condemned to immobility" as he explained it to an SAA informant.[65] It was a nameless local officer who located Mohand and determined that his excuse for truancy was insufficient. Mohand described his responsibility as the father of six young children and asked to be repatriated. Demands for repatriation, however, proved difficult to coordinate, with the port clogged with war-related shipments. As weeks dragged into months and winter approached, the SAA noted that North African detainees lacked winter clothing, and the bureau urged officials to either repatriate the men immediately or allow them to leave the camp and find jobs.[66] In advocating for the stranded North Africans, we can see the intermediary role of services like the SAA, at once an oppressive surveillance organization and a bureau that understood itself as a genuine resource to North African migrants.

Camp Lyautey, in addition to sheltering Algerian workers awaiting repatriation, also housed a small group of women and children. In January 1941, the Vichy minister of the interior forwarded an anonymous note to the prefect of the Bouches-du-Rhône, calling attention to the terrible living conditions of the nineteen women and twenty-four children housed in Camp Lyautey. These women and children, the note scolded, lived in filth, covered in lice and at risk for disease.

French authorities had reserved Camp Lyautey for "Arab" men waiting to be sent home but had decided against continuing the repatriation of women, given the wartime dangers of maritime travel.[67] The letter demanded that the women and their children be released to civil care, lest the "risks of immorality" in the camp increase.[68]

The anonymous letter's scathing critique is unclear on one point. Were the women in Camp Lyautey North African? Or Europeans married to North African men? Or women and children from European settler families attempting to regain their homes in North Africa? Given Camp Lyautey's classification as a "colonial" camp, it is likely the women were the wives of North African colonial subjects, if ambiguously North African themselves. Police records show, for example, that at least one European woman, a Belgian national married to a Moroccan, was held in Camp Lyautey while awaiting repatriation.[69] But it is surprising that the horrified note does not call more attention to the racial identity of these women, if they were indeed European.

The prefect responded by issuing a request for an investigation, calling on the police services that worked with Camp Lyautey to refute the accusations. Commissioner Gaubert, the chief of the special police of Marseille, proceeded with an investigation of the "Arab families" in Camp Lyautey. Gaubert noted that the families were housed in a separate barrack. In a nod to tropes about precocious Arab sexuality, he carefully emphasized that boys over the age of thirteen slept in the men's quarters, while girls over thirteen had their own barrack connected to the family one. Addressing accusations of malnutrition and poor food quality, Gaubert retorted that the food was prepared by a group of "devoted" Moroccan men, as if devotion negated inadequate nutrition. While he admitted that the camp had no showers, Gaubert lamely countered that there were "a sufficiently large number of faucets" for inhabitants to bathe.[70] When Gaubert wrote his letter, only seven women and thirteen children remained in the camp, along with a population of about six hundred North African men. Gaubert insisted that his investigation had revealed no trace of the "immorality" hinted at in the letter.

Although the letter was anonymous, Gaubert knew that Alice Gianotti, an employee of the Foyer Marin, had sent it.[71] The police easily identified her from an almost verbatim letter she had written (and signed) to the medical commander of the MOI. According to the police, devoutly Catholic Gianotti sought to discredit the police and military staff of Camp Lyautey to get the women transferred to Catholic-run services. The squabble over housing therefore played out as a familiar battle between church and state for the souls of North African couples.[72] Gaubert sought to defend the camp and its paternalistic role. The police investigation of Camp Lyautey, however, contains a resounding silence—the voices of the women and children living there. Gaubert cited not a single woman in his report, although presumably he interviewed them during his investigation. The debate raged over who could best take care of these women—church or state— yet little is said about the women themselves or their North African partners. What brought them to Marseille? What did they think of life in Camp Lyautey? Gaubert did not ask, so I can only wonder.

French authorities sent North Africans, and their families, to Camp Lyautey to restrict their mobility, but workers proved adept at escaping. Despite the gendarmes stationed as guards, North Africans frequently slipped out. The gendarmerie almost never found these men and instead forwarded lists of names and descriptions of escaped North Africans to the police of Marseille. The police used their overlapping vision of race and space in Marseille to track escaped Algerians, conducting searches on Rue des Chapeliers, which they noted as "the gathering point for Arabs in the city."[73] As the North African population of Marseille ballooned, the police linked the change to an uptick in petty crime in the central neighborhoods of Marseille. Police tactics for controlling the supposed crime wave, however, proved heavy-handed and controversial. Instead of targeting specific crimes, the police conducted indiscriminate sweeps behind the Bourse. The North African men, and at times women, who fell into police nets had not necessarily behaved suspiciously. Rather, the police used tactics like verification of ID cards to control all North Africans' movement, using contract-dodging requis or Lyautey escapees who had fled to Marseille as probable cause.

Attempts to control Algerian mobility during the war at times provoked arguments between the various bureaus and departments that surveilled North Africans. In December 1939, as soldiers hunkered down on the stalled warfront, inspectors of the Sûreté conducted a sweep on Rue Longue des Capucins, located "behind the Bourse" near Rue des Chapeliers. The officers stopped an Algerian man named Bachatene. Bachatene presented the police with an ID that had been issued to him by Marseilles' SAINA, but the officer told him the ID was worthless and arrested Bachatene for shirking his military obligations.[74] The police report noted that Bachatene said he had been drafted in 1929 but had not been called to arms since. Bachatene therefore believed he had already fulfilled his military duties.[75] Bachatene reached out to SAINA, expressing his evident confusion over the "invalid" ID. The chief of SAINA, Poussardin, shot off an irritated letter to the prefect of the Bouches-du-Rhône saying that this behavior "destroys in the spirit of the indigènes the prestige of the metropolitan administration." Algerians, he warned, had already been taught to distrust the French by "agitators" and hardly needed additional encouragement.[76] Poussardin also rebuked the police for arresting the "interpreter chaouch" of his office, Mohamed Ben Hadj. Ben

Hadj had produced a photo ID established by SAINA, as well as his employment papers, but the officers declared the ID invalid and arrested him.[77]

The police denied the version of events laid out by Poussardin. They said Bachatene's ID had only been supplied by his mistress the following day, after he spent the night in jail.[78] As for Ben Hadj, the chief of the Sûreté, after initially denying all culpability, eventually admitted that it was possible officers questioned Ben Hadj during a raid and then later released him.[79] Even Ben Hadj's position within the French bureaucracy could not save him from being treated like a suspect. The incident demonstrates the essentially racial parameters of police strategies for patrolling behind the Bourse, investigating North Africans regardless of their "respectability" or relationship to the state. Justifying the targeted policing, the chief protested that the police aimed their raids at North African populations because of their mobility, seeking out those who "left, without authorization, the places where they had been."[80] The police defended targeting North Africans by referring to illicit mobility, but this framing ignored the longer pattern of North African residence in Marseille, positioning all North Africans as requis or Camp Lyautey escapees.

The Vichy-era policing of North Africans followed old patterns in its emphasis on illicit mobility and labor but added a newly open language of racial discrimination. In October 1942, the police launched "one of their habitual raids" on Rue des Chapeliers. The raid proceeded with the questioning and arrest of North Africans who had the misfortune to have chosen to shop, eat, or gather there.[81] This time, however, among the dockers and day laborers interviewed by the police, there was an "honorable" merchant. Caught between the police barriers, he was questioned and then "rudely pushed" and brusquely told to follow the police to the station to verify his ID. The merchant told Commandant Wender of the SAA that he offered to show the officer his papers immediately, but the officer refused, saying "All Arabs are liars." When the merchant expressed his shock at this racist statement, the officer replied, "If you aren't happy, you can just get the hell out of here and go back to your country, you are all bastards." Violence oozes from the officer's offensive language, but the insult also came from the officer's choice to employ the informal *tu*.[82] Although the merchant noted that the superior officer in charge of the raid behaved politely, he refused to reprimand the offending agent, "affirming that he had received orders to treat North Africans severely."[83] The passive verb tense hides the origin of this order, but the police had evidently been instructed to target North Africans and even been encouraged to be rough with them. Wender noted that other North Africans made similar complaints. Although targeted raids were common in the interwar, Vichy ideology permitted racial language that had previously been veiled in a rhetoric of crime and insecurity.

No laws restricted access to Rue des Chapeliers, and North Africans went there to conduct business or meet friends, ordinary interactions of daily life. Although Wender noted that the merchants generally supported police efforts to "rid this artery of the herds of undesirables who give the street a detestable reputation," he urged caution in treating all North Africans with such indiscriminate disdain.[84] To solve the problem, Wender suggested increasing training and encouraging agents to be firm but fair. Wender foresaw worrisome outcomes of the police raids on Rue des Chapeliers, casting a wide net that ensnared even law-abiding, elite North Africans, who might otherwise be sympathetic to Vichy.

Police tactics relied on an imagined map of North African spaces of the city. The police search for North Africans who had abandoned their jobs legitimized raids on spaces seen as central to North African daily life. Conversely, it also empowered police to stop North Africans they deemed out of place. Whether or not the person in question was actually North African, whether or not the police observed any crime, proved beside the point. Characterizing all North Africans as potential deserters, police officers in Marseille crafted an excuse for racial profiling. Field notes reveal that officers stopped North Africans for any reason, or no reason at all. In January 1943, a group of gendarmes arrested a North African man named Rabah K. as he walked along a national highway toward Marseille. To justify the arrest, the report merely noted that Rabah was "a North African subject who looked like a beggar."[85] Interrogated in the police station, Rabah admitted that he had no steady job and had been wandering in search of employment. Rabah did not, however, admit to leaving a work contract, the reason the gendarmes had been theoretically empowered to stop him. Rabah's only crime was being unemployed and Algerian.

Cases like Rabah's occurred frequently. Although sometimes the police did indeed catch recalcitrant requis with their "random" stops, in other cases, these men had committed no crime besides being in a public space and, perhaps, being unemployed. The structure of wartime labor laws, punishing laborers who operated outside the regulated state system, granted police this freedom. If the Vichy government broadly sought to find and repatriate North African vagrants, local police officers in Marseille defined, by their actions, who was North African, a racialized group rendered visible by skin tone, language, and clothing but also by the ways in which they moved through the urban landscape. Vagrancy and draft dodging were illegal for Europeans, too, but the police treated them on an individual, case-by-case basis. In contrast, the police interacted with North Africans in Marseille as a singular unit, whose very presence in public space provoked suspicion.

The Vichy regime did not invent a new way of policing North Africans. Vichy policies built on more than a century of racialized strategies of rule that the

French had enacted in Algeria, laws and policies that reproduced an understanding of North Africans as an "Other." Targeted police tactics, however, had been previously justified by discourses of criminality that claimed Algerians posed a threat to the French populace and to each other. Wartime manufacturing needs pushed the police in Marseille to see North Africans not as potential criminals but as units of labor, workers that the police had the right to ensure remained productive. Policing North Africans in wartime Marseille, then, became about locating "out of place" North Africans. In identifying potential requis on the run, the police fell back on their preexisting knowledge of North African urban spaces, singling out Rue des Chapeliers and the neighborhood "behind the Bourse." If racial profiling had already been a de facto practice of the interwar years, the war gave the police a blanket excuse to control North African bodies in urban space, reliant not on narratives of crime but an implicit understanding of North Africans as truants. The constant raids on Rue des Chapeliers placed police into the daily lives of North Africans, disrupting patterns of sociability in the name of wartime production.

Scarcity and Social Conflict in Algiers

In Algiers, the advent of Vichy rule did not radically alter politics. The local government had long leaned right, unlike historically leftist Marseille, setting up the city for a smooth transition to Vichy rule.[86] But the realities of life during war created new social and economic pressures that it fell to the police to stabilize. European and Algerian communities competed for scarce resources and the right to public space in Algiers. Racial tensions boiled over in the marketplace, with conflicts over food mapping onto claims of European racial privilege. Fights over resources only increased as the Algerian population of Algiers climbed, inflated by rural migrants fleeing famine in the countryside.[87] In some ways, Vichy's precarious hold on the French Empire and need for colonial resources opened a possibility of negotiation for Algerians. If Vichy fragility made officers tread carefully, however, they did not police Europeans and Algerians equally, and colonial structures of racial repression continued to define policing.

As the war ramped up, the markets used by both Algerian and European residents became increasingly contentious spaces, and police officers characterized Algerians' presence there as suspect. On December 3, 1940, for example, Police Commissioner Susini filed a report in which he described with pride the efforts of his brigade. They had spent the day questioning crowds gathered near the main markets of Algiers, and Susini celebrated that his men had arrested twelve Algerians, sending them to the police station to verify their IDs. Describing the operation, Susini explained that to stop daily thefts, he had rounded up all "indigènes" near the markets "who did not have a reason to be there."[88] To the police, the Algerian men they stopped, questioned, and brought to the police station had no right to be near the markets. Their physical presence in this space, and their proximity to sources of food, made them suspicious.

But from the perspective of the arrested Algerians, things must have looked different. Although various markets served Algerian and European neighborhoods, both populations mixed in the marketplace, and even in European neighborhoods, vendors were often Algerian men. This made the markets a space of contact in colonial Algeria. Although some loiterers perhaps intended to pilfer vegetables, most Algerians came to the market to buy food. Arriving to purchase carrots or couscous, they found themselves taken aside by a police officer and questioned simply for existing. The Algerians in this report seemed suspicious, indeed criminal, to Susini and his brigade because of how they moved through the city. As with the policing of requis in Marseille, the Algiers police sought to circumscribe Algerians' urban mobility and everyday actions.

The policing of access to food in Algiers played out in conflicts framed through gender. As in France, both European and Algerian women in Algiers had to navigate long lines, rationing rules, and soaring prices to provide food for their families. Rather than treating Algerian women as mothers, providers, or individuals operating in difficult circumstances, however, police painted them as greedy and violent, a danger to European women.[89] In one incident, Commissioner Gauthier of the 5ème arrondissement recounted a tense encounter at a bakery in the Spanish immigrant neighborhood of Bab El Oued.[90] The commissioner reported that an Algerian woman named Fatma had threatened to send her husband to cut off the baker's head if he did not give her priority access. He noted that "of course" this threat was not carried out, but he linked the incident to a series of violent exchanges between Algerian shoppers and European bakers.[91] This moment of tension over baguettes shows the high stakes of rationing in a starving city. The fragile colonial state, weakened by military loss and regime change, might also have empowered Algerians to resist daily inequalities more boldly. Police reports in Algiers obsessed over popular concern about food scarcity and the exorbitant prices of the black market.[92] Rather than seeing the exchange between Fatma and the European baker she "threatened" as evidence of desperation, however, the police report knitted a narrative of Algerian violence. Gauthier took the angry exclamations of Fatma at face value, relying only on the version of events proffered by the nameless European baker.

Although the police were supposed to serve a neutral, intermediary role in market conflicts, police officers and their families felt the same squeeze of wartime scarcity that other residents of Algiers did. On August 24, 1944, Principal Commissioner Lainyech wrote a scathing letter to the general secretary for Muslim affairs of Algiers, describing the experience of his wife in the Phillipe market. Lainyech complained that his wife had been insulted by a *"mauresque"* during her shopping. Quickly extrapolating, Lainyech claimed that this was not an isolated misunderstanding, but exemplary of a pattern of Muslim women "mistreating" European housewives.[93] He asserted that Algerian women routinely arrived late to the markets and then tried to force their way to the front of the line "by violence."[94] This, Lainyech implied, allowed Algerian women to skip ahead of European women who had followed the rules. Evoking racial solidarity, he asserted that the "indigènes" merchants selling the goods supported the Algerian women. Lainyech portrayed Algerian society as "us versus them," with scarcity revealing the racialized social divisions administrators tended to deny. Lainyech called for a police detail to be added to the market during high-traffic hours, and his complaint ultimately led to an investigation into the market's surveillant.[95]

Lainyech defended not just the right of his wife to priority but the right of all European women over all Algerian women. Lainyech's account reflected his own personal priorities, but because of his position of power as a police officer, Lainyech's voice carried added weight. Unlike many complaints in the police archives that ended without further action, Lainyech's letter led to an investigation and a severe reprimand for the market guard. Lainyech understood rationing as a zero-sum battle between Europeans and Algerians and, as a police officer, he had the authority to intervene in favor of his side. As Lainyech's example shows, policing access to food and behavior in public space could become personal, especially with supplies restricted by war and poor harvests.

Lainyech's description of "violent" Algerian housewives mirrored complaints from European women. In a letter to the general secretary of the police, a Mme Llobert listed a litany of faults with the Messonier market in downtown Algiers. Among her objections, she emphasized the "insolence of the Arabs" and the "mauresques" who applied for milk rations for their children, only to turn around and resell the milk.[96] Llobert also ridiculed police surveillance of the markets, calling the agents "indolent." The police fell into an uneasy intermediary role, called on by Europeans to teach Algerians proper civility, which is to say proper submission. They fulfilled this civilizing task imperfectly, at least according to Europeans. Although letters complained about "Arab" neighbors, colons like Llobert grumbled just as loudly about ineffective, corrupt police agents.

Even when Algerians called on the police to intervene in social conflicts within the Algerian community, officers tended to see tensions between Algerians and Europeans as the "real" problem. In December 1941, a group of Algerian shopkeepers from Rue Randon presented a petition to Abderrahmane Boukerdenna, a pharmacist and influential municipal councilor. The businessmen complained about a mobile secondhand clothing market that invaded their street at night. They informed Boukerdenna that cars could no longer enter the street and "honest women" feared shopping there because of pickpockets and pushy crowds. They concluded that the market prevented customers from entering their stores, even alleging that they had seen daring thieves tear banknotes from their clients' hands.[97]

When confronted by Boukerdenna on the issue, the central commissioner of Algiers angrily responded that these merchants were exaggerating. The police had received no complaints from Algerian women about pickpockets or inappropriate jostling on Rue Randon. Reflecting the building racial tensions in wartime Algiers, he argued, "This situation is besides infinitely less tense and delicate than the situations provoked by the indigènes in European neighborhoods, in public transport and in the markets, towards European women."[98] The commissioner framed the *important* concern as the aggression of Algerians toward Europeans, and specifically European women. If conflict between Algerians did happen, he implied, it paled in comparison to the danger Algerians posed for Europeans.

Addressing the merchants' concern about crowded sidewalks, the commissioner explained that the police received criticisms from all sides—store owners, street vendors, politicians—all of whom wanted to "oust the one that bothers him." What, the commissioner asked, should the police do? "Should we leave these unfortunates to earn their living on Rue Randon or should we chase them out? As far as forbidding pedestrian traffic, which is to say indigènes, and preventing them from meeting, from stopping to speak about their affairs . . . It should not even be considered."[99] The economic scarcity of war had made Algerian residents desperate. The commissioner felt unable to deny their desire to gather, to commiserate in an "Algerian" space. Like earlier attempts to police Rue des Chapeliers in Marseille, the Algiers police had decided that Rue Randon could be used by Algerians as they wished. This decision, however, left some Algerian merchants disgruntled.

Conflicting demands of police intervention occurred outside the marketplace, too, especially in neighborhoods where Algerians and Europeans lived in intimate proximity. European requests for police action demonstrated a belief that they owned public space, just as they assumed their right to priority with rationed food. One particularly virulent example came to the police in 1942 in a four-page letter written by Hubert M. He listed an address on the Cervantes stairs, adjacent to an enclave of working-class Algerians near the Muslim cemetery in El Hamma, an area sometimes referred to as the "Little Casbah."[100] Living on the edge of one of the few Algerian spaces of Algiers, Hubert displayed a particular anxiety to defend his authority as a European. He whined that his neighborhood was overrun by "Muslims, whose arrogance, often anti-French attitude, and disagreeable fantasies take the place of laws."¹⁰¹ He framed his complaint around public space and gender, saying that Europeans could not walk in the neighborhood without being insulted and that young "indigènes" pushed old women on the stairs. His letter began with general complaints, but he quickly got to the point. He wanted the police to stop the "indigènes parties" that ignored wartime edicts ordering gatherings to end at midnight. Hubert noted that his European neighbors refused to file a complaint because they believed it would lead nowhere. Hubert laid on the guilt, calling it disappointing that taxpaying citizens could not depend on the functionaries they paid to protect their interests.

Hubert made clear what other complaint letters only hinted. His annoyance about the parties was partially about noise, but it was also about who had the right to make claims on the state, to make claims on space. He, Hubert, was a *citizen*, while his Algerian neighbors were not.¹⁰² Hubert believed the police should defend a specific subset of Algerian society—Europeans. Not all Europeans shared his view. Indeed, he noted that a European neighbor, a woman he dismissed as "of Italian nationality" and thus not truly French, took up against the police when they came to shut down the party.¹⁰³ The police responded to Hubert, questioning the party host and reminding him of the midnight rule. In their intervention, the police officers mediated not just a noise complaint, but the racialized, interpersonal tensions created by divergent opinions about whom the police served and who owned urban space.

The unruly youths briefly evoked in Hubert's letter fit into a broader narrative identifying Algerian children as a public problem. The police of Algiers laced their reports with complaints about the *yaouleds* of Algiers. The word yaouled comes from Arabic. The phonetic segment *ya* proceeds statements directed at an individual, indicating the person whom the speaker is addressing. *Ouled* is a French transliteration of اولد, the Arabic word for *boys* or *children*. The police, and French settlers, adopted the term, presumably from hearing Algerians use it while speaking to each other. Calling someone child, daughter, or brother in Algerian dialect reflects codes of familiarity and kindness, rather than literal familial lineages. This term of endearment in Arabic, however, turned bitter in the mouths of Algiers's police. The police framed yaouled not as children of a community but as troublemakers and delinquents.¹⁰⁴

Policing the yaouled often focused on what police saw as the correct use of public space. One such contested space was the stone arches and staircases below the Beaux-Arts Museum. The Beaux-Arts Museum featured prominently among the elite cultural institutions of Algiers, with a collection that rivaled peer institutions in France. The museum, still open today, sits across from Algiers's botanical gardens, the Jardin d'Essais. The museum was also adjacent to El Hamma's Little

Casbah. The uneasy presence of these two European cultural institutions, the Beaux-Arts Museum and the botanical gardens, next to a working-class Algerian neighborhood set up potential for spatial conflict.

In 1944, the mayor of Algiers gathered a special delegation to discuss criminality in the city. A European delegate, M. Alazard, complained that due to poor police organization, the area near the Beaux-Arts Museum lacked security.[105] As proof of this claim, he included a letter from the museum's director. The director began with an account of a recent attack on one of the museum guards by "an indigène with haggard eyes." The director continued that "the young yaouleds who come from who knows where" threw stones at museum staff and the stairs leading up to the museum "are transformed into a delousing center for a large number of indigènes." The director asked for a new police station to clean up this neighborhood "infested by an underworld of low quality."[106] The police of Algiers, constantly lacking staff, could not create another commissariat, but they did respond to the complaints with an increased police presence near the museum.

In this case, municipal officials called on the police to enforce a French vision of how public space should be used. The museum director made a direct complaint about yaouleds throwing stones at staff members, an actual misdemeanor, but he also expanded into a more general grievance about how youths inhabited the area around the museum. He decried that they had turned the stairs leading up to the museum into a space of gathering, of sociability. The "delousing" of the Algerians on the stairs was unacceptable to him because he saw the museum as a venue of European civility, where visitors could come observe art and culture. That the stairs near the museum could be used by dirty, "uncivilized" Algerian workers and youths became criminal in his vision, a source of insecurity real enough to demand police protection. This battle over the museum stairs cannot be chalked up to Vichy, as it took place after Vichy's fall from power in Algiers. Instead, it shows how the war deepened existing cracks within Algerian society, pushing Algerians and Europeans to view each other ever more antagonistically and in openly racial terms.

World War II increased the pressure on Algerian society. Racial divisions, already visible in times of plenty, became violent clashes as supplies decreased and Europeans sought to translate their social privilege into priority access. The police of Algiers were pulled into these conflicts. The personal beliefs of police officers, often members of Algiers's European community, influenced how they policed the markets and whose stories they chose to believe. In reprimanding what they saw as dangerous Algerian women, suspect Algerian men, and unruly yaouleds, the police acted as agents of colonial hierarchy, seeking to cultivate docile Algerians who did not threaten European privilege. Yet even as the police intervened on their behalf, Europeans relentlessly critiqued officers for not doing enough. The war made clear that the Algiers police had been built to protect citizens, not subjects, prioritizing European complaints over Algerian needs.

Violence and Vichy Policing

Critics of the Zeralda affair would point to the tragedy as emblematic of Vichy policing, but this framing downplayed the reality of racialized violence prior to the war. Colonial police forces always used violence as a tool for maintaining colonial order, particularly in places where the Indigenous population outnumbered Europeans.[107] Although the Algerian police theoretically followed the professional norms of all French police, in reality, policing in Algeria reflected colonial standards, and this continued to be true under Vichy. In Marseille, the everyday violence of verbal assaults, shoves, and "random" ID checks remained typical, but more extreme police violence against North Africans during the war proved rare, or at least remained undocumented in police files and newspaper reports. Instead, the most notable incidents of police brutality during the war were directed against other political and religious groups, including Jews and Communists. In Algiers, however, Vichy rhetoric reframed racial violence.

Vichy propaganda sought to win over colonial elites by emphasizing how Vichy's "traditional" policies mirrored the cultural heritage of colonial peoples.[108] In the case of Algeria, the colonial elites Vichy sought to woo were twofold. Like preceding governments, Vichy catered toward European settlers, but Vichy officials also cultivated relationships with Algerian notables, appealing to a traditional, rural vision of Algeria.[109] By restoring favor to older Algerian elites, Vichy tried to co-opt their networks of influence in support of the fledgling regime. However, if the government made modest overtures to Algerian elites, Vichy also openly accepted an idea of racial difference that had always hovered as a contradiction within the imperial policy of their republican predecessors.[110] The reinforced belief in regimes of difference was evoked to explain episodes of police violence against Algerians, incidents whose racial tone leftist critics later characterized as "Vichy" policing.

Algerians themselves sounded the alarm on police racism.[111] In a letter to the governor general of Algeria in April 1942, a *"Français Musulman"* complained about the commissioner of the 3ème arrondissement of Algiers. According to the letter, this commissioner would use racial slurs and mistreat Algerians when they came to the station to obtain IDs. The letter warned that, "these acts, unworthy of a Frenchman, create a dangerous effect on the indigènes."[112] The anonymous letter reminded the governor general that Algerians were "French at heart" and had loyally supported Maréchal Pétain. The prefect found the complaints of this anonymous letter credible enough to issue a formal response, sending an admonishing note to the commissioner. However, the letter downplayed the racism in the accusation, saying only that the prefect had been informed that the staff of the station did not always receive Algerians appropriately. He asked the commissioner, the one specifically accused of misconduct, to remind his staff of the correct procedure.[113] This weak reprimand failed to indict the commissioner, but it did suggest a wider problem.

The concerns over racialized tensions between Algerians and the police took center stage in a controversial incident on March 28, 1942. According to the official police report, Guardians of the Peace Viel and Klein heard cries coming from a restaurant on Rue des Tanneurs and discovered three intoxicated Algerians causing a scene. The policemen attempted to bring them to the station, but they resisted, refusing to show their IDs. Viel and Klein said that one Algerian started name-dropping connections with a police commissioner, while another listed his political acquaintances. The third man insisted that because of his job as a scribe in the courts of Algiers, he knew the police were violating the law in arresting them. The officers put the young men in jail to sober up, releasing them the next day.[114]

The story differed, however, according to the three arrested Algerians. Belgacem A., a medical student, Amar C., a scribe, and Mohamed D., president of the Association of Muslim Students, claimed they had paid in advance for a meal at the restaurant on Rue des Tanneurs. When they arrived, the restaurant owner informed them that they could not be served due to the late hour. Upset about losing their money, the men insisted they get their food. Belgacem admitted to raising his voice, but all three men confirmed that the incident remained peaceful until the police arrived.[115] The students, contradicting the police, insisted that they had not been drinking.[116] They accused the police of forcing them, roughly, to go to the police station. Once the station doors closed, the student alleged that the officers brutally kicked and punched Mohamed, until he had a bloody lip and eye. Belgacem, the medical student, treated Mohamed's wounds while the police hurled racist insults at them.[117] Demonstrating knowledge of French law, all three men insisted that they had been jailed without being charged, a violation of their rights.

The police quickly put together a paper trail to support their version of the story. Viel and Klein submitted reports, affirming that they never hit Mohamed. The *planton* on duty, another European, submitted testimony that he never saw his colleagues abusing the three young men, all of whom he described as visibly drunk.[118] The case quickly became the word of three Algerian youths against the sworn testimony of a whole unit of police officers. Police officials pointed to the holes in the Algerians' records. Mohamed, for example, never filed a formal complaint, nor did he produce a medical certificate of his injuries. The police immediately, and suspiciously, produced a dossier discrediting the students, even before they lodged a grievance.

The police story grows even more doubtful in light of the events in the following days. Mohamed went for advice to Municipal Councilor Abderrahmane Boukerdenna, who wrote to the central police commissioner, criticizing the officers. According to Mohamed, when Officers Viel and Klein heard about this, they came to Boukerdenna's pharmacy and offered to apologize to prevent a scandal.[119] Viel admitted to going to Boukerdenna's store but reversed the accusation. According to Viel, Boukerdenna said that Mohamed, about to embark on an official visit to Vichy, would report the violence to Vichy representatives. Boukerdenna knew that Vichy officials were courting support from Algerian elites and warned he could expose Viel's misconduct. Viel further alleged that Boukerdenna threatened to use the incident to rally Algerians. According to Viel, Boukerdenna shouted, "If you come upon a knife [*boudjadi*], do what you want, I don't care, I would even help you hit me. I will break you, I will behead you in putting this affair on a political level."[120] In this quote, Boukerdenna flips the script, threatening to metaphorically turn the violence perpetrated on Algerian bodies into a weapon against the officers and, by extension, the French colonial state.

Ultimately, the case had no repercussions for the officers involved. Commissioner Fachot, in charge of the investigation, noted that given the "particular character" of the case and the personality of the students, he was content to collect testimony but make no arrests.[121] The final police report implied the police had been lenient in not prosecuting the young men for rebellion. In the last letter in the archive on this evocative case, the central commissioner noted that he had passed the report along to the prosecutor. The case presented in that dossier staunchly supported the police version of events.[122]

The violence perpetrated on Belgacem, Amar, and Mohamed offers a glimpse into daily police practices in Algiers under Vichy. According to the officers, these three Algerians tried to avoid arrest by naming police commissioners and other officials they knew personally. This sort of name-dropping is hardly surprising. In Algiers, police commissioners often remained in charge of a specific neighborhood for years. Locals knew these men, especially educated Algerian elites like the three students. The use of personal relationships to twist rules or broker exceptions formed part and parcel of police practice, in Algiers but also in France. In this case, however, the police presented it as evidence that the Algerian students had tried to impede the law. Although the police denied any violence, the aftermath suggests otherwise. Viel would have been unlikely to visit Boukerdenna if he had never harmed the students. And yet, the police received no punishment, backed by a system that operated to protect them.

Police officers' strategic use of violence was hardly new, but something did seem to shift under Vichy. The students framed this violent encounter explicitly in terms of race, referencing the racial tones of the police officers' insults. Viel, too, offered a racial understanding of the incident, accusing Boukerdenna of threatening an all-out war of the "indigènes" against French sovereignty. The experience of these students also shows the narrow window of negotiation opened by Vichy rule. Boukerdenna and the injured Algerian students had political leverage to denounce violence because of Vichy's precarious hold on Algeria and the need for buy-in from Algerian communities. Yet Algiers authorities grounded the conflict not in national politics but in local chains of authority, managing to dismiss the incident. If the imperatives of Vichy rule changed the language, ultimately local relationships and continuing priorities of colonial order prevailed.

In the context of the tense and violent negotiations of power between police and Algerians in Algiers, the scandal of the Zeralda affair seemed to solidify boundaries.[123] Police sources in Algiers characterized the Algerian reaction to the twenty-five lives lost in Zeralda as despair, but not shock. They reported an Algerian interlocutor saying:

> An affair of this type, would it have been possible with Europeans, even ex-convicts, even those arrested with weapon in hand after an act of mischief? You know very well the answer is no. And if in the impossible case that it did happen, wouldn't we have seen an explosion of indignation in the press? Wouldn't the authorities have required prompt and rapid justice, to satisfy public opinion? You know very well the answer is yes.[124]

As this quote emphasizes, the specter of racial discrimination loomed over the tragedy. The disregard for human life, the exaggerated police action against people who had committed no crime besides walking on a public beach, could not have happened to European colons. Part of Algerians' outrage stemmed from the slow response of the government. The state eventually opened trials against the mayor of Zeralda and the three-person police force, all four of them European. The half-hearted trials dragged on for years, pushed back because of disorder in the court system during the war. Ultimately, all four men were sentenced to less than two years of prison.[125]

The Zeralda affair came to symbolize Vichy policing for republican observers after the war. Zeralda was a small town, policed by its own small force, but the event resonated in nearby Algiers, seeming to give grotesque example of the daily acts of police brutality that Algerians there, too, associated with the Vichy regime. Algerians understood the Zeralda affair as a racist attack, violence that would have been condemned if perpetrated against Europeans. The discriminatory laws at the root of this affair, forbidding access to the beach for Muslims and Jews, certainly reflected Vichy's legal prerogatives. But if republican newspapers and Algerian observers linked the violent excesses of the Zeralda affair to Vichy, the trials show that the regime change had less impact than they might have wanted to believe. When the sentencing of the mayor and police officers finally took place in 1944, Vichy had already been pushed out of power in Algiers. Vichy politics permitted the Zeralda affair, but the Fourth Republic brushed the event under the rug.[126]

Vichy practices built on the racialized policing of North Africans pioneered during the Third Republic. Vichy did not invent racialized policing, but the war created conditions in which the French state, acting through the local police, could expand its control over North Africans. The police zeroed in on regulating North African movement, identifying North Africans they deemed out of place and monitoring North Africans' access to resources. The visual and spatial markers used by the police to identify misplaced North Africans demonstrate how the police coded North African bodies through space.[127] This spatial, racial policing shaped interpersonal conflicts over labor, public space, and access to food.

When France entered the war in 1939, the police felt the reverberations. The forces of Algiers and Marseille underwent rapid turnover, with hundreds of men mobilized to the fronts and untrained civilian recruits stepping in to fill the gaps. As the needs of wartime production ramped up, the Marseille police doggedly tracked North Africans who slipped out of the regimented labor order. Surveilling Camp Lyautey and reprimanding requis, the Marseille police treated all North Africans as potential truants. In Algiers, Europeans called on the police to protect their access to rationed goods and public space. As daily police encounters with disgruntled citizens, truant laborers, and harried shoppers demonstrate, Algerians' daily life changed under Vichy rule. These differences, however, stemmed more from the realities of war than a distinct Vichy style of policing.

Even as the Vichy government set about building a new France, a movement of resistance had already started to form. General Charles de Gaulle established the "Free French" army from his exile in London, opposing Vichy and working with Allied leaders. From 1940 to 1942, Vichy entrenched its control of Marseille and Algiers, stitching together a distinct vision of the French Empire. Then in November 1942, Allied troops descended, storming Algiers to gain a foothold in the Mediterranean. This campaign would change the tide of the war and was a moment, too, of dramatic rupture for Algerians in both metropole and colony. Despite the now opposing governments in power in Marseille and Algiers, the police of both cities developed a monolithic picture of Algerians. Previously positioned as criminal enclaves, the North African neighborhoods of Algiers and Marseille now became imbued with a new characterization—that of being "anti-French."

4
MAPPING THE ENEMY WITHIN

On November 8, 1942, a ragtag band of 400 "Free French" resistance operatives coordinated with Allied troops to overthrow Vichy control of Algiers. With the relatively bloodless coup, part of Operation Torch, Algiers switched sides. Instead of an Axis port, Algiers now became an important Allied base. Residents of Marseille and Algiers reeled as the invasion severed the links that had woven together the Mediterranean for centuries. Inextricably connected by trade and migration, the two cities had existed, in many ways, in parallel. Now, for a brief period between November 1942 and August 1944, Marseille and Algiers charted separate courses.

The Allied conquest of Algiers placed Marseille and Algiers on opposite sides of the ongoing war, but the police of both cities worried about more than just the international conflict. In the winter of 1943, as the war raged on, Commissioner Marabuto of the Marseille police reported to his superiors on a different kind of enemy. Rather than an update on the German or American troops, Marabuto described the city's unbreachable Algerians. Marabuto noted that "Algerians ... are very reserved, mixing very little with the French population. It is therefore difficult to penetrate [their community] to clarify their feelings."[1] Marabuto described Algerians as a bloc, closed off to the police and of undiscernible loyalty. Officers like Marabuto served as quintessential representatives of the French state, but the shifting political alliances of World War II meant French police had to decide when to be loyal to which state. Throughout changes from Axis to Allied allegiances, as loyalties of the entire nation shifted, police in Marseille and Algiers remained constant in their wary treatment of Algerians.

This chapter spans the political turnovers and ruptures in communication that shook Marseille and Algiers from 1940 to 1945, events that toppled governments but ultimately saw a solidification of French mistrust of North Africans in both cities. The Allied victory in Algiers disrupted the maritime flow that connected Marseille and Algiers, leaving the ports silent and families unable to reach loved ones across the Mediterranean. This forced immobility placed the police in the position of managing the intimate lives of North Africans trapped in the metropole. Amid political change in Marseille and Algiers, police worried that wartime rivals could sway North Africans' allegiance and tried to track North Africans' contact with Germans, Italians, and Americans. Fear of imperial opponents primed police to understand North Africans as a threat to the French cause. Police also described North Africans as denizens of the flourishing wartime black market, mapping illicit trade onto the Casbahs of Marseille and Algiers.

The tensions of war fueled a police obsession with "anti-French" behavior among North Africans, a vague term used to condemn an array of behaviors. Weaving existing discourses of North African criminality into new contexts, the police constructed a model of the "anti-French" North African that fit, regardless of the changes in the aims and alliances of France itself. If Allied-occupied Algiers and Vichy-led Marseille proposed distinct visions of what loyalty to France meant, all seemed to agree that North Africans posed a danger to the "true" France. The loose parameters of anti-French laws and the administrative chaos of war granted interpretive power to officers on the ground, rooting requirements of proper nationalism in local contexts and spurring new carceral practices.

Families in Rupture

The Allied victory in Algiers and the resulting silence in communication with mainland France had serious consequences for Algerians and Europeans caught on either side of the Mediterranean. European functionaries on vacation, Algerians soldiers heading home from the front, businessmen, tourists, families, and workers—all got stuck. Though the problem of transport affected both Marseille and Algiers, the situation felt more dire in Marseille given the flow of migration, with thousands of Algerians brought to the metropole for the war. Vichy officials negotiated with the Americans and Germans, using the intercession of international aid organizations, but various schemes for repatriation all stalled. By the end of the war, hundreds of North Africans had gathered in Marseille, awaiting transport for months or even years. On the other side of the Mediterranean, French functionaries also waited anxiously to return home.

The blockage took a personal toll, but it also had a severe impact on the economic life of both Marseille and Algiers. These two port cities relied on seaborne trade for their local economies. Factories in Marseille needed raw materials shipped in from the colonies, and Algiers, the principal port of French North Africa, reaped profits as a center of colonial trade. With the Allied takeover, not just the movement of people but also the movement of goods faltered. In both cities, business in the ports dramatically declined and left Algerians, many of whom worked on the docks, without a job. Marseille's Service des Affaires Algériennes (SAA) expressed worry about the effect the quiet docks would have on the North Africans employed as porters, dockers, and sailors, fretting that these men would become beggars wandering the streets of Marseille.[2]

North Africans trapped in the metropole worried about more than just the loss of income. As the SAA acknowledged in a note shortly after the Allied takeover in November 1942, North African workers who came to the metropole did so to send money back to their families. Cut off from all contact with family members and unable to provide for their loved ones' needs, North Africans expressed a growing sense of alarm.[3] These men hoped that the government would provide for their families in their absence. Which government however—Vichy or Gaullist—seems unclear in their demands. Facing the rift in communication between France and Algeria, French officials in Vichy-controlled Marseille now had to think about the needs of Algerians not just as individual laborers but as part of family networks that spanned the Mediterranean. In turn, Algerian men pushed the government by narrating their demands in a language of fatherhood that reflected Vichy ideals.[4]

Marseille was already a site of triage for Algerians seeking to return to Algeria, many of them filtering through Camp Lyautey. With the rupture in 1942, those awaiting repatriation got stuck. Many Algerians resented French attempts to sequester them in Camp Lyautey, which they viewed as a prison.[5] As the blockage dragged on, more and more North Africans arrived in Marseille, sent south by police services across France but unable to get home. The local police estimated that five thousand Algerians lived in Marseille in 1943 along with about two hundred Moroccans and few dozen Tunisians. Not all these North Africans had immediate intentions to regain the Maghreb, but all of them lost contact with their connections across the Mediterranean.[6] Police reports declared, or perhaps more accurately speculated, that the primary concern of these stranded men was their inability to reach family members in North Africa.

The police, along with aid services like the SAA and the Bureau des Affaires Musulmanes Nord-Africaines (BAMNA), had long served as middlemen in cross-Mediterranean family disputes. Communication between Algerians in France and their families in Algeria had always been imperfect and police units in the metropole often failed to find the Algerian immigrants sought by their families.[7] As communication crawled to a halt in 1942, long-standing issues of connection became increasingly grim. The silence caused by the Allied arrival in Algiers created a corresponding archival silence. There are no letters in the police archives detailing the concerns of families in Algeria, as the letters could not be sent. Instead, cases from immediately before the rupture demonstrate the typical intermediary role of the police and suggest the consequences this sudden stoppage would have had on daily life for North Africans in both metropole and colony.

One such case was Tahar A., who traveled to the metropole early in the war to work in the mines of the Hautes-Pyrénées. In August 1942, Tahar received a troubling letter from his mother in Algeria, informing him that his wife had fled with their child to her parents' house. Tahar's mother warned that his wife planned to divorce him and marry a rival if he did not return to Algeria immediately. Tahar requested a forty-five-day vacation to travel home and fix this personal problem, but the mine administrators refused. Desperate, Tahar fled his post and headed for Marseille, hoping to slip onto a boat bound for Algeria. The Marseille police caught Tahar and sent him to Camp Lyautey. In an interview, Tahar lamented, "If the gendarmes must take me back to the mine without me being able to go home, it would be better for them to kill me right now."[8]

Tahar's case demonstrates the intimate stakes of mobility for Algerians, living a life that spanned two continents. Although financially able to provide for his family with the remittances from his work in the mine, Tahar's absence clearly left a void for his wife, who refused to accept an absentee husband. Her decision to leave forced Tahar's hand, but the strict policing of Algerian movement during the war prevented him from reaching her. Although Tahar's plea showcases the restrictions already in place, the rupture would have only solidified the powerlessness of Algerian fathers like Tahar. Trapped in France, they could not remedy marital problems, aid ill children, or weigh in on arguments over inheritance. With the rupture, the letter from Tahar's mother would have been unlikely to arrive in the first place. Notably, it was the police officer on the dock who prevented Tahar from going home, a moment of professional discretion but one with intensely personal consequences for Tahar.

In other cases, police interceded on behalf of loved ones writing from Algeria. In June 1942, the two wives of Djerdi B. lodged a complaint against their husband. Djerdi, a forty-seven-year-old Algerian laborer who lived on Rue des Chapeliers, had resided in Marseille for years. In the letter, Djardi K. and Atar H. informed the prosecutor of Marseille that Djerdi had abandoned them and their five children for more than six years, sending no news and leaving them to "die of hunger."[9] The women asked the police to send Djerdi home to resume his responsibilities. Though the letter was addressed to the prosecutor, the women explicitly called for police intercession. Their demands, couched in terms of paternal responsibility, generated a quick response. Djerdi and his wives practiced polygamy, a marital status legally ordained for Muslim Algerians but relentlessly critiqued by French observers as an example of Algerian "backwardness."[10] This case, then, provides an intriguing example of the French police being called on to enforce ideas of family duty and masculine responsibility that matched Algerian, rather than French, norms.[11]

Within two months, the police had located Djerdi. Guardian of the Peace Félix Vincentelli recorded his interview with Djerdi, who admitted to abandoning his wives. Djerdi explained that he had been gassed during World War I and still suffered from the resulting injuries. Without work, he had been unable to provide for his own existence, much less send money to his wives. However, Djerdi told the police he had recently been approved for repatriation to Algeria to "return to conjugal life."[12] Djardi and Atar had successfully wrangled the police into serving their interests. The police cajoled this recalcitrant Algerian father, "teaching" him the proper role of a husband. This exchange took place in June 1942, and perhaps Djerdi did indeed go home. But had the police taken longer to find him, had the repatriation order come through a bit more slowly, Djerdi, or others in his situation, would have been unable to return.

To be stuck in Marseille and unable to provide for their families made it impossible for Algerian fathers in the metropole to coordinate their trans-Mediterranean lives. If these examples speak to the difficulty of fathers and sons stranded in Marseille, families in Algiers also suffered from a lack of communication and the loss of much-needed income. The police had served as intermediaries in the dialogue between colonial subjects and the imperial government, the go-between tasked with facilitating contact across empire. This was intimate work, with Algerians revealing personal issues of love, family, and livelihood to police in the hope of getting official support. The rupture cut off police connectivity, too, and local officers in Marseille and Algiers now sought to manage disjointed Algerian families rather than finding ways to connect them.

France's Secret Police

As governments crumbled and reformed, both Vichy and the Free French relied on France's infamous political police to surveil the loyalty of the nation during regime change. In the nineteenth century, the Third Republic, trying to distance itself from the authoritarianism of previous regimes, declared an end to the hated "political police." Still, the new republican government continued to rely on the misleadingly named *Police spéciale des chemins de fer*. Originally created in 1855 under the Second Empire to surveil France's bustling train stations, the service gradually gained broad responsibility for monitoring organizations deemed threatening to the French nation, including foreigners, anarchists, and Communists. By 1911, the unit had been renamed simply the *Police spéciale*.[13] The "special police" of Marseille and Algiers diligently documented the rumors, accusations, and suspect organizations swirling in the port cities. A second political police, the Renseignements Généraux (RG), emerged in Paris in the early twentieth century, tasked with "confidential" administrative investigations. As this service expanded during the interwar years, a national network of information-gathering police units arose.[14] In Marseille and Algiers, RG brigades collected information on organizations or individuals deemed suspicious by the French government. Though the RG and special police both cooperated with the police d'état of Marseille and Algiers, they remained administratively separate from each other and differed in their mandates.[15] The special police, for example, prevented or investigated crimes that took place in train stations, but the RG were supposed to collect information only. The Third Republic indeed distinguished the RG from older forms of political policing by emphasizing its passivity.[16]

In both Marseille and Algiers, the RG and special police featured centrally in police initiatives to "penetrate" the Algerian community. As was often the case in the complicated system of French policing, the duties of the special police and RG overlapped. Both services produced at times redundant reports on Algerians, seemingly just as confused as the modern observer about who had primary responsibility. Though designed to gather intelligence on political movements, in practice, the special police and RG collected a much broader range of information. In their copious notes on Algerians, the two police entities treated even benign, daily events in the lives of colonial subjects as potentially subversive. The RG, for example, monitored public meetings organized by Algerian nationalists, but they also sent in reports about rumors, conversations, and the "mood" of Algerians in both cities.[17] In assigning RG and special police details to monitor ordinary Algerians, the police began to politicize the very category of "Algerian," layering a rebellious political identity onto a racialized colonial population.

Because the RG and the special police sought an insider view, they relied heavily on Algerian informants.[18] Playing with language barriers, Algerians could communicate in Arabic or Amazigh in public, languages they knew the police rarely understood. While particularly true in Marseille, this lack of expertise in local languages also proved problematic in Algiers. Unable to break into Algerian circles, the political police's information came from Algerians who proved willing, for a fee, to pass on gossip. Police sources reveal little about these informants, whose secrecy was maintained even in internal reports. Police records do, however, hint at their methods. The head of the Marseille special police, Commissioner Gaubert, noted in a letter that a "collaborator" of the police had been surveilling the Porte d'Aix, a monumental arch adjacent to Rue des Chapeliers. Noticing a large gathering of North Africans talking animatedly, the informant said, "I slipped in among them."[19] The informant's wording suggests someone who could disappear into a crowd of North Africans, someone who spoke the language and could gain their trust. It seems likely, then, that this mysterious "collaborator" was a North African. In other cases, the police leveraged the social position of café owners, offering North African restaurateurs exemptions to rationing rules in exchange for a steady stream of information.[20]

In Algiers, too, the political police relied on largely invisible informants. Special police and RG reports regularly began with the passive "we were informed," hiding the source of their information. Despite this archival erasure, the mountain of notes on meetings, speeches, and rumors attest to the indispensable role of Algerian informants. As in Marseille, police spies appear in the archives most clearly when caught between government services. In 1945, the prefect of Algiers asked the RG to investigate an Algerian named Mohammed ben H., only to have the RG return a note defending him as a loyalist and an informant.[21] Little can be gleaned about the personal lives and motivations of these informants. Some police reports scathingly describe spies as living on the margins of Algerian society, lacking stable jobs and mired in a seamy underworld of prostitution and crime.[22] Marginal or adjacently criminal agents benefited the police, giving them entry to this world. The social precarity of informants might also explain their motivation for exchanging information for money.[23]

If some Algerians participated in information gathering, others loudly critiqued the mission of the RG and special police. Algerian nationalists denounced the *mouchards*, literally flies, sent by the police to report on their gatherings. Some organizers went further still. M'haer ben Abdallah, an Algerian Communist and member of the Congrès Musulman, opened a speech in Marseille with a tongue-in-cheek nod to the police. As the anonymous informant at the event noted, M'haer announced that he had important statements to make, and therefore "he would use French, to allow the representatives of the police, presumed to be present in the room, to understand very precisely the meaning of his words and be able to inform their bosses."[24] M'haer acknowledged the police presence, but he turned the tables on them, speaking French so the police could accurately note all his demands. Algerians knew about police informants but could redirect this spying as a means of getting a message to the French government, switching languages not to hinder police comprehension but to help it. Organizers unraveled the power of espionage by accepting its presence and adapting it to their own purposes.

Though ostensibly created to police political behavior, the purview of the RG and special police expanded well beyond typical definitions of politics. In Marseille, the RG compiled frequent reports on "our Muslim subjects," reports that listed not just participation in political parties but also issues of health, hygiene, and living conditions.[25] When it came to Algerians, the definition of "dangerous politics" became diffuse. In 1941, the "special service of North African affairs" within the RG investigated a man named Boulou at the request of the Service des Affaires Algériennes (SAA), who misspelled his name as "Bollon." Boulou had been reported to the SAA for trafficking in bread rations. The RG could not prove black-market participation but emphasized his association with a criminal underworld. Boulou, they said, lived with prostitutes before taking up with his current European "concubine" and had a long criminal record for assault and weapons possession. The RG report declared Boulou "undesirable" and concluded that he would remain the object of close surveillance.[26] Boulou had no proven link to politics or the black market. Instead, the RG deemed him dangerous because of their judgment of his morality, his sexual relationships, and his previous criminal record. This collapse of moral and political concerns occurred frequently. Undeniably, the RG concentrated its efforts on policing left-wing political groups, especially in occupied France. But with North Africans, "undesirable" politics seemed to take on added meanings.[27] One wonders, after all, if a French worker would have been signaled to the RG or special police for drunkenness, a criminal record, or association with prostitutes.

In addition to tracking nationalist meetings, special police officers in Algiers also whiled away their evenings at the theater. In May 1941, the îlotier of the Casbah, Agent Akli of the Algiers special police, attended a theater performance. While there, Akli arrested a fellow Algerian named Alidji A. for shouting, "Enough already, change!" [Aia baraka beddel] after a song dedicated to Maréchal Pétain. Alidji's exclamation was in darija, the local Arabic dialect. Akli's language abilities and local knowledge were therefore imperative for policing this evening of art, as a European officer trained in classical Arabic might not have understood this dialectical expression.[28] Alidji insisted that he had been shouting "baraka" at a friend, who had been pinching his elbow to direct his attention to a row of attractive women seated in front of them. Still, Akli hauled Alidji off to the nearest police station and kept him overnight in jail before releasing him without charges.[29] Alidji's offense was shouting, at worst, a confusingly vague insult. It was Akli's explanation that imbued this exclamation with political heft. Akli could understand Alidji's dialect, no doubt the reason his superiors selected him for theater duty. It was Akli's personal interpretation, not just his translation, that had weight, showing the essential labor performed by Algerian police officers.

Between 1940 and 1944, Marseille and Algiers underwent radical shifts in government. The RG and special police served different military goals, different political projects, and even different governments in these two cities. There were also key demographic differences. In Marseille, both units overwhelmingly employed Europeans.[30] The Algiers police d'état hired mostly Europeans, but the RG units recruited a higher percentage of Algerians, perhaps in recognition of the crucial role language played in gathering information. Police placed a higher priority on policing "politics" in Algiers, whereas the police in Marseille worried more about Algerian mobility. Yet in both cities, the methods and preoccupations of the political police blurred the limits of "political" behavior for Algerians, identifying threats in quotidian activities deemed apolitical for French populations.

Competing Colonialisms

In 1940, with Paris occupied by the German army and Marseille and Algiers under Vichy control, the special police and RG turned their attention to a competing colonial power that threatened to undermine France's precarious imperial stability.[31] Hitler's government proved adept at selling the Third Reich as an Arab world power, producing Nazi propaganda in Arabic and emphasizing German respect for Arab culture.[32] German officials proposed an alternative imperial power in North Africa, threatening to usurp France.[33] Then in 1942, the Allied invasion of Algiers again shifted the relationship with Germany, turning a reluctant ally into an enemy. Throughout the war and despite regime changes, the French police on both sides of the Mediterranean paid close attention to Algerian communities' relationship with Germany, certain that Algerians harbored sympathies for this colonial competitor.

For decades prior to World War II, the police of both Marseille and Algiers had insisted that Algerians lacked interest in politics. The police saw Algerian participation in political organizations as a sign of European influence, rather than genuine political agency. French officials, for example, dismissed the Étoile Nord-Africaine (ENA), the most vocal Algerian nationalist group of the interwar period, as nothing but a subsidiary of the French Communist party.[34] By framing Algerian nationalism as really just an expression of Communism, the police placed the political power in the hands of European actors—French Communists.[35] Officers in Algiers insisted that Algerian voters, a small elite group, voted for nationalist parties because they were afraid of nationalists' bullying, rather than because they held sincere political convictions.[36] Police reports denied that Algerians had the ability to produce their own political movements or articulate worldviews outside of European frameworks. Algerian masses preoccupied with basic needs simply could not, police narratives claimed, worry about the injustice of the French colonial system or push for systemic change. This insistence, of course, ignored the ongoing political organizing and anticolonial protests of Algerians in both Algeria and metropolitan France.

Why dedicate so much time to the surveillance of Algerians if the police argued they had no independent political ambitions? The two narratives jostled within police discourse during World War II, presenting Algerians as politically undeveloped but nonetheless threatening, not least because of the influence Germany might have over these supposedly hapless subjects. Following French defeat in 1940, Germany and France entered an alliance, albeit a tense one where Germany, as the occupying force, retained the upper hand. Vichy's family policies, emphasis on tradition, and ideas about gender and race often aligned with Nazi worldviews. And yet, there was evident rivalry between Vichy and Germany when it came to the hearts and minds of Algerians.

The French obsession with German propaganda stemmed from a fear of precarious French colonial power. If France lost the colonies, it would lose manpower needed for the army and industrial production. On an ideological level, too, Vichy France clung to the colonies as proof of France's international prestige after the humiliating defeat in 1940. If the police believed that Algerians lacked the intellectual maturity to participate in politics, they also recognized the military weakness betrayed by the French loss. Vichy officials feared that colonial populations, perhaps particularly North Africans, would take advantage of French vulnerability and side with Germany to challenge the established colonial order.[37] The insistence that Algerians did not care about politics reveals police fears of Algerian political action, denying Algerians' agency precisely because the police sought to undermine it. Police officers carefully documented each interaction between Algerians and German soldiers or authorities, calling Algerians "pro-German" and fretting that Germany might provoke armed revolt against France.

Police fears had a basis. In Paris, especially, some Algerians saw the Third Reich as a viable alternative. The Algerian newspaper *Er-Rachid*, for example, supplied a steady stream of pro-German content in Paris.[38] If some Algerians did display sympathy for the German cause, this relationship shifted over time, in part due to Algerians' discomfort with the racial content of German propaganda.[39] Hitler may have presented his regime as "pro-Arab," but Nazi racial hierarchies still understood Arab populations as inferior to the Aryan race. This dissonance discouraged some would-be Algerian sympathizers. How much ordinary Algerians supported the German occupiers proves difficult to assess, but whatever the reality of pro-German sentiment, police representations built an idea of collaborationist Algerians.

After defeat in 1940, French officials in Algiers worried about German propaganda agents infiltrating the mass of demobilized Algerian soldiers returning to

North Africa. In response, police began to ramp up surveillance.[40] The increased policing did not go unnoticed by Algerians. Commandant Wender, head of the SAA in Marseille, reported a conversation with an Algerian who had recently returned to the metropole after a trip to Algiers. This Algerian, who had lived in Paris for fifteen years, complained that the police of Algiers treated him like a common criminal, tracking him relentlessly. This sort of police behavior, Wender warned, "profoundly agitates and dangerously sickens the feelings of the Algerian Muslims who are most attached to France."[41] Just as dangerously, obvious surveillance, the report suggested, would be recounted to the German authorities upon the Algerian man's return to Paris, adding fuel to German propaganda against the French. This case demonstrates the difficulty of the police in monitoring Algerian attitudes and emotions, fluid categories inherently difficult to pinpoint. Police struggled to prevent Algerians from expressing support for Germany without employing the heavy-handed colonial tactics that the Germans critiqued in their propaganda aimed at Algerians. The police of Marseille and Algiers did not find an effective compromise, leaving superiors to fret over optics while officers on the ground remained convinced of the need for close surveillance.

Claims of a Germano-Algerian alliance in Marseille centered on the idea that Germany would be able to attract the loyalty of Algerians with promises of greater freedom. The minister of the interior warned the prefect of the Bouches-du-Rhône that German forces in occupied Paris spread pernicious rumors among Algerians, liable to travel to Marseille, that Hitler would give North Africans independence if they fought alongside Germany. The propaganda, his note explained, had extra weight because German officers spoke Arabic "admirably" and were well-versed in North African culture.[42] The police also explained Algerians' preference for Germany by saying Germany catered to their antisemitism.[43] French authorities identified Algerian antisemitism as a centuries-old hatred, engrained in Algerian, and Arab, culture. This reified, simplistic, and often inaccurate interpretation of the historical relationship between Algerian Muslims and Algerian Jews offered a ready excuse for the appeal of German propaganda.[44] The fixation on Algerian antisemitism seems ironic given that the Vichy government in power in Marseille and, until 1942, in Algiers actively promoted antisemitic policies.[45] Police reports conveniently ignored the overall tenor of French policy under Vichy, instead identifying antisemitism as a particularly Algerian vice.

Official framing deflected blame away from French colonial policy and the systemic inequality of colonial Algeria. In April 1942, Commandant Wender wrote a note detailing the anger of the hundreds of North African veterans in hospitals in Marseille, awaiting repatriation to Algeria. These men had spent time in prisoner-of-war camps in Germany, an experience that perhaps naturally would have led to anti-German attitudes. According to police reports, however, German authorities wooed Algerian prisoners-of-war by treating them well in hopes of sowing discontent in the French Empire.[46] Wender wholeheartedly blamed the recovering veterans' "bad attitude" on the German propaganda they had imbibed as prisoners. Only in passing did he mention other factors that might contribute to their anger, namely that the soldiers had been paid only irregularly, were being forcibly held in Marseille, and resided in hospitals with "personnel insufficiently aware of the North African mentality."[47]

Meanwhile, in Algiers, the fear of foreign propaganda among "naive" Algerians intensified during the war. In part, the police blamed the surge of pro-German propaganda in Algiers, tracked in pamphlets and coffee-shop conversations, on the actions of returning Algerian prisoners of war. In August 1940, the commissioner of the 7ème arrondissement of Algiers, for example, credited repatriated prisoners of war for a marked "arrogance" in the Algerian community. The men returned to Algeria following crushing defeat, the collapse of the Third Republic, and the rise to power of Pétain's Vichy government. The soldiers, the commissioner said, declared that Germany had proven its strength and would soon take over North Africa. When the Germans gained power, Algerians would be given the same rights as French citizens.[48] The police association of German propaganda and Algerian "arrogance" toward Europeans is telling. A loyal Algerian, it implied, would show deference to Europeans, but an Algerian indoctrinated by the German sales pitch would rebel against French authority. In their discussion of prisoners of war, the police in both Marseille and Algiers ignored the ways in which France had failed these soldiers, instead blaming their attitude on German propaganda. They could not, or would not, recognize that Algerians did not need foreign influence to be critical of French rule or demand equality.

Fear of German propaganda intensified after the Allied capture of Algiers in November 1942. With this military victory, Algiers switched sides in the war effort, and Germany became a clear enemy rather than quasi-ally. In December 1942, frenzied reports from the RG of Algiers noted intense German propaganda aimed at Algerian workers and worried that Algerians continued to secretly listen to German radio broadcasts at night. This report emphasized that the propaganda circulated primarily "in ignorant communities," crediting Algerian stupidity for German success.[49] The RG of Algiers insisted that the "Muslim masses" in Algeria supported Germany because of Germany's military strength and the fortunes Algerians had made through illicit trade in the occupied zone.[50] Pro-German sentiments, then, could be explained as blind submission to the most powerful force or a selfish desire for profit. Algiers police also used the familiar narrative of Algerian antisemitism to explain German sympathy.[51] All these reasons deflected blame for Algerians' "pro-German" attitudes away from French actions.

Algerians, however, offered different explanations. The RG of Algiers kept a copy of a short booklet by the Algerian Islamic reformer, socialist, and editor of *La Défense*, Lamine Lamoudi, written in 1943 for American authorities. The Americans wanted to understand what they saw as the success of German outreach among Algerians.[52] According to Lamoudi, Algerians had responded to Axis propaganda because German authorities devoted special attention to them. Germany created Arabic-language radio programs and promised Algerians "mountains and marvels" if Germany won the war. Lamoudi alleged that at the moment of French defeat in 1940, 95 percent of Muslim Algerians were pro-German. However, he offered a strikingly different explanation for this sympathy than police sources. "Muslim sympathies for the Germans can be explained by the fact that Muslims, who had so many injustices to complain about, had endured so much suffering, experienced so much bullying and humiliation . . . saw in HITLER . . . an avenger armed by Providence."[53] In his explanation, Lamoudi blamed French colonialism for Algerians' "pro-German" stance.

Whatever the reason for the supposed Algerian-German alliances, officers in both Marseille and Algiers treated German propaganda as an ever-present worry. Marseille had a larger contingent of German soldiers and officials present, creating more potential for contact with the city's North African population. Algiers, while geographically distant, proved a significant target of German propaganda. These structural differences meant police fears of German influence played out in different contexts and spaces. In Marseille, "pro-German" Algerians printed pamphlets sympathetic to Germany and drank with German officers in neighborhood bars. In Algiers, after Allied victory, a "pro-German" Algerian might simply have been someone less than thrilled about the arrival of the Allies. Despite changing politics, the police of both Marseille and Algiers remained convinced that gullible Algerians had fallen into Germany's rhetorical trap. Warning of the consequences of German propaganda, the French police evoked a broad category to reassert control—the "anti-French" Algerian.

"Anti-National" Algerians

In response to the looming danger of German colonial ambitions, the French police turned their attention to the imagined enemy within their empire—Algerians. The war empowered the police to punish "anti-national" or "anti-French" actions, criminalizing any criticism of the French government.[54] The Vichy regime implemented laws to suppress dissidents, building on legal codes that had been previously weaponized against "dangerous" political groups like anarchists.

The police suspected several populations of "anti-national" attitudes, including Jews, Italian and German immigrants, Communists, Freemasons, and Algerians. The power of "anti-national" policing lay precisely in its vague parameters. What was anti-national? Who decided? Following the Allied takeover of Algiers in 1942, anti-French could even refer to two different Frances. Both Vichy and the Free French, led by de Gaulle abroad, claimed to represent the "true" France. At a moment of crisis in the very conception of the French nation, the meaning of "anti-French" behavior became difficult to decipher. French Resistance fighters became terrorists in the eyes of the Vichy government, while Allied officials decried Vichy authoritarianism as a betrayal of France. Laws promulgated by Vichy punished "anti-national" behavior, but even after the change in government in Algiers, the police continued to use these laws to bolster the uncertain legitimacy of the new Gaullist government. With the opposing visions of France promoted by Vichy and de Gaulle and the vague legal language, the actual definition of "anti-French" action often fell to the police.

In Vichy-controlled Marseille, police officers built a case against "anti-national" North Africans, a charge leveled at North Africans for everything from support for Germany, to endorsement of Algerian nationalism, to disagreements between disgruntled neighbors. In May 1940, the Marseille police compiled a list of all the men charged with anti-national rhetoric. This list contained a distinct overrepresentation of North Africans.[55] In part, racialized police mapping of urban space contributed to this overrepresentation. Attached to the list of names, a note explained that the police paid special attention to raids on the quays in their repression of anti-national behavior. North Africans, employed on the docks as porters and sailors, might have been more likely than other populations to get caught in these sweeps. But the focus on "anti-French" North Africans was not limited to the docks. The SAA's Commandant Wender emphasized a general need to track anti-French sentiments within the Algerian community.[56] Agents should not just identify agitators, he advised, but also develop relationships with them, to infiltrate their networks. Constructed as "pro-German" in the wake of French defeat in 1940, North Africans easily fell under police suspicion for anti-national behavior.

While police reports in Marseille demonstrate a targeting of North Africans for anti-French actions, the reports remain opaque about what exactly the term meant.[57] In one example, an Algerian man, Djerdi D., wrote to the SAA of Marseille, advocating for a pension he felt he was due as a World War I veteran. In their response, the SAA hinted at the potential anti-French ties of individuals around Djerdi who used his case to promote a "xenophobic movement of emancipation."[58] The common framing of Algerian nationalism as "xenophobic" refused the legitimacy of Algerian anticolonialism but also paradoxically acknowledged

Algerians as the "natural" inhabitants of Algeria as opposed to the "foreign" French. In Djerdi's case, his "anti-French" attitude had no immediate connection to the war. Instead, anti-French, in this case, meant suspected nationalist.

National directives offered few details on how to police anti-French action, and local officials proved adept at molding the expansive power of the laws to address local concerns. In December 1942, Commandant Wender of the SAA wrote a letter of complaint to the Vichy minister of the interior, explaining that several Algerians had approached him about the plight of an Algerian named Laroubi. The Marseille police tried to charge Laroubi with anti-French behavior, but "lacking sufficient material proof" they could not bring him to trial. Instead, the police fell back on special powers over anti-nationals granted by the war, putting Laroubi under administrative internment.[59] Faced with insufficient proof of Laroubi's anti-French action, the police shifted from the courts to internment, a system designed to be as fluid as the category of anti-French itself.[60]

Under Vichy, charges of anti-national conduct had heavy consequences for Algerians. A law of April 17, 1942, stripped all "indigène" citizens of their citizenship if found guilty of "anti-French intrigues" or otherwise condemned to administrative internment.[61] This law, applied only to "indigènes," treated citizenship as a privilege based on absolute loyalty to the French state. The smallest critique, adherence to a nationalist organization, or resistance to authority, all framed as anti-French action, could result in this hard-won civic right being casually stripped away.[62] The risk of an anti-French condemnation, then, was high-stakes, but the punishment could be doled out with few checks on police authority.

Across the Mediterranean in Algiers, many of the reports on anti-national acts came from altercations in which Algerians defied or insulted the police. The police positioned any rebellion against them as an act against France and thus dangerous to the French war effort. In January 1941, for example, a group of police officers arrived at the Hotel Provençal in a central European quarter of Algiers to calm a "completely drunk indigène." The officers found Ahmed O., a mechanic from Algiers. As the police arrested him, Ahmed yelled "Long live Germany; they came and straightened you out [*vous arrangèrent la cravate*]. You aren't French. You are nothing but dirty Italians and Spaniards."[63] The police dragged Ahmed to the commissariat and charged him with a litany of offenses, including "public drunkenness, attacking and insulting a police officer, and sedition against France."[64] Ahmed's case demonstrates the flexibility of anti-French laws. His insults seem more a reflection of anger over his arrest than any real critique of French power. Moreover, in 1941, Algiers remained under Vichy control, collaborating, if testily, with Germany. This made Ahmed's support of Germany theoretically less subversive. Interestingly, Ahmed called into question the "Frenchness" of the arresting officers, pointing out the diverse immigrant origins of Algeria's European population. In fact, many police officers in Algiers were from Spanish and Italian migrant communities that had gained French citizenship only a generation or two prior. The police used accusations of anti-French action to rack up the charges against Ahmed, whose crime otherwise amounted to being drunk and, just as importantly, drunk in a European neighborhood. His presence in this European space defied colonial segregation, prompting police to intervene in the name of "order."

The policing of Algerian "sentiments" in Algiers underwent a rapid switch in November 1942 with the Allied takeover of the city. For two years, the government of Algiers had enthusiastically endorsed Vichy politics and maintained a tenuous alliance with Germany. Overnight, a republican government headed by resistance figures set up shop in Algiers, and propaganda in favor of the Germans became a betrayal of the "true" French cause. If Algiers now renounced Vichy, political power remained in flux, with different factions grappling for control.[65] In December, Mohamed A., the chauffeur of the Free French General Henri Giraud, relaxed at a café while waiting for his boss' car to be fitted with new leather seats. Next to Mohamed, an Allied soldier reclined. A young Algerian approached the soldier and lashed out in Arabic, a language he knew this soldier could not understand, saying "Bunch of bastards, if the Germans were here, you would not be lounging around like that."[66] If the Allied soldier did not understand this insult, Mohamed did, and he promptly grabbed the young man and took him to the police station. The police charged the eighteen-year-old with "sedition." The reproaches of a disgruntled teenager could hardly disrupt the larger war effort. But in an atmosphere of shifting loyalties, when the Allied hold on Algiers remained unsure, police officers interpreted anything in favor of the Germans as a danger to the French cause.

Anti-French laws could also be mobilized to police other political threats. In the fall of 1943, a fight broke out as four Algerians descended from the Casbah's brothels to the commercial thoroughfare of Rue Randon. The police report vaguely claimed that these men got into a fight with their "coreligionnaires," and Inspector Akli intervened to break it up. Akli, the same Algerian îlotier who had arrested a man at the opera, reported that he heard cries of "Down with France, Long live the PPA, Long live Islam."[67] Though Akli described this incident as "sedition" against France, he denied the political ambitions of the Algerians involved. Despite the Algerians naming a nationalist political party, the PPA, Akli's report concluded that the shouts were not political propaganda but "an isolated act of individuals whose emotions burst out in the middle of the fight."[68] The report classified the men's shouts as anti-French, a threat to the French government, but in the same breath denied the anger as an intellectually informed political position. We might also read this incident as an Algerian officer protecting fellow

Algerians, downplaying the severity of the crime by writing it off as a simple fight. Either way, Akli's intervention makes clear the personal leeway in the interpretation of anti-national action. As governments changed and the war raged on, individual officers held the power to decide when an incident constituted a real threat and when shouts against France were merely hotheaded nonsense.

As the case of the chauffeur, Mohamed, shows, the police of Algiers were not alone in evoking the idea of anti-French or anti-national sentiments. Algerians, too, played on French fears for their own purposes. In March 1945, as the war in Europe drew to a bloody close, the RG of Algiers received an anonymous letter denouncing Mohamed T. as a "real anti-French" individual who "spreads a scandalous propaganda among us."[69] The RG investigation into this venomous letter, however, revealed a motivation decidedly more personal than national. After investigating Mohamed and his family, the police concluded that although Mohamed had questionable moral conduct and was a known drunk, nothing about his behavior seemed anti-French.[70] The police also discovered that Mohamed's brother-in-law wrote the letter after an argument. Officers had been drawn into what amounted to a private family dispute. Officers used the idea of anti-French behavior to punish any statement against French authority, including the police. But Algerians, too, could appropriate the nebulous definition of anti-French actions to involve the police in their own concerns, albeit in this case unsuccessfully.

Though national directives gave the police the power to surveil anti-French behavior and Vichy laws added consequences for the crime, ultimately the policing of anti-French Algerians relied on local preoccupations and individual relationships, interactions rooted in space. The local police, and not just the national government, decided the contours of anti-French action. Drawing on broader governmental and press discourses that pointed to Algerian sympathy for Germany and hinted at their doubtful loyalty, police officers became disposed to see Algerian anti-French action everywhere. As the cases from Algiers show, many of those accused of anti-French behavior attacked, more specifically, the police. Officers could use the poorly defined category to maintain authority over Algerians, especially Algerians who challenged their power.

Charges of anti-French action did not fall solely on Algerians. Such accusations had been used in the interwar period, for example, to repress anticolonial organizing.[71] Horrifically, both Nazi occupiers and the Vichy government labeled Jews as a threat, and specialized police brigades rounded up and deported thousands of Jews to be sent to their death in concentration camps.[72] In these deportations, the impact of Vichy politics on policing is most evident. Immigrants from Italy or Germany and "dangerous" political groups also preoccupied police services.[73] Yet in the eyes of the police, Italians, Algerians, and leftist political organizations all posed the same threat of being inherent enemies to France. Policing anti-French sentiments among Algerians reflected a predetermined denial of Algerians' "Frenchness." Given an opportunity, the police seemed to believe, Algerians would undermine France to the benefit of its enemies. This understanding of Algerians, paired with the individual discretion embedded in laws on anti-national action, gave the police extraordinary power. Anti-French behavior depended not just on what Algerians did in public but also on what they believed, the type of company they kept, and where they drank their coffee. Policing the private in the name of public safety and wartime loyalty enabled the police to probe the personal lives of Algerians, an invasion that would become ever more important in the postwar.

Tracking Black-Market Traffickers

Police suspicion of Algerians' loyalty also shone through in the targeted policing of the black market. As the war squeezed supply chains, France rolled out rations on meat, milk, oil, vegetables, cloth, cigarettes, sweets, soap, wine, and more, regulating access to both luxuries and essentials. As rationing started, a flourishing black market also emerged, an omnipresent feature of life in France and its empire during World War II. Conflicts over scarce resources heightened social divisions.[74] French citizens mobilized categories of the "undesirable" in battles over food and housing, stigmatizing refugees, foreigners, and French Jews in an effort to guard resources.[75] At first, Vichy authorities described black-market traffickers as enemies of the state, greedy individuals stealing food from the starving populace. As the war lumbered on, however, Vichy begrudgingly accepted the black market as a practical necessity. Within French Resistance circles, the black market was even celebrated as an act of rebellion.[76] Exchanges that violated regulations often served the needs of families, reinforcing popular disapproval of strict enforcement.[77] Acknowledging the popularity of the black market, official Vichy policy pivoted in 1942 toward tracking large-scale operators rather than punishing occasional traffickers.[78]

This tacit acceptance and focus on kingpins, however, was not true for North Africans in Marseille and Algiers. Police officers knew that demand from European customers drove the black market. Government officials knew that the "kings of the black market" running large operations made the bulk of the profits.[79] And yet, police repression of North African participation in the black market focused on small-scale, one-off trades on the streets. This strategy targeted North Africans not because they made the most money from the black market, but because they were the most visible and vulnerable to surveillance. As the policing of the black market became unpopular among French citizens, police could point to their pursuit of North African traffickers as an uncontroversial battle against internal enemies.[80] In their hunt for North African black marketers, the police treated North Africans not as individual criminals but as a racialized bloc of potential profiteers. In doing so, the police made North Africans' alleged participation in the black market a proxy for their inherent disloyalty, despite a more fluid idea of what engaging in the black market meant for other populations.

The disproportionate focus on a "North African" black market is evident in the surveillance files of Marseille's North African aid bureaus. In February 1942, Commandant Wender described an urgent problem in the "indigène" life of Marseille. Speaking of a wave of unemployed North Africans arriving in Marseille, Wender suggested that these newcomers might be behind the recent uptick in theft, trafficking, and other infractions.[81] Wender's note listed 163 condemnations of North Africans for these crimes between September and December 1941. Of the 163 cases, 59 charges related to black-market infractions like trafficking in forbidden or restricted products, overcharging for price-controlled foods, or fencing stolen goods. Daily reports from the various commissariats of Marseille from 1941 show that a striking number of North Africans arrested by the police during the war were charged with the sale of black-market goods.[82] In reports like this, officials linked alleged black-market participation to broader stereotypes about North African criminality.

The police suspicion of North African black marketeers in Marseille also related to the perceived danger of North Africans' mobility and connection to the port. For example, the SAA forwarded a report to the police from a "Kabyle" informant who accused a fellow Algerian of trafficking merchandise through the port of Marseille to be sold in Paris.[83] Reports emanating from Algeria also pointed to suspicious movement within and to Marseille. A letter from the prefecture of Constantine, for example, alerted the North African services of Marseille that an Algerian who had recently returned to Constantine claimed his "coreligionnaires" had given up regular work altogether in favor of profits from the black market. The source cited a friend who shuttled between Paris and Marseille with contraband cigarettes, pulling in a staggering profit of twenty-five thousand to thirty thousand francs per trip.[84] The police criminalized what they saw as the transient nature of Algerian life in the metropole, positioning Algerians as the "usual suspects" for black-market trafficking.

The police of Marseille never claimed that North Africans dominated the black market in their city. If North Africans represented only a small portion of black-market operators, however, the police implied that the black market "employed" a large percentage of North Africans. Based on this belief, the policing of the black market in Marseille narrowed in on spaces considered particularly North African, like Rue des Chapeliers. Commandant Wender wrote a long, disparaging letter in November 1942, warning of the dangers lurking in this, in his mind, insufficiently policed North African space. Recently, Wender testily remarked, the street had become encumbered with "gatherings of often unsavory indigènes, traffickers who arrived to unload their wares."[85] Wender noted that police attempts to arrest traffickers consisted of blocking the ends of Rue des Chapeliers and then searching those caught between the barricades, verifying IDs and confiscating suspect goods. However, these periodic descents sowed discontent among shopkeepers on the street. Wender suggested that the police should instead station a permanent detail on Rue des Chapeliers, until the "undesirables" lost the habit of coming there.[86] In the chaos and short staffing of the war, however, the Marseille police lacked the resources to carry out Wender's plan, and officers instead continued their periodic raids, lumping all North Africans on the street into the same category of potential black-market trafficker.

After the rupture, uncertain immigration status compounded the effects of the constant raids on Rue des Chapeliers. In 1943, the police described what they saw as a crisis of vagrancy and black-market operations on Rue des Chapeliers. Trying to clear this street of illicit activity, police brigades frequently raided the businesses, and even sidewalks, of Rue des Chapeliers. Many of the North Africans stuck in Marseille lacked proper paperwork, having only intended to stay in Marseille for a short visit or a stopover on the journey back to Algeria. The "safe passage" (*sauf-conduit*) they possessed, however, was not a residency card. Algerians were unable to rectify their immigration status administratively because it required communicating with their "home" administrator in Algeria, made impossible by the war. Their cases thus fell to police to adjudicate.[87] Blocked in France, Algerians, according to the SAA, had become bitter and disappointed, especially with their "difficulties" with the police.[88] Police certainty of black-market activity around Rue des Chapeliers constantly thrust officers into the lives of Algerian workers already vulnerable because of the rupture, a familiar and violent presence.

The police of Marseille seemed to base their assumption of North African participation in the black market in part on letters from local residents. Many complaints sent to the Marseille police during World War II displayed a marked distrust of North Africans. Some letters evoked religion, as in one in which the anonymous writer claimed an Algerian bar owner, Issa A., had stockpiled mutton illegally "for the month of fasting" and participated in black-market sales of bread, meat, wine, butter, and oil.[89] Officers dutifully responded to accusations, although they rarely discovered suspicious activities. Complaints against North Africans frequently linked black-market activity with a broader idea of anti-French action. In the case of Issa, for example, the anonymous letter also accused him of employing a foreign woman in his restaurant, stealing a job from a French citizen.[90]

In another anonymous letter denouncing an Algerian woman, Hada J., and her boss, the writer stated, "While many Frenchmen suffer, Belkacem and Hada J. and her lover, Marcel, partake in the black market."[91] The writer insisted on his own French identity, declaring his French nationality and his four years of military service. The accusation against Hada, however, seemed to stem from a personal vendetta rather than national loyalty. The man also accused Hada of "seducing" him into sleeping with her with her "good manners" and then stealing 2,300 francs while he slept.[92] His letter, then, reads more as an attempted defamation of character than a patriotic defense of France. The grouping of black-market activity with other crimes created an idea of the "anti-French" Algerian that resonated with existing police beliefs about Algerian criminality and sympathy for Germany.

If Muslim Algerians fell under police and public scrutiny in Marseille, Algerian Jews, caught between colonial stereotypes and antisemitic laws, faced even more pointed accusations. Angry letters from the public accused the police of turning a blind eye on Algerian Jews making a windfall on the black market in Marseille. These accusations rang with antisemitism, in keeping with Vichy norms. It was also an accusation with deadly penalties, as Vichy began deporting Jews to Nazi death camps in the summer of 1942.[93] Just months prior, Madame Germaine came to the police to report on her neighbor, a Jewish widow from Oran named Perle D. Germaine complained that Perle had attacked her, and she demanded that the police intervene. When the police interviewed Perle, however, she said that Germaine started the fight and had already written two letters to the police accusing Perle of black-market activity. These letters had resulted in raids on Perle's hotel that, she defiantly added, found no suspect activity. Perle said her neighbor hated her because she had forced Germaine to leave the hotel following the Frenchwoman's bad behavior. A neighbor who overheard the fight confirmed that Germaine had started the confrontation and had yelled, "What are you butting in for you dirty Jew. Just go to Palestine. Besides, you are involved in the black market and I will have your café closed."[94] Germaine's acerbic insults mixed antisemitism with accusations of black-market activity. She clearly assumed that the police would believe and act on her accusations. And to some extent, Germaine was right. While the police seemed to accept the testimony clearing Perle, Germaine's two earlier letters had indeed resulted in raids on Perle's business.

As the Marseille police battled the black market at the port and on Rue des Chapeliers, officers across the Mediterranean in Algiers also worried about the black market in their city. Administrators and police officers in Algiers placed full blame on the local Algerian population for the flourishing black market.[95] An official report on the activity of the Economic Brigade, responsible for enforcing rationing laws, noted that the black market "is still and above all practiced by the indigène population."[96] As in Marseille, the policing of the black market in Algiers focused on Algerian urban spaces. In police reports, officers described black-market sales as taking place in the Casbah, particularly the main commercial arteries of Rue Randon and Rue des Chartres.[97] Police depicted black-market participation as anti-French, casting Algerians as greedy profiteers seeking their own benefit at the expense of Algiers's European population. What the notes on black-market activity do not acknowledge, however, are the inequalities built into the rationing system. Only Europeans could purchase certain goods, including chocolate and alcohol, and Europeans and Algerians had different ration cards, creating uneven access to food.[98] The desire of Algerians to provide for their families became, in the eyes of the police, a crime against France. The strain on scarce resources in Algiers became even more dire due to the explosion of Algiers's population during the war, an increase caused not only by Allied troops and metropolitan refugees but also the steady arrival of rural migrants fleeing famine in the countryside.[99]

The targeted policing of the black market led to a series of conflicts between Algerians and the police in the markets of Algiers. The chief of the Economic Brigade, Friand, characterized these conflicts as a problem of the "attitude of the Muslims towards police."[100] Friand claimed that in the past, Algerians had accepted police intervention meekly. Now, however, merchants and peddlers "have become aggressive. . . . arrogant and ready to rebel."[101] Friand described incidents in which young Algerians threw stones at the police when they tried to arrest an Algerian for selling overpriced zucchini or when a crowd gathered in solidarity in front of the house of an Algerian accused of operating a clandestine slaughterhouse. Friand lamented, "All this demonstrates a total lack of respect and fear towards the police among Muslims and their attitude risks to seriously compromise the internal security of the country."[102] Friand complained that Algerians had become disrespectful, less fearful of police authority, and thus a threat to France.

Although the police defined black-market activity as a crime, they policed this crime unevenly in Algiers. In November 1944, with Paris newly liberated from German occupation, the same Officer Friand and a colleague came upon Kouidri A. selling a European woman a leg of lamb.[103] According to the report, Kouidri fled at the sight of the police, handing off the compromising meat to a child. The police managed to catch the fleeing man and admitted that in the struggle to subdue him, Kouidri "may" have been hit in the face with handcuffs. The commotion attracted the attention of other Algerians, and as a crowd gathered, the officers took out their guns. The official report justified this by noting, "Force must rest with the law."[104] The police report accused Kouidri of unsuccessfully grabbing for the gun and in the struggle, one of the officers hit him in the face with the butt of the gun. Kouidri's intake paperwork lists a horrific litany of contusions, evidence that he was beaten to a pulp by the police during his arrest. The official response, which doctored the record to protect the officers, proves the impunity with which police could exercise violence on Algerians. Kouidri went to jail, but the officers would not even be questioned for their use of force.

And what of the European woman to whom Kouidri sold the lamb? She dropped out of the story entirely. An internal report to the governor general of Algeria in 1942 admitted, "Black market buyers are mostly Europeans. Without these buyers, the black market would disappear."[105] Despite this recognition, police officials and individual officers continued to target Algerian sellers. In doing so, the police of Algiers criminalized Algerians while treating their European clients as victims of wartime circumstances. Police reports in Algiers rarely cited Europeans for black-market crimes.[106] Officers in Algiers operated under the belief that the black market existed principally in the Casbah, dedicating their limited manpower to patrols there. This spatial understanding resulted in a predictable overrepresentation of Algerian traffickers. In part, the focus on Algerians reflected a socioeconomic reality. Land expropriation and systematic pauperization of Algerians in the nineteenth century encouraged a proliferation of street vendors in urban centers, struggling to survive by selling fruits and vegetables.[107] These mobile merchants no doubt recognized they could earn higher profits by sidestepping the laws regulating prices and quantities to meet demand. Still, social realities alone do not explain the police obsession with Algerian traffickers.

Though they had identified Algerians as the center of the black market, the police of Algiers despaired of methods to suppress it. The police could fine black-market traffickers, but they complained that those who participated in the black market were impossible to track. Many traffickers were homeless, meaning the police could seize suspect goods but could not collect fines.[108] The situation came to a head in 1944, as reflected in a letter from Assistant Central Police Commissioner of Algiers Georges Lafond. Lafond had served in the police d'état of Algiers for years but was promoted to adjoint central commissioner in the fall of 1944, after the Allies took control. Although Lafond represented the new republican government, he reinforced ideas about the black market steeped in old prejudice against Algerians. In a letter to the central commissioner, Lafond referred to black-market traffickers as "parasites" who posed a danger to the city. "They live from the proceeds of the robberies they commit, the black market that they practice, and increase the too numerous idlers who wander the streets, ready to be led astray by any and all Muslim troublemakers, to the profit of Muslim anti-French movements."[109] In his letter, Lafond drew a direct link between stereotypes of Algerian thieves, anti-French movements, and the evils of the black market.

Responding to the situation described by Lafond, the prefect of Algiers proposed a new plan. In a note to the governor general of Algeria, the prefect said that police raids on the Casbah had led to the arrest of numerous delinquents. However, current laws blocked the police from jailing traffickers, so all the culprits had to be released shortly after. The prefect described this as "discouraging" to police officers. He requested that the recent law from April 25, 1944, which allowed the requisitioning of agricultural laborers, be adapted as a tool for punishing the black marketeers. By the prefect's suggestion, all "black market fraudsters" between the ages of fifteen and fifty caught trafficking and unable to prove "regular" employment would be sent to agricultural labor camps.

The prefect defended this strategy as "effective as well as legal" and said it would give the police the power to discipline those who refused to report to the camps.[110] The black-market traffickers would be sent to a triage center in the Algiers suburb of Kouba, where they would be matched with employers.[111] The RG of Algiers had recently reported that Europeans in the countryside lacked sufficient labor for their farms, blaming the shortage on the temptations of the black market and the higher wages offered by the Americans. The report also blithely acknowledged that the inability of European farmers to provide sufficient food for their workers contributed, perhaps, to the reluctance of Algerian farmhands. These settlers' demands for workers matched the prefect's proposal to requisition Algerian traffickers and thereby "prevent us from seeing so many idlers in the cafés maures" of Algiers.[112] The plan to co-opt Algerian black-market sellers as laborers suited multiple agendas.

By September 1944, the proposal had been implemented. A large dossier discusses the fate of a group of Algerian men, all "Muslim indigènes" arrested for selling on the black market.[113] When I first encountered the manila folder in the archives, the silences drew me in as much as what was written on the page. On formulaic sheets, some nameless police officer carefully recorded the name, filiation, birthplace, age, and occupation of each of these men. Separate columns listed how long they had lived in Algiers, their local address, and level of education. For all this information, more was left unsaid. These men, although arrested in Algiers, had often lived in the city for only a few weeks or months before their arrest. What brought them to Algiers? What were the circumstances of their arrest? How did they experience their encounter with the police? The men likely came to Algiers as part of the wave of rural immigrants pushed into urban centers by wartime poverty.[114] These migrants, new to Algiers and likely to work in day laborer positions because of their level of education, could hardly be expected to have a steady job contract within weeks of their arrival. According to their directives, the police could arrest and requisition any Algerian they caught selling on the black market who could not prove regular employment. In practice, this meant the police targeted the most vulnerable Algerians, those without deep roots in the urban environment.

No law or decree formally legalized this plan. Rather, the context of the war gave the police the ability to operate purely by internal policy, to create a program of unfree labor that targeted the most precarious segment of Algerian society. Although all these men were accused of black-market activity, none were tried in a court of law. Given the lax parameters, it seems likely that many of them had been arrested while simply wandering the streets of Algiers, selling a personal item, a marked-up bundle of carrots, or a contraband pack of cigarettes, when the police happened upon them. Though it is unclear from the records how much these requisitioned laborers would be paid, there can be no doubt about their lack of freedom. Arrested for a crime that legally could not be punished with incarceration, these men nonetheless lost their freedom of mobility and of choice.

The sequestering of the "delinquents," as the police called them, immediately ran into problems. According to a harried letter from the director of the camp in Kouba, when the first group of men arrested in Algiers arrived at the triage center, their convoy had not thought to bring along food rations. The Labor Ministry also encountered delays in placing requisitioned workers with employers. Potential employers expected the government to continue to house and feed the Algerian laborers in Kouba, which was not the government's plan. To make matters worse, the alleged traffickers refused to work.[115] Of the seventy-five men held in the camp, several had been classified by police files as "dangerous" ex-convicts, and four men had already escaped. As a stopgap measure, the director ordered the men locked in their rooms, under guard.

As the camp director pointed out, all of this was illegal. The camp at Kouba had been intended to temporarily house requisitioned "<u>agricultural workers</u>" (underline in original) who had refused to answer an individual requisition order.[116] These unemployed black-market traffickers legally could not be detained in Kouba. The director further added that the camp did not have the funding to feed these men, who besides had "no utility" for the French cause, as employers refused to hire them, and the men refused to work. Despite the failure in Kouba, the police continued to send Algerians caught trafficking to army recruitment centers or public works projects.[117] The archival records are unclear about the destiny of the Kouba program, but the example reveals an expansion in the scope of police power. The police criminalized unemployment, made their opinion law, and policed public order in the Casbah with a predetermined idea of Algerian culpability.

The police construction of Algerians at the center of the black market created patterns and relationships that persisted after rationing ended. The idea of Algerians as denizens of the black market dovetailed with other police fears about Algerians during the war, including their supposed pro-German sympathies. Black-market links to Algerians in the popular and police culture of Marseille had tangible ramifications. The police focused on the port and Rue des Chapeliers, concentrating intensely on the space of Algerian daily life. Weekly, at times daily, raids of the restaurants and stores on Rue des Chapeliers placed Algerians in direct proximity with the police, guilty until proven innocent. If the police of Marseille considered Algerians likely participants in the black market, in Algiers, the policing of the black market implicated almost exclusively Algerians. Identifying Algerians as *the* black-market profiteers, the police treated Algerians as an internal enemy France needed to guard against.[118] In Algiers, the image of Algerians as "anti-national" black-market operatives enabled practices that bestowed total authority to the police, bypassing the courts and even the law.

Despite the differences in magnitude, police officers in both cities cultivated a spatial understanding of black-market activity that centered North Africans. The police arrested individual traffickers, but they targeted neighborhoods that they understood as North African in their hunt. Considering North Africans as a bloc and emphasizing their sympathy for Germany, French authorities in both Marseille and Algiers treated North Africans as an internal danger. This remained true regardless, ironically, of whether the Germans were erstwhile allies, as when Vichy ruled Algiers and Marseille, or declared enemies, once each city joined the Allied cause.

The police angled wartime anxieties into an expanded power over these perceived enemies within, with vague legal language delivering powers of interpretation to the individual îlotiers walking their beats in Marseille and Algiers. The meaning of loyalty morphed over the course of the war. Debates raged over whether true patriotism was expressed through adherence to Pétain or de Gaulle. In a contradictory stance, the police demanded absolute loyalty from North Africans, despite confusion over which competing French government represented the "true" France. When they jailed North Africans for shouting "Down with France," even the police might have been unsure which France they meant. Though created to protect France during a time of war, the capacious structures of policing developed in World War II would allow officers to surveil the "national" attitudes of North Africans in times of peace. Policing loyalty meant policing not just crimes, but personal thoughts, daily patterns, family life, and informal exchange, encouraging an expansion of dangerously intimate police work.

During the war, scarcity and political instability prompted the police to see North Africans as a threat, both to Europeans and to the French state. The Vichy regime's antisemitic, racist priorities encouraged the police, and North Africans, to describe social conflicts in terms of race. In the interwar period, police reports had labeled North African neighborhoods as spaces of crime. They now marked these same neighborhoods as the center of black-market profiteering and anti-French sentiment. Having conceived of North Africans as the enemy during the war, the police of both Marseille and Algiers would continue to treat them as such afterward.

In August 1944, Allied troops took Marseille, once again opening channels of Mediterranean communication and connecting Algiers and Marseille in a singular effort of liberation. The end of the war uprooted the logic behind police mistrust of "anti-French" Algerians, as Algerians could not undermine a victorious war effort. Peace, however, did not bring an abrupt change in police practice. As French officials set about restoring a republican government after liberation, they sought to reclaim mythic ideals of liberty, equality, and fraternity. The police of Marseille and Algiers were called to put these principles to work in their daily practices. The dramatic postwar shift in rhetoric would prove to be less than revolutionary, however, in its effect on everyday policing.

5
A NEW POLICE FOR A NEW REPUBLIC

On May 8, 1945, headlines across France and Algeria trumpeted Allied victory. Shortly after the armistice, Algerian politician Ferhat Abbas released a pamphlet provocatively entitled *J'accuse l'Europe*. In it, Abbas referenced the Atlantic Charter, underlining its promise to provide liberty to all peoples, regardless of "race, color, or religion."[1] Drafted by Allied leaders during the war, the charter promised self-determination and a new world order in which freedom, rather than imperialism, would be the status quo. Evoking the text, Abbas vowed, "These engagements will not remain, like in 1918, without a future. In waiting for the New France to take them up for itself... it falls to us to remind ourselves of them and to yoke ourselves from this day forward to the heavy task of making them respected."[2]

Abbas's pamphlet highlighted the possibilities of the postwar. Having positioned themselves as spreading freedom to those oppressed by Nazi Germany, the victorious Free French now faced an implicit challenge to follow through on their professed ideals. Postwar reforms promised a reevaluation of the relationship between France and Algeria, a moment of change that also influenced policing. Attempts to resuscitate the image of the French police, tarnished by association with the Vichy regime, prompted institutional changes in Marseille and Algiers. As the Fourth Republic dismantled police brigades known for discrimination, Algerians greeted reforms with a mixture of hope and doubt, a watchful attitude visible in Abbas's pamphlet. Guardedly, they waited to see if the promises of politicians could really change their everyday life.

As the postwar order took shape, the reforms elaborated in debates in Paris proved less radical in their application on the streets of Marseille and Algiers. As officers monitored "illegal" immigration, mediated conflicts between colonial populations, and stamped out the embers of the black market, recognizable patterns of racialized space continued to define police practice in both cities. Police officials noted, with alarm, moments of Algerian resistance to colonial rule, citing crowds and collective action as evidence that "anti-French" Algerians had now become a political problem. In the France being (re)created after the war, police continued to be a constant presence in the lives of North Africans, unmoved by the sweeping reinvention reformers like Abbas had hoped for.

Reinventing Colonial Order

After World War II, France began a long process of rebuilding. Allied troops finally captured Paris in August 1944 and declared victory in Europe on May 8, 1945. The Vichy government crumbled, and General de Gaulle and his allies set about reconstructing a deeply divided France. Although de Gaulle had managed to cobble together a broad coalition of political and social interests in the resistance, the fault lines began to show as the war drew to a close.[3] During the war, de Gaulle's Free French army recruited heavily among colonial populations. It was in Africa that de Gaulle rallied international support for his cause, established a provisional government, and convinced Allied troops to launch an invasion of France.[4] Thousands of Algerian soldiers served the French, fighting for a *mère patrie* that had treated them as little more than ugly stepchildren. After the war, the sacrifices of these Algerian soldiers, and of the men and women of other French colonies, could not be ignored.

In an embrace of universalism, French officials in the provisional government publicly disavowed distinctions based on religion, class, or race. Legislators made a studious attempt to erase all Vichy-era language of racial hierarchy from the new constitution.[5] Politicians claimed this "color-blind" ethos as a tradition that harkened back to the French Revolution, but in doing so, they ignored France's troubled history of slavery, antisemitism, colonialism, and racialized oppression.[6] France had never *been* color-blind. Positioning this egalitarian ethos as a return, however, allowed legislators to claim an imagined political heritage that reflected the postwar international consensus on the evils of Nazi racial ideology. New policies also changed the legal relationship between Algerians and the French state. On March 7, 1944, the provisional government decreed all Algerians to be "Français Musulmans," a status that theoretically granted Algerians equality with all French citizens.⁷ The new reform ended restrictions that had forced Algerians to give up personal legal status to gain citizenship. Now, Algerians could choose to follow Qur'anic law in matters of family law but also have the right to vote and to circulate without restriction between France and Algeria.⁸

A decree on August 17, 1945, granted Algerians who had French diplomas, honorific titles, or awards that demonstrated "an evolution under the influence of French culture" the right to vote in the same capacity as European French citizens.⁹ The new citizenship law exemplified a larger shift within French bureaucratic discourse from a language of *racial* difference to one of *cultural* difference. Nothing prevented Algerians from being French, this rhetoric suggested, if they proved themselves to be culturally aligned with French norms. Already, however, these reforms hinted at the limits of postwar changes. By 1947, legislation granted Algerian men who did not fit this elite category the right to vote only in a second college, creating a two-tiered system that gutted the political agency of most Algerians.¹⁰ In addition, although most French women could now vote, Algerian women could not.¹¹

The reforms in Algerian citizenship eroded traditional tools of the police, including officially eliminating the indigénat code in Algeria.¹² Laws that had imposed special penalties on Algerians for gathering in public or carrying weapons could no longer be used, although the governor general of Algeria retained special powers to repress incidents "of an insurrectional nature."¹³ Structural changes in Algeria also brought about the end of the Direction of Muslim Affairs in 1945, a department born of the Arab Bureaus that had coordinated the surveillance of and aid for Algerians in nineteenth-century Algeria.¹⁴ Algerian newspapers such as the *Voix Indigène* had called for the dissolution of this service for years, and the decision to disband it represented a victory for Algerian reformers.¹⁵ French Minister of the Interior Adrien Tixier also turned his attention to the Secretary General for Indigène Affairs and Police in Algeria, a department that had been thus labeled for decades. The title must be changed, Tixier advised, "as this association between 'indigène affairs' and 'police' is very politically inopportune."¹⁶ Tixier's attention to optics represented an important move, as the blending had seemed logical, even natural, to colonial officials up until this postwar moment.

In Marseille, too, liberation called into question the state's relationship with North Africans. Since the 1920s, the Service des Affaires Indigènes Nord-Africaines (SAINA) had been charged with the surveillance of North Africans in Paris, Marseille, and other French cities. Although designated political intelligence bureaus surveilled other colonial populations, SAINA and its accompanying police agents were unique in the breadth of their mission and targeted nature, focusing only on North Africans.¹⁷ In 1945, the provisional government shut down SAINA's Vichy equivalent, the Bureau des Affaires Musulmanes Nord-Africaines (BAMNA) and dissolved its police detail.[18] An organization that proposed to police a segment of the French population based on a racialized category simply could not exist in the new political environment.[19] Tixier acknowledged Algerians' assertions that SAINA and other specialized services "perpetuated in France a policy of the indigénat long condemned in Algeria."[20]

The fresh start, however, proved to have its own controversies. Previously, the BAMNA had been responsible for establishing ID cards for North Africans in Marseille. After liberation, the prefecture required that the newly minted Français Musulmans establish new IDs to replace the "temporary" ones provided during the war by the BAMNA.[21] Algerians had to go through a special procedure to get IDs, including obtaining documents from administrators in Algeria. The prefecture decided to keep ID services for Algerians in a separate building because of this extra paperwork, but could only find space in the Foreign Services building.[22] The irony, as even the prefecture recognized, was not lost on the Algerians lining up to obtain their IDs. Postwar reforms sought to remove discriminatory legal structures and administrative bureaus in Marseille and Algiers. Yet the new arrangements borrowed heavily from prewar models and, as the ID services show, French officials failed from the start to truly integrate Algerians as French citizens.

A Crisis of Legitimacy

After the war, the nascent Fourth Republic entered a period of political reckoning. Resistance figures throughout France and Algeria insisted on a purge of Vichy officials. This process included a complicated seizure of power at the local level and was not as homogenous, nor as smooth, as the winners sought to portray.[23] The tenuous transition of power proved especially fraught for the police. As the face of French authority, the police had been clearly tied to the Vichy regime. The fall of Vichy shook the police, who were blamed by many for violent excesses and enforcing discriminatory laws. Epuration trials scrutinizing police practices during the war called into question the moral authority of the police.

Officers in both Marseille and Algiers protested vigorously against portraying their rank and file as collaborationist. In fact, in both Marseille and Algiers, segments of the police had proven instrumental to Allied success. In Algiers, a cell of four hundred resistance fighters had famously planned the "coup of Algiers" on November 8, 1942, including several police officers. But if some officers participated in the Allied takeover, subsequent epuration trials brought others under fire. In response, a group of police agents in Algiers banded together to create the Association of Republican Police Resistors of November 8, with a stated goal to "destroy all that could be said or written, contrary to the truth."[24] The association's goal to defend the "true" history of police participation betrays a fear that the public would label all police officers as pro-Vichy.[25] In Marseille, police officers' loyalty to Vichy was similarly varied. The police of Marseille initially accepted Vichy because of promises of increased power and resources, but enthusiasm waned as the war continued. The policing of certain groups, like Jews and Communists, intensified under Vichy directives, but in Marseille, police officers, for both personal and political reasons, disproportionately participated in the resistance.[26]

The legacy of resistance in Marseille also extended to the BAMNA, led by Louis Poussardin. On January 12, 1943, the police of Marseille arrested Poussardin for creating fake ID cards for ten Jewish foreigners.[27] According to the report, Poussardin had used his right to establish IDs for North Africans as a cover. He issued the cards to Jews of "non-French" nationality, giving them Arabic-sounding names to disguise their true origins. Under Poussardin's pen, Guillaume Steinberger became Ali Becher and Jeanne Vialée became Madame El Biadoui.[28] Poussardin's act of insubordination shows the power of individual resistance, but the success of his plan also relied on the uncertainty of police, and French society, of how to define what it meant to be "North African."[29]

Regardless of documented police resistance in both Algiers and Marseille, accusations of collaboration plagued police departments in both cities. In Marseille, the police d'état union complained that strict epuration, along with wartime casualties, had reduced the size of the police force dramatically.[30] Across the sea in Algiers, popular opinion viewed the process of epuration as corrupt. In 1944, even the police d'état union of Algiers voted a motion calling for a more thorough purge.[31] Local newspapers declared that epuration had been unjust and trials against collaborationist officers had stalled without punishments.[32] The lingering association with Vichy-era policies allowed critics, especially those on the left, to voice complaints about police abuse of power. Both leftist and Algerian nationalist newspapers decried incidents of police violence by calling it evidence of "fascism" and "Hitlerian methods."[33] By framing violence and discrimination as Vichy legacies, detractors used the ongoing process of epuration to add weight to their demands for police accountability.

Vichy-era associations also had an important afterlife when it came to public perceptions of the Algerian community, both in Algeria and the metropole. Police reports and official correspondence throughout the war had emphasized the sympathy of Algerians for Nazism.[34] If critiques of collaboration within the police could be officially addressed by epuration trials, the recurrent theme of North African collaboration proved harder to confront. General Georges Catroux, briefly in charge of Algeria during the liberation, noted a "malaise" in the Algerian population over the unequal sentencing for the crime of "carrying arms" against France. The courts of Algiers consistently doled out harsher punishments to Algerians as compared to Europeans guilty of this same crime.[35] The widespread belief that Algerians were pro-German seemed to lead judges to believe that they had more willingly served the enemy.

In 1945, the prefecture of Algiers charged individuals who had belonged to "anti-national" groups with the crime of "national disgrace." This charge was intended to be used against those who had participated in collaborationist or fascist groups, but the prefect asked, "How could we not consider parties like the PPA and the Amis du Manifeste as anti-national?"[36] The governor general of Algeria ultimately refused to allow this extension of anti-national laws to punish Algerian nationalism, but Algerians still complained that they had been unfairly targeted in epuration. The legacies of Vichy and doubts over epuration undermined police authority in their dealings with Algerians, but the rumored pro-German sympathies of Algerians also aided police denigration of Algerian nationalism.

The piecemeal nature of records on police epuration make it difficult to know whether the process of purging collaborationists looked different in metropole and colony. Clearly, however, the police on both sides of the Mediterranean faced a crisis of legitimacy and sought to (re)build a reputation as "guardians of the peace" instead of a repressive force. Epuration trials brought police misconduct to the public's attention and forced officers in both Marseille and Algiers to account for their actions during the war. Though the purges weeded out some collaborationists within the French state, there could be no such "epuration" of Algerian loyalties, and rumors of Algerian treachery during the war persisted.

Policing Colonial Conflicts

The turmoil of liberation also forced the police of both Algiers and Marseille to mediate between colonial populations brought together by war. Tirailleurs sénégalais, West African units serving in the French army, occupied barracks in both cities.[37] These soldiers, like Algerian tirailleurs, arrived as part of the effort to reconquer occupied France. Though de Gaulle triumphantly declared victory in 1945, demobilization proved painstakingly slow, and tirailleurs sénégalais remained stationed in Algeria and Marseille for years after the official end of the war. West African soldiers and sailors had blended into the Mediterranean melting pots of Marseille and Algiers for decades, a small but constant presence. Now, they entered the cities in greater numbers. European neighborhoods proved no more welcoming to the tirailleurs than they were to Algerians and, perhaps inevitably, West African soldiers gravitated toward North African neighborhoods, strolling the winding streets of the Casbah in Algiers and sampling the cafés maures behind the Bourse in Marseille.

These two populations shared a common story of colonial subjugation, but police documented a conflictual relationship between Algerians and West Africans, rather than anticolonial solidarity. Reports cite incidents of murder, theft, and brawls that filled the streets of Marseille and Algiers with battered soldiers and broken glass. The violence between colonized populations in Marseille and Algiers speaks to the power of colonial hierarchies, never a simple division but rather an ever-evolving constellation used to divide and conquer. As fights broke out, police struggled to navigate the contradictory demands of Algerians, West Africans, Europeans, and civil and military authorities.

In Algiers, encounters between Algerians and tirailleurs sénégalais began long before World War II, as seen in the conflicts over policing religion discussed in chapter 2. But these recurrent tensions took on new intensity during World War II, including a series of bloody incidents in the Casbah in 1939. Municipal councilors blamed the conflicts on the brothels relegated to the top of the Casbah.[38] Newspapers in Algiers echoed this argument, calling for the red-light district to be moved away from the honest, working-class Algerian families in the Casbah.[39] Police evoked the "passions" of colonial subjects to explain fights, but officers also discerned deeper animosity between the two communities.[40] In August 1944, for example, a fight broke out between West African soldiers and Algerian civilians on a trolleybus between the suburb of El Biar and central Algiers. The police confronted an Algerian, Benouafi T., who admitted to provoking the fight by shoving past the soldiers as they waited to board the trolley, saying "blacks [*les noirs*] should not get on with whites."[41] In this formulation, Benouafi fashioned himself as "white," in opposition to the Blackness of the West African soldiers, using his violence against the tirailleurs as a mark of his whiteness.[42] No European would have accepted Benouafi's implicit claim. How could Algerians, themselves the victims of colonial racism, happily participate in such stereotyping? Benouafi, it seems, accepted the colonial hierarchies that ranked him above Black Africans, even if these same hierarchies denied his own equality with Europeans.

Then, as the haze of war began to clear in the summer of 1945, violence between Algerian civilians and tirailleurs sénégalais rocked Algiers. Three tirailleurs were climbing up Boulevard de la Victoire, a wide thoroughfare at the top of the Casbah, to return to their barracks. Visibly drunk, the soldiers attracted the attention of a crowd of Algerian children, who followed them and began pelting them with insults and the occasional rock. When the soldiers turned to fight, the adult Algerians living on Boulevard de la Victoire jumped to the youths' defense. Then, a patrol of West African soldiers arrived and took the side of their compatriots, attacking any Algerian they came across. The police report on the fight said that the soldiers' reaction stemmed from a false rumor that Algerians had killed two soldiers.[43] Algerians in the Casbah fled into their homes, hiding from the soldiers' "hunt" until police patrols later that night managed to corral the men back into their barracks.

This brawl was not created by rumors alone. The police related the fight to a pattern of conflict between Algerians and West Africans. Tirailleurs sénégalais often complained about being the victim of theft in the Casbah, led astray by locals and continually taunted by Algerian children who mocked them for their unfamiliar languages and dark complexion. Commenting on the fight on Boulevard de la Victoire, a police report claimed that even before the incident, a "sharp discontent" reigned among the soldiers because of a rash of thefts.[44] Algerians, on the other hand, blamed the fights on the liberties West Africans took on their days off, drinking too much and idling in the Casbah's brothels before staggering home through respectable neighborhoods.

The police of Algiers got caught between the soldiers and the civilians, both groups seeking to validate their vision of the Casbah. The police tried to intercede between, as they put it, Algerian "coreligionnaires" and West African soldiers.[45] The use of the term coreligionnaire in this context is interesting given that many Algerians and West Africans in fact shared an Islamic faith. In this slippage, we see how coreligionnaire served as a colonial shorthand for a racial, rather than religious, categorization. Though post-Vichy reforms may have precluded the use of racial language in official reports, this racial-religious category continued to do the work of racialization in police discourse. The reports of violence between West African soldiers and Algerians eventually died down, presumably as soldiers returned home, but similar conflicts occurred throughout the 1940s.[46] Pulled in multiple directions, police sought, unsuccessfully, to protect civilians from hotheaded soldiers and to preserve the dignity of soldiers who had sacrificed for France.

Across the Mediterranean, similar conflicts pitted West African soldiers against North African migrants in Marseille. After the war, Marseille remained the principal point of debarkation for demobilized soldiers returning to the colonies. West African soldiers languished in the south, as the French state sorted through the logistics of sending everyone home. While awaiting transfer, West African soldiers explored Marseille, enjoying the city's vibrant nightlife. Building on established residential patterns of Black life in Marseille, the tirailleurs were drawn to the same colonial immigrant spaces that police reports associated with North Africans, including Rue des Chapeliers.[47]

Violence between tirailleurs and Algerian civilians simmered on Rue des Chapeliers in the summer of 1945, at the same time as similar incidents in

Algiers. The context of the war caused the mirrored timing, as West African soldiers funneled through both Marseille and Algiers on their way home. Police reports warily noted an uptick in confrontations between Algerians and West African soldiers throughout the summer, but the most notable "brawl between indigènes" broke out on the night of June 5, 1945. The police report explained that the conflict began when a West African soldier gestured obscenely at a woman in a bar and her "Arab" lover sprang to her defense.[48]

The angry exchange devolved into a fight between two "clans," as West African soldiers and North African civilians closed ranks. Outnumbered, the West African soldiers went in search of reinforcements, spreading the fight for fifty meters along Rue des Chapeliers and eventually involving, by police estimates, a hundred and fifty people. The police described a bloody scene, with shots fired by the soldiers and residents throwing bottles from apartments overlooking the street. "The Senegalese battled armed with straight razors. The injured Arabs lay lifeless on the pavement."[49] Informed of the bloodshed, the police sent eleven officers, but required backup from the military police to eventually disperse the crowd of nearly a thousand people that had formed near the Porte d'Aix. Though the police managed to subdue the fight, violent incidents continued for several days, as West African soldiers returned to Rue des Chapeliers to "correct the Arabs."[50] Dozens of Algerians and West African soldiers ended up in the hospital, and one tirailleur died. In the days following the fight, the police proposed a ban on West African troops entering Rue des Chapeliers, a prohibition enforced by both police and military patrols.[51]

The fight on Rue des Chapeliers, however, also sparked a moment of cooperation between the police and North African shopkeepers. Officials had considered forcing all public establishments on Rue des Chapeliers to close until tensions calmed. Seeking personal profit and collective security, a delegation of North African restaurant and bar owners came to the commissariat on June 7, offering to voluntarily close for three or four days, per police suggestion.[52] The shopkeepers likely collaborated with the police out of self-interest—their businesses could hardly prosper with ongoing bloodshed. Though quotidian police raids interrupted business and bothered customers, North African businessmen still proved willing to work with police in mitigating this conflict with the tirailleurs.

Police officers in both Algiers and Marseille repeatedly read stereotypical understandings of colonial masculinity into the motives behind the fights. The police of Marseille believed the June 5 brawl on Rue des Chapeliers had been caused by a West African soldier insulting a North African's mistress. Correspondence between police officials in Marseille stated outright, "One must see the real cause of all these incidents in the rivalry that exists between Algerian and Senegalese soldiers over the women, more or less prostitutes, who haunt this neighborhood."[53] This statement reveals officials' derogatory understanding of European women who chose to have relationships with colonial subjects. They also denied, implicitly, the validity of the interracial relationships that had existed in Marseille for decades, relationships that produced marriages, partnerships, and families. In characterizing women who dated, loved, and lived with North and West African men as "more or less prostitutes," the French police absorbed these women into a category of criminality that legitimized police control over family and romantic life. In Algiers, the police also often identified conflicts between men pursuing the same woman as the "true" cause of violence between tirailleurs and civilians.[54] The reports, however, never included testimony from the women supposedly at the heart of these fights, nor did police do more than a perfunctory investigation into motives. Fights between Arabs and Africans over prostitutes matched the colonial stereotypes that already colored police expectations.

Officers seemed to miss a different cause for the violence between Algerians and West Africans. The fights between Algerians and tirailleurs sénégalais, in both Marseille and Algiers, occurred in Algerian neighborhoods. Shut off from European sections of Algiers and Marseille, West African soldiers gravitated toward the areas marked as a space for colonial subjects. The fights broke out between Algerians and West Africans following a divergent interpretation of how this space should be inhabited. West African soldiers perused Marseille and Algiers on leave, stretching their legs and freeing their bodies from regimented life in the barracks. Wandering the cities, West African soldiers drank, they yelled, they caroused. French and Allied soldiers stationed in Algiers and Marseille got up to the same antics, and there were also incidents of conflicts between North Africans and American or British soldiers.[55] But the conflicts with West African tirailleurs occurred more frequently, and with more vicious reprisals, because these fights occurred within the spaces North Africans had carved out as their own. This was perhaps particularly true in Algiers. The Casbah housed middle-class, "respectable" families who looked on aghast as their neighborhood catered to European fantasies of Orientalist debauchery, with bars, brothels, and cabarets next to mosques, homes, and schools. The arrival of West African pleasure-seekers in the Casbah disrupted Algerian residents' vision of the rare urban space they considered their own. An analogous phenomenon might have occurred in Marseille, too, although the bars and restaurants of Rue des Chapeliers had always attracted a more diverse population.

The police of Marseille and Algiers played an uneasy intermediary role in these conflicts. They sought to impose calm on public thoroughfares, but faced with two colonial populations, two different language barriers, and two different types of authority—military backing as opposed to local accountability—the police did not have a clear path to resolve the controversy. Instead, they fumbled their way through, breaking up fights as they occurred but unable to prevent them. Police control of these conflicts played out in the familiar racialized spaces of Marseille and Algiers, neighborhoods where colonial soldiers and North African civilians rubbed shoulders because of the urban segregation of both cities. The police interpreted the conflict between tirailleurs sénégalais and Algerian civilians through their assumptions about Algerians' jealousy and West Africans' rage. Even as the "color-blind" Fourth Republic shifted the language of policing, reforms had little impact on the categories of race deployed by police in practice. Officers haphazardly breaking up fights between tirailleurs and North Africans understood the conflicts in enduringly colonial, racialized terms. If the law was now blind to race, police officers were not.

Postwar Mobility

Liberation ended the rupture between Algiers and Marseille, restoring maritime traffic to its normal circular pattern. As France began to reconstruct its economy and urban infrastructure after the war, the government sought out new sources of labor and encouraged Algerians to come to the metropole. The postwar changes in Algerians' legal status also prompted growing numbers of men to bring their wives and families to the metropole with them. This mobility, however, was not without its limits. Even as legislators declared a new era in immigration, the French police continued to track Algerian movement, convinced that the migrants would bring with them crime and conflict. Despite reforms allowing freedom of movement for Algerians, police worried about "illegal" immigration, connecting Algerian mobility to a broader network of smuggling and stowaways.[56]

The reopening of movement between metropole and colony did not end the problems of the hundreds of North African workers and soldiers who had been stranded in Marseille during the war. Although many trapped North Africans had been housed in Camp Lyautey, by October 1944, the French government converted the camp to hold German prisoners of war. Officials in Marseille scrambled to find a tenable housing solution for the displaced North Africans.[57] In addition to these blocked and now homeless workers, the French army sent Algerian soldiers to Marseille to await demobilization and repatriation, adding additional strain to Algeria-bound boats. Officials in Marseille worried about stranded North Africans, describing them as ill-prepared for life in the metropole and therefore a potential social problem.[58]

Algerians voiced their displeasure with the slow pace of repatriation.⁵⁹ The Association des Musulmans Algériens (AMA) of Marseille, for example, made repatriation one of their central demands.⁶⁰ The Renseignements Généraux (RG) of Marseille reported that North African soldiers had staged two protests in Marseille in September 1945 to agitate "against the insufficient means of transportation" for returning home.⁶¹ Some soldiers and workers likely took matters into their own hands, slipping onto boats bound for Algiers as stowaways.⁶² The anger of these soldiers may have stemmed in part from the bias evident in repatriation policy, as the French government awarded Europeans from Algeria priority for return.⁶³ Algerians slowly filtered home from Marseille through the fall of 1945, and the police in the port of Algiers carefully tracked their arrival. Repatriation efforts would continue through the spring of 1946, more than a year after Mediterranean traffic reopened.⁶⁴

In the past, various legal regimes had circumscribed Algerian immigration to France, but the decree of March 7, 1944, gave Algerians full liberty of movement within French territory.⁶⁵ Beginning in 1947, the numbers of Algerians in France began to sharply increase. Algerians, lured by job opportunities and perhaps motivated by their wartime experiences in France, boarded boats by the thousands. As in the past, this immigration filtered through the ports of Marseille and Algiers. Many Algerians found jobs in the refineries and docks of Marseille, but thousands more headed for industrial zones in the North or the bustle of Paris. Still, Marseille remained a center of North African immigration, with an estimated fifteen thousand Algerians living in the city in the late 1940s.⁶⁶ Studies of immigration typically describe post–World War II Algerian migration as circular, with workers cycling between France and Algeria. These men (and the scholarship focuses almost exclusively on men) formed transient communities without deep ties to their local surroundings, living in miserable conditions to pool money for remittances.⁶⁷ While true for most Algerian migrants, this characterization misses the long-standing history of Algerian life in Marseille, including Algerian residents who had lived in the city for decades.

Algerians also increasingly brought their families to live in France with them. By 1952, the RG of Marseille noted roughly three hundred Algerian women living in Marseille and another fifty in nearby Aix-en-Provence.⁶⁸ Police analysis of Algerian women's life in Marseille quickly veered into gendered stereotypes. The RG report called Algerian women "children." The gender restrictions of Arab society, it claimed, made them incapable of the more active social role of French women. The police concluded, "Traditionalist, the Muslim woman does not dream of innovation, on the contrary she is pleased with the passive existence reserved for her."⁶⁹ The police report suggested that the difference in "evolution" between French and Algerian women led Algerian men to despise their wives, as compared to the more "advanced" wives of their French colleagues.

Racist and gendered attitudes about the growing numbers of North African women in the metropole had implications for policing. In December 1949, the Marseille RG filed a report on the "rivalries" that had developed between Algerians and Moroccans over a Moroccan woman named Hadda. Citing an anonymous informant, the report explained that Hadda had arrived from Casablanca without her husband to work as a domestic servant for a French family.[70] Eventually, however, she left this position and moved to Rue Sainte-Barbe, a hub of North African life adjacent to Rue des Chapeliers. The police condescendingly noted that Hadda dressed "correctly" but claimed tensions had arisen because of her popularity among Algerian and Moroccan men, who both pursued her assiduously. Hadda created discord, the police said, because both Moroccans and Algerians "lust after the possession of a young Moroccan mauresque."[71] The police casually explained the hostilities by leaning on familiar tropes about North African men, like their jealousy and possessiveness.

But the alleged rivalry had real repercussions for Hadda. The police and unnamed "Muslim representatives" of Marseille decided that Hadda should be repatriated to ease the conflict, a request her husband apparently supported. Hadda was effectively deported because of the perceived jealousies her independence caused in the heavily male North African immigrant community. We see the consequences of intimate policing in Hadda's example. Discretionary decisions of the Marseille police limited not just her livelihood but her ability to be in the metropole altogether. Policing North Africans often had little to do with crime. Indeed, Hadda was accused of no criminal activity. Rather this was about the regulation of everyday life and social norms, the police imposing their own ideas about gender and mobility.

As Algerians, of all genders, streamed to the metropole in greater numbers, old concerns about controlling Algerian movement resurfaced. The police of Algiers worried that departing Algerian immigrants would be unprepared for life in France. Commissioner of the Port of Algiers François Mercadal noted in 1947 that the hundreds of Algerians leaving each day often spoke only Arabic or Amazigh, not French. Mercadal reported hearing a Frenchman also traveling to the mainland exclaim, "What are these men without an occupation going to do in the metropole? . . . Surely augment the already elevated number of unemployed people at the charge of the collective!"[72] Reproducing this quote in his report, Mercadal reinforced the idea that Algerian workers heading for France would become unemployed vagrants. The "problem" of North African immigration gained coverage in government reports, academic publications, and national newspapers. Articles focused on the sheer numbers of North Africans arriving and highlighted their cultural difference. They fretted over Algerians' lack of industrial training and general education, portraying this as a problem of Algerian society rather than a failure of colonial education.[73]

Old fears of "illegal" Algerian immigration also reappeared. In the fall of 1945, Jules Bourgeois, head of the soon-to-be-disbanded BAMNA, wrote a letter complaining about "clandestine" Algerian immigration to Marseille. When Algerian stowaways arrived in Marseille, the gendarmerie arrested and jailed them for fifteen days. However, after fifteen days, the gendarmes simply released the men, at which point the Algerians would turn up at Bourgeois's service asking for an ID. Bourgeois pointed out the confusion of both his service and the police as to whether the "illegal" Algerian immigrants should be immediately repatriated, triaged in Marseille, or given an ID and allowed to seek work.[74] Algerian migrants seemingly profited from this bureaucratic confusion. Part of the disarray came from overlapping police structures. Who controlled the right of Algerians to enter France? Customs officers? The port police? The specialized services for North Africans? The gendarmerie? In some ways, the answer was yes to all of these. The ability to remain in the metropole depended on the individual encounter between a migrant and one of many possible police services.

By 1948, the police seemed to have solved their earlier procedural dilemma. All North Africans caught in Marseille without proper paperwork were sent back to Algeria on the next available boat.[75] What remains unclear, however, is what exactly the police meant when they described "clandestine" immigration. The Fourth Republic had granted Algerians citizenship. How could a citizen "illegally" enter their own country?[76] The reports implied that these Algerians were stowaways who did not pay for their ticket. Yet police records do not describe European French citizens as "clandestine," nor did I find reports of other Frenchmen being sent back to their point of origin for failing to purchase a ticket. Instead, the treatment of "clandestine" Algerians put them in the same category as foreigners.

If Marseille saw a new wave of Algerian immigration, the postwar also changed patterns of mobility in Algiers. Algiers underwent stunning urban growth during World War II and its aftermath. In the agglomeration of Algiers, the population leapt from 266,268 in 1929 to 473,261 in 1948.[77] This rapid increase was made up mostly of Algerian migrants from the countryside, pulled to the capital by employment opportunities. The influx shifted the city's demographics. Algiers had a large European majority throughout the 1930s, but by 1954, Europeans made up only 49 percent of the Algiers metropolitan region, although they remained a majority within city limits.[78] Some of the Algerian newcomers moved into the already crowded neighborhoods of the Casbah and the "Little Casbah" in El Hamma, but many also settled in *bidonvilles*, shantytowns that began to dot

Algiers and nearby suburbs, like Hussein Dey.[79] The Algiers police did shift some of their focus to policing the bidonvilles, but in central Algiers, officers remained concentrated on the Casbah as the primary space of Algerian life.[80]

Marseille's Brigade de la Bourse

Vichy-era restructuring had changed the organization of the French police force, and in an effort to start anew, the Fourth Republic dismantled many, but not all, of these institutional changes.[81] At the local level, police services sought to keep some elements of Vichy's streamlined system, while also carefully distancing themselves from the unpopular regime.[82] Police departments also faced a crisis of manpower, with their forces sapped of men by mobilization and epuration.[83] Reforms changed the face of policing in Marseille, but the reorganization of police services still re-created familiar prewar patterns of racial profiling.

After the war, the new French government sought to eradicate discriminatory policing, dissolving specialized police units like Paris's Brigade Nord-Africaine (BNA). In Marseille, the small police detail assigned to the BAMNA was disbanded when that service was closed. However, in 1949, just a few years after the government shuttered these specialized bureaus, the police d'état of Marseille moved to create its own Brigade Nord-Africaine.[84] According to an RG report, the idea of creating a police brigade to specifically surveil the "Arab milieus of Marseille" provoked angry reactions from Marseille's North African population, especially among Algerians.[85] Algerians framed their concerns through their newly won citizenship. According to police surveillance of a protest at Cinéma Roxy, Algerians found "a police service that appears specially directed against them unacceptable, while other groups, even foreigners, would be surveilled by ordinary local police services."[86] Why single them out, they asked, if they were now supposedly citizens of France? The protestors had a point. In the nineteenth century, Marseille had never established an "Italian brigade" nor a "Corsican brigade" to tackle previous waves of immigration. Officials never even proposed a "West African" or "Indochinese" brigade.[87] Only with North Africans had the state proven willing to use racial labels, linking the need for specific policing to stereotypes about specific criminality. But in the postwar, with Algerians now citizens, such targeting created an image problem for the French government.

Protests organized by Marseille's North African community prompted the police to shift tactics. The administration canceled the proposed Brigade Nord-Africaine and instead created the Brigade de la Bourse. Rather than designating a specific population, this brigade zeroed in on a neighborhood, the "behind the

Bourse" area so closely associated with North Africans. According to an internal RG report, the Brigade de la Bourse's mission would be the same as the scrapped Brigade Nord-Africaine, "but its name no longer has the bullying character that the Arabs had discovered in it and this rectification sufficed to produce calm in these milieux."[88] The report baldly stated that the police had no intention of changing their approach. Municipal authorities had effectively pulled a bait and switch on Algerian protestors, presenting a new spatial label while maintaining the brigade's mission of racially targeted repression.[89] This linkage of race and space had always been key to policing North Africans in Marseille, but it became all the more obvious in postwar attempts to hide racial targeting.

The new unit, staffed with a commissioner, a secretary, and nine inspectors, quickly took responsibility for policing North Africans in Marseille.[90] Several of the officers assigned to the brigade spoke Arabic.[91] A report highlighted that this knowledge of Arabic and other North African dialects would permit officers to "easily penetrate in these famously closed groups."[92] This internal note, written in April 1949, also suggested that the "Muslim" community of Marseille trusted the Brigade de la Bourse and approved of its efforts to control the "undesirable coreligionnaires" who gave North Africans a bad reputation among Europeans.[93] The police account of the Brigade de la Bourse framed the service in terms of perception—how North Africans perceived the brigade and how the European community and police officials perceived North Africans.

Although named for a neighborhood, the brigade's real mission was racial control. In a 1949 letter to the central commissioner of Marseille, the commissioner of the Brigade de la Bourse outlandishly claimed that only half of the North Africans in the city lived off honest labor. The rest, he asserted, supported themselves with charity from fellow Muslims or a life of crime.[94] The commissioner praised his officers for restoring calm to the city center where the "toxic" part of the North African population lived and where, he claimed, the greatest number of violent crimes took place.[95] The commissioner justified the existence of the Brigade de la Bourse by explicitly evoking racialized stereotypes of Algerian criminality. In another letter, the regional director of police services noted that police units across Marseille could come to the Brigade de la Bourse with crimes that implicated North African "indigènes."[96] By 1949, Algerians were citizens of France, not "indigènes." This language, then, reveals not just the racial parameters but also the colonial mentality embedded in the new brigade.

The Brigade de la Bourse got to work, operating rounds of surveillance in North African neighborhoods and responding to requests from other police units on cases involving North Africans.[97] Their regular descents on streets associated with North African daily life resulted in mass roundups of North

Africans, taken to the station for an "examination of situation" without any evidence of wrongdoing. The Brigade de la Bourse became the primary face of the police for North Africans in Marseille. In this sense, the brigade operated like the police detail of SAINA, the visible members of the police force who went into the "closed" North African community. Other police services also turned over accused criminals to the Brigade de la Bourse, as in the case of a knife fight on Rue Poids de la Farine in 1949. Local police tracked down two Algerians involved in the fight and promptly turned the "antagonists" over to what the report called the Brigade Nord-Africaine.[98] As no such brigade existed in 1949, the officer writing the report almost certainly meant the Brigade de la Bourse. Internal police reports from the early 1950s continued to refer to the Brigade de la Bourse as the Brigade Nord-Africaine, making clear the unit's true aims.[99] The slippage between race and space in the naming and practice of the brigade reveal the emptiness of the Fourth Republic's promise of egalitarian governance and the reality of continued racialized control of North Africans.

Although the Brigade de la Bourse targeted Algerians based on racialized categories, North Africans could also turn to this specialized brigade for help. In June 1949, an RG report noted that the president of Marseille's Association des Musulmans Algériens (AMA), Hamouda Talmoudi, received daily visits from Algerians complaining about the law requiring two forms of ID to board a boat for Algeria. Many illiterate North African workers relied on scribes within the North African community for immigration paperwork, who charged speculative prices for their services. These abuses, the report noted, had already been signaled to the Brigade de la Bourse, "that specifically takes care of North Africans."[100] This note was a call from within the North African community for the brigade to serve its purpose, rooting out fraudsters. If the Brigade de la Bourse would be an intrusive presence in the lives of North Africans, Talmoudi implied, then at least officers could protect the community, too.

As Algerian immigration increased, the North African population began to spread from Rue des Chapeliers toward Marseille's central train station, Gare St. Charles. Tensions over the demographic changes in the neighborhood around Gare St. Charles boiled over in the summer of 1949, only a few months after the creation of the Brigade de la Bourse. A group of residents sent a letter to the mayor complaining about a rash of thefts. The director of police services noted that the complaints were justified concerning "the interloping idlers, prostitutes, North Africans, and Black soldiers and civilians in this neighborhood."[101] If postwar reforms removed racial language in law, this letter again shows that it did not eliminate racial prejudice in policing. The director listed North Africans and African soldiers in the same category as prostitutes and "idlers," implying a criminality and immorality based on race. Notable too is the intermixing of colonial populations in this space, with the police report highlighting the presence of both North African and multinational Black populations.

When the central commissioner of Marseille's police responded to the criticism, he provided a list of police operations in the streets near Gare St. Charles. Though the report did not list the names of arrested individuals, the commissioner specified that fifteen North Africans were arrested and turned over to the Brigade de la Bourse.[102] Residents had demanded police intervention because of a surge of crime near the Gare St. Charles, but the North Africans arrested in the police raids had committed no crime. Rather, they were taken to the station to verify their IDs, a tactic used to catch illegal immigrants in the interwar years and to hunt down escaped requis during World War II. With the Brigade de la Bourse, Marseille officials camouflaged racial policing with a label of space, while nonetheless continuing the same old discriminatory practices.

A "Climate of Insecurity" in Algiers

In Algiers, too, the police used familiar techniques to police Algerians, despite a national change in rhetoric and Algerians' new citizenship status. The social and political changes after World War II forced the police to confront their assumptions about Algerians. Some Europeans in Algeria clung stubbornly to the idea that Algerians were incapable of self-governance.[103] Police reports, too, tended to emphasize the material concerns of the Algerian masses, denying their interest in politics.[104] Still, though they tried to deny the appeal of nationalism, the police could not ignore that the dynamics of colonial rule were changing. The amendments announced in the postwar gave Algerians hope, but the slow, incomplete nature of these reforms left many frustrated. In addition to political disappointment, material scarcity marked life in Algiers in the years following the war. As the police watched Algerians navigate these struggles, both personal and political, they interpreted conflict as evidence of deepening racial divisions within the colony, despite official language that emphasized the unity of all French citizens.

The political shifts of the postwar were immediately apparent in Algiers. On May 1, 1945, just a few days before armistice, a group of Algerian protestors gathered on Rue d'Isly, a street that wound from the edge of the Casbah to the center of the administrative quarter of Algiers.[105] The marchers called for the release of Messali Hadj, still being held in administrative internment years after Algeria's liberation from Vichy control.[106] Tracts circulated by the protestors referenced "Hitlerian provocations" in Algeria, equating ongoing police repression with Nazi Germany. The peaceful march devolved into a violent clash when protestors encountered the police. In the fray, police killed two protestors and injured twelve others, while the police listed fifteen injured officers. In a letter to the minister of the interior, the governor general of Algeria explained:

> The investigation on the circumstances in which the encounter between police and protestors took place, in the middle of a European neighborhood of Algiers, has not yet had definitive results. It seems however that the Prefect of Algiers failed to take the necessary measures in time and should have prevented the Muslims from spilling out [*déboucher*] of the indigènes neighborhoods.[107]

Here, the question of space looms large. The protests turned violent, the governor alleged, precisely because the police had allowed Algerian protestors to leave "their" space in the Casbah and enter the European neighborhood below.

A few days later, on May 8, 1945, the Allied forces declared victory in Europe. As the French flag flew and church bells jubilantly tolled the triumph of the Allies, a procession of Algerian nationalists gathered in the towns of Guelma and Sétif, in the Constantine department. As in Algiers, the protestors, unarmed and orderly, encountered police barricades. Scuffles broke out and when the police opened fire, the protests turned deadly.[108] In the following days, police and European vigilante groups retaliated for police casualties with an orgy of bloodletting, resulting in staggering Algerian death tolls numbering in the thousands.[109] The massacres of Guelma and Sétif, as they became known, emerged as a rallying cry for Algerian nationalists.[110] Algerian residents of Algiers reacted in anger and sorrow to the news from Sétif and Guelma, including staging a protest at the Grande Poste, the post office at the heart of Algiers's administrative district.[111]

The violence that met these protests presaged a new era in Algerian policing, one in which the police would deploy ever more force against Algerians as a strategy to suppress nationalism. Though national political discourse spoke of reforms, police actions on the ground demonstrated a hardening of repression and responded to what the police saw as increasing divisions between Europeans and Algerians. In June 1945, the police d'état union of Algeria issued a formal letter to the minister of the interior calling on the government to reinforce the Algerian police force in the light of the "events" in Constantine. The letter declared, "Only a powerful police, well-armed, well-organized and provided with means of transport can prevent the return of such events and guarantee the integrity of French sovereignty in ALGERIA."[112] The letter used explicitly colonial language, insisting that only the police could preserve the future of the French Empire in Algeria.

In the months leading up to the massacres in Guelma and Sétif, the police of Algiers had commented on a hardening of the divisions between European and "indigène" populations in everyday encounters. One report from February 1945 claimed that propaganda sought to divide Europeans and Muslims "in giving a religious and racial character" to disagreements.[113] Ignoring years of racialized policing and discriminatory laws, the police blamed foreign propaganda for the rift. Further displacing fault, they argued that Algerian nationalists valorized "racist and anti-French" divisions within Algeria.[114] Now that the war had ended, the tensions only got worse.[115] A police report from 1946, for example, described a rumor that Algerian elected leaders had been telling constituents to shop only at Muslim-owned grocery stores. The police could not prove the truth of this accusation but did note that both "Muslims" and Europeans tended to shop "at their coreligionnaires."[116] Although quick to blame "racial" differences on nationalist agitators, the police adopted the same racialized labeling in their own reports.

The growing Algerian population in Algiers during World War II had already sparked some residential conflicts. Residents of the working-class neighborhood Clos Salembier, for example, had demanded a new police station, citing "insecurity." The police, however, lacked the officers to create new posts and denied the request. Outraged, O. J. H., the president of the neighborhood association, fired off a letter to the prefect of Algiers in 1944. He seethed, "I must, Monsieur le Préfet, repeat here what I have already written several times: The Arab hatred towards the Europeans."[117] O. J. said that European residents were afraid to let their children wander the neighborhood alone and asserted that the "little indigènes" who roamed the streets committed theft in broad daylight. He concluded ominously that if tensions continued, European residents would have to leave the neighborhood "as quickly as possible."[118] This letter came in the context of a large public housing structure built in Clos Salembier in the mid-1930s specifically to house "indigènes." The complex was one of several initiatives to tackle the overcrowding of the Casbah and the proliferation of bidonvilles, while maintaining racial segregation.[119] The creation of these segregated housing units brought Algerians into the predominately European neighborhood, and the European locals reacted with a demand for more policing, a sign of their recognition that the police existed to serve them. As the racialized geography of Algiers shifted in the postwar, friction over urban space began to reach a breaking point.

The police of Algiers paid close attention to incidents that might reinforce divisions between "Europeans" and "Muslims." Brigadier Pierre Marquillanes, for example, reported an incident in which he encountered a hundred and fifty "indigènes" boisterously gathered on Rue de Lyon. He established that the crowd formed after a European sexagenarian beat up a homeless Algerian man, resulting in his hospitalization. Tellingly, Marquillanes titled his report "Mood of the Muslim Population."[120] The violence against this homeless man mattered to the police only because it had the potential to have a negative impact on the attitude of the Algerian populace. For the police, the group of Algerians on Rue de Lyon, reportedly seeking revenge on the European author of the crime, represented a greater threat to stability than the crime itself. The police report highlighted the reinforcements sent to patrol Rue de Lyon but did not specify whether officers arrested the European man for assault. The report noted only that the police had opened an investigation. Police officials worried about incidents of violence between neighbors like this because they feared it would become fodder for Algerian nationalists. As in Marseille, the police of Algiers had become increasingly concerned with optics. In interpreting this fight between neighbors, police understood their role of enforcing order through their fears of Algerian dissent and their understanding of colonial racial categories.

It was not just the police who worried about the potential for racial conflict in Algeria. Critics of the police, too, saw cause for concern. An article in the leftist *Alger Républicain* from 1947 described a "Climate of Insecurity for the Muslims." The article said that if the riots in Guelma and Sétif had created a feeling of uncertainty for Europeans, now the situation was reversed. Algerians watched with fear as innocent Algerians were murdered and the authorities protected the European perpetrators. The article protested that if Europeans had been killed in similar circumstances, there would be a public outcry.[121] In postwar Algiers, the police functioned in a state of cognitive dissonance, responding to national directives that rejected racialized categories while at the same time viewing conflicts between Europeans and Algerians in starkly racialized terms. The racial divisions mattered to the police not because of the actual discrimination faced by Algerians but because of the opportunity that racial violence offered for nationalist propagandists.

The fragile promise of postwar reforms shattered completely in 1948. When Algerian nationalist parties threatened to gain a majority of seats in the second college, French authorities rigged elections, ensuring a majority of seats would go to pro-French candidates.[122] The blatant tampering with elections left many Algerians disillusioned with the possibility for gradual reform. The police, acknowledging this frustration, shifted their tactics, begrudgingly recognizing Algerians' political agency. Increased nationalist agitation, paired with new taboos about racial discourse, pushed the police of Algiers to worry about perception. Though police violence in the postwar era continued with widespread impunity, police reports show that officers began to consider how their initiatives and arrests would be viewed by the Algerian public, cautious of actions that might further nationalist claims.

In both Algiers and Marseille, postwar reforms changed the official norms and labels of police action but did not alter the daily experience of policing for North Africans. Though the conversations about race, colony, and citizenship following World War II created a moment when reform seemed possible, new policies did not undo the racialized discrimination that reinforced colonial power structures. In Marseille, the police disguised old methods with new names and hidden agendas. In Algiers, police units continued to understand conflict in terms of racial divisions, in direct contradiction to the new "color-blind" republican order. Policing North Africans, now more than ever, became a matter of targeting spaces layered with racial subtext.

The Black Market . . . Again

In both Marseille and Algiers, policing the black market in the postwar revealed continuity in police practices, despite political change.[123] As Mediterranean trade started to regain its normal cadence in 1945, once-scarce products became increasingly available. Rationing continued, however, on goods such as cloth, chocolate, and cigarettes, all still sold in a vibrant black market. In Marseille, the police continued to target and criminalize North Africans selling on the street, despite official acknowledgement that they were not the "kingpins" of the black market. The policing of North African traffickers served as a shorthand to prove police efficiency in a port city still recovering from the war. In Algiers, in contrast, police insisted that Algerians were solely to blame for the black market. In both cities, police officials designed their repression of the black market to target specific spaces associated with North Africans.

In Algiers, the police had viewed Algerians as the central operators of the black market throughout the war. Officers held Algerians responsible for trafficking everything from cigarettes to flour, watermelon to cloth, chocolate to zucchini. In the miles of paperwork written by the police of Algiers on the suppression of the black market, European criminals stood out for their scarcity, despite the majority European population of the city. For example, in November 1944, the Algiers police received a letter about a European butcher allegedly selling meat on the black market. Rather than arresting him, however, the police report suggested that "public rumors have a tendency to exaggerate the facts." The note concluded by saying that the butcher had simply deployed the "liberty of commerce" allowed to everyone and refused to investigate his case further.[124]

The focus on Algerian participation in the black market cropped up in the popular press, too. On January 24, 1947, the local newspaper *Écho d'Alger* ran an exposé lamenting the scale of the local black market.[125] This article resulted in an investigation, carried out by Inspector Godard of the Economic Service. Godard concluded that the state of affairs was even worse than the article claimed, listing a variety of black-market goods sold near the Bab El Oued market. Godard described the sellers as "young indigènes, veritable thugs who insult and steal from the housewives."[126] Moreover, while the black market had previously been focused near the Casbah, it was now expanding to other parts of the city. Godard closed his report with a pointed admonishment of the police. Instead of pursuing the young Algerian sellers, Godard alleged, local agents and market guards simply let them carry on.[127] As the geography of the black market shifted, officials remained certain of Algerians' central role.

Many of the daily reports from the police of Algiers focused on policing Algerians selling cigarettes. Report after report from 1945–1947 listed almost daily cases of Algerian men arrested for trafficking foreign cigarettes, recognized as such because the products lacked the official band printed on rationed tobacco products.[128] The gendered nature of these arrests was no accident. Cigarette sellers were almost invariably men, both because of the mobility and visibility needed to sell cigarettes and the social stigma against women who smoked. Algerians could also be fined for the sale of cigarettes in a "forbidden zone" of the city, an issue not just of product but of space.[129]

Conflicts between police and Algerians over black-market accusations could become moments of anticolonial solidarity. In August 1946, an Algerian man informed two European police officers near the Randon Market, at the base of the Casbah, that a stall was selling beans at an elevated price. The stall was owned by Youcef L., an Algerian municipal councilor. After the officers forced the stall to change the pricing, Youcef tracked down the two agents to complain.[130] The police report noted that when Youcef confronted the officers, a group of nearly a hundred people gathered to watch. The police tried to arrest him, but Youcef threatened to organize a protest of vegetable sellers in front of the commissariat in response. The officers retreated, although they planned to pursue charges against Youcef later. This incident is unique. Rather than the typical story of a young Algerian caught selling cigarettes in an alleyway, Youcef owned a legitimate business in the market. Moreover, Youcef was not an impoverished street vendor, but an elected official. The difference is evident, too, in how the story played out. Instead of confiscating Youcef's goods, the police were forced to retreat in the face of an unfriendly crowd. The retreating officers had reason to fear. Throughout metropolitan France in the previous summer, price-control officers had been pelted with vegetables, mobbed by angry crowds, or otherwise assaulted.[131] In this case, the threat of collective action, not outright violence, proved powerful enough to force police to withdraw. Still, the structures of colonialism meant this was only a temporary reprieve for Youcef, who surely faced the wrath of the two officers later on if they pursued charges.

In Marseille, the police believed the "North African" black market continued to lurk in Rue des Chapeliers.[132] The police referred to the street as the primary gathering spot of "all the black market traffickers" and insisted that locals viewed it as a "veritable gangrene."¹³³ Reports noted that rarely a week passed without special police raids of this area frequented by "indigènes traffickers." Police scrutiny of North Africans selling cigarettes in Marseille began during the war, but the crackdown on cigarettes continued steadily through 1947. The police carried out daily "operations" on Cours Belsunce and Rue des Chapeliers, streets strongly coded as North African.¹³⁴ In one typical raid, the police arrived with a group of thirty officers to scour Rue des Chapeliers, searching a hundred people, "mostly North Africans." Of these one hundred individuals, the police sent nearly half to the station for an extended examination but managed to discover just eleven North Africans trafficking cigarettes, resulting in a fine.¹³⁵ The sheer size of this raid demonstrates a marked difference from Algiers, where the police constantly griped about the lack of personnel for black-market repression. Marseille, a larger city with a larger police force and also far fewer North Africans, had greater manpower. It might indicate, too, a difference in priorities. The raids on specific streets produced a predictable overrepresentation of North Africans in arrests for black-market trafficking, an intentional strategy to tackle what police saw as a "North African" crime.

Despite police operations, the general secretary for the police in Marseille worried about an untenable situation on Rue des Chapeliers, clogged with bodies to the point where it became "impossible to move" and rife with black-market sales of military goods and rationed food. Describing the chaos on Rue des Chapeliers, the secretary warned that drunk, "irascible indigènes" lurked looking for a fight, even insulting and assaulting police officers.¹³⁶ The police linked the black-market trades on Rue des Chapeliers to a broader idea of North African criminality and violence, including violence against the police. The secretary general also highlighted a worrisome trend of solidarity among North Africans. When the police tried to arrest an offending Algerian, the crowds on Rue des Chapeliers resisted. The secretary described how "a hostile and menacing group flocks, cries are proclaimed against the police, and finally, to avoid more serious incidents that could lead even to spilling blood, the guardians of the peace are obligated to withdraw."¹³⁷ As this incident shows, police shied away from some interventions on Rue des Chapeliers, afraid to arrest supposed traffickers because of the anticipated reaction. When faced with a crowd of angry North Africans in this North African space, the police retreated. These moments of resistance speak to the ways that North Africans managed to make and claim space in a city where local authorities constantly painted them as transient, criminal, or foreign.

The language of police reports betrays the racial and colonial thinking behind the raids on North African space. In one descent on Rue des Chapeliers and Rue Longue des Capucins in 1948, officials noted that a thousand "North African subjects" were questioned, with forty-seven brought to the station.[138] The report anachronistically used the term *sujet*, mischaracterizing Algerians as subjects rather than citizens. A similar "vast operation" occurred in 1949 behind the Bourse, an area described in the report as "frequented in particular by North African immigrants, idlers, and traffickers."[139] This same link was echoed in citizen letters that arrived at police headquarters. The owner of a hotel on Rue Poids de la Farine wrote to the police to notify them that his hotel was frequented by "a gang of parasites and North Africans who traffic American cigarettes."[140] The police response said they had stepped up surveillance on "hot" streets in the center of Marseille, to prevent "nocturnal aggressions."[141] Here, police officials easily shifted from cigarettes to violence and from a particular street to a network of crime and insecurity.

North Africans deployed the new egalitarian language of the French state to protest these constant raids. In 1948, Talmoudi, president of the Marseille AMA, railed against the familiar police practices in a letter to the prefect:

> The successive raids unleashed in the city, exclusively in the neighborhoods where North Africans live, at all hours of the day, have provoked massive and arbitrary arrests . . . The police, rapidly examining ID cards of people they stop, arrest and take to the commissariat all natives of North Africa upon simple examination of their origin, without regard for their honorability, nor their profession . . . We believe it is a grave error to discriminate between the children of the same fatherland [*patrie*].[142]

As Talmoudi pointed out, the overtly racialized police discrimination against Algerians belied the Fourth Republic's assertion that Algerians were all now French. The endless raids behind the Bourse and on Rue des Chapeliers rarely resulted in more than a handful of fines. Yet in the police narrative, these "toxic" spaces presented an ominous danger for the citizens of Marseille. Policing cigarettes became a stand-in for controlling the unwelcome presence of North African immigrants in Marseille. As Talmoudi points out, these raids brought police into the daily lives of all North Africans, regardless of their age, class, or "honorability." Through the constant operations, the police became an unwelcome, intimate presence for North Africans.

In Algiers, the police targeted Algerians for all black-market crimes, carrying over the wartime stereotype of "anti-French" Algerian profiteers. In Marseille, in contrast, conversations about the black market were more likely to evoke Corsican smuggling than North African traffickers. Instead, police pursuit of North African cigarette sellers in Marseille evolved within a police mandate to control North African spaces. Fines for selling cigarettes provided a tangible success to point to when the prefect or the public raised issues of insecurity in these neighborhoods. French politicians became wary of racial language in the wake of Vichy, but the tentative shift in discourse did not diminish an existing category of race that functioned in police surveillance. Police conceptions of North African criminality rendered North African urban spaces inherently dangerous and thus necessitating tighter surveillance, a continuity of long-standing strategies of racialized colonial control. In both Marseille and Algiers, fines for black-market sales could be dutifully logged, offered as evidence of efficacy in the police fight against an amorphous vision of North African delinquency.

The intense focus on neighborhoods not just of North African residency, but also of North African social interaction brought the police into contact with a diverse range of North Africans. In police framing, crime overran the Casbah and Rue des Chapeliers, but these neighborhoods formed the space of law-abiding Algerian social activity too. Police raids outed some criminals, but they also made the police a regular feature of the lives of ordinary North Africans, a dangerous intimacy. The overt targeting of Algerian traffickers developed within a set of police assumptions. European customers, Allied soldiers who supplied products, sellers who did not fit the standard police profile—all received far less attention than North Africans in police efforts to repress the illegal trade in tobacco. Controlling contraband cigarettes and lingering black-market exchanges illustrates police strategies that collapsed race and space, reproducing old tactics of racialized control despite a postwar language of reform.

In 1945, French political leaders resurrected the ideal of a "republican" France, a nation that proclaimed equality for all citizens. Ferhat Abbas's accusatory pamphlet called on this nation to make good on its promises. The attempts to create a more equal France opened a moment of possibility in France's relationship with its colonies, especially the three departments of Oran, Constantine, and Algiers. The French government made Algerians citizens, promised freedom of circulation, and ended brigades and bureaus that had provided specialized, and discriminatory, services. The new republican government removed racial language from the constitution and from official discourses.

The frustration of this moment came in how little these legal reforms changed lived reality. Algerians became French citizens, but the second-class citizenship created by colonial lobbying undermined their political agency. The postwar order's repugnance for racial categorization did not prevent the police from acting based on racialized assumptions about North Africans. Targeting North Africans through where they lived and how they moved through Algiers and Marseille, the police replicated enduring practices of racializing space. In part, attempts to change the relationship between France and Algeria failed because of a disconnect between national policy and local practices. If the postwar government disavowed ideas of race, this shift did not change what the police continued to construe as on-the-ground problems of criminal North African enclaves and racialized colonial conflicts.[143]

Unbeknownst to French observers, the protests and violence in Constantine in 1945 proved only a precursor to the revolution that would soon sweep Algeria. Rising waves of Algerian nationalism threatened the stability of France's colonial order, a system that the French relied on the police to protect. Algerian nationalists saw police officers as a symbol of French repression, brashly noting that if Algeria spent more money on teachers and doctors and less on police officers, "Algeria would not be the worse for it."[144] The overlap of politics and policing, always evident in the policing of colonial subjects, became more marked as Algeria spun closer to revolution. As the physical embodiment of colonial order, police officers became both targets and key players in the battle for the future of Algeria, seeing politics in Algerians' every personal choice and daily action.

6

POLICING POLITICS AT
THE END OF EMPIRE

In November 1952, the prefect of Algiers received a letter from the Service des Liaisons Nord-Africaines (SLNA), an intelligence bureau that functioned as a collective archive and a close collaborator of the police. In the note, the chief of the SLNA alerted the prefect to a recent performance of an Algiers theater troupe led by Algerian musician Abdelhamid Ababsa. A few weeks before, while on tour in Oran, the company had closed the soirée with a rendition of "Ia Ouled el Orbane, Chaalou el Niran," which the service translated as "Oh Sons of Arabs, Light the Fire." This, the SLNA relayed, was no ordinary song. It was a "PPA hymn" and one that Ababsa's group had previously performed in Bouira in 1947.[1] The note warned the prefect about Ababsa's nationalist political leanings, as evidenced by this support of the PPA, an Algerian nationalist party. The note implied that the administration should mobilize its regime of permits to prevent the troupe from giving future performances.

But all was not as it seemed. Just a few months later, in January 1953, another SLNA note came through. According to this report, the lyrics to the controversial song were:

> O children of the Arabs, light the fire
> Sing songs together, live happily
> Come, sons of the desert
> Here are the nights of the moon
> With the songs of tam-tams

And the *zukra*[2]
Make her dance
The most beautiful of beautiful women
The graceful Bedouin
Life is beautiful
With her[3]

As the letter went on to explain, "Ia Ouled El Orbane" was not a nationalist hymn but a love song, composed by a Tunisian Jew, Idias Kakino, and popularized by the acclaimed Egyptian singer Umm Kulthum. Though the SLNA, the prefecture, and the police eventually caught their mistake, they had apparently been tracking this song since 1947 as if it were a nationalist anthem.[4] Police officials' inability to distinguish between a love song about Bedouins and nationalist agitation demonstrates the incoherence of colonial political policing. But this (mis)interpretation proved more the rule than the exception.

In postwar Marseille and Algiers, police officers frequently struggled to define the contours of anticolonial resistance. In the years following World War II, police officers watched nervously as Algerian nationalism developed into a powerful, organized political movement. Officers in Marseille and Algiers fought a shadowy foe. How could the police determine who was a nationalist? Was nationalism adherence to a political party? Or did a song critiquing alcohol count too? Was the movement of Algerians within and between Marseille and Algiers inherently political? What of daily gatherings, religious rituals, café culture, and art? Police officers looked for nationalism in intimate spaces, defining "politics" in ever more capacious terms.

In the 1940s, Algerians gained French citizenship and new laws allowed relative freedom of movement, ratcheting up the pace of circular migration between Marseille and Algiers. As Algerian mobility increased and fears of nationalist politics deepened, the police deployed statistics to "prove" Algerian criminality and justify targeted policing. In both Marseille and Algiers, police officers responded to nationalist organizing by increasing their surveillance of Algerian politics, using tactics pioneered in policing other political groups. The policing of Algerian nationalism, however, expanded beyond ordinary party politics. Surveillance invaded spaces of Algerian sociability, personal moments of celebration, relaxation, or consumption. The policing of daily life in the name of politics played out in a familiar geography. As police came to view North Africans monolithically as a nationalist threat, they mapped these fears onto the "Casbahs" of Marseille and Algiers. In broadening their definition of the political when it came to Algerians, the police co-opted the power to define political action, a precedent with grave ramifications during the Algerian War of Independence. Police strategies effectively racialized politics, lumping all Algerians into a suspect category of "nationalist" to justify increased violence and invasive surveillance.

Battling Nationalism

In the 1940s, nationalist movements swept the French and British Empires. In this global context of anti-imperialism, Algerian nationalism came into its own. In the interwar period, Messali Hadj's Parti du Peuple Algérien (PPA) developed an anticolonial ethos, the 'Ulamā promoted an Islamic Algerian identity that rejected French influence, and elected officials like Ferhat Abbas pushed for expanded rights for educated Algerians. Following World War II, divergent threads of Algerian nationalism united in calls for change. Abbas founded the Association des Amis du Manifeste et de la Liberté, demanding political representation for Algerians. It was this organization that galvanized protestors in Guelma and Sétif in 1945. Following the tragic massacres in these cities, Abbas formed the Union Démocratique du Manifeste Algérien (UDMA) party, rejecting assimilation but continuing to imagine an Algerian future linked to France. Meanwhile, Messali Hadj's PPA rebranded as the Mouvement pour le Triomphe des Libertés Démocratiques (MTLD). While the MTLD worked in elected politics, its leaders continued to secretly support radical revolution and armed revolt through the now-underground PPA. By the 1940s, Algerian political organizations had moved from limited calls for reform, to demands for democratic representation, to open advocacy for an independent Algerian nation-state.[5]

Police officers in metropole and colony used traditional tools of political policing to combat Algerian nationalism. As they did with Communists, trade unions, and far-right groups, police officers targeted Algerian nationalists by suppressing their publications, arbitrarily arresting militants, and harassing audience members at meetings.[6] The surveillance of Algerian political parties fell to the Renseignements Généraux (RG) and the special police, traditional bastions of antileft policing in France.[7] Nor was the policing of Algerian nationalism new to the postwar period. Paris's Brigade Nord-Africaine, for example, had utilized the same strategies to police the Étoile Nord-Africaine in the 1930s.[8] The police of Marseille and Algiers, however, were trapped in an inherent contradiction when tasked with controlling nationalist politics in the postwar. Officers were responsible for brutally repressing anticolonialism but were also theoretically tasked with upholding the legitimacy of the state by dealing "fairly" with Algerians, now French citizens.

Some differences distinguished the policing of nationalism in Marseille and Algiers. In Algiers, fear of nationalism eclipsed all other political concerns. In

Marseille, however, the police insisted that nationalism did not have mass appeal. Their repeated dismissal of Algerian politics was ironic given that nationalist leaders, including Messali Hadj, first built support among Algerian workers in the metropole.[9] The ability of the police to effectively surveil nationalism also depended on officers who spoke Arabic and Amazigh. The hiring practices of the Algiers police shifted after World War II to include more Algerians, although the force remained heavily European. Marseille, in contrast, relied on only a handful of officers and translators who spoke Arabic for both political surveillance and criminal cases.

The policing of Algerian nationalism pushed boundaries, empowering officers to blur the line between the political and the personal. One telling example of this comes from the surveillance of Messali Hadj. In 1945, Hadj settled into a villa in the town of Bouzaréah, near Algiers.[10] Inspector Lucien Bernardie of the Algiers police tracked Hadj's movements, keeping a daily vigil at the villa. This intimate surveillance implicated Bernardie in the everyday life of the Hadj family. In May 1948, Messali Hadj contemplated a strategic move. The MTLD had been shifting toward a Pan-Islamic message of unity through a shared Muslim faith. This narrative did not fit the life of Messali Hadj, who had spent decades in France, dressed in European clothes, and worst of all, was married to Émilie Busquant, a French feminist anarcho-syndicalist. According to police surveillance, these "Westernized" traits made Hadj suspect in the eyes of some Algerian nationalists.[11]

To revamp his reputation, Hadj contemplated divorcing his French wife and finding a Muslim partner.[12] Police reports document the fraught, emotional conflict that ensued. On May 5, an intelligence report noted that Hadj planned to repudiate his wife to marry a young Muslim woman. Aware of the plan, Busquant blocked the marriage broker from entering their home. The officer on duty at the villa noted that "violent domestic scenes" exploded between the spouses afterward.[13] Bernardie filed a subsequent report on May 27, reproducing quotes from a fight he had overheard between Hadj and Busquant. Busquant had apparently slapped one of Hadj's bodyguards and the Algerian man, in turn, hit her in the face. Busquant insisted that the man be fired, but Hadj instead blamed his wife, saying that the conflict began because Busquant treated the bodyguards like servants.[14] As the fight continued, underlying tensions surfaced. Recalling a time when Busquant had called the guards "scum," Hadj lanced angrily, "Don't forget that I am Arab and I am also part of that same scum." Infuriated, Busquant responded, "I consider you as less than that [scum] and lower than the most vulgar assassin."[15] Scum, or *racaille*, was a pejorative term typically used to denigrate the working class. In this fight, however, the word implied the racialized category of "indigène." When Messali Hadj informed his wife that he, too, was part of the racaille, he reminded her of the implications of choosing to share her life with him, an Algerian man.

What fascinates me about this fight is how it entered the historical record. The profoundly personal nature of the argument is self-evident, the bitterness of a couple struggling against external pressures.[16] But we only know about this emotional exchange because somewhere outside the villa, Lucien Bernardie skulked, scribbling down every conversation, every private moment of anger, every personal exchange of remorse. Bernardie became a de facto member of the Hadj household, a witness to a rocky marriage and a man in the throes of reinvention. This episode speaks to the intimacy of policing Algerian nationalism. The French police obviously did not place all Algerians under the same level of scrutiny as Hadj. Still, as nationalism gained strength and the police expanded their definition of politics and loyalty, Algerians of all walks of life felt the consequences.

Stereotypes and Statistics

For decades, French authorities had painted Algerian men as a particularly criminal, violent population. Algerian women were their constant victims, terrorized by Algerian masculinity. These racist tropes informed police strategies. Algerian immigration picked up after 1945, both to colonial cities like Algiers and metropolitan destinations like Marseille, because of changes in citizenship laws and the need for labor. But as the numbers of Algerians in both Marseille and Algiers grew and fears of nationalist organizing swirled, the police began to warn of an invasion of dangerous Algerian criminals. Reports blended familiar caricatures with a new tool—statistics. By crafting and manipulating data on Algerian criminals, the police justified redoubled surveillance of Algerian communities. The heightened surveillance, in turn, could be deployed to track and repress activities that the police understood as nationalist organizing.

The vilification of North Africans went beyond generalized xenophobia. The National Ministry of Information claimed that in Marseille, 53 percent of all crimes were committed by foreigners. But some foreigners were more threatening than others. "As with sanitary concerns, it is the exotics and the immigrants the most ethnically distant from the French who produce the most criminals: in summer come the North Africans, with a criminality fifteen times higher than the French population, then the Polish, four times, the Italians and Portuguese, three times, the Spanish, double."[17] The least "French," despite their French citizenship, North Africans allegedly posed by far the greatest threat. The national director of the judicial police concurred in a 1951 report, claiming that Algerian immigrants, woefully unprepared for a life in the metropole, inevitably turned to a life of crime.[18] Reproducing colonial stereotypes, he described the Algerian mentality as "characterized by instantaneous, unforeseeable, and violent changes" and labeled Algerian criminals as both ferocious and primitive.[19] The report concluded that while European gangs had "disappeared," Algerian violence was on the rise, now accounting for 81 percent of total assaults.[20] Officials treated these statistics as conclusive, but as Emmanuel Blanchard has shown in Paris, reports on North African criminality were often manipulations of the data or outright fictions.[21]

The press, however, did little to question official statistics. Like the faits divers of the 1920s, Paris newspapers in the late 1940s described an invasion of the Algerian "criminal underworld" and claimed North African criminality was a "national problem."[22] In Marseille, newspapers alleged that Algerians were flooding the city and bringing with them a new set of problems. In an article from 1950, journalist Jean-Marie Garraud criticized the French government for not curbing Algerian immigration. Evoking the imagined criminality of North African neighborhoods, Garraud questioned, "Is it admissible that at their arrival in Marseille, Algerians wash ashore into that sordid Rue des Chapeliers, the veritable 'Casbah of Marseille' where all forms of trafficking take place?"[23] Clearly, his answer was no. Commentaries on the misery and criminality of Marseille's "Casbah" continued for years, and Marseille's major dailies, *Le Provençal* and *La Marseillaise*, produced faits divers that painted North Africans as a criminal element in an already vice-ridden port town.[24]

North Africans fought back against these negative stereotypes. In October 1949, an RG report in Marseille recorded the reactions of North Africans to a series of negative articles in local newspapers. North African workers expressed their indignation, calling the attacks against them "clearly racist."[25] The workers pointed out the inconsistency between coverage of North African and European criminals. North Africans "deplored" that poverty and unemployment drove their fellow countrymen to crime, but why "outrageously publish these crimes when similar misdeeds committed by Europeans very often benefit from a more hidden publicity?"[26] Criticizing French colonial policy, these North African interlocutors argued that if the French government improved social safety nets for unemployed North Africans, the newspapers would have nothing to report. In a meeting of the Association des Musulmans Algériens (AMA) of Marseille that same year, Association President Talmoudi emphasized the impact of these journalistic attacks on Algerians' daily lives. According to the police spy present at the meeting, Talmoudi said that the "violent" press campaign being waged against Algerians had "led to a severe police control" and recurrent insults from officers during questioning and arrests.[27]

The figure of the "criminal" North African loomed so large that in 1952, the Marseille police compiled a specific report on North African delinquency. The report intentionally included only North African "specialties."[28] Clearly, police officials already understood North Africans as inherently prone to certain types of crime. The report claimed that North Africans represented nearly 14 percent of total delinquency while accounting for only 4 percent of the population.[29] In every category of crime discussed, North Africans were grossly overrepresented. In 1951, for example, the police claimed that North Africans made up 82 percent of arrests for carrying prohibited arms, 75 percent of theft in cars, and 80 percent of violent theft.[30] Surprisingly, the police acknowledged the social problems underlying crime, noting that "the causes are multiple and are founded at once on the mentality of those concerned and the social conditions in which they find themselves placed."[31] Even so, the report qualified the causality of "social conditions" by crediting the "mentality" of North Africans with equal explanatory power. Moreover, while the police recognized the problem of poverty, they did not interrogate what role they themselves played in the overrepresentation of North Africans in criminal reports. If the police found North Africans carrying prohibited weapons, it was not just a function of who carried weapons, but also of whom the police stopped and searched, whom they deemed too dangerous to carry a gun, a pocketknife, or a cane.[32]

In Algiers, too, crimes committed by the "indigènes" consistently fueled the local press. In the main European papers of Algiers, such as the *Écho d'Alger* and *Journal d'Alger*, crime reports featured the usual parade of Algerian criminals. Some of the headlines could have been plucked directly from the 1920s, reflecting lasting stereotypes of Algerian criminality. For example, a *Journal d'Alger* story from February 1947 titled "A Knight of the Bousaadi" echoed almost exactly the Algerian "Knights of the Knife" criticized in the interwar press.[33]

As in Marseille, the Algiers police mobilized statistics to justify their suspicion of Algerians. The police of Algiers routinely created monthly criminal reports. These overviews categorized criminals and victims as "European," "indigène," or "unknown." Given the dissolution of the legal category of "indigène" after World War II, the choice to continue using these divisions in postwar statistic is contradictory. The data reflected the categories the police cared about. The genders of the criminal and victim, for example, are not noted. Nor was class a salient category, as no mention is made of profession. Reflecting the primary divide of colonial society, the relevant duality was "indigène" and European. Statistics from Algiers show that the majority of crimes were committed by unknown criminals, a simple reality of crime in general. Within crimes with known authors, however, Algerians regularly made up more than 75 percent of accused criminals, particularly for crimes such as theft.[34] Although the Algerian population of Algiers increased in the 1940s, Europeans remained the majority, making this a disproportionate representation of Algerians.

The police produced statistics like this for a reason. The percentages cited over and over reflected arrests, but the data did not indicate the real spectrum of crime, much less guilt. The numbers, after all, did not show who was convicted of a crime—just who the police arrested. If inspectors disproportionately charged Algerians with theft, it might also have been because the police disproportionately looked for Algerian thieves. The long history of racialized space also contributed to the overrepresentation of North Africans in arrest data, as officers conducted raids for Algerian "criminals" in the neighborhoods where they believed they would find them. What these statistics do not tell us is the number of people questioned, searched, forced to show their papers but then simply let go. In targeting specific spaces and populations, police found North African criminals while paying less attention to those committing crimes in other places and within other communities. Police officers have always had a role in determining criminality, as evidenced in the wartime policing of black markets and requis laborers. The postwar statistics, however, allowed police officials to produce neutral "facts" about Algerian criminality without acknowledging the ways in which their own priorities and presumptions shaped the data.

Gun-Smuggling Nationalists

As Algerian nationalism gained popularity, police officials became convinced that the Algerians traveling between Marseille and Algiers would provide an arsenal for a nationalist revolt. In treating all Algerian migrants as potential nationalist gunrunners, the police criminalized Algerian trans-Mediterranean movement, contradicting post–World War II reforms that allowed Algerians freedom of mobility. In Algeria, Europeans could easily obtain a gun license, but Algerians had to meet a long list of requirements to obtain permission for even a hunting rifle.[35] Algerians living in the metropole also needed special permission from the administrator of their douar, or home region, to obtain a gun license. As nationalist organizing picked up in the 1940s, the police began to target Algerian "smugglers" circumventing these restrictions. The policing of suspected gun traffickers, like many stories of policing in Marseille and Algiers, was also about mobility and space. Police officials fixated on the dangers of contraband passing through their ports, using the chokepoint of customs to control the trade. The connection of North Africans to areas of the city seen as centers of the black market, particularly Rue des Chapeliers, also shaped police conceptions of gun smuggling.

The fixation on guns affected both sides of the Mediterranean. In Marseille, the police claimed that North African veterans frequently trafficked arms on Rue des Chapeliers.[36] Officers suspected that African American soldiers stationed in Marseille also sold guns to North Africans, since they socialized in the same behind the Bourse neighborhood.[37] With this alleged trafficking in mind, the Marseille RG expressed concern over the massive return of Algerians to Algeria. In September 1949, for example, more than ten thousand Algerian workers left for Algeria, as compared to less than five thousand who arrived in Marseille. According to the RG's informants, the movement could be partially explained by holiday travel for Eid Al-Adha, but other Algerians affirmed that they planned to head home for good.[38] The RG feared that gun smugglers lurked among the voyagers, including Algerians who had acquired hunting rifles while in France and veterans who had managed to keep their military-issue pistols. According to the RG report, Algerians risked little in transporting guns home, as the customs police conducted only "superficial" luggage checks and, it was rumored, could be bribed into looking the other way.[39] The note ominously concluded that the PPA watched the returning Algerians with excitement, indicating police certainty that the alleged gun smuggling was part of a nationalist plot.

Almost certainly, nationalist sympathizers did use the fluid border between Marseille and Algiers to bring arms to Algeria. Not all Algerians with guns had nationalist ambitions, however. Take for example, Saïd C., whose story opened this book. After years of cyclical migration, Saïd decided to return home to Algeria in 1953. Saïd had purchased three hunting rifles for himself and his brothers in the Seine-et-Marne department and had declared the weapons before boarding his train in Paris. The Parisian customs officers apparently happily allowed Saïd to bring his guns south, leaving it to their colleagues in Marseille to inform Saïd that he had no right to purchase the weapons in the first place. The Marseille police seized the rifles and fined him five thousand francs.[40]

Marseille's port police then conducted a full investigation, trying to uncover the motive behind Saïd's "smuggling." They found Saïd's explanation for purchasing the guns unlikely, suggesting that he secretly intended to sell the weapons in Algeria at a significant markup. The police ultimately decided that Saïd had no nefarious intentions, emphasizing that he did not belong to any political party. Still, the report concluded, since guns brought to Algeria in this way were likely to fall into the hands of "separatist elements," it was necessary to step up surveillance on the ferries bound for Algeria.[41] If Saïd had no nationalist intentions, other Algerians might. Saïd's case reveals a central discord. Police cared about the physical possession of guns, but they worried much more about the intentions of the Algerians who carried them. These internal questions of loyalty, however, were ultimately unknowable. The police could not prove what gun owners planned to do with their weapons, just as they could not regulate thoughts and beliefs. Officers disrupted Saïd's day, restricted his mobility, and affected his livelihood, trying to police his access to guns but also, more intimately, his intentions.

If reports on gun smuggling were scattered throughout police correspondence in Marseille, the port police of Algiers seemed to think of little else. In Algiers, police officials grew concerned about stopping the flow of guns at the port, fearing that once Algerians slipped into the urban sprawl of the city or the cordoned world of the Casbah, the weapons would fall into the hands of nationalists. Port police in Algiers filed report after report on Algerians returning from Marseille with weapons in 1949 and 1950.[42] In one report from March 1949, for example, customs officials caught twenty-six Algerians bringing guns through the port of Algiers. Police had confiscated seven rifles, seven revolvers, nine pistols, and more than a hundred rounds of ammunition.[43] These twenty-six Algerians were a tiny minority of the thousands of North Africans who traveled between metropole and colony each month, but the trend still alarmed authorities. The police described various methods for smuggling guns. One Algerian man arrived from Marseille with an automatic pistol hidden in his belt and five rounds of ammunition in his pocket.[44] Another Algerian impressively attempted to hide a hunting rifle under his clothes.[45] Customs officers caught someone else with a revolver hidden "between his legs."[46] Fines for illegal arms possession could be as high as twelve thousand francs, in addition to criminal charges. It is unclear how officials selected whom to search, but finding arms smuggled under clothes or between someone's legs necessarily involved invasive, violently intimate searches.[47] If the police caught some Algerians smuggling guns, they surely searched many more innocent travelers whose humiliating, public experience generated no police report.

Algerians also could take advantage of French fears of gun smuggling to serve their own ends. In October 1950, Brahim B., in jail for fraud, gave the police a tip on a militant nationalist, Bengrine. As was often the case, the police confused the identity of this purported agitator, writing "Bengrine, not Belgrine" in a report title.[48] The police raided Bengrine's house in Hussein Dey, a suburb of Algiers just beyond El Hamma. Officers discovered a gun and six cartridges of ammunition, but ultimately decided that Bengrine was no nationalist agitator. In reality, Brahim's jail-cell accusation was motivated by personal revenge, not loyalty to France. Brahim had feuded with Bengrine and sought vengeance by accusing Bengrine of trafficking arms.[49] If Brahim wanted revenge, he succeeded. The police arrested Bengrine for possessing a gun, although they lacked the evidence to charge him with trafficking. We often (and rightly) think of the colonial police primarily as repressive enforcers of state priorities, but this case shows a more complicated reality.[50] Officers imposed the will of the colonial state, but they also reacted to demands made by Algerians, including navigating incidents in which Algerians wielded police against each other.

As Algerians circulated between Algiers and Marseille, the police worried about the criminality they believed came with these migrants. Police obsessively tracked arrivals and departures, quantified Algerian criminality, and fought against a mysterious, if not entirely imaginary, ring of gun smugglers. In their crusade against guns, and more broadly against the spread of Algerian nationalism, the police of Marseille and Algiers relied on one another, forming a circular exchange of information.[51] The pursuit of guns was also about controlling mobility, tracking Algerians as they moved between metropole and colony. This trans-Mediterranean movement had long defined life in Marseille and Algiers, a transience that police on both sides perceived as dangerous. French officials fretted about the potential for this flow of goods and people to become a network for traffickers, linking what they saw as black-market smugglers skulking on Rue des Chapeliers to nationalists hidden in the Casbah. The indiscriminate targeting of Algerian travelers demonstrates how policing Algerian nationalism came to mean, quite simply, policing Algerians, a fusion that was even more evident in matters of art, culture, and daily life.

Redefining Politics in Algiers

Unable to pinpoint nationalist agitation, the police in Algiers developed all-encompassing and inconsistent definitions of political action. The policing of nationalism followed patterns established in the policing of other political groups, both in the metropole and colony. But while policing nationalism might have been business as usual in some ways, it also redefined politics, folding identity, religion, and recreation into the same category as voting, strikes, and party membership. Religion could always be a political choice, as could the decision of how to spend one's leisure hours. In both France and Algeria, the police also tracked Communist sports leagues and Catholic political organizations. Algerian nationalists did use social and religious gatherings to proselytize their cause. The difference, however, was how police read political meaning onto all Algerian sociability, basing politics on a racialized Algerian identity rather than expressed ideologies.

The police of Algiers saw suspicious behavior everywhere, asserting control over personal and familial events. In April 1947, for example, two police officers were patrolling Rue Randon at the base of the Casbah. The officers heard a male voice singing in Arabic coming from the house of an Algerian woman. Though the agents could not understand Arabic, they insisted that the chorus, sung in French, included the line "Long live the charming PPA, down with the *trois couleurs* [the French flag]."⁵² The officers learned from a local market guard that the singing was at a baptism, though it was likely actually a circumcision, recast by the guard in Catholic terminology. Unsure how to proceed, the two officers went to the 2ème commissariat to report the incident. The commissioner came to the house, but the host calmly proved he had all the necessary permits to hold the party. Meanwhile, the guests had already quietly filed home. The police report ends, leaving it unclear whether officers pursued this "suspicious" incident or let it go. The two police agents wanted to gain entrance to this family gathering, convinced that a religious ceremony had been repurposed as a nationalist meeting. But their uncertain knowledge of Arabic and Islamic custom, as well as the personal nature of the party, slowed police efforts at control.

The mysterious baptism reveals the haphazard police definition of politics. Singing a song with a suspect refrain during a circumcision could be political. The act of arranging a circumcision party itself could be political. A year later, Commissioner LaJeunesse of the 2ème commissariat filed a report about a rumor. He had learned that during parties in the Muslim community, such as "baptisms" and marriages, guests took up collections for the PPA. According to an unnamed source, fundraisers had recently amassed 65,000 francs for the nationalists at one such party. LaJeunesse admitted, "Still, I could not learn the name and address of the person's home where this collection took place."⁵³ Although the police had identified parties as a cause for concern, their knowledge remained limited. LaJeunesse, as police commissioner of the Casbah, sought to understand the influence of nationalism within this famously "closed" neighborhood. Yet his ambitions were frustrated. Police officials did not have enough information to combat the threat they saw hidden in religious and family celebrations, nor could they disband parties without cause. Rendering Algerian celebrations as suspect, however, meant the police had an excuse to surveil them. Nationalists, too, played with the fine line between private and political, using family gatherings to drum up support.

Police had long tracked religious organizations in Algeria, seeking to unravel the relationship between Islamic faith and political resistance.⁵⁴ The French administration regularly surveilled religious meetings, even sending a police agent on the hadj with Algerian pilgrims.⁵⁵ The police's muddy distinction between religion and politics also appeared in requests for state funding by religious groups. Discussing the requests, the governor general of Algeria noted that there was no reason to abstain from supporting "reformist" organizations "if their reformism is purely religious, if it plays a useful social role, and if its directors adopt a loyal attitude towards us."⁵⁶ In this revealing statement, the governor distinguished between "purely religious" organizations and those with political motives. Yet in his understanding, "purely religious" groups were loyal to France. Being *disloyal* to France, on the other hand, constituted political action. Decisions about "loyalty" notably relied on police officers' observations of the meetings and events held by these societies. The blurry edge between religion and politics existed in the interwar years, but in the increasingly tense political atmosphere of the postwar, both nationalists and police picked at the already unclear distinction between politics and faith.

As nationalism grew in influence, the police saw danger in many leisure activities. The French state had required the creation of separate, parallel sporting and civic organizations for Europeans and Algerians, but now these distinct "Muslim" associations became a threat. This included Algerian soccer teams, athletic clubs, and even Scouting troops.[57] In 1948, Commissioner Georges Costes of the Algiers RG filed a report on the proliferation of political propaganda within the Muslim Scouts. Costes alleged that some Muslim troops spread nationalist propaganda to their young recruits, but the law prevented him from stopping it.[58] To solve this problem, Costes suggested a work-around. The French Ministry of Youth and Education controlled the finances of Scouting organizations. While the police could not disband troops sympathetic to nationalism, the government could use police intelligence to "favor apolitical scouting troops."[59] But Costes had a decidedly political definition of "apolitical." A pro-French troop, after all, was not devoid of politics. In cultivating "apolitical" social and religious activities, the police in fact sought a political goal of producing loyal Algerian subjects.[60]

The police also tracked the artists who offered entertainment in the theaters and cafés of Algiers. In the interwar period, Algerian artists, playwrights, and composers created a flourishing Arabic-language theater scene.[61] While French authorities at times offered financial support and official encouragement for this artistic production, they also used laws restricting tours and censoring plays to carefully monitor for nationalist sympathies.[62] In 1947, for example, Méziane Aizel wrote to the Prefecture of Algiers for permission to put on a Ramadan show with music, sketches, dancing, and food. The prefecture rejected his request, noting internally that, in the past, known prostitutes had attended Aizel's shows.[63] Subsequent requests from Aizel, however, suggest a different reason for official reticence. A police report in the same file labeled Aizel as an MTLD sympathizer, even if he did not openly discuss politics.[64] Though by all accounts Aizel's shows were politically neutral, police fears that he secretly harbored nationalist sympathies proved enough to prompt official rejection. The police also collapsed morality and politics, labeling Aziel a threat both because of his alleged nationalism and the presence of "loose women" at his performances.

Artists and playwrights found themselves compelled to couch any new ventures in terms palatable to police. In 1948, for example, Mostefa Kasderli wrote to the Prefecture of Algiers to ask for permission to produce a new show. In his letter of request, Kasderli explicitly described the production as "strictly artistic," heading off any police fear of political motivations.⁶⁵ The prefecture, however, was not convinced. A report compiled by the police of Algiers cautioned that Kasderli's troupe, the Hillal el Djezairi, had previously gotten in trouble for inserting ad-libbed nationalist songs in between scenes of a historical drama. The police could not actually stop performers from deviating from the censored script on stage, but they could prevent actors who took such risks from performing again. And in this case, they did precisely that. Kasderli's request was rejected.

Although the administration could weaponize bureaucracy against performers like Kasderli and Aziel, police control over less formal cultural production proved elusive. In 1948, the governor general of Algeria issued a special report calling attention to a new trend in PPA recruitment tactics. The nationalists would send groups of children to wander the streets and markets of Algiers, with at least one of the children physically disabled. These youths, the governor alleged, sang songs about French repression in Sétif in 1945, accompanying themselves with drums and flutes. The songs implied that the disabled or blind child had been wounded in the massacres that followed peaceful nationalist protests in that city.⁶⁶ Evoking recurrent problems of translation, the governor noted, "These songs, sung in a sad tone, vividly capture the imagination of passers-by, while the agents, who often do not understand the meaning [of the songs], remain unaware of this clever propaganda."⁶⁷ By using children, the nationalists could rally support under the noses of police officers, who would be unable to distinguish between a ballad about star-crossed lovers and a hymn detailing French violence. The police responded to the governor general's warning with assurances that any musicians of this kind would be arrested.

A month later, the Algiers police were informed that two fourteen-year-old "indigènes" were singing songs that attacked "the integrity of French territory and sovereignty" on the sidewalk.⁶⁸ The commissioner specifically sent Officer Albert Safrana, head of the "indigène" information service, to investigate. Again, the very existence of an *indigène* information service in 1948 belies the postwar reforms that made all Algerians "Français Musulman" and recognized them as citizens of France. Safrana, likely an Algerian Jew, spoke Arabic fluently and therefore could assess the subversion of the songs. Safrana reported that the youths' song criticized France for sending soldiers off to serve in World War II. Just as the governor had warned, one of the young singers was blind, and the lyrics blamed this disability on French cruelty. Interrogated by the police, the teens said they had learned the song from an Algerian named Hadouche whom they had met in downtown Algiers. The police, however, suspected that Hadouche was an imaginary scapegoat and arrested the boys. In strategies like this, Algerian nationalists recognized the power and persuasion of art and the limits of police control. Consider the optics, as nationalists surely did, of the police harassing these two children, homeless and disabled, for singing. This abusive display of power could only feed nationalist messaging that highlighted French oppression.

In Algiers, policing politics took on a new meaning in the postwar period. Before World War II, the police could convincingly argue that nationalism remained an elite persuasion. By the 1940s, however, this comforting narrative was evidently false. As Algerian nationalism gained mass appeal, the police began to see it everywhere.[69] In religion, in parties, in theater, and in music, the police wondered whether "anti-French" sentiments lurked within prose or skulked behind closed doors. The fear of nationalism drove the police to exert greater control over the cultural and social life of Algerians. As Omar Carlier has shown, politics did exist in these spaces. Nationalists organized protests and boycotts over coffee in the Casbah's cafés maures, youth clubs and religious organizations doubled as recruitment hubs, homes became not just gathering spaces but clandestine mailboxes for nationalist materials.[70] Soccer clubs, scouting organizations, and musical theater could all be real sites of resistance to French colonial rule.[71] The police seemed to miss, too, the active role of Algerian women in nationalist organizing, instead focusing on what they perceived as a dangerous Algerian masculinity.[72] But not every Algerian was a nationalist and not every home, meeting, or performance had political ambitions. The inability of the police to define the edges of politics benefited nationalist organizers, but it also meant that the police unleashed blanket repression based on a racialized category—Algerian.

Discovering Politics in Marseille

In Marseille, the police reacted differently to the growth of Algerian nationalism. For decades, the metropolitan police had professed skepticism about anticolonial movements. They tended to blame French Communists, seeing Algerian organizers as little more than pawns manipulated by European masterminds.[73] The Marseille police insisted that Algerians followed nationalists not out of a genuine desire for reform but due to gullibility and concerns about material needs. A police report from 1950 argued that when "indigènes" attended political meetings, it was "more a material question than a spiritual, moral, religious, or especially political, question."[74] Even as late as 1952, police continued to frame Algerian nationalism as the folly of an elite minority.[75] The police sent informants to nationalist meetings, but policing Algerian politics was not initially the same all-consuming obsession it was in Algiers. After World War II, however, the Marseille police scrambled to counteract decades of denying nationalism and to infiltrate the political networks they had once deemed inconsequential. As in

Algiers, the Marseille police came to treat a North African identity and North African neighborhoods as synonymous with suspect politics.

Despite denials of North African political ambitions, the police had to confront the reality of growing anticolonial movements. On September 17, 1950, two hundred Algerians marched along the Canebière, Marseille's main thoroughfare. Protestors carried signs criticizing the censorship of *L'Algérie Libre*, a nationalist newspaper, and calling for "Korea for Koreans," a reference to other anticolonial struggles.[76] The line of protestors "collided" with a group of twenty patrolmen and a fight broke out.[77] Nationalist publications reported police brutality and police records confirmed that two "Arabs" were hospitalized after clashes with the police.[78] Even as the police denied Algerian nationalism, they faced it marching down main street. In that encounter, the officers' first response was violence.

Other confrontations with Algerian nationalism, however, were less obvious. In September 1950, a guardian of the peace "surprised" three Algerians selling copies of the banned *L'Algérie Libre* on Cours Belsunce and Rue des Chapeliers. The location of these arrests suggests long-established police tactics of trolling North African neighborhoods, searching for "dangerous" criminals but usually issuing nothing more than minor fines. The arrested men protested that they had no political affinity and were simply selling the newspaper for profit, but to no avail.[79] Police continued to target *L'Algérie Libre*. Reacting to concerned notes from Paris in 1952, the Marseille police assigned three officers to conduct a search for the forbidden newspaper. Their quest was fruitless:

> Despite the large number of establishments patronized by North Africans or owned by them, which were visited with all the desirable meticulousness, it was not possible to find a single example of the newspaper. Additionally, the surveillance carried out in the streets of the city frequented by North Africans and the searches of all those found carrying suitcases, briefcases, or any kind of package were also without result.[80]

This letter is telling of police methods. The officers, dressed in plainclothes, stopped and searched any person they found in what they deemed "North African streets." This indiscriminate targeting of those the police believed to be North African shows the consequences of racialized space in Marseille. Officers needed no probable cause to search any North African they happened upon in these neighborhoods, nor any real confirmation that the person being stopped was North African. By criminalizing space, the police created a suspect community rather than trying to identify individual culprits.

The overlap of political policing and racial profiling that became common practice in Marseille is perhaps most evident in police action prior to a diplomatic visit by the king of Morocco, Mohammed V, in 1950. The sultan had already developed a reputation for colonial resistance and would go on to lead his country to independence in 1956.[81] In preparation for his visit in 1950, the Marseille police conducted a series of "preventative operations" among North Africans, to avoid any nationalist disturbances. The police carried out raids in the week before the visit, focused on nodes of North African mobility in Marseille. Groups of plainclothes officers stopped and questioned North Africans at the arrival of trains at Gare St. Charles and near car rental kiosks. The police also increased the frequency of their habitual raids on the *meublés*, furnished rooms rented by North African workers on streets like Rue des Chapeliers. In their descents, the police stopped more than seven hundred North Africans "or foreigners."[82] This phrasing demonstrates the fluidity of racial divisions in Marseille. The police could not neatly identify North Africans, accidentally picking up Egyptians, Syrians, and other "Arab" foreigners in their raids, as well as miscellaneous Europeans. These were not raids of "usual suspects" or known nationalists; these were descents on North African space that politicized and thereby criminalized anyone found in the area. Despite extensive and invasive raids, the police apprehended only a handful of men on charges for improper immigration paperwork, most of them not even North African.

In addition to preemptive raids in the "neighborhoods frequented by North Africans" such as Rue des Chapeliers, the police expanded their searches to new North African spaces, like the Quartier des Crottes by the industrial port and Boulevard Oddo and Rue de Lyon in the north of Marseille.[83] In these targeted raids, the police stopped and questioned an additional 1,400 North Africans and brought more than 300 men into the station to examine their papers. This "examination of papers" occurred despite the fact that French law had granted Algerians freedom of movement to France. Of the huge number of North Africans stopped, the police charged only thirty-five people with minor infractions.[84] Police relied on their understanding of North African spaces of Marseille to track down potential nationalists, but the police also responded to changing residential patterns, expanding beyond Rue des Chapeliers to search new North African enclaves in the north. The reliance on sporadic raids on North African neighborhoods was a decades-old tradition in Marseille, one that differed from police tactics in Algiers. The supposed "impenetrability" of the Casbah, as well as the larger size of the Algerian population there, made raids less practical as a tool for fighting nationalism in Algiers.

The visit of King Mohamed V was extraordinary in its stakes, but the case reflects quotidian police practices of racial profiling in Marseille. When the king visited, the police knew where to look for North Africans, they knew which brigades to mobilize, and they knew what crimes they could use to bring suspects in, because these massive roundups were only an extension of everyday tactics.

The impetus was political—the police wanted to prevent demonstrations during the king's visit. Yet police actions had intimate consequences. The men collected in police sweeps had their days disrupted, their right to be in Marseille questioned, their plans, meals, and conversations interrupted, without any evidence of wrongdoing. The police treated all North Africans as nationalists, and therefore criminals, criminalizing not just political activity but an assumed North African identity itself.

The policing of nationalism in Marseille slipped into policing religion, too. In 1949, for example, an RG note accused Kabyle PPA sympathizers of gathering in the basement of an Algerian restaurant on Boulevard des Dames.[85] "Under cover of Qur'anic prayers," the police asserted, the Algerians secretly assembled to listen to PPA propaganda.[86] The police desire to penetrate these meetings is palpable in the report, but it contains no concrete information, reproducing only vague rumors. How could the police determine whether the prayer meetings were a nationalist plot or earnest religious gatherings? The police had relatively little knowledge of Islam, especially in Marseille, which perhaps increased their distrust.[87] But the police also had reason to fear. In Algeria, as in Morocco, Egypt, and Senegal to name just a few, Islam and anticolonialism were closely connected.[88] Lack of familiarity with Islamic practices and general mistrust of North Africans fed the police's suspicion that Islam was a cover for nationalism.

The uncertain boundaries of political activity and art seen in Algiers also troubled the police in Marseille. In 1952, artist and playwright Mahieddine Bachetarzi's traveling troupe, Tournée Mahieddine, undertook one of its frequent tours in France, including an obligatory stop in Marseille. Mahieddine was a prominent figure in Algerian theater, the organizer of the Arabic-language season at the Algiers Opera and a star tenor of the music halls and theaters of the Casbah. He also had a troubled relationship with the French colonial government, alternatively viewed as a collaborator or a threat.[89] On October 8, 1952, the prefect of the Bouches-du-Rhône reported on the show to the minister of the interior. The troupe had performed in the Cinéma Colisée, in a street adjacent to the Porte d'Aix and a short walk from Rue des Chapeliers, where they had put on a three-act comedy titled *Bou Houdba*. Drawing on an RG report, the prefect summarized the play, which centered on police persecution of an Algerian peasant farmer. The play began, the prefect recounted, with police officers discovering an Algerian farmer playing drums. The officers assumed the farmer was sending coded messages, a riff, perhaps, on the blurry line between politics and art in colonial Algeria. The police harassed and abused the Algerian until he "admitted" to knowing the location of a secret stash of weapons. The officers then tried to force the peasant to bring them to the imaginary stockpile, but when they realized the guns were a fiction, the police put the Algerian on trial for lying. The play concluded with a dream sequence in which the Algerian people have overthrown the "ex-torturer-colonist" police. The prefect warned that the spectacle "has an anti-French and biased character, likely to negatively impact the opinions of the North African workers in the metropole."⁹⁰

The departmental director of police in Marseille quickly issued a letter calling for a "strict surveillance" of subsequent performances and forbade future shows by this troublesome troupe.⁹¹ In many Arabic-language plays, the "anti-French" element the police sought to control remained subtle, displayed only in allusions, ad-libs, or veiled references. By 1952, the Tournée Mahieddine dared a more direct attack. Although never denouncing colonialism outright, the play's critique of the police served as a metonymy for the colonial state. It seems surprising that the police did not immediately put a stop to such an overtly subversive show. But in part, this could be due to the limitations of the French legal code. In Algeria, a regime of permits allowed the police to monitor troupes, but in Marseille, the police lacked these legal tools.⁹² Algeria also had laws repressing "anti-French" actions, but these laws did not apply in the metropole. Authorities in Marseille could observe, worry, and prevent future performances, but in the moment, officers had little legal room for maneuver. The police also proved unwilling to bend the laws for the ill-defined threat of theater, perhaps in part because they continued to discredit the political viability of Algerian nationalism.

French officials despaired over the "flood" of North African immigration in the postwar and remained convinced that these migrants harbored criminal tendencies. Yet North Africans were hardly the only, or even the most concerning, colonial population milling around Marseille. In the late 1940s, the police's more immediate concern was the Indochinese community. Though smaller in number, Indochinese immigrants in Marseille posed a threat because of the ongoing war of decolonization in Indochina. Despite downplaying Algerian nationalism, however, the police in Marseille did shift their strategies for repressing it, doubling down on racial profiling that turned all North African people and spaces into targets. The policing of North Africans in Marseille was not restricted to surveilling meetings, protests, and rallies. Instead, the police sought to combat nationalism with an intense police presence in spaces of North African daily life. The uncertain boundaries between culture and dogma, between the intimate and the political, empowered the police, with tangible effects for North Africans in Marseille.

Violence and "Legitimate Defense"

In the years following World War II, reports of police violence proliferated. Violence itself was nothing new. Police officers had strategically deployed violence as a tool of social control throughout French rule in Algeria.[93] This violence was unidirectional. The police could brutalize Algerians, but Algerians had no right to resist or respond.[94] Officers mobilized a variety of excuses to justify violence, logics eerily familiar from today's headlines. The French police excused vicious beatings by saying the accused had "resisted arrest" or justified shootings by saying they had seen the North African suspect reaching for a gun hidden in their pocket.[95] Although the police almost never found the alleged gun, the mere act of reaching down gave permission for the officers' trigger-happy response. When surveillance turned into bloodshed, the colonial administration mobilized to prove the police officer had acted in "legitimate defense," excusing agents' violent excesses.[96]

In Marseille, evidence of violence against North Africans cropped up in postwar police records. In 1949, Talmoudi, president of the AMA of Marseille, brought police brutality to the attention of the Marseille prosecutor in a letter. Talmoudi alleged that two North Africans had been called over by police on the street for an ID check. When they handed over their IDs, "they were beaten, without having pronounced a single word."[97] The police denied the incident and said the two North Africans had been unable to identify their alleged attackers in a lineup. The charges against the officers were dropped. Another letter accused the police of beating up "an Arab" on the street. The Marseille police admitted to the beating but defended themselves by saying the Algerian had been found "dead-drunk" on the sidewalk.[98] In these incidents, and others like them, the police denied or excused their violence and the state backed their assertions.

Encounters between police and Algerians could become dangerous in even the most banal circumstances. In April 1954, just months before the beginning of the Algerian War of Independence, Officer René Bardin returned home from shopping. On his doorstep, Bardin encountered a North African who asked him how to enter the building.[99] Suspicious, Bardin asked why he wanted to get in, and the stranger replied that he was hoping to rest at a friend's apartment. Bardin asked for the man's ID and went inside with the card.[100] When he returned, he told the stranger that he was a police officer and demanded to see his work papers. According to Bardin, the North African man responded by attacking him.[101] Bardin called for help from his European neighbors to "master" the stranger, and while his neighbors held the North African man down, Bardin ran inside to get his gun. As Bardin returned, the man struggled free and fled. Bardin claimed he pursued him, yelling "Stop, police!" and shooting into the air several times to "intimidate" him. Finally, Bardin shot at the stranger, claiming that he intentionally missed. The man fell, and "in his fall, he injured his right leg."[102] By Bardin's own account, then, an off-duty police officer had staged a vigilante arrest and then chased and shot at a man accused of no crime.

But the story is different according to the North African victim, Mohamed S. Born in Constantine, Mohamed had worked as an industrial laborer in Marseille for two years before being placed on sick leave. Mohamed wanted directions to downtown Marseille, since he now had time to explore, and had asked the first person he encountered. The stranger, Bardin, asked for his papers, and Mohamed willingly handed them over. When Bardin returned, however, Mohamed said the man "grabbed me by the throat and called several other people, who threw themselves on me and hit me."[103] Mohamed fell to the ground, frightened and in pain. When he saw the man returning with a gun, Mohamed ran. He heard several shots and felt a shock in his leg, causing him to fall.

When he first gave testimony, Bardin stated that Mohamed had injured his leg by falling. But police arriving on the scene found a bullet in Mohamed's leg, irrefutable evidence contradicting Bardin. Faced with this development, Bardin suddenly claimed that before he went to get his gun, he had seen that the "Arab" had a knife. Bardin insisted that as Mohamed ran away, he was brandishing the knife. The sudden appearance of a knife framed Bardin's actions as self-defense. In fact, the police did find a knife on Mohamed.[104] Two of Bardin's neighbors also confirmed that they saw the "Arab" with a closed pocketknife in his hand *after* he was shot.[105] In his interview, Mohamed also acknowledged that he was carrying a knife. However, at the bottom of the report, the interviewing officer wrote "refused to sign, on excuse that he was injured."[106] The *procès-verbal* is written as if it were an exact transcript of Mohamed's testimony, but with this simple, final sentence, I was reminded of how police officers shape the archive. This interview was not Mohamed's "voice," as much as I wanted it to be. It was simply what an officer wrote down. It could be, as the statement suggests, that Mohamed was too injured to sign. He was indeed hospitalized immediately after being questioned. But it might also hint that Mohamed did not agree with the report's narrative. In his refusal to sign, we might also see an act of resistance.

Surprisingly, the official report from Bardin's superiors seemed to support Mohamed. The report confirmed that Bardin shot Mohamed and criticized Bardin for not stating that he was a police officer before asking for Mohamed's ID.[107] Though police officials blamed Mohamed for starting the fight, they also confirmed that his knife had remained unopened and unused. The report concluded that Mohamed had not behaved aggressively and was shot while fleeing. Bardin was charged with "involuntary injury." In both Marseille and Algiers, the system usually mobilized to support officers, especially when the victim was Algerian. Officials' willingness to believe Mohamed flipped the typical outcome.

The surprising final decision might have been due in part to Bardin's personality. As his superior noted, "Guardian Bardin is a barely passable employee. The last professional notes given to him—10/20—convey a lack of professional consciousness ... Bardin cannot in any way legitimate an arbitrary intervention which, in fact, resulted in an attack on the life and liberty of another."[108] In this categorical reprimand, police authorities confirmed that Bardin had no right to ask for Mohamed's papers, much less shoot him. After this initial investigation, the archival trail ends. Bardin was given a suspension with half salary, and there were whispers of judicial proceedings, but what followed remains unclear. Quite likely, Bardin simply returned to the police force. He would not be the first, nor the last, officer to do so. The postwar period gave Algerians new leverage in their dealings with police. The looming threat of nationalism increased the stakes of police misconduct, and Algerians, as French citizens, had a new language through which to make demands on the French state. Yet the shallow nature of Bardin's punishment shows the limits of police accountability.

In Algiers, the police justified even homicide with "legitimate defense." In 1948, Guardian of the Peace Edouard Benchebana found two "indigènes" sleeping on public stairs. Benchebana tried to make the men move, but one of the sleeping Algerians "played deaf." To encourage him to get up, Benchebana nudged him with his foot.[109] What the report describes as a light push, of course, might have been called a kick by the Algerian on the receiving end. The dozing man, surprised, jumped up and hit the officer with a matraque, a wooden baton associated with Algerians. Benchebana struggled with the man and then "in legitimate defense," took out his gun and shot the Algerian man in the "sinus."[110] In other words, Benchebana shot a man point-blank *in the face* for sleeping on the stairs and reacting to the provocation of an officer. The Algerian, Mohamed ben Ahmed Belkheir, died before reaching the hospital. Belkheir's murder at the hands of a police officer was far from an anomaly in the records of the Algiers police.

The violence unleashed against Algerians in Algiers was born of shared space and unequal power, a dangerous intimacy. A little after noon on July 23, 1948, off-duty Guardian of the Peace Julien Dazard left his house to buy a newspaper. While ambling along, a stray ball from a group of "Muslim youths" playing nearby arced over and hit Dazard in the face. Dazard tried to seize the offending toy, but the boys resisted and scattered up into the "Little Casbah" of El Hamma. Dazard took off in pursuit, signaling to his neighbor and fellow police officer, Gabriel Bultel, seated on his balcony, to come help. Dazard took off after his "young aggressors," as the report put it, but encountered a group of Algerian adults on the stairs up to Boulevard Cervantes who "advanced towards him to do him harm."[111] The police officer's next actions revealed the real aggressor. Citing the ominous crowd of Algerians on the stairs, Dazard took out his pistol to "intimidate" the crowd. Dazard claimed to have been on his way to buy a newspaper while off-duty. Why, then, did he have a gun in his pocket? Dazard said his gun did not sufficiently frighten the Algerians, and as they advanced toward him trying to grab his weapon, he fired into the crowd, hitting one man in the hand. Officer Bultel attempted to follow Dazard up the stairs when he heard the gunshot but was blocked by another group of "Muslims" who hit him with a baton and threw rocks. Forced to retreat, Bultel telephoned for backup.[112]

The man Dazard shot, however, recounted a very different version of events. Aloui B. was a thirty-three-year-old manager at the Transatlantic Company, a respectable middle-class job. Interviewed by the police, Aloui said that he had seen a European man advancing toward the children, by all appearances drunk. Aloui insisted that he was unaware that Dazard was a police officer and explained that Dazard had ordered him to put his hands up, but then immediately fired when Aloui complied. According to Aloui, the injury to his hand occurred when Dazard shot him as he disarmed the drunk officer. Aloui, along with another "coreligionnaire," brought Dazard into the station, as well as turning over the gun they had pulled out of his hands.

Faced with an embarrassing incident, in which an off-duty and perhaps drunk officer attacked a group of schoolchildren and their parents, the police administration mobilized to downplay the event. The report, for example, notes that Dazard was sent to get bloodwork to "cut short" Aloui's allegations of drunkenness.[113] Police authorities carefully wrote Dazard's version of events into the official record, adding justifications for his every misstep. The report evoked a "threat" from the Algerians and insisted that Dazard had warned his "aggressors" that he would shoot. Though the case has no clear resolution within the archival record, the official reaction speaks to the police institution's willingness to protect officers over civilians.

This tense moment of conflict illustrates a spatial problem at the crux of policing Algerians. Dazard and Bultel, both European officers, lived in El Hamma near the "Little Casbah," a working-class Algerian enclave adjacent to the Muslim cemetery. Dazard could hardly have been surprised to see children in the street, running on the wide boulevard that offered an inviting playing field.[114] How could an innocently misdirected ball, or even a maliciously aimed ball, lead to gunshots? Would Dazard have pulled a gun on European parents who rushed to defend the right of their children to play? The answer is almost certainly no. Dazard took out his gun because he saw the crowd of Algerian adults as a threat. Whereas misbehaving European children might have been reported to a parent, with Algerians, colonial racism led to violence. Dazard's reaction to an incident that started with children at play shows the underlying police, and European, assumption of who owned public space in Algiers. Algerians who dared to use urban space on their own terms, who protected their children's right to the city, were deemed hostile, and containing them meant police officers were acting in "legitimate defense."

If police violence became more public in the postwar, critics also became more vocal about denouncing police abuse. In the Communist newspaper, *La Liberté*, full sections were dedicated to exposés on police brutality toward French Communists and ordinary Algerians. In a story from 1951 titled "The Scandalous Abuses of the Algiers Police," the paper railed against the police for invading a villa housing ten Algerian families. The article accused the police of conducting this intrusive raid without a search warrant or any evidence of criminal activity.[115] Other articles referred to police as "uniformed killers" or charged officers with using torture.[116] Harsher censorship regimes typically kept Arabic-language newspapers silent on the police, but after the war, even this seemed to change. In 1948, for example, *El Maghreb el Arabi* printed an article criticizing an unwarranted police raid on their office.[117] The reports on police repression in Algiers reflected more assertive police efforts to counteract nationalist organizing, but also perhaps a growing spirit of protest among Algerian dissidents.

The patterns of police violence in both Marseille and Algiers did not begin after World War II. Violence was essential to French conquest of Algeria, an endeavor that for all the gloss of "civilizational" goals remains a story of military conquest, expropriated land, and exploited labor and resources. A preexisting system of state violence protected the right of the police to harm Algerians without question and without consequences. As the case of Dazard shows, the police sprang into action to protect their own. The violence evidenced in these stories represented both a continuation and an escalation of the violence that regularly appeared in police reports and personnel dossiers earlier in the twentieth century. Paradoxically, however, what makes the postwar moment unique is also the limit of violence. Algerians could file grievances, could demand justice, even if justice did not always come. Officers could be punished for excesses, even if punishment rarely amounted to more than an administrative slap on the wrist. This violence was not yet the violence the police would deploy during the Algerian War of Independence. Then, police would torture and slaughter Algerians under direct orders from the state. But before the war, a relationship of exchange, albeit a tense and restricted one, still existed between police and policed.

After World War II, colonized peoples around the world demanded change. The tide of anticolonialism swept Algeria along with it. As political leaders in France grappled with the implications of shifting global discourses on colonialism, police officers, too, had to respond to the change. Reiterating old colonial narratives, police in both Marseille and Algiers insisted that Algerians were criminals, a population that required close policing and strict rules. Police certitude of Algerian criminality only deepened as fears of Algerian nationalism took root. Policing nationalism resembled the policing of other political groups, but the police adopted an increasingly capacious understanding of what "politics" meant when it came to Algerians. In the postwar, the police forces of Marseille and Algiers faced an impossible task of repressing nationalist organizing while also upholding a narrative of "color-blind" republican justice. As the police searched for smuggled guns, reinforced discourses of Algerian danger with statistics, and searched for subversion in every song, they created an increasingly adversarial and violent relationship with Algerians. In tracking nationalism, the police relied on their spatial understanding of Algerian urban life. Their intimate policing of Algerian daily life, in pursuit of nationalism, made police an unavoidable and dangerous presence in the lives of Algerians in Marseille and Algiers. Yet as policing became more interventionist, Algerian resistance to police intrusion also became more vocal.

As dawn broke on November 1, 1954, members of the Front de Libération Nationale (FLN) launched a series of attacks across Algeria. This coordinated assault catapulted smoldering conflict into an all-out war for Algerian independence. In the following years, the FLN wrenched control of the Algerian nationalist movement from competitors and unified, at times violently, the Algerian people behind a singular independence struggle. Already attempting to extricate themselves from a failed war of decolonization in Indochina, some French politicians were less than eager to begin another war. Algeria's European population, however, refused to cede, and the French government launched a bloody response to the FLN offensive. The Algerian War of Independence, infamous for its brutal cycle of terror and torture, raged from 1954 to 1962, paving the way for the collapse of the French Fourth Republic and costing tens of thousands of lives.

Police relationships to Algerians, in Marseille and Algiers, in Algeria and France, morphed during the war. If scholars often debate the distinction between the military and the police, even the facade of distinction disappeared during this war.[118] In Algeria, police officers became part of the military, serving alongside soldiers in operations targeting the FLN. In Marseille, too, the police launched vicious campaigns of repression against Algerian nationalists.[119] This violence and militarism had a history. In the interwar period, the police labeled Algerians as inherent criminals. During World War II, this "criminal" population was painted as disloyal, the internal enemies of France. Having built an idea of enemy Algerians, the postwar police politicized this same racialized group, seeing them as a threat to French sovereignty. Racial practices of policing Algerians created precedents for police control over even the most mundane, intimate aspects of Algerian life. This omnipresent policing, justified by the belief that all aspects of Algerian life could be political and that all Algerians were inherently criminal, fed the extremes of policing that became commonplace during the Algerian War of Independence. As the war raged on, the police and French army deployed existing ideas of racialized urban space to repress the North African populations they saw as universally nationalist and ubiquitously dangerous.

Epilogue

After World War II, the dynamics of race and space began to change in Marseille and Algiers, as urban planners tried to raze "dangerous" North African neighborhoods and patterns of North African residency shifted. In 1949, the Algiers municipal council decided to demolish 462 *mauresque* homes in the upper Casbah, deemed unfit for residency. The Defense of the Casbah Committee, run by residents, protested that the decision had been made without considering the preservation of historic homes or providing alternate housing for affected homeowners.[1] The municipal council eventually backtracked, offering to grant loans to homeowners to pay for repairs and avoid demolition. Nonetheless, the council's message was clear - the Casbah needed to be modernized. Faced with overcrowded, dilapidated housing stock in the Casbah, many Algerians instead began to settle in the bidonvilles that had sprung up around the city.[2]

A similar shift occurred in Marseille. In 1952, local municipal councilors voted for the demolition of the "Arab quarters" near Place Jules Guesde, including Rue des Chapeliers and adjacent streets. The council sought to combat the "insalubrity" of the neighborhood but promised that the residents would be given new housing.[3] Despite opposition from residents, the project proceeded.[4] Today, the once-vacant lot "behind the Bourse" houses a shopping mall and the Marseille city museum. Vibrant shops and noisy crowds no longer fill Rue des Chapeliers. Instead, the "Casbah" of Marseille is a truncated, deserted alley. As North Africans continued to make a home in Marseille in the 1950s and 1960s, many families moved instead to public housing in the quartiers nord.[5]

As the geography of North African life changed in the 1950s, police adapted techniques that had been piloted in the "Casbahs." Through decades of discriminatory policing, the streets of the Casbah and around Rue des Chapeliers had been marked as North African and therefore as spaces of delinquency and danger. Officers did arrest some thieves, censure some traffickers, and break up some fights. But just as important as the reality of crime was the police certitude of its existence in these racialized spaces. By demarcating and racializing space, the French police created repressive methods for controlling North African bodies while proclaiming to uphold universalist ideals of justice. In constructing the Algerian criminal, through arrests, statistics, and reports, police officers in both Marseille and Algiers contributed to an ongoing process of racialization.

The policing of North Africans in Marseille and Algiers operated in a connected Mediterranean world, a web within which people and strategies of policing circulated. Yet policing North Africans in these two cities often looked different. In Algiers, the sheer number of Algerians and the population density of the Casbah prevented the police from relying on the raids favored in Marseille. In Marseille, the police could not deploy the indigénat code to bolster their power over Algerians. Differences like these illustrate the importance of understanding urban policing in context. In assuming that police discrimination looks the same in all places, we miss how relationships of violence and cooperation were personal or locally determined.

For all their differences, however, the stories of policing North Africans in Marseille and Algiers can be startlingly similar. Police officers in both cities operated with a shared understanding of North African criminality, a supposedly inherent tendency toward theft, violence, and jealousy. These stereotypes, which circulated throughout the French Empire and particularly within this Mediterranean network, had real costs. In both cities, police officers also served a complex variety of roles in North Africans' lives. Police could be violent intruders, breaching homes, roughing up suspects, and defending a racist colonial order. At times, however, officers could also be called upon by North Africans for protection, mediation, or aid.

The relationship between police officers and Algerians in Marseille and Algiers shifted in the decades between World War I and the Algerian War of Independence. In the interwar period, the police built a system of surveillance aimed at controlling Algerian mobility. In both cities, officers focused on defining and delineating "North African" neighborhoods, locating Algerian bodies in the Casbah in Algiers and behind the Bourse in Marseille. During World War II, the tensions of war altered policing. Tracking laborers, monitoring German propaganda, or chasing black-market profiteers, the police increasingly saw all

Algerians as "anti-French." In the postwar, policing again adapted in response to Algerian nationalism. In their efforts to repress nationalism, officers layered a political identity onto the racialized, colonial category of "Algerian." Police now perceived the spaces of Algerian life as dangerous not just because of delinquency, but because officers believed that in the depths of the Casbah and in the heart of Rue des Chapeliers lurked nationalists eager to overthrow French rule.

These changes, however, were only possible because of what remained constant. Between 1918 and 1954, sweeping political and juridical changes transformed the experience of immigration, political participation, and labor for Algerians. France and Algeria and their relationship to each other morphed in response to global forces of war and whispers of decolonization. The postwar could have been a moment of change. Instead, old racial categories hardened. Police officers continued to exoticize and villainize the spaces of North African sociability, and they continued to emphasize the inborn criminality of North Africans themselves. Despite broader social changes, policing still relied on a consensus among police officials and officers that North Africans were dangerous and required special surveillance. By labeling North Africans as others, colonial discrimination permitted policing that refused North Africans' humanity and denied their inclusion in an imagined French nation.

Policing the Algerian War

On July 24, 1953, the *Ville d'Alger* cut through the crisp waves of the Mediterranean. As generations of ferries had, it traveled from Marseille to Algiers, shuttling between metropole and colony. The watery world of the French Mediterranean had been built with boats like this, but this ferry was remarkable not for the workers or merchandise it carried, but the bodies concealed in its hold. On July 14, Algerian nationalists had led an anticolonial march through Paris.[6] Though initially peaceful, the crowd of Algerians clashed with police and fights broke out. In the end, police killed at least seven Algerians and injured dozens more. The French government quickly emphasized police injuries and alleged Algerian aggression, directing attention away from gratuitous police violence.[7] In the following days, the bodies of the murdered Algerians were quietly transported to Marseille and loaded on the *Ville d'Alger* to be returned to Algeria for burial. The ferry docked in Algiers on July 25, met by crowds of mourners who held an impromptu vigil.[8] Once again, Marseille and Algiers linked metropole and colony, this time in a tragedy that pitted police violence against anticolonial mobilization.

In November of the following year, the Front de Libération Nationale (FLN) launched a series of coordinated attacks across Algeria, opening an armed struggle against French colonial rule.[9] The French government refused to acknowledge the brutal conflict as a war, instead referring to the "events" in Algeria. The power of the Algerian police ratcheted up in 1955, when the French government declared a state of emergency in Algeria. This granted authorities extraordinary power to use police operations as part of a larger military strategy.[10] The French government also began to send police officers from the metropole to address the Algerian "problem." Metropolitan officers participated in local police duties, including military operations, forced resettlement of Algerian civilians, and torture.[11] Frantz Fanon reflected on the psychological impacts of this new role in *The Wretched of the Earth*, discussing a police officer who sought treatment for violent outbursts against his family. Pushed by Fanon, the officer admitted that his troubles began during the "events" in Algeria when his job shifted from catching criminals to torturing suspected FLN militants.[12] Not coincidentally, FLN attacks often targeted police, especially Algerian officers.[13]

The distinction between police officers and soldiers also slipped in the metropole. By 1958, the FLN had declared a "second front" in France, and de Gaulle responded by granting Parisian Prefect of Police Maurice Papon a "blank check" for repression.[14] Police officers became the front-line soldiers in the battle against the FLN.[15] Police violence in the metropole appears most starkly in the infamous massacre of Algerians in Paris on October 17, 1961. On this night, the police attacked Algerians marching to protest the curfew imposed on them.[16] Though accounts differ on the death toll, even conservative estimates suggest that the Parisian police killed dozens of Algerians, allegedly dumping their bodies in the Seine. In Marseille, too, the local government turned to the police to repress FLN operatives.

The militarization of the police during the Algerian War of Independence changed the form and function of policing. Although the relationship between the police and North Africans had always been influenced by racialized colonial power structures, there had been a real distinction between military and police in both Marseille and Algiers. And if police violence was ubiquitous, it was not unrestrained. Particularly after World War II, the police navigated the contradiction of needing to appear to treat Algerians like any other French citizens, while also being asked to use authoritarian tactics to quash anticolonial organizing. Despite broad impunity and clear evidence of discriminatory practices, the police still had checks on their power, including formal resistance from Algerians themselves. During the war, these limits evaporated.

The rapid militarization of the police during the Algerian War was a significant transformation, but it did not happen without context. The relationship between police officers and Algerians had always been predicated on unequal power. Police officers had a monopoly on violence, one that they wielded to defend the colonial status quo in both metropole and colony. For decades, French police officers engaged with discourses that presented Algerians, and specifically Algerian men, as intrinsically criminal. By imagining Algerians as an inherent, collective threat, all while denying their political agency, the police created precedents for their wartime treatment of Algerians as at once dangerous rebels and gullible masses. The violence of the war, too, had precedents. Police officers had routinely profiled, targeted, and physically assaulted Algerians. Critics in mainland France claimed that torture was a tactic as old as the Algerian police itself.[17] Understanding the history of policing North Africans prior to the Algerian War of Independence, then, allows us to see policing at a crossroads, the power and limitation of controlling a colonial situation on the brink of collapse.

Colonial Legacies

The Algerian War of Independence is not the end of the story. The signing of the Evian Accords in 1962 launched unprecedented waves of migration. In the aftermath, nearly all of Algeria's more than one million European residents left, most to France. As always, many of these migrants arrived in France via Marseille.[18] Among the exodus were police officers. The "returning" officers, both Europeans and Algerians, joined police units throughout the south of France, some of them settling in Marseille.[19] Repatriated officers' personnel files ended up in the departmental archives of the Bouches-du-Rhône, creating a fragmentary but telling record. Their presence in French police forces would be just one legacy of colonial policing in metropolitan France.

Algerian immigration to France also increased, buoyed by the freedom of circulation guaranteed in the Evian Accords. Scholars often describe the 1960s and 1970s as a second era of Algerian immigration, in which migrants began to put down roots in France.[20] Marseille's North African population, already substantial, swelled.[21] This increase in Algerian immigration was met with aggression. Changing labor markets, racism steeped in colonial tropes, and bitter memories of the Algerian War created hostility toward North Africans.[22] The tensions reached a breaking point in Marseille in August 1973, after a mentally-ill Algerian man fatally stabbed a bus driver and injured several passengers. Some French residents retaliated by forming vigilante mobs that murdered ten Algerians unconnected to the original crime.[23] The editor of Marseille's right-wing paper, *Le Méridional*, shrieked:

> We have had enough! Enough Algerian thieves, enough Algerian hooligans, enough swaggering Algerians, enough Algerian troublemakers, enough crazy Algerians, enough Algerian killers . . . One of these days,

we must employ the CRS, the *gardes mobiles*, the police dogs to destroy the Casbahs of Marseille.[24]

This racist rant reproduced the same tropes of Algerian criminality that had been prevalent for decades, evoking the danger of Marseille's "Casbah." The attacks on Algerians, in Marseille and elsewhere in France, spurred the Algerian government to suspend immigration to France in protest.[25] These patterns of mobility, violence, and policing reflect the longevity of the colonial practices explored in this book.

Across the Mediterranean, the Algerian police deny any French influence. In the National Police Museum in El Biar, posters narrate the history of policing in Algeria dating back to the Almoravid dynasty. But the retelling skips directly from a poster on the Ottoman Beyliks to one detailing the postindependence police and its origins among FLN fighters. Notably absent, of course, are the French. Despite this silence, the legacy of more than a hundred years of French policing is undeniable. To this day, Algeria has a gendarmerie and a Sûreté, a distinctly French structural model. It is also likely that there was continuity in police personnel, although this information is, perhaps deliberately, difficult to obtain. As I watched protestors fill the street beneath my apartment in Algiers during the Hirak revolution in 2019, I saw how questions of who the Algerian police serve—the people or the "Power"—continue to loom large.

When I began this research in 2015, policing dominated American headlines. Following the murders of Rekia Boyd, Eric Garner, Michael Brown, Freddie Gray, and too many others, the Black Lives Matter movement challenged Americans to rethink policing. These same conversations again came to the fore following an extraordinary and yet all too ordinary summer of police violence against African Americans in 2020. But scandals of police brutality have preoccupied France, too. French protestors have rallied since 2016 for "Justice for Adama" and since 2017 for "Justice for Théo." Leaders of these movements have forced the French public to reckon with the incomplete nature of France's universalist republican model.[26] French minority populations, especially those issuing from postcolonial migration, are disproportionately affected by the criminal justice system.[27] Police discrimination in France today is often coded through a language of dress and space, with officers describing targets as youths from the *banlieues*.[28] This spatial pattern of racialization, as we have seen, was already commonplace in colonial police tactics more than seventy years earlier.

The legacies of colonial policing were clear, too, on June 27, 2023, when a police officer shot and killed seventeen-year-old Nahel Merzouk during a traffic stop in Nanterre, France. Protests erupted across France, and almost immediately, press coverage zeroed in on "rioting" protestors, rather than the actions of the officer. In a public statement the day after the shooting, President Emmanuel Macron described Nahel's death as "inexcusable" and "inexplicable." But his characterization of Nahel's murder as a tragedy without explanation erased a long history of colonial racism in French policing. This was not an anomaly, but part of a heartbreakingly familiar cycle. As French activists have been screaming until their lungs can take no more, police racism kills. In encounters with North Africans and their descendants living on the urban periphery, the French police today recycle the same colonial tactics of omnipresent surveillance and blanket criminalization.

Police accountability remains just as vital today as it was to North African colonial subjects in the twentieth-century French Empire. To understand police discrimination, we must recognize the historical dynamics that shaped the police as an institution.[29] The French colonial state, and its representatives, interacted with North Africans with a systemic understanding of this population as criminal, backward, and violent. Individual police officers operated within a legal apparatus that disciplined North Africans differently and in a carceral world designed to uphold French imperial power. Police forces are the products of the societies that create them, and police violence cannot be reduced to "bad apples" in a good system.

But there are limits to studying the police *only* as an institution. In February 1946, an Algerian woman named Houria wrote a desperate letter to the prefect of Algiers. In fluent, if somewhat misspelled, French, Houria explained that her husband beat her and complained that this was the second letter she had written to authorities, with no result. Employing the informal *tu* and speaking directly to the police services that had failed to help her, she cried, "It's you who makes the law—come get him."[30] Houria's point was simple. Since police officers enforced the law, it was they who made it a reality. The stories in this book show how right she was. Police embodied the French state, but they also inflected colonial power with their own choices.

By looking at the quotidian in two Mediterranean cities, I offer an analysis of the social relations of policing. I highlight the choices, center the daily interactions, and sit in the uncomfortable truth that Algerians feared, needed, respected, and hated police officers and that police officers could be racist, helpful, sadistic, and idealistic. These complicated realities are reflective of humanity. Try as we might to reduce history to dialectics and theories, generalizations and trends, people tend to defy our attempts to classify and contain them. By focusing on specific urban spaces and daily-level choices, we can see how discrimination was built into routine practices of policing. In patrols and tactics that merged ideas of race, space, and criminality, police officers on their beats in Marseille and Algiers helped to define and produce criminal North Africans. There is an opportunity in paying attention to how racialized policing operated historically in particular places. In doing so, we learn that policing as we know it today is not inevitable, but a product of historical currents, of change over time, and of colonial imperatives. It can also, therefore, be reimagined.

Notes

INTRODUCTION

1. In this case, customs searches were carried out by the Brigade de la Surveillance du Territoire under the jurisdiction of Marseille's central police commissioner.

2. ADBR. 148 W 193. Commissaire Divisionnaire à M. l'Inspecteur Général pour le 9eme Région Militaire. "Objet: Examen de situation du nommé C. Saïd." April 28, 1953.

3. These numbers are from a specific report, but there are dozens, perhaps hundreds of similar reports. ADBR. 150 W 160. Commissaire de Police à M. le Commissaire Central. "Objet: Opérations de police . . . du quartier de la rue des Chapeliers." April 25, 1947.

4. *Kabyle* denotes someone from the Kabylia region of Algeria, including the Babor mountain range where Saïd was born. Kabyle natives typically spoke Amazigh, and French colonial policy at times celebrated the Kaybles as more civilized than the Arab majority. On the "Kabyle myth": Patricia Lorcin, *Imperial Identities: Stereotyping, Prejudice and Race in Colonial Algeria* (I. B. Tauris, 1999).

5. These are all spaces and forms of policing explored in this book.

6. For example, Sheila Crane has written about the parallels between Marseille and Algiers for French architects. Sheila Crane, "On the Edge: The Internal Frontiers of Architecture in Algiers/Marseille," *Journal of Architecture* 16, no. 6 (2011): 941–973.

7. On Paris: Danielle Beaujon, "Policing Colonial Migrants: The Brigade Nord-Africaine in Paris, 1923–1944," *French Historical Studies* 42, no. 4 (2019): 655–680; Emmanuel Blanchard, *La police parisienne et les Algériens (1944–1962)* (Nouveau Monde, 2011); Amit Prakash, "Colonial Techniques in the Imperial Capital: The Prefecture of Police and the Surveillance of North Africans in Paris, 1925–circa 1970," *French Historical Studies* 36, no 3 (2013): 479–510; Amit Prakash, *Empire on the Seine: The Policing of North Africans in Paris, 1925–1975* (Oxford University Press, 2022); Clifford Rosenberg, *Policing Paris: The Origins of Modern Immigration Control Between the Wars* (Cornell University Press, 2018). On Lyon: Azouz Begag, *Place du Pont, ou la médina de Lyon* (Autrement, 1997); Geneviève Massard-Guilbaud, *Des Algériens à Lyon: De La Grande Guerre au Front Populaire* (L'Harmattan, 1995).

8. The North African population of Marseille rarely constituted more than 3 percent of the city's population.

9. On this process: Didier Guignard, *1871: Algérie sous séquestre* (CNRS, 2023).

10. See David Prochaska, *Making Algeria French: Colonialism in Bône, 1870–1920* (Cambridge University Press, 1990); Jennifer Sessions, *By Sword and Plow: France and the Conquest of Algeria* (Cornell University Press, 2015).

11. Algerians were never more than one-third of the population of Algiers between 1920 and 1940. Mahfoud Kaddache, *La vie politique à Alger de 1919 à 1939* (SNED, 1970), 11.

12. *Communes de plein exercise* were Algerian municipalities with a majority European population. In these areas, French legal and administrative systems operated as they did in the metropole.

13. The Jewish population of Algiers had lived in Algeria for centuries prior to French conquest. Naturalization did not preclude virulent antisemitism in Algeria, but it did assimilate local Jews toward whiteness and give them privileged access to education, public employment, and civil rights. See Sessions, *By Sword and by Plow*, 321; Michael

Laskier, *North African Jewry in the Twentieth Century: The Jews of Morocco, Tunisia, and Algeria* (New York University Press, 1994), 28; Ethan Katz, *The Burdens of Brotherhood: Jews and Muslims from North Africa to France* (Harvard University Press, 2015).

14. On whiteness in Algeria: Charlotte Legg, *The New White Race: Settler Colonialism and the Press in French Algeria, 1860–1914* (University of Nebraska Press, 2021); Yuval Tal, "The 'Latin' Melting Pot: Ethnorepublican Thinking and Immigrant Assimilation in and Through Colonial Algeria," *French Historical Studies* 44, no. 1 (2021): 85–118.

15. Algerians were French nationals, but only a small group obtained citizenship until after World War II.

16. On the indigénat: Olivier Le Cour Grandmaison, *De l'indigénat: Anatomie d'un "monstre" juridique; Le droit colonial en Algérie et dans l'Empire Francais* (Zones, 2010); Gregory Mann, "What Was the Indigénat? The 'Empire of Law' in French West Africa," *Journal of African History* 50, no. 3 (2009): 331–353; Emmanuelle Saada, "La loi, le droit et l'indigène," *Droits* 43 (2006): 165–190; Judith Surkis, *Sex, Law, and Sovereignty in French Algeria, 1830–1930* (Cornell University Press, 2019).

17. Vincent Milliot, Emmanuel Blanchard, Vincent Denis, and Arnaud-Dominique Houte, eds., *Histoire des polices en France: Des guerres de religion à nos jours* (Belin, 2020), 416.

18. On Algerian immigration: Emmanuel Blanchard, *Histoire de l'immigration algérienne en France* (La Découverte, 2018); Neil MacMaster, *Colonial Migrants and Racism: Algerians in France, 1900–62* (Palgrave Macmillan, 1997); Abdelmalek Sayad, *La double absence: Des illusions de l'émigré aux souffrances de l'immigré* (Seuil, 1999).

19. This number comes from postwar government reports on the conditions of North African life in France. AN. F 60 202. Rapport du Haut Comité Méditerranéen. "Les Nord-Africains en France." March 1937.

20. Blanchard, *Histoire de l'immigration algérienne en France*, 30; Mary Lewis, *Boundaries of the Republic: Migrant Rights and the Limits of Universalism in France, 1918–1940* (Stanford University Press, 2007), 191–192.

21. Yaël Simpson Fletcher, "'Capital of the Colonies': Real and Imagined Boundaries Between Metropole and Empire in 1920s Marseilles," in *Imperial Cities: Landscape, Display and Identity*, ed. Felix Driver and David Gilbert (Manchester University Press, 1999).

22. Only a few hundred migrants came from France's protectorates in Morocco and Tunisia. AN. 20010216 233. Chef de la Police Spéciale, Sallet à M. Directeur des RG. "A/s de la surveillance des Nords Africains." June 11, 1937.

23. See Jean-Marc Berlière, *Le monde des polices en France: XIXe-XXe siècles* (Complexe, 1996).

24. Simon Kitson, for example, describes a *"guerre des police"* in Marseille caused by personal tensions between the heads of branches. Simon Kitson, *Police and Politics in Marseille: 1936–1945* (Brill, 2014), xv.

25. ANOM. 1 F 443. Commissaire Central à M. le Maire. April 18, 1920. The census suggests a smaller total population of 205,000 in 1921. Kaddache, *La Vie Politique à Alger*, 11.

26. BWA. *Bulletin Municipal Officiel de la Ville d'Alger*. May 25, 1928.

27. On policing slavery: Gene Ogle, *Policing Saint Domingue: Race, Violence, and Honor in an Old Regime Colony* (University of Pennsylvania, 2003); Hurard Bellance, *La police des Noirs en Amérique (Martinique, Guadeloupe, Guyane, Saint-Domingue) et en France aux XVIIe et XVIIIe siècles* (Ibis Rouge, 2011).

28. Malcolm Anderson, *In Thrall to Political Change: Police and Gendarmerie in France* (Oxford University Press, 2011); Berlière, *Le monde des polices*; Jean-Marc Berlière and René Lévy, *Histoire des polices en France: De l'Ancien Régime à nos jours* (Nouveau Monde, 2011).

29. Milliot et al., *Histoire des polices en France*, 396, 422.

30. Stéphane Beaud and Michel Pialoux, *Violences urbaines, violence sociale: Genèse des nouvelles classes dangereuses* (Fayard, 2003).

31. On policing anarchism in nineteenth-century France: John Merriman, *Ballad of the Anarchist Bandits: The Crime Spree That Gripped Belle Époque Paris* (Nation Books, 2017). On policing communism: Frédéric Charpier, *Les RG et le Parti Communiste: Un combat sans merci dans la guerre froide* (Plon, 2000). On Vichy: Kitson, *Police and Politics in Marseille*; Jean-Marc Berlière and Laurent Chabrun, *Les policiers français sous l'Occupation: D'après les archives inédites de l'épuration* (Perrin, 2001).

32. On Italian violence in Marseille: Céline Regnard-Drouot, *Marseille la violente: Criminalité, industrialisation et société (1851–1914)* (Presses Universitaires de Rennes, 2009), chap. VI.

33. Indeed, Samuel Kalman argues that the colonial police in Algeria almost exclusively investigated crimes with European victims. Samuel Kalman, *Law, Order, and Empire: Policing and Crime in Colonial Algeria, 1870–1954* (Cornell University Press, 2024).

34. I found examples of this racial division of crime data in Algiers from the 1930s to the 1950s, although in the 1940s it sometimes lapsed. ANOM, 1F series.

35. There is a vast literature on political policing, some cited previously.

36. On legibility: James C. Scott, *Seeing Like a State: How Certain Schemes to Improve the Human Condition Have Failed* (Yale University Press, 1998).

37. A similar process occurred in West Africa. Kathleen Keller, *Colonial Suspects: Suspicion, Imperial Rule, and Colonial Society in Interwar French West Africa* (University of Nebraska Press, 2018).

38. I do not discuss the policing of European populations in Marseille and Algiers, except as a contrast to the primary North African case study.

39. On accountability: David Arnold, *Police Power and Colonial Rule, Madras 1859–1947* (Oxford University Press, 1986). On capitalism and colonial policing: Martin Thomas, *Violence and Colonial Order: Police, Workers and Protest in the European Colonial Empires, 1918–1940* (Cambridge University Press, 2012).

40. The notable exception is Samuel Kalman, whose book offers an overview of policing in Algeria, with an emphasis on politics. Kalman, *Law, Order, and Empire*. See also Thomas, *Violence and Colonial Order*, chap. 4.

41. For example: Beaujon, "Policing Colonial Migrants"; Blanchard, *La police parisienne et les Algériens*; Prakash, *Empire on the Seine*; Rosenberg, *Policing Paris*.

42. For example: Julian Go, *Policing Empires: Militarization, Race, and the Imperial Boomerang in Britain and the US* (Oxford University Press, 2023); Georgina Sinclair and Chris A. Williams, "'Home and Away': The Cross-Fertilisation between 'Colonial' and 'British' Policing, 1921–85," *Journal of Imperial and Commonwealth History* 35, no. 2 (2007): 221–238.

43. Egon Bittner, *The Functions of the Police in Modern Society: A Review of Background Factors, Current Practices, and Possible Role Models* (Oelgeschlager, Gunn & Hain, 1979), 40.

44. Micol Seigel, *Violence Work: State Power and the Limits of Police* (Duke University Press, 2018).

45. *Tu* is the French informal second person, used to address subordinates or friends. The police would normally be expected to use the respectful *vous* but often called Algerians *tu* as an insult or assertion of power.

46. Joan Mars, *Deadly Force, Colonialism, and the Rule of Law: Police Violence in Guyana* (Greenwood, 2002).

47. Noel A. Cazenave, *Killing African Americans: Police and Vigilante Violence as a Racial Control Mechanism* (Routledge, 2018).

48. For example: Michelle Alexander, *The New Jim Crow: Mass Incarceration in the Age of Colorblindness* (New Press, 2010); Adam Malka, *The Men of Mobtown: Policing Baltimore in the Age of Slavery and Emancipation* (University of North Carolina Press, 2018).

49. Steven Pierce and Anupama Rao, eds., *Discipline and the Other Body: Correction, Corporeality, Colonialism* (Duke University Press, 2006).

50. For example: David Anderson, *Histories of the Hanged: Britain's Dirty War in Kenya and the End of Empire* (Phoenix, 2006); Caroline Elkins, *Imperial Reckoning: The Untold Story of Britain's Gulag in Kenya* (Henry Holt, 2006).

51. Blanchard refers to the "*chèque en blanc*" metaphorically issued to the French police during the Algerian War, allowing them to use any means necessary to suppress Algerian nationalism in Paris. See Blanchard, *La police parisienne et les Algériens*, chap. 11.

52. See Victor Román Mendoza, *Metroimperial Intimacies: Fantasy, Racial-Sexual Governance, and the Philippines in U.S. Imperialism, 1899–1913* (Duke University Press, 2015); Emmanuelle Saada, *Les enfants de la colonie: Les métis de l'empire français entre sujétion et citoyenneté* (La Découverte, 2007); Ann Laura Stoler, ed., *Haunted by Empire: Geographies of Intimacy in North American History* (Duke University Press, 2006); Ann Laura Stoler, *Carnal Knowledge and Imperial Power: Race and the Intimate in Colonial Rule* (University of California Press, 2002).

53. Jennifer Boittin has explored policing and intimacy in empire, but her definition of intimacy is focused on passion, the key theoretical framework of her project. Jennifer Anne Boittin, *Undesirable: Passionate Mobility and Women's Defiance of French Colonial Policing, 1919–1952* (University of Chicago Press, 2022).

54. Kathryn Takabvirwa similarly focuses on the intimacy of policing as "familiarity," and I take this articulation of closeness from her. Kathryn Takabvirwa, "Citizens in Uniform: Roadblocks and the Policing of Everyday Life in Zimbabwe," *American Ethnologist* 50, no. 2 (2023): 236–246.

55. As Alex Vitale, among many others, argues, police organizations have never been primarily concerned with crime. Alex S. Vitale, *The End of Policing* (Verso, 2021).

56. Ilana Feldman, *Police Encounters: Security and Surveillance in Gaza under Egyptian Rule* (Stanford University Press, 2015), 13.

57. These other colonial migrants remained numerically much smaller than the North African population of both Marseille and Algiers. A distinct bureau surveilled West African and Indochinese migrants—the Service de Contrôle et d'Assistance en France des Indigènes des Colonies (CAI). My focus on North Africans, then, as opposed to a larger story of colonial surveillance, reflects the divisions of the French colonial state. On the CAI see Vincent Bollenot, "Maintenir l'ordre impérial en métropole: Le Service de Contrôle et d'Assistance en France des Indigènes des Colonies (1915–1945)" (PhD diss., Université de Paris I Panthéon Sorbonne, 2022). On West Africans in France: Jennifer Boittin, *Colonial Metropolis: The Urban Grounds of Anti-Imperialism and Feminism in Interwar Paris* (University of Nebraska Press, 2010); Jennifer Boittin, "The Militant Black Men of Marseille and Paris, 1927–1937," in *Black France/France Noire: The History and Politics of Blackness*, ed. Tricia Keaton, T. Denean Sharpley-Whiting, and Tyler Stovall (Duke University Press, 2012); Philippe Dewitte, *Les mouvements nègres en France, 1919–1939* (L'Harmattan, 1985), 26; Sylvain Pattieu, "Souteneurs noirs à Marseille, 1918–1921: Contribution à l'histoire de la minorité noire en France," *Annales: Histoire, Sciences Sociales* 64, no. 6 (2009): 1361–1386.

58. For example: Angela Hattery and Earl Smith, *Policing Black Bodies: How Black Lives Are Surveilled and How to Work for Change* (Rowman & Littlefield, 2017); Khalil Muhammad, *The Condemnation of Blackness: Race, Crime, and the Making of Modern Urban America* (Harvard University Press, 2010).

59. For example: Véronique Le Gaoziou and Laurent Mucchielli, *Quand les banlieues brûlent: Retour sur les émeutes de novembre 2005* (La Découverte, 2006); Sebastian Roché, *Le frisson de l'émeute: Violences urbaines et banlieues* (Seuil, 2006).

60. Henri Lefebvre, *The Production of Space* (Blackwell, 1991), 116.

61. Katherine McKittrick, *Demonic Grounds: Black Women and Cartographies of Struggle* (University of Minnesota Press, 2006), xi.

62. On the United States: George Lipsitz, "The Racialization of Space and the Spatialization of Race," *Landscape Architecture* 26 (2007): 10–23; Katherine McKittrick and Clyde Woods, eds., *Black Geographies and the Politics of Place* (South End, 2007); Rashad Shabazz, *Spatializing Blackness: Architectures of Confinement and Black Masculinity in Chicago* (University of Illinois Press, 2015).

63. On segregation: Carl Nightingale, *Segregation: A Global History of Divided Cities* (University of Chicago Press, 2012).

64. These "carceral landscapes" are studied in the United States but are largely absent in the French scholarship. For example: Simon Balto, *Occupied Territory: Policing Black Chicago from the Red Summer to Black Power* (University of North Carolina Press, 2019); Shabazz, *Spatializing Blackness*. One exception is Amit Prakash's discussion of police "mapping" of the North African community in Paris's Goutte d'Or neighborhood. Prakash, *Empire on the Seine*.

65. Jodi Rios, *Black Lives and Spatial Matters: Policing Blackness and Practicing Freedom in Suburban St. Louis* (Cornell University Press, 2020).

66. This language of "coding" space comes from Rios, *Black Lives and Spatial Matters*, 2.

67. Arlette Farge makes similar arguments about the allure and risk of judicial archives. Arlette Farge, *Le goût de l'archive* (Seuil, 1989).

68. On the archival "grain": Ann Laura Stoler, *Along the Archival Grain: Epistemic Anxieties and Colonial Common Sense* (Princeton University Press, 2009).

69. Saidiya Hartman, *Lose Your Mother: A Journey along the Atlantic Slave Route* (Farrar, Straus & Giroux, 2007). A similar method is deployed by Marisa Fuentes, *Dispossessed Lives: Enslaved Women, Violence, and the Archive* (University of Pennsylvania Press, 2016).

70. On analysis of spectacular violence: Joshua Cole, *Lethal Provocation: The Constantine Murders and the Politics of French Algeria* (Cornell University Press, 2020); Jim House and Neil MacMaster, *Paris 1961: Algerians, State Terror, and Memory* (Oxford University Press, 2006).

71. For example: Blanchard, *La police parisienne et les Algériens*; Jean-Paul Brunet, *Police contre FLN: Le drame d'octobre 1961* (Flammarion, 1999); House and MacMaster, *Paris, 1961*; Prakash, *Empire on the Seine*. In Algeria: Kalman, *Law, Order and Empire*.

72. Emmanuel Blanchard and Sylvie Thénault, "Quel 'monde du contact'? Pour une histoire sociale de l'Algérie pendant la période coloniale," *Le Mouvement social* 236 (Juillet–Septembre 2011): 3–7.

1. CONTROLLING MEDITERRANEAN MOVEMENT

1. The Arabic word *casbah* (قَصَبَة) can be translated as fort, citadel, or watchtower. In Algiers, casbah means the old town, the equivalent of a *medina* (مدينة) in Morocco or Tunisia.

2. Zeynep Çelik, *Urban Forms and Colonial Confrontations: Algiers under French Rule* (University of California Press, 1997), 28.

3. Zeynep Çelik, "Historic Intersections: The Center of Algiers," in *Walls of Algiers: Narratives of the City Through Text and Image*, ed. Zeynep Çelik, Julia Clancy-Smith, and Frances Terpak (Getty Research Institute, 2009). On "urbicide": Nightingale, *Segregation*, 123.

4. Mahfoud Kaddache, "La Casbah" (unpublished manuscript, Les Glycines, Le centre d'études diocésain, 1950?), 42.

5. Kaddache, "La Casbah," 14.

6. René Lespès, *Alger: Étude de géographie et d'histoire urbaines* (Félix Alcan, 1930), 220.

7. Kaddache, *La vie politique à Alger*, 10–11.

8. Lespès claims that 78 percent of Algerians in Algiers lived in the Casbah in 1926. Lespès, *Alger*, 557.

9. Lespès, *Alger*, 274.
10. Larbi Icheboudene, *Alger: Histoire et capitale de destin national* (Casbah Editions, 1997), 132–133.
11. Kaddache, "La Casbah," 16.
12. Kaddache, "La Casbah," 20. French observers claimed that these Black populations worked for public works projects or as masseurs but really practiced witchcraft. Lucienne Favre, *Dans la Casbah* (Collette d'Halluin, 1949), 171.
13. Kaddache, "La Casbah," 38.
14. Robert Descloitres, Claudine Descloitres, and Jean-Claude Reverdy, *L'Algérie des bidonvilles: Le tiers monde dans la cité* (Mouton, 1961), 60.
15. Elizabeth Crouse, *Algiers* (Pott, 1906), 23.
16. For example: Crouse, *Algiers*; Favre, *Dans la Casbah*.
17. The Jewish quarter of Algiers abutted the synagogue at Place Rabbin Bloch, adjacent to the Casbah.
18. Çelik, *Urban Forms and Colonial Confrontations*, 14.
19. Icheboudene, *Alger*, 142.
20. In 1935, French officials listed five European *maisons de tolérance* in the Casbah of Algiers, as compared with thirty-five "indigène" establishments. The brothels were typically racially segregated. Christelle Taraud, *La prostitution coloniale: Algérie, Tunisie, Maroc (1830–1962)* (Payot, 2003), 133.
21. On Algerian immigration: Blanchard, *Histoire de l'immigration algérienne en France*; Sayad, *La double absence*.
22. On Jewish immigration to Marseille: Katz, *The Burdens of Brotherhood*.
23. AN. F 60 720. René Janon, "Colonisation de la Métropole." *De la France Outre-Mer*. November 11, 1937.
24. On Syrians in Marseille: Céline Regnard, *En transit: Les Syriens à Beyrouth, Marseille, Le Havre, New York, 1880–1914* (Anamosa, 2022).
25. Neil MacMaster notes that 84 percent of Algerians in France in 1923 were Kabyle. Although this proportion decreased over time, Algerians from Kabylia remained the majority. Neil MacMaster, "Patterns of Emigration, 1905–1954: 'Kabyles' and 'Arabs,'" in *French and Algerian Identities from Colonial Times to the Present: A Century of Interaction*, ed. Alec Hargreaves and Michael Heffernen (E. Mellen, 1993), 22.
26. ADBR. 4 M 2369. Commissariat Spécial. "Les indigènes Algériens à Marseille." February 21, 1913.
27. ADBR. 4 M 2369. Commissariat Spécial. "Les indigènes . . ." February 21, 1913.
28. ADBR. 4 M 2306. Rapport de Rafle. September 2, 1921; Rapport de Rafle. August 25, 1921.
29. Albert Londres, *Marseille, Port du Sud* (Les Éditions de France, 1927), 19.
30. This sentiment was echoed by other travel writers. See Louis Roubaud, *Pays de Marseille* (Gallimard, 1933).
31. The center of this community was Rue Baignoir, slightly above Rue des Chapeliers.
32. ADBR. 4 M 2313. Commerçants de la Rue des Chapeliers à M. le Préfet. September 18, 1937.
33. The commissariat of the 2ème was located at Halle Puget from 1927 to 1942, when it was moved slightly north to 7 Rue des Convalescents. AMM. *Indicateur de Marseille*.
34. The Casbah would come to be seen as a space that lent itself to revolution due to its narrow streets and social solidarity. See Farouk Benatia, *Alger: Agrégat ou cité; L'intégration citadine de 1919 à 1979* (SNED, 1980), 39; Sheila Crane, "Housing as Battleground: Targeting the City in the Battles of Algiers," *City and Society* 29, no. 1 (2017).
35. Berlière, *Le monde des polices*, 129.

36. Berlière, *Le monde des polices*, 89–90. Other cities with nationalized police forces included Lyon, Nice, Toulon, and Strasbourg.

37. In the personnel dossiers available in the ANOM, I did not find any Algerian commissioners in Algiers, although there were Algerian officers at the rank of *inspecteur* in the Sûreté and *brigadier* in the police d'état.

38. ANOM. 1 F 443. "Personnel des Services de Police, Règlement" (n.d.).

39. On martial races, see Arnold, *Police Power and Colonial Rule*. In Indochina, see Melissa Anderson, "For 'the Love of Order': Race, Violence, and the French Colonial Police in Vietnam, 1860s–1920s" (PhD diss., University of Wisconsin–Madison, 2015).

40. My estimates are based on officers' names. I cite what I consider to be the maximum possible number of Algerian officers, but some of these officers may have been Algerian Jews, as Jewish families often had Arabic surnames. ANOM. 1 F 443. "Contrôle du personnel de la police d'état." Undated [likely 1943].

41. Samuel Kalman notes that Algerians were widely recruited in rural police forces, but these Algerian agents were rarely promoted beyond entry-level positions. Kalman, *Law, Order, and Empire*, 40.

42. BWA. *Bulletin Municipal Officiel de la Ville d'Alger*. April 29, 1938.

43. BWA. *Bulletin Municipal Officiel de la Ville d'Alger*. June 27, 1938.

44. On education in colonial Algeria: Fanny Colonna, *Instituteur algériens, 1883–1939* (Presses de la Fondation nationale des sciences politiques, 1975). Kalman also argues that colonial inequality and malnourishment meant many Algerians did not meet the physical qualifications to be a police officer. Kalman, *Law, Order and Empire*, 41.

45. For example, the position of *garde champêtre* required a minimum salary of 7,200 francs and free lodging for Europeans but offered only 6,300 francs and no housing for Algerians. ANOM. 1 F 411. Maire de la Commande Montenotte à M. Le Préfet d'Alger. May 9, 1936. See also Kalman, *Law, Order and Empire*, 40–44.

46. ANOM. 3 F 8 *Dossier Hamidi Mohamed*.

47. ANOM. 3 F 8 *Dossier Hamidi Mohamed*. Hamidi would serve in the police of Algiers until 1954, when he was killed by FLN fighters.

48. ANOM. 1 F 400. *Dossier Hebert*. Lettre. Aissa ben el Hadj Amar. May 1921.

49. Women were only admitted to the French police beginning in the 1970s.

50. Pop culture associates Marseille's Corsican and Italian residents with criminal syndicates. For the pre–World War I period, however, historian Céline Regnard disputes the stereotype: Regnard-Drouot, *Marseille la violente*. On organized crime in Marseille: Laurence Montel, "Espace urbain et criminalité organisée: Le cas marseillais dans le premier XXe siècle," in *Villes en crise?*, ed. Yannick Marec (Créaphis, 2005).

51. On police training, see BNF, *Récit des Vies des Policiers*.

52. Kitson, *Police and Politics in Marseille*, chap. 2.

53. AN. 19940493 181. Rapport on Bretin. 1938.

54. ADBR. 1 M 751. "Dans la police marseillaise . . ." *Le Radical*. November 21, 1938.

55. There is one officer with no connection to Algeria, Louis Décanis, who spoke Arabic. ADBR. 4 M 81. *Dossier Décanis Louis*.

56. Jewish families had built import-export businesses to channel goods between France and Algeria since at least the 1700s. See Aïcha Guettas and Fatima Zohia Ghechi, "La communauté juive dans les relations rive nord–rive sud," in *Parlez-moi d'Alger: Marseille-Alger au miroir des mémoires*, ed. Abderrahmane Moussaoui and Florence Pizzorni (Réunion des musées nationaux, 2003).

57. Traditionally, Algerian Jews spoke a dialect of Arabic, although most would have been educated in French by this period. ADBR. 4 M 70. *Dossier Benichou Salomon Ange*; ADBR. 10 W 4. *Dossier Benichou Salomon Ange*.

58. ADBR. 4 M 70. *Dossier Benichou Salomon Ange.*
59. ADBR. 10 W 4. *Dossier Benoit Eugène.*
60. See, for example, Benjamin Lawrence, Emily Osborn, and Richard Roberts, eds., *Intermediaries, Interpreters, and Clerks: African Employees in the Making of Colonial Africa* (University of Wisconsin Press, 2006).
61. A *café maure* refers to a traditional North African café but was also used in Marseille to describe any café or restaurant frequented by Algerians.
62. On cultural translation and colonial intermediaries: Danielle Beaujon, "The Chaouch of Marseille: Metropolitan Intermediaries and Colonial Control, 1928–1945," *French Politics, Culture, and Society* 41, no. 1 (2023): 345–389.
63. The inability to translate darija would continue to plague the police, with a letter written in "notions" of different dialects stumping the police translator in 1950. ADBR. 148 W 191. Letter. November 18, 1950.
64. ADBR. 4 M 2352. Procureur de la République à M. le Commissaire Central. December 23, 1916.
65. ADBR. 4 M 2352. Procureur de la République . . . December 23, 1916.
66. ADBR. 4 M 11. Commissaire Divisionnaire de la police spéciale, Sallet à M. Le Sécretaire Général pour la Police. "A/s d'agents auxiliaires Nords Africains." November 17, 1937.
67. ADBR. 4 M 11. Le Général Gogues, Résident Général de France au Maroc à M. le Préfet des Bouches-du-Rhône. "Recrutement de deux agents Marocains." December 13, 1937.
68. In 1924, police ID records indicate that there were 105,000 Italians in Marseille. See Emile Témime, Pierre Échinard, Renée Lopez, Marie-Françoise Attard-Maraninchi, and Jean-Jacques Jordi, eds., *Migrance: Histoire des migrations à Marseille*, vol. 3, *Le cosmopolitisme de l'entre-deux-guerres: 1919–1945* (Edisud, 1990), 35.
69. For example, Officer Albert Maury's personnel dossier listed that he was born in Algeria and spoke Arabic. A note, however, clarified that he "parle et comprend suffisamment l'Arabe pour interroger un indigène." ANOM. 1 F 401. *Dossier Maury Albert.*
70. A *garde champêtre* is a cross between a forest ranger and a police officer, typically used to police rural spaces.
71. ANOM. 2 I 41. Commissaire Central de Police à M. le Secrétaire des Affaires Indigènes et Police Générale. August 16, 1939.
72. BWA. *Bulletin Municipal Officiel de la Ville d'Alger.* October 30, 1931.
73. BWA. *Bulletin Municipal Officiel de la Ville d'Alger.* October 30, 1931.
74. On French criminology, see Laurent Mucchielli, ed., *Histoire de la criminologie française* (L'Harmattan, 2004).
75. See Laurent Mucchielli, "Criminology, Hygenism, and Eugenics in France, 1870–1914: The Medical Debates on the Elimination of 'Incorrigible' Criminals," in *Criminals and Their Scientists: The History of Criminology in International Perspective*, ed. Peter Becker and Richard Wetzell (Cambridge University Press, 2006). On "degeneration," see Daniel Pick, *Faces of Degeneration: A European Disorder* (Cambridge University Press, 1989).
76. Richard C. Keller, *Colonial Madness: Psychiatry in French North Africa* (University of Chicago Press, 2007), 124. See also Robert Berthelier, *L'homme maghrébin dans la littérature psychiatrique* (L'Harmattan, 1994).
77. Adolphe Kocher, *De la criminalité chez les Arabes* (J. B. Baillière, 1884). On this text see Fabien Gouriou, "Le sexe des indigènes. Adolphe Kocher et la médecine légale en Algérie." *Droit et cultures* (2010): 59–72.
78. Kocher, *Criminalité*, 106.
79. Kocher, *Criminalité*, 232.
80. These stereotypes endured. Frantz Fanon, for example, quotes similar attitudes from a psychology text from 1949. See Frantz Fanon, *Pour la révolution africaines. Écrits politiques* (F. Maspero, 1969), chap. 1.

81. On this earlier racialization, see Sue Peabody, *There Are No Slaves in France: The Political Culture of Race and Slavery in the Ancien Régime* (Oxford University Press, 2002).

82. On faits divers, see Anne-Claude Ambroise-Rendu, *Petits récits des désordres ordinaires: Les faits divers dans la presse française des débuts de la IIIe République à la Grande Guerre* (Seli Arslan, 2004); Thomas Cragin, *Murder in Parisian Streets: Manufacturing Crime and Justice in the Popular Press, 1830–1900* (Bucknell University Press, 2006); Laetitia Gonon, *Le fait divers criminel dans la presse quotidienne française du XIXe siècle* (Presses Sorbonne Nouvelle, 2012).

83. Dominique Kalifa, *L'encre et le sang: Récit de crimes et société à la Belle Époque* (Fayard, 1995).

84. BNA. "Les chevaliers du couteaux." *Alger Républicain*. December 19, 1938.

85. The Algerian press could be divided into two categories—newspapers written for Europeans and newspapers written for Algerians. Algerian-produced newspapers appeared in both French and Arabic, but due to censorship of the Arabic-language press, Arabic newspapers tended to focus on culture. The faits divers appear largely in European press sources. On the press and settler identity, see Legg, *The New White Race*.

86. BA. "Un drame de la jalousie à Mende: Un Algérien tue sa femme à coups de hache et de couteau." *Petit Provençal*. February 27, 1930.

87. BA. "Encore les Arabes." *Petit Marseillais*. July 24, 1926.

88. ADBR. 4 M 2369. Rapport. "Les Algériens dans les usines de Marseille." February 11, 1914.

89. ADBR. 4 M 2369. Rapport. "Les Algériens . . ." February 11, 1914. *Apaches* is a translation of the Native American tribes, the Apache. Drawing on American discourses, French faits divers used this term to denote youth gangs in urban spaces. In Algeria, it typically meant rural bandits. On banditry in Algeria: Samuel Kalman, "Criminalizing Dissent: Policing Banditry in the Constantinois, 1914–1918," in *Algeria Revisited: Contested Identities in the Colonial and Postcolonial Periods*, ed. Rabah Aissoui and Claire Eldridge (Bloomsbury, 2016), Kalman, *Law, Order and Empire*, chap. 2.

90. ADBR. 4 M 379. *Dossier Haddadi Ahmed, Blanc Marcel*. Le Commissaire de Police Mobile, Nouges à M. le Commissaire Divisionnaire. July 30, 1918.

91. This segregation was less rigid in Marseille, where some wealthier North Africans lived outside of "North African" spaces.

92. On colonial law and polygamy: Surkis, *Sex, Law, and Sovereignty*.

93. He also labeled Algerian women as homosexual. Kocher, *Criminalité*, 169.

94. Kamel Kateb, *Européens, "Indigènes" et Juifs en Algérie (1830–1962): Représentations et réalités des populations* (INED, 2001), 143.

95. Favre, *Dans la Casbah*, 87.

96. Taraud, *La prostitution coloniale*, 133.

97. Favre, *Dans la Casbah*, 89.

98. BWA. Bulletin Municipal Officiel de la Ville d'Alger. Séance du March 21, 1919.

99. Sihem Bella, "Le voyage à Alger dans les guides touristiques français au XXe siècle," *Diacronie* 36, no. 4 (2018).

100. BWA. Bulletin Municipal Officiel de la Ville d'Alger. Séance du March 21, 1919; Séance du March 3, 1939.

101. Algerian men had to obtain a letter from their future employer, assuring authorities that the family could survive on his salary, and permission from the local mayor. ANOM. 9 H 113. Le Ministre de l'Intérieur à M. le Gouverneur Général de l'Algérie. "Règlementation de la main d'œuvre indigène dans la Métropole." August 8, 1924. Freedom of movement for Algerian women began in 1936. See Muriel Cohen, *Des familles invisibles: Les Algériens de France entre intégrations et discriminations 1945–1985* (Editions de la Sorbonne, 2020), 48.

102. There were only 265 such marriages in Algeria between 1880 and 1906. Kateb, *Européens, "Indigènes" et Juifs en Algérie*, 204.

103. This attempt to "protect" European women from colonial husbands motivated changes to French nationality laws in 1927. See Elisa Camiscioli, *Reproducing the French Race: Immigration, Intimacy, and Embodiment in the Early Twentieth Century* (Duke University Press, 2009).

104. ADBR. 5 W 360. Commissaire Divisionnaire Gaubert à M. Le Préfet des Bouches-du-Rhône. October 21, 1940.

105. The Renseignements Généraux are the French political police, a subunit of the Sûreté.

106. ADBR. 76 W 205. Commissaire Divisionnaire des RG à M. L'Intendant Régional de Police. "Liste de familles musulmanes de Marseille." May 13, 1942.

107. For example: ADBR. 149 W 137. "Impression d'un indigène libéré d'un camp d'internement." November 12, 1941.

108. ADBR. 5 W 423. Commissaire de la Sûreté à M. le Commissaire Chef de la Sûreté. April 25, 1941.

109. ADBR. 63 W 985. Lettre. Pauline B. à M. le Procureur. April 23, 1939.

110. ADBR. 63 W 985. Lettre. Pauline B. à Chérif K. February 4, 1939.

111. ADBR. 63 W 985. Procès-Verbal. Chérif K. May 13, 1939.

112. For discussions of this persistent stereotype, see Emmanuel Blanchard, "Le mauvais genre des Algériens: Des hommes sans femme face au virilisme policier dans le Paris d'après-guerre," *Clio: Histoire, femmes et sociétés* 27, no. 1 (2008): 209–224; Todd Shepard, *Sex, France and Arab Men, 1962–1979* (University of Chicago Press, 2018).

113. This case came from Kouba, a suburb of Algiers. ANOM. 1K 212. Commissaire Principal de Kouba, Spiteri. "Objet: Attentat à la pudeur avec violences." November 19, 1949.

114. ADBR. 63 W 1027. Procès-Verbal. "Affaire d. Benaissa B." January 30, 1941.

115. ADBR. 63 W 1027. Procès-Verbal. "Affaire d. Benaissa . . ." January 30, 1941.

116. ADBR. 63 W 1027. Procès-Verbal. "Affaire d. Benaissa . . ." January 30, 1941.

117. Blanchard, *Histoire de l'immigration algérienne en France*, 24.

118. ANOM. 9 H 113. Gouverneur Général de l'Algérie à MM. le Préfets d'Oran et Constantine. "A.s. de la réglementation de l'exode des indigènes vers la Métropole." November 8, 1924.

119. ANOM. 9 H 113. "Exode des indigènes se rendant dans la Métropole." April 4, 1928.

120. ANOM. 9 H 113. Gouverneur Général de l'Algérie. "Exode des travailleurs indigènes." December 27, 1927.

121. On immigration in 1930s Marseille: Lewis, *Boundaries of the Republic*.

122. ANOM. 9 H 113. *Journal Officiel*. 1928.

123. AN. F 60 704. Haut-Comité Méditerranéen et de l'Afrique du Nord. "Rapport de M. Laroque et Ollive, Auditeurs au Conseil d'État." March 1938.

124. AN. F 60 720. Préfet des Bouches-du-Rhône à M. Ministre de l'Intérieur. April 8, 1937.

125. ADBR. 4 M 11. Commissaire Divisionnaire de Police Spéciale, Sallet à M. Le Préfet des Bouches-du-Rhône. "A/s de la réorganisation des services de la police spéciale de Marseille." November 25, 1935.

126. ADBR. 4 M 2369. Commissaire Spécial à M. le Préfet des Bouches-du-Rhône. "Travailleurs indigènes arrivés clandestinement." June 2, 1925.

127. ADBR. 4 M 2369. Commissaire Spécial. "Contrôle Général des Services de Police Administrative, Clandestins." November 30, 1925.

128. ADBR. 4 M 950. Le Commissaire Spécial Adjoint, Bondurand à M. Le Commissaire Spécial, Saint-Etienne. "Au sujet de l'entrée frauduleuse en France d'indigènes Marocains."

December 2, 1927. There had been an even more scandalous affair in 1926, when several Moroccan migrants died while stowaways on the *Sidi Ferruch*. See Emmanuel Blanchard, "Des contrôles migratoires aux conséquences funestes: Le 'drame du Sidi Ferruch,' avril 1926," in *Encyclopédie d'histoire numérique de l'Europe*.

129. ADBR. 4 M 950. "Affaire Francisi." January 18, 1928.

130. ADBR. 4 M 950. Procès-Verbal. Commissaire de Police, Clément Menard. December 18, 1928.

131. ADBR. 4 M 950. Francisi à M. Le Commissaire Central. January 5, 1928.

132. ADBR. 4 M 2361. Commissaire Spécial à M. le Préfet des Bouches-du-Rhône. "Refoulement d'indigènes Algériens." March 21, 1929.

2. LOCATING DANGEROUS ALGERIANS

1. AN. F 60 720. René Janon. "Colonisation de la Métropole." *De la France Outre-Mer*. November 11, 1937.

2. This context comes from a conversation with his daughter-in-law, whom I met at the Centre de Documentation Historique sur l'Algérie in Aix-en-Provence, France.

3. AN. F 60 720. Janon. "Colonisation de la Métropole."

4. On controlling interwar migration, see Lewis, *The Boundaries of the Republic*; Rosenberg, *Policing Paris*.

5. Amit Prakash shows a similar pattern in Paris. Prakash, *Empire on the Seine*.

6. On Algerian nationalism: Martin Evans, *Algeria: France's Undeclared War* (Oxford University Press, 2012); Mahfoud Kaddache, *La vie politique à Alger*; Mahfoud Kaddache, *Histoire du nationalisme algérien: Question nationale et politique algérienne, 1919–1951* (EDIF, 2000); James McDougall, *History and the Culture of Nationalism in Algeria* (Cambridge University Press, 2008).

7. Joshua Cole argues that Mohamed El Maadi was responsible for organizing a gang that committed up to twenty of the twenty-five murders. See Cole, *Lethal Provocation*.

8. ANOM. 4 I 1. Le Gouverneur Général de l'Algérie à MM. les Préfets. "Rôle et attributions des S.L.N.A. départementaux." August 29, 1950.

9. ANOM. 4 I 1. Le Gouverneur Général à MM. les Préfets. "Rôle des S.L.N.A départementaux." December 4, 1952.

10. This exchange can be seen in the ANOM series on the CIE and its successor, the SLNA. For example: ANOM 4 I and 2 I.

11. AN. F 60 186. Président de la Ligue Française pour la Défense des Droits de l'Homme et du Citoyen à M. le Président du Conseil. July 30, 1935.

12. AN. F 60 186. Ministre de l'Intérieur, Marcel Régnier à M. le Président de la République Française. "Pression des manifestations contre la souveraineté française en Algérie." March 30, 1935.

13. AN. F 60 733. Chambre des Députés. "Reprise de la discussion du projet de loi portant amnistie." June 8, 1939.

14. AN. F 60 186. Ministre de l'Intérieur, Marcel Régnier à M. le Président de la République Française. "Pression des manifestations contre la souveraineté française en Algérie." March 30, 1935.

15. *La Défense* was an Algerian nationalist newspaper, published in French. ANOM. 91 4I 32. "Un nouveau décret." *La Défense*. June 15, 1938.

16. AN. F 60 718. "Il ne faut pas prendre le Pirée pour un homme ni l'administration pour la France elle-même." *Alger Républicain*. January 22, 1939.

17. The phrase *passage à tabac* derives from the French verb *tabasser* or "to beat up." On the ubiquity of this practice in Algeria, see Kalman, *Law, Order, and Empire*, 113.

18. On police professionalization: Berlière, *Le monde des polices en France*.

19. Scholars have examined the "circulaire logic" of immigration law: Lewis, *The Boundaries of the Republic*, 214; Alexis Spire, *Etrangers à la carte: L'administration de l'immigration en France, 1945–1975* (Grasset, 2005).

20. ANOM. 1 F 144. Arrêté. Bouinan. June 26, 1936.

21. ANOM. 1 F 144. Maire de la Ville d'Alger à M. Le Préfet. "Police générale." June 20, 1936.

22. On the police power of the indigénat: Milliot et al., *Histoire des polices en France*, 416.

23. In 1921, nearly 80 percent of Algerians in Algiers lived in the Casbah. Kaddache, *La vie politique à Alger*, 13.

24. ANOM. 4 I 39. "Intervention de notre Camarade Boukroufa Messaoud au conseil municipal." *La Lutte Sociale*. December 30, 1938.

25. While it was not a *quartier réservé*, the Casbah was the only area of Algiers where soliciting was authorized. Taraud, *La prostitution coloniale*, 149.

26. BWA. *Bulletin Municipal Officiel de la Ville d'Alger*. September 27, 1935.

27. For example: BWA. *Bulletin Municipal Officiel de la Ville d'Alger*. January 13, 1939; March 3, 1939.

28. Lucienne Favre, *Tout l'inconnu de la Casbah d'Alger* (Baconnier Frères, 1933), 18.

29. Favre, *Dans la Casbah*, 19.

30. These two streets were contiguous halves of the same boulevard, creating the confusion.

31. ANOM. 2 I 38. Commissaire de Police du 2ème à M. le Commissaire Central. July 31, 1934.

32. This was likely Mohamed Akli, who served in the special police and RG of Algiers between at least 1941–1943.

33. While I do highlight moments of conflicts between tirailleurs and North Africans, ultimately the policing of the tirailleurs largely fell to military authorities. On tirailleurs: Gregory Mann, *Native Sons: West African Veterans and France in the Twentieth Century* (Duke University Press, 2006); Sarah J. Zimmerman, *Militarizing Marriage: West African Soldiers' Conjugal Traditions in the Modern French Empire* (Ohio University Press, 2020).

34. ANOM. 1 K 130. Akli. "A/s d'un rassemblement d'indigène autour de tirailleurs sénégalais." August 4, 1941.

35. For example: ANOM. 1 K 130. "A/s Soirée donnée par la Troupe Rachid Kssantini." May 24, 1941.

36. BNA. "Où la police d'Alger veut-elle en venir?" *La Justice*. April 25, 1936.

37. BNA. "Agents tortionnaires" *La Défense*. December 21, 1934.

38. BNA. "Où la police d'Alger veut-elle en venir?" *La Justice*. April 25, 1936.

39. BNA. "Les dessous d'une rafle." *La Défense*. February 23, 1934.

40. Favre, *Dans la Casbah*, 198.

41. ANOM. 1 F 62. Rapport Mensuel. January 1935.

42. In 1931, 78 percent of all "colonial" migrants in France came from North Africa. See Laure Blévis et al., *1931: Les étrangers au temps de l'exposition coloniale* (Gallimard, 2008), 17.

43. On the Rue Fondary murder, see Blanchard, *La police parisienne et les Algériens*, 52–53; Amit Prakash, "Colonial Techniques in the Imperial Capital: The Prefecture of Police and the Surveillance of North Africans in Paris, 1925–circa 1970," *French Historical Studies* 36, no. 3 (2013) 487–488; Rosenberg, *Policing Paris*, 141–147.

44. See Emmanuel Blanchard, "Des Kabyles 'perdus' en région parisienne: Les 'recherches dans l'intérêt des familles' du Service des affaires indigènes nord-africaines (années 1930)." *Revue du Monde Musulman et de la Méditerranée* 144 (2018): 29–44; Emmanuel Blanchard, *Des colonisés ingouvernables: Adresses d'Algériens aux autorités françaises (Akbou, Paris, 1919–1940)* (Presses De Sciences Po, 2024).

45. On the BNA and SAINA: Beaujon, "Policing Colonial Migrants"; Blanchard, *La police parisienne et les Algériens*; Prakash, *Empire on the Seine*; Rosenberg, *Policing Paris*.
46. On the CAI: Bollenot, "Maintenir l'ordre impérial."
47. Lyon's SAINA was a one-man show run by J. Azario and housed under the special police. The service closed in 1936 when his ill health forced him to retire. Massard-Guilbaud, *Des Algériens à Lyon*, 395–412; Lewis, *The Boundaries of the Republic*, 202–205.
48. By the same logics, Marseille was also a key hub of CAI operations. See Bollenot, "Maintenir l'ordre impérial."
49. ADBR. 1 M 759. *Journal Officiel*. October 30, 1928.
50. ADBR. 1 M 759. Conseil Général des Bouches-Du-Rhône. "Création d'un office Nord-Africaine." Envelope marked October 7, 1927.
51. *Communes mixtes* were municipalities in rural Algeria where Algerians were a majority. In these zones, appointed administrators had broad powers of policing.
52. ADBR. 1 M 759. Le Ministre de l'Intérieur à M. le Maire de Marseille. June 2, 1927.
53. ADBR. 1 M 759. Arrêté. Sarraut. November 5, 1928.
54. Kateb, *Européens, "Indigènes" et Juifs en Algérie*, 94.
55. This idea of "imperial capital" is developed by Bollenot in "Maintenir l'ordre impérial."
56. The original budget for SAINA sat in city coffers for a full year before expiring and requiring a second vote, as administrators struggled to coordinate logistics.
57. *Chaouch* is an Arabic term meaning bailiff, but in colonial Algeria it meant a janitor, guard, or *garçon de bureau*. ADBR. 1 M 759. Chef du SAINA, Zannetacci. "Demande de subvention." March 31, 1931.
58. In 1928, a North African veteran, Fayah Othman, requested to work at SAINA, but his application was refused. ADBR. 1 M 759. Letter. Sergent Fayah Othman. July 16, 1928.
59. ADBR. 1 M 759. Ministre de l'Intérieur. November 1928.
60. APP. H A 88. "Arrêté concernant le recrutement." December 12, 1930.
61. ADBR. 1 M 759. Ministre de l'Intérieur à M. le Préfet. March 16, 1931.
62. ADBR. 1 M 759. Préfet des Bouches-du-Rhône à M. Ministre de l'Intérieur. September 21, 1927.
63. ADBR. 1 M 759. Commissaire Spécial Dhubert à M. le Préfet. April 9, 1931.
64. ADBR. 5 W 360. Chef du SAINA, Poussardin à M. le Général Commandant de la XVe Région. "Rapport sur les Services des Affaires Indigènes Nord-Africaines de Marseille." August 12, 1940.
65. On the complicated relationship between Algerian Muslims and Jews, see Katz, *The Burdens of Brotherhood*.
66. The 1936 Blum-Viollette project proposed to grant certain Algerians citizenship while allowing them to retain personal status. However, it restricted citizenship to Algerians in elite positions. AN. F 60 729. Chambre des Députés. "Projet de Loi relatif à l'exercice des droits politiques par certaines catégories de sujets français en Algérie." December 30, 1936.
67. AN. F 60 729. "Plutôt la mort." *La Défense*. March 15, 1939.
68. On the shift with the Popular Front: William Hoisington Jr., "The Mediterranean Committee and French North Africa, 1935–1940," *Historian* 53, no. 2 (1991): 255–266.
69. AN. F 60 720. Secrétaire-Adjoint du Haut-Comité Méditerranéen, Fernand Vrolyk à M. Le Ministre de l'Intérieur. June 6, 1939.
70. AN. F 60 720. Secrétaire-Adjoint du Haut-Comité Méditerranéen . . . June 6, 1939.
71. On Mohamed Ben Hadj, see Beaujon, "The Chaouch of Marseille."
72. AN. F 60 720. Secrétaire-Adjoint du Haut-Comité Méditerranéen . . . June 6, 1939.
73. The 1938 Laroque Report suggested eleven thousand Algerians lived in Marseille, but local police documents asserted that fifteen thousand was more accurate. AN. F 60 704. Haut-Comité Méditerranéen. "Rapport de MM. Laroque et Ollive, Auditeurs au Conseil d'État." March 1938.

74. Kaddache cites 76,627 "indigènes Musulmans" out of a total of 264,232 residents of Algiers in 1936. Kaddache, *La Vie Politique à Alger*, 11.

75. Sources on Algerians' perception of Marseille's SAINA are difficult to find, but the rare sources preserved among police records belie the claim of SAINA's chiefs that their service was seen as an ally.

76. The workload of the service exponentially increased between 1935 and 1938. ADBR. 5 W 360. Chef du SAINA à M. le Général Commandant de la XVe Région. "Rapport sur les Services des Affaires Indigènes Nord-Africaines de Marseille." August 12, 1940.

77. ADBR. 5 W 360... "Rapport sur les Services des Affaires..." August 12, 1940.

78. *Chleuh* is a dialect of Amazigh, synonymous with a population from Morocco.

79. ADBR. 1 M 759. Chef du SAINA à M. le Préfet. June 17, 1938.

80. This was the same Jewish Algerian officer fired for his ill-treatment of Muslims. ADBR. 1 M 759. Chef du SAINA à M. le Préfet des Bouches-du-Rhône, Bouet. October 7, 1939.

81. *Sabir* could refer to North African Arabic dialects or North Africans speaking creolized French. ADBR. 1 M 759. Chef du SAINA... October 7, 1939.

82. ADBR. 5 W 360. Chef du SAINA à M. le Général Commandant de la XVe Région. August 12, 1940.

83. ADBR. 5 W 360. Chef du SAINA... August 12, 1940.

84. AN. F 60 720. René Janon. "Chez le 'hakem' de Marseille." *De la France Outre-Mer*. November 5, 1937.

85. A "bogato" seems to be a creolization of the Spanish word "abogado" meaning lawyer, taken from Algerian dialect. AN. F 60 720. René Janon. "Colonisation de la Métropole." *De la France Outre-Mer*. November 26, 1937.

86. A *caïd* was a local Muslim administrator, a powerful position in colonial Algeria. Their responsibilities could include judicial and policing, as well as administrative, functions.

87. ADBR. 4 M 2313. Lettre. Drif el Mahfoud à M. le Préfet. Marseille. August 10, 1937.

88. ADBR. 4 M 2313. Commissaire Divisionnaire à M. le Préfet. October 23, 1937.

89. ADBR. 4 M 2313. Note. August 20, 1937; Ministre de l'Intérieur à M. le Préfet. Paris. October 11, 1937.

90. The police also discovered that Mahfoud's brother, the caïd, had extorted between fifty and three hundred francs from Algerians for ID papers and permission to travel to France. ADBR. 4 M 2313. Commissaire Divisionnaire à M. le Préfet. "Affaire D. el Mahfoud escroqueries et tentatives." October 23, 1937.

91. ADBR. 4 M 2313. Lettre. Commerçants de la Rue des Chapeliers à M. le Préfet. September 18, 1937.

92. ADBR. 4 M 2313. L'Officier de Paix Gelibert à M. le Commissaire de Police du 11ème. September 1937.

93. ADBR. 4 M 2313. Commissaire de Police Lebas à M. le Commissaire Central. October 1, 1937.

94. Lettre des commerçants algériens au Préfet des Bouches-du-Rhône. February 22, 1921. Cited in Emile Témime, *Marseille transit: Les passagers de Belsunce* (Autrement, 1997), 72.

95. ADBR. 12 W 23. "Coups et blessures volontaires aux agents de la force publique." September 18, 1939.

96. An Algerian witness corroborated Abdallah's version of the story. ADBR. 12 W 23. "Coups et blessures volontaires..." September 18, 1939.

97. The two Algerians were sent to court for "outrages" against an agent, but it is unclear whether they were convicted.

98. Historians have explored the role of different bureaucrats and religious leaders in France's "civilizing mission." Alice Conklin, *A Mission to Civilize: The Republican Idea of Empire in France and West Africa, 1895–1930* (Stanford University Press, 1997); J. P. Daughton,

An Empire Divided: Religion, Republicanism, and the Making of French Colonialism, 1880–1914 (Oxford University Press, 2006); Amelia Lyons, *The Civilizing Mission in the Metropole: Algerian Families and the French Welfare State during Decolonization* (Stanford University Press, 2013).

99. BWA. *Bulletin Officiel Municipal de la Ville d'Alger*. February 28, 1936.

100. BWA. *Bulletin Officiel Municipal* . . . February 28, 1936.

101. BWA. *Bulletin Officiel Municipal* . . . February 28, 1936.

102. On the masculine sociability of cafés maures: Omar Carlier, "Le café maure: Sociabilité masculine et effervescence citoyenne (Algérie XVIIe-XXe siècles)," *Annales: Histoire, Sciences Sociales* 45, no. 4 (1990): 975–1003.

103. Neil MacMaster, "The Algerian Café-Hotel: Hub of the Nationalist Underground, Paris, 1926–1962," *French Politics, Culture and Society* 3, no. 2, (2016): 72.

104. ANOM. 1 K 201 contains a series of records on this subject.

105. ADBR. 5 W 360. Chef du SAINA à M. le Général Commandant de la XVe Région. "Rapport sur les Services des Affaires Indigènes Nord-Africaines de Marseille." August 12, 1940.

106. ADBR. 76 W 205. SAA. Wender. "Statistiques des indigènes Algériens en France." October 13, 1941.

107. For example: ADBR. 4 M 950. "Au sujet de l'entrée frauduleuse en France d'indigènes Marocains." December 2, 1927.

108. ADBR. 12 W 2. *Dossier Saouli Ahmed*. Rapport de l'Inspecteur Valfré sur "SAOULI Ahmed."

109. ADBR. 4M 2339. Habitants de Rue Bernard du Bois à M. le Maire de Marseille. May 16, 1938.

110. ADBR. 4 M 2339. Commissaire de Police à M. le Commissaire Central. June 29, 1938.

111. BNA. "Le Harem violé, le hijab bafoué impunément par la crapule policière." *La Voix du Peuple*. July 27, 1934. "Crapule" could also be translated as thug or scoundrel.

112. Tighrine appears several times in the police records of Algiers as an "information agent." See ANOM. 2 I 33.

113. For example: BNA. "Toujours la Police à Alger." *La Voix du Peuple*. February 10, 1935.

114. This is commented on in many SAINA reports and also discussed in the scholarship on Algerian immigration. For example: Sayad, *La double absence*; MacMaster, *Colonial Migrants and Racism*.

115. ADBR. 1 M 759. Rapport. July 21, 1936.

116. Though the quartiers nord are now racialized as a postcolonial immigrant space, this was not yet the case in the 1920s. ADBR. 1 M 759. Chef du SAINA, Zannettacci à M. le Préfet. May 15, 1929.

117. ADBR. 1 M 759. Arrêté. September 1928.

118. ADBR. 1 M 759. Arrêté. September 1928.

119. On Islam and political organization: Julia Clancy-Smith, *Rebel and Saint: Muslim Notables, Populist Protest, Colonial Encounters (Algeria and Tunisia, 1800–1904)* (University of California Press, 1994); Cheikh Anta Mbaké Babou, *Fighting the Greater Jihad: Amadu Bamba and the Founding of the Muridiyya of Senegal, 1853–1913* (Ohio University Press, 2007).

120. For example: Robert Crews, *For Prophet and Tsar: Islam and Empire in Russia and Central Asia* (Harvard University Press, 2006); Moses Ochonu, *Colonialism by Proxy: Hausa Imperial Agents and Middle Belt Consciousness in Nigeria* (Indiana University Press, 2014).

121. See Kaddache, *Histoire du nationalisme algérien*, vol. 1, 204.

122. ANOM. 2 I 44. "Des musulmans manifestent contre un arrêté préfectoral." *La Dépêche*. March 4, 1933.

123. This is confirmed in internal government documents. ANOM. GGA 2CAB 12.

124. ANOM. 2 I 44. "Un déplorable incident cause en Algérie une légitime indignation." *Le Quotidien.* March 24, 1933.

125. ANOM. 2 I 44. Rapport. March 4, 1933.

126. ANOM. 2 I 44. Rapport. March 4, 1933.

127. ANOM. 2 I 44. "Un déplorable incident . . ." March 24, 1933.

128. The circulaire would become law in 1934. ANOM. GGA 2CAB 12. Commission Interministérielle des Affaires Musulmanes "Procès-Verbal de la Séance du 9 Mai 1934."

129. Police continued to target El Okbi, including framing him for the murder of the mufti of Algiers in 1936. On the political implications of this murder: Christian Phéline, *La terre, l'étoile, le couteau: Le 2 août 1936 à Alger* (Editions du croquant, 2021).

130. See Aliénor Cadiot, "Vichy et les Algériens: Indigènes civils musulmans algériens en France métropolitaine (1939–1944)" (PhD diss., EHESS, 2020), 353.

131. An annual report from 1940, for example, listed the hadj as one of SAINA's "civil" responsibilities. ADBR. 5 W 360. Chef du SAINA à M. le Général Commandant de la XVe Région. "Rapport sur les Services des Affaires Indigènes Nord-Africaines de Marseille." August 12, 1940. See also ADBR. 3194 W 1. Dossier "Culte de Marseille."

132. This struggle to build a mosque would continue well into the 1940s. For example: ADBR. 76 W 206. SAA. "A.s. de la Construction d'une Mosquée à Marseille." January 10, 1942. On the failure to build a mosque in Marseille under Vichy, see Cadiot, "Vichy et les Algériens," 245.

133. AN. 20010216 173. Commissaire Divisionnaire des Services de Police Spéciale à M. le Préfet. "Meeting organisé par la section Marseillaise du Congrès Musulman." July 26, 1937.

134. By 1953, Marseille still did not have a mosque. ADBR. 148 W 193. Commissaire Principal des RG à Constantine à M. le Commissaire Principal des RG à Marseille. February 18, 1953.

135. Omar Carlier emphasizes the importance of precisely these types of spaces in the development of Muslim civil society in Algiers. Omar Carlier, "Medina and Modernity: The Emergence of Muslim Civil Society in Algiers between the Two World Wars," in *Walls of Algiers: Narratives of the City Through Text and Image*, ed. Zeynep Çelik, Julia Clancy-Smith, and Frances Terpak (Getty Research Institute, 2009).

3. POLICING AN EMPIRE AT WAR

1. A police inspector and a team of garde champêtre policed Zeralda. On the Zeralda affair: Jean-Louis Planche, "Violences et nationalismes en Algérie, 1942–1945," *Les Temps modernes* no. 590 (1996): 112–134.

2. Women and children were also arrested, but only men were jailed overnight. ANOM. 9 H 27. "Affaire de Zeralda." August 1942.

3. For example: ANOM. 9 H 27. Gouverneur Général de l'Algérie. "Asphyxies mortelles à Zeralda." August 3, 1942.

4. ANOM. 9 H 27. Commissaire de la PRG. "A.S. des incidents de Zeralda." August 10, 1942.

5. Robert Paxton ignited debates when he exposed how Vichy policies continued in the Fourth Republic, framing the legacy of Vichy as one of continuity. Robert Paxton, *Vichy France: Old Guard and New Order, 1940–1944* (Columbia University Press, 1972). See also Gérard Noiriel, *Les origines républicaines de Vichy* (Hachette, 1999).

6. Annie Rey-Goldzeiguer, *Aux origines de la guerre d'Algérie 1940–1945: De Mers-el-Kébir aux massacres du Nord-Constantinois* (La Découverte, 2002), 18; Pierre Darmon, *L'Algérie de Pétain* (Perrin, 2014), chap. 8.

7. On the persecution of North African Jews under Vichy: Aomar Boum and Sarah Abrevaya Stein, eds., *The Holocaust and North Africa* (Stanford University Press, 2019).

8. On far-right politics in Algeria: Samuel Kalman, *French Colonial Fascism: The Extreme Right in Algeria, 1919–1939* (Palgrave Macmillan, 2013). Although far-right parties gained ground in Marseille, leftist leaders had been in power since the 1930s. See Kitson, *Police and Politics in Marseille*, 10–11.

9. *Tirailleurs algériens* were drafted into segregated units commanded by European officers.

10. Soldiers were recruited from throughout the French Empire, including tirailleurs sénégalais from French West Africa. See Ruth Ginio, *The French Army and its African Soldiers: The Years of Decolonization* (University of Nebraska Press, 2017); Eric Storm and Ali Al Tuma, eds., *Colonial Soldiers in Europe, 1914–1945: "Aliens in Uniform" in Wartime Societies* (Routledge, 2015).

11. ANOM. 1 F 444. Inspecteur Divisionnaire de la Police d'État à M. Le Commissaire Central. February 9, 1940.

12. My estimate of the numbers of requis officers comes from a randomized search among police personnel dossiers in the 12 W series of the ADBR archives.

13. ADBR. 12 W 12; 12 W 27.

14. The archives of Algiers do not have the same density of personnel records available, so it was difficult to determine how many men were recruited.

15. Alice Conklin, Sarah Fishman, and Robert Zaretsky, eds., *France and Its Empire Since 1870* (Oxford University Press, 2015).

16. Ruth Ginio, "The Implementation of Anti-Jewish Laws in French West Africa" in *The Holocaust and North Africa*, ed. Aomar Boum and Abrevaya Stein, 82. On Vichy and empire: Jacques Cantier and Eric Jennings, eds., *L'Empire colonial sous Vichy* (Odile Jacob, 2004).

17. Only North Africans who owned property in France, had a legitimate marriage to a French woman, or recognized children in France could stay. ADBR. 76 W 204. Lettre. Préfet de la Loire à M. Yacef Ameur. February 12, 1941.

18. Germany held more than 1.5 million French prisoners of war. Many Algerians spent years in the prisoner-of-war camps in Germany and occupied France. See Sarah Ann Frank, *Hostages of Empire: Colonial Prisoners of War in Vichy France* (Nebraska University Press, 2021).

19. Miho Matsunuma, "La politique du gouvernement de Vichy vis-à-vis des militaires coloniaux rapatriables," *Outre-Mers: Revue d'histoire* 362 (2009): 230. There is some mention of Indochinese soldiers participating in a strike in Marseille in 1944, suggesting their presence in the city, but they were typically sent to other camps, such as Sorgues near Avignon. See Tobias Rettig, "From Subaltern to Free Worker: Exit, Voice, and Loyalty among Indochina's Subaltern Imperial Labor Camp Diaspora in Metropolitan France, 1939–1944," *Journal of Vietnamese Studies* 7, no. 3 (2012): 21.

20. ANOM. 2 I 35. Circulaire. Préfet d'Alger. August 28, 1940.

21. ADBR. 76 W 131. Commissaire Divisionnaire Gaubert à M. Le Préfet des Bouches-du-Rhône. August 30, 1940.

22. As the war wound down, the police chief of Algiers continued to protest the lack of officers. ANOM. 1 K 81. Louis Laperrière à M. le Préfet. March 8, 1944.

23. Kitson says this was the reason police officers in Marseille initially proved willing to cooperate with Vichy. Kitson, *Police and Politics in Marseille*, chap. 3. See also Berlière and Chabrun, *Les policiers français sous l'Occupation*.

24. Vichy also centralized the Renseignements Généraux (RG). Berlière and Chabrun, *Les policiers français sous l'Occupation*, 29.

25. Berlière, *Le monde des polices*, 164.

26. Berlière and Chabrun, *Les policiers français sous l'Occupation*; Berlière, *Le monde des polices*, 176–184; Laurent Joly, *L'antisémitisme de bureau: Enquête au cœur de la préfec-*

ture de police de Paris et du commissariat général aux questions juives (1940–1944) (Grasset, 2011).

27. Vichy did create a "North African Brigade" in Paris, staffed with North Africans and tasked with hunting members of the French Resistance. See Benjamin Stora, *Ils venaient d'Algérie: L'immigration algérienne en France (1912–1992)* (Fayard, 1992), 87–88.

28. SAINA had moved from its original building on Rue Garibaldi to the new Rue Barbaroux location in 1940. ADBR. 150 W 170. Adjoint au BAMNA, J. Bourgeois à M. le Préfet. "Intérimat du BAMNA." September 25, 1944.

29. Wender came to Marseille after serving as head of the Centre d'Informations et d'Études of Algiers, an organization designed to collect information on Algerians. ADBR. 76 W 205. SAA. Chef de Service par intérim, Bourgeois à M. le Chef du Gouvernement. "A/S de l'OFALAC." May 15, 1943. On the SAA, see Cadiot, "Vichy et les Algériens," 181–183.

30. ADBR. 76 W 205. SAA. "A/s du Service des Affaires Indigènes Nord Africaines de Marseille." April 3, 1941.

31. A law from June 1941 restricted Jewish access to white-collar jobs as lawyers and doctors, capping their overall percentage in these professions at 2 percent. In Algiers, the administration forced nearly two-thirds of Jewish doctors to resign, creating a crisis in the Casbah because young Jewish doctors were the only ones willing to serve the Muslim community. ANOM. 4 I 73. CIE. "Élimination des médecins juifs à Alger." May 18, 1942.

32. Jewish officers would be reinstated in January 1943, a few months after the arrival of Allied troops in Algiers. In Marseille, Jewish police officers would have to wait for Allied arrival in August 1944. Incomplete personnel records make it difficult to determine exact numbers but suggest that most "North African" officers in Marseille were Algerian Jews. ANOM. 1 F 437. Le Général de l'Armée à M. Le Préfet du Département d'Alger. "Réalisation de mon arrêté du 28 Janvier 1943." July 5, 1943.

33. ANOM. 91 3 F 4. *Dossier Mamane Salomon*. Several other police officers fired for being Jewish show up in the files of the ADBR, because their personnel dossiers were transferred to the metropole when they left Algiers for France during the Algerian War.

34. For example: ADBR. 13 W 16. *Dossier Bel-Aïss David*.

35. Because rounding up Jewish families in France began roughly simultaneously with the Allied invasion of Algiers in 1942, the police in Algiers did not necessarily play this role. See Donna Ryan, *The Holocaust and the Jews of Marseille: The Enforcement of Anti-Semitic Policies in Vichy France* (University of Illinois Press, 1996). On Vichy policing in Algeria: Kalman, *Law, Order, and Empire*, chap. 4.

36. See Paul Fenton and David Littman, *L'exil au Maghreb: La condition juive sous l'islam, 1148–1912* (Presse de la Université de Paris-Sorbonne, 2010); Sarah Taïeb-Carlen and Amos Carlen, *The Jews of North Africa: From Dido to de Gaulle* (University Press of America, 2010).

37. Florence Berceot notes that nearly 19 percent of foreign-born Jews in Marseille were North African, particularly Algerian. Florence Berceot, "Renouvellement sociodémographique des juifs de Marseille, 1901–1937," *Provence historiques* 44, no. 175 (1994): 45. Ethan Katz argues that there was significant commercial exchange between Muslims and Jews in Marseille but less personal interaction. Katz, *The Burdens of Brotherhood*, 83.

38. ADBR. 76 W 161. Chef du SAA, Wender. "A.S. Israélites Nord Africains." November 9, 1942.

39. The dossier misspells his name as "Mohamed," but he is called Mahmoud in the file. ADBR. 13 W 17. *Dossier Ben Chaouch Mohamed ben Amar*. On his career in the BNA: APP. 350 W 188-96650. *Dossier Benchaouch Mahmoud ben Omar*.

40. ADBR. 13 W 17. *Dossier Ben Chaouch*. Caisse Régionale d'Assurance à M. le Directeur des RG. November 23, 1966.

41. ADBR. 13 W 17. *Dossier Ben Chaouch*. Commissaire Divisionnaire des RG à l'Intendant Régional de Police. "A/s de l'Inspecteur auxiliaire Ben Chaouch..." March 23, 1942.

42. Ben Chaouch had first been placed in the police d'état before being transferred in February 1942. ADBR. 13 W 17. *Dossier Ben Chaouch*. J. Iversenc au Directeur de la Caisse Régionale d'Assurance. January 10, 1967.

43. ADBR. 13 W 17. *Dossier Ben Chaouch*. Inspecteur de Police Dabonville. January 30, 1943.

44. ADBR. 13 W 17... "A/s de l'Inspecteur auxiliaire Ben Chaouch..." March 23, 1942.

45. Nearly identical accusations were leveled at other Algerian police officers recruited during the war and Algerian officers in Algiers.

46. Ben Chaouch eventually lost his job when he went to Algeria for vacation in October 1942 and was blocked there by the Allied invasion.

47. On Vichy labor organization of Algerians in the *zone libre*, see Cadiot, "Vichy et les Algériens."

48. ADBR. 4 M 2361.

49. For example: ADBR. 76 W 205. Service de la MOI. "Arrivée de 128 travailleurs indigènes Algériens." August 19, 1942. On German recruitment in Marseille, see Cadiot, "Vichy et les Algériens," 296; Darmon, *L'Algérie de Pétain*, 257. Algerian recruitment for German industries paralleled similar initiatives aimed at French workers, like the Service de Travail Obligatoire. Patrice Arnaud, *Les STO: Histoire des Français requis en Allemagne nazie, 1942–1945* (CNRS, 2010).

50. ADBR. 76 W 206. SAA. "A/s action de l'office de placement allemand." June 23, 1942.

51. ADBR. 4 M 2361. Commissaire Divisionnaire de police spéciale à M. le Préfet. "A/s du personnel Nord-Africain des Établissement Vermink..." February 28, 1940.

52. ADBR. 4 M 2361. Commissaire Divisionnaire de Police Spéciale à M. le Préfet. March 27, 1940.

53. The record does not specify what happened to these escaped workers. ADBR. 4 W 2361 Commissaire Divisionnaire de Police Spéciale à M. le Préfet. "A/s du personnel Nord-Africain des Établissement Vermink..." February 28, 1940.

54. ADBR. 76 W 205. SAA. "État d'esprit aux mines de la Grand-Combe." June 24, 1941.

55. ADBR. 5 W 371. Commissaire, Chef du 1er Secteur à M. le Commissaire Principal. March 14, 1942.

56. News of this came to the SAA, who wrote to the prefect of the Bouches-du-Rhône in protest. ADBR. 76 W 206. Wender. "A/s travailleurs indigènes avec contrat." April 23, 1942.

57. ADBR. 76 W 206. SAA. Wender. "A/s travailleurs indigènes Algériens à contrat." July 13, 1942.

58. ADBR. 4 M 2361. Commissaire de Police de la Sûreté à M. le Commissaire Central. January 9, 1940.

59. ADBR. 76 W 207 contains stacks of reports on searches for North Africans who had left work contracts.

60. ADBR. 5 W 371. Commissaire de Police, Chef du 1er Secteur à M. le Commissaire Principal. March 14, 1942.

61. A system of internment camps had existed in the south of France for years, used previously to house refugees from the Spanish Civil War. These same camps would later hold prisoners of war and FLN sympathizers. See Nicolas Lebourt and Abderahmen Moumen, *Rivesaltes, le camp de la France: 1939 à nos jours* (Trabucaire, 2015).

62. For example: ADBR. 76 W 204. Inspecteur de Police Nationale Klein à M. le Commissaire Principal des RG. July 16, 1942.

63. ADBR. 76 W 204. Secrétaire Général de la Police à MM. les Préfets. "Au sujet des nord africains." August 1, 1942.

64. ADBR. 76 W 206. SAA. "A/s travailleurs indigènes en rupture de contrat." October 9, 1942.

65. ADBR. 76 W 206. SAA. "Mécontentement parmi les travailleurs à contrat." August 3, 1942.

66. ADBR. 76 W 206. SAA. "A/s travailleurs indigènes . . ." October 9, 1942.

67. ADBR. 5 W 365. Secrétaire d'État à l'Intérieur à M. le Préfet. "Indigènes algériens du camp Lyautey." January 2, 1941.

68. ADBR. 5 W 365. . . "Indigènes algériens du camp Lyautey." January 2, 1941.

69. ADBR. 76 W 206. SAA. Wender. "Rapatriement de travailleurs indigènes." January 10, 1942.

70. ADBR. 5 W 365. Commissaire Divisionnaire de Police Spéciale Gaubert à M. le Directeur des Services de Police. "Hébergement de familles arabes au Camp Lyautey." January 17, 1941.

71. ADBR. 5 W 365. . . "Hébergement de familles arabes au Camp Lyautey." January 17, 1941.

72. On tensions between church and state in empire: Daughton, *An Empire Divided*.

73. This point was made in reference to searches for Algerians who escaped Camp Lyautey. ADBR. 76 W 207. Chef du Centre d'Hébergement Nord-Africain à M. le Préfet des Bouches-du-Rhône. September 17, 1941.

74. This was shortly before SAINA was renamed BAMNA. ADBR. 1 M 759. Chef du SAINA à M. le Préfet. December 12, 1939.

75. ADBR. 1 M 759. Procès-Verbal. Bachatene Hacene. December 1, 1939.

76. ADBR. 1 M 759. Chef du SAINA à M. le Préfet. December 12, 1939.

77. A *chaouch* was an "office boy" or menial bureaucrat in colonial Algeria. On Ben Hadj's vital role in SAINA: Beaujon, "The Chaouch of Marseille."

78. His girlfriend, a European, had arrived at the police station as soon as she learned where he was. ADBR. 1 M 759. Sous-Chef de la Sûreté à M. le Chef de la Sûreté. December 16, 1939.

79. ADBR. 1 M 759. Chef de la Sûreté à M. le Commissaire Central. December 17, 1939.

80. ADBR. 1 M 759. Chef de la Sûreté à M. le Commissaire Central. December 17, 1939.

81. ADBR. 76 W 205. SAA. "A/s d'une rafle Rue des Chapeliers." November 4, 1942.

82. Officers often used the informal *tu* with Algerians, but *vous* with Europeans. Complaints of this grammatical insult were also common in Algiers.

83. ADBR. 76 W 205. SAA. "A/s d'une rafle Rue des Chapeliers." November 4, 1942.

84. ADBR. 76 W 205. SAA. "A/s d'une rafle Rue des Chapeliers." November 4, 1942.

85. ADBR. 76 W 204. Procès-Verbal. "Arrestation du Nord-Africain K. Rabah." January 18, 1943.

86. On interwar politics in Algiers: Kaddache, *La vie politique à Alger*.

87. Descloitres, Reverdy, and Descloitres, *L'Algérie des Bidonvilles*, 93–94.

88. ANOM. 1 K 25. Rapport. Commissaire de Police, Susini. December 3, 1940.

89. In Paris, the policing of marketplaces was also highly gendered, but the struggles of women to provide food for their family was only viewed negatively in Communist-led protests. See Paula Schwartz, *Today Sardines Are Not for Sale: A Street Protest in Occupied Paris* (Oxford University Press, 2020).

90. On Bab El Oued: Benjamin Stora, *Histoire de l'Algérie coloniale (1830–1954)* (La Découverte, 1991), 58.

91. Fatma was also a generic name for Algerian women, like "Jane Doe." ANOM. 1 F 119. Commissaire Central Gauthier à M. le Préfet. "A.S. du ravitaillement en pain." January 31, 1942.

92. For example: AN. F 60 811. Rapport du Commandant Blot. February 20 to March 20, 1943.

93. ANOM. 1 F 119. Lettre. Commissaire Principal Lainyech à M. le Secrétaire Général pour les Affaires Musulmanes. August 24, 1942.

94. ANOM. 1 F 119. Lettre. Commissaire Principal Lainyech... August 24, 1942.

95. ANOM. 1 F 119. Lettre. Préfet d'Algiers à M. le Maire. September 2, 1942.

96. ANOM. 1 F 435. Mme. LLobet à M. Le Secrétaire Général pour la Police. September 14, 1944.

97. ANOM. 1 F 119. Commerçants de la Rue Randon à M. Boukerdenna. December 18, 1941.

98. ANOM. 1 F 119. Commissaire Central à M. le Préfet. "A/s marchands indigènes ambulants." January 10, 1941.

99. ANOM. 1 F 119... "A/s marchands indigènes ambulants." January 10, 1941.

100. Descloitres, Reverdy, and Descloitres, *L'Algérie des Bidonvilles*, 42.

101. ANOM. 1 F 119. Lettre. Hubert M. à M. le Directeur. July 14, 1942.

102. His assertion about taxes was false. Until 1918, Algerians actually paid a disproportionate amount because Europeans were exempt from many taxes. Kateb, *Européens, "Indigènes" et Juifs en Algérie*, 82.

103. ANOM. 1 F 119. Lettre. Hubert M. à M. le Directeur. July 14, 1942.

104. Christelle Taraud argues that the yaouleds were the children of prostitutes and thus linked to vice, but this was not consistently the case in police files. Christelle Taraud, "Les *yaouleds*: Entre marginalisation sociale et sédition politique," *Revue d'histoire de l'enfance "irrégulière"* 10 (2008): 59–74. On youth "gangs" in France: Miranda Sachs, "'But the Child Is Flighty, Playful, Curious': Working-Class Boyhood and the Policing of Play in Belle Époque Paris," *Historical Reflections/Réflexions Historiques* 45, no. 2 (2019): 7–27.

105. ANOM. 1 F 125. Maire de la Ville d'Alger. October 31, 1944.

106. ANOM. 1 F 125. Musée National des Beaux-Arts d'Algiers à M. le Secrétaire Général. October 12, 1944.

107. See Pierce and Rao, eds., *Discipline and the Other Body*; Thomas, *Violence and Colonial Order*.

108. Ruth Ginio, "La propagande impériale de Vichy," in *L'Empire colonial sous Vichy*, ed. Jacques Cantier and Eric Jennings (Odile Jacob, 2004).

109. Vichy efforts to woo "traditional" Algerian elites were also about restricting the power of more radical political elites, particularly nationalists. See Jacques Cantier, *L'Algérie sous le régime de Vichy* (Odile Jacob, 2002), 256–263; Cadiot, "Vichy et les Algériens," 95.

110. On the tension of republican empire, see Gary Wilder, *The French Imperial Nation-State: Negritude and Colonial Humanism between the Two World Wars* (University of Chicago Press, 2005).

111. In one such case, a police informant complained that he had been called a "*sale bicot*" by an officer after refusing to bribe him while in line for a ration card. ANOM. 1 F 119. Lettre. Mohamed Missaoui à M. le Gouverneur Général. November 28, 1942.

112. The same anonymous author sent a letter to the prefect of Algiers on April 25, 1942, signed "un Musulman d'Alger." ANOM. 1 F 119. "Un Français Musulman" à M. le Gouverneur Général de l'Algérie. April 23, 1942.

113. ANOM. 1 F 119. Préfet d'Alger, Lavaysse à M. le Commissaire Central. "Plainte contre le commissaire du 3ème Arrondissement." May 8, 1942.

114. ANOM. 1 F 119. Gardiens de la paix Viel et Klein à M. le Officier de la Paix. March 28, 1942.

115. ANOM. 1 F 119. Procès-Verbal. Belgacem A. April 2, 1942.

116. They listed a local notable they had spent the evening with as a witness to their sobriety. ANOM. 1 F 119... Belgacem A. April 2, 1942.

117. ANOM. 1 F 119. Procès-Verbal. Mohamed D. April 18, 1942.

118. A *planton* is the front desk officer of the police station. ANOM. 1 F 119. Procès-Verbal. Jampy. April 4, 1942.

119. ANOM. 1 F 119. Procès-Verbal. Mohamed D. April 18, 1942.

120. ANOM. 1 F 119. Gardien de la Paix Viel à L'Officier de la Paix. April 15, 1942.

121. ANOM. 1 F 119. Commissaire Fachot à M. le Commissaire Central. April 21, 1942.

122. No record indicates that Viel and Klein were prosecuted. ANOM. 1 F 119. Commissaire Central à M. le Préfet. "Violences par des gardiens de la paix sur indigène musulman." April 22, 1942.

123. Jacques Cantier, for example, frames the Zeralda affair in relation to other incidents of "intercommunity" violence. Cantier, *L'Algérie sous le régime de Vichy*, 189-192.

124. ANOM. 9 H 27. CIE. "Affaire de Zeralda." August 26, 1942.

125. ANOM. 9 H 27.

126. The trials were delayed because a civil court was slated to be created in Algiers, but the project fell through during the war. The delay was so long that Mayor Fourcade left house arrest and enlisted in the Free French Army. It was several months before the authorities realized. The four men were eventually tried by military tribunal in Oran. ANOM. 9 H 27.

127. I take this idea of bodies and space "coding" each other from Jodi Rios, *Black Lives and Spatial Matters*.

4. MAPPING THE ENEMY WITHIN

1. ADBR. 76 W 187. Commissaire Principal Marabuto à M. Le Commissaire Divisionnaire des RG. January 12, 1943.

2. ADBR. 76 W 205. SAA. Wender. "Population musulmane nord-africaine de Marseille." January 6, 1943.

3. ADBR. 76 W 206. SAA. "Relation des travailleurs indigènes avec leur famille." November 25, 1942.

4. Miranda Pollard argues that restoring French men and women to traditional gender roles was a key tenet of Vichy social policy. Miranda Pollard, *Reign of Virtue: Mobilizing Gender in Vichy France* (University of Chicago Press, 1998). Kristen Stormberg Childers focuses on the contradiction of Vichy's valorization of family structures while also separating families for the war effort. Kristen Stromberg Childers, *Fathers, Families, and the State in France, 1914-1945* (Cornell University Press, 2003).

5. ADBR. 76 W 205. SAA. Wender. "Population musulmane nord-africaine de Marseille." January 6, 1943.

6. ADBR. 76 W 205. SAA. Wender. "Population musulmane..." January 6, 1943.

7. See Blanchard, "Des Kabyles 'perdus' en région parisienne." Blanchard further explores these exchanges in *Des colonisés ingouvernables*.

8. ADBR. 76 W 206. SAA. Wender. "Indigène ayant abandonné son travail." August 6, 1942.

9. ADBR. 63 W 1060. Lettre à M. le Procureur. May 10, 1942.

10. On polygamy and law in French Algeria, see Surkis, *Sex, Law, and Sovereignty*.

11. Similar moments also occurred with Senegalese men. See Boittin, *Undesirable*, chap. 5; Zimmerman, *Militarizing Marriage*.

12. ADBR. 63 W 1060. Procès-Verbal. Djerdi. June 20, 1942.

13. See Berlière, *Le monde des polices*, 140-141. See also E. G. Perrier, *La police municipale, spéciale et mobile: Historique & organisation*. (M. Giard & É. Brière, 1920), 155-161.

14. Berlière, *Le monde des polices*, 142–146. On the political policing of the RG: Patrick Rougelet, *RG: La machine à scandales* (Albin Michel, 1997); Charpier, *Les RG et le Parti Communiste*.

15. Some historians describe the special police as the precursor of the RG, but the services coexisted for a period, and Berlière argues that they jealously guarded information from each other. In 1941, Vichy reorganized police intelligence services under a new Direction des Renseignements Généraux. See Berlière, *Le monde des polices*, 146, 166–168.

16. Berlière, *Le monde des polices*, 147.

17. RG reports also discuss other colonial populations in Marseille, although they tended to feature North Africans most prominently.

18. On informants in Algerian policing, see Kalman, *Law, Order, and Empire*, 30.

19. ADBR. 5 W 361. Commissaire Divisionnaire Gaubert à M. le Préfet. July 1, 1940.

20. ADBR. 5 W 372. Délégué Régional à la Propagande, Klotz à M. l'Intendant de Police. April 21, 1943. This surveillance was the main function of the CAI. On CAI informants: Bollenot, "Maintenir l'ordre impérial," chaps. 7, 8, 9.

21. ANOM. 1 K 201. Commissaire Principal des RG, Carcenac à M. le Préfet. "A.s. du nommé Mohamed ben H." June 19, 1945.

22. ANOM. 91 3F 2. *Dossier Mailhou Jacques Camille*.

23. Bollenot also suggests anti-Communist sentiment as a motivation or, conversely, Communist sympathizers who joined to subvert the state. Bollenot, "Maintenir l'ordre imperial."

24. ADBR. 1 M 801. Commissaire Divisionnaire Police Spéciale à M. le Préfet des Bouches-du-Rhône. "Réunion de propagande de la section de Marseille du Congrès Musulman." May 26, 1931.

25. ADBR. 76 W 204. Commissaire Principal des RG à M. le Commissaire Divisionnaire des RG. "A.s. de la situation matérielle et morale de nos sujets musulmans de l'empire de la région de Marseille." February 9, 1943.

26. ADBR. 76 W 205. Commissaire Seignard, Chef des RG à M. l'Intendant Régional de Police. "A/s du nommé Boulou A." December 17, 1941.

27. On *undesirable* and its gendered connotations, see Boittin, *Undesirable*. This category of "undesirable" is similar to the idea of "suspect" traced by Kathleen Keller in West Africa. Keller, *Colonial Suspects*.

28. For example, the word بَرَكة (*baraka*) in classical Arabic means a blessing rather than "enough" or "stop."

29. ANOM. 1 K 130. Police Spéciale d'Alger. "Soirée donnée par la Troupe Rachid Kssantini." May 24, 1941.

30. I found only one North African RG officer in Marseille, and he served just four months before being transferred to the SAA. For the RG of Algiers, personnel records are in ANOM 3 F 1–16.

31. On the stakes of Algeria for Vichy, see Cantier, *L'Algérie sous le régime de Vichy*.

32. AN. F 1a 3297. Bulletin de Renseignements. Service des Affaires Musulmanes. January 20, 1945. See also Ageron, "Les populations du Maghreb face à la propagande allemande." Aliénor Cadiot also notes the German propaganda aimed at North Africans. Cadiot, "Vichy et les Algériens," 119.

33. There were similar fears about the influence of Italy in North Africa. For example, the police arrested an Algerian man found carrying a pamphlet that said "على السلامة في افريقية عطف اطالية [Italian Sympathy for Peace in Africa]." ANOM. 2 I 32. Rapport de police. August 18, 1937.

34. ADBR. 1 M 801. Le Ministre de l'Intérieur. "Propagande antifrançaise parmi les nord-africains." April 18, 1934.

35. In reality, the ENA had a tense relationship with the Communists and eventually broke with them. This denial of political ambitions did not stop the Prefecture of Police in Paris from disbanding the ENA and arresting its leaders in 1937.

36. ANOM. 1 F 77. Renseignements Généraux. November 1936.

37. See Cantier, *L'Algérie sous le régime de Vichy*; Cantier and Jennings, *L'Empire colonial sous Vichy*.

38. On the collaboration of Algerians, see Cadiot, "Vichy et les Algériens," chap. 8.

39. Lamoudi, for example, said that Algerians would lose interest in the German cause when they realized that German racism also considered them inferior. ANOM. 4 I 29. Lamine Lamoudi. "Le Statut Algérien" Citoyens et Sujets. May 31, 1943.

40. ADBR. 76 W 204. Ministre de l'Intérieur à M. le Préfet des Bouches-du-Rhône. "Propagande auprès des indigènes algériens." February 12, 1941.

41. ADBR. 76 W 205. SAA. Wender. "A/S Surveillance effectuée à Alger sur certains indigènes." January 19, 1942.

42. ADBR. 76 W 204. . . "Propagande auprès des indigènes algériens." February 12, 1941.

43. ADBR. 76 W 206. SAA. "État d'esprit de musulman algériens de Marseille." December 13, 1941.

44. On Algerian Muslim-Jewish relations, see Katz, *The Burdens of Brotherhood*.

45. On Vichy antisemitic policies in Marseille: Ryan, *The Holocaust and the Jews of Marseille*.

46. On German propaganda among North African prisoners of war: Frank, *Hostages of Empire*; Raffael Scheck, "Nazi Propaganda towards French Muslim Prisoners of War," *Holocaust and Genocide Studies* 26, no. 3 (2012): 447–477. On German propaganda in the Middle East: Jeffrey Herf, *Nazi Propaganda for the Arab World* (Yale University Press, 2009).

47. ADBR. 76 W 206. Wender. "Rapatriés nord-africains en traitement à Marseille." April 27, 1942.

48. ANOM. 1 F 112. Rapport Mensuel. August 1940.

49. ANOM. 1 K 130. RG. December 19, 1942.

50. ANOM. 1 K 130. RG. "A.s de la population musulmane." December 8, 1942.

51. ANOM. 1 K 130. RG. "A.s de la population musulmane." December 8, 1942.

52. Lamoudi was an acolyte of Ben Badis and a member of the 'Ulamā. ANOM. 4 I 29. Lamine Lamoudi. "Le Statut Algérien" Citoyens et Sujets. May 31, 1943.

53. ANOM. 4 I 29. . . "Le Statut Algérien" Citoyens et Sujets. May 31, 1943.

54. These antinational laws joined other "exceptional" justice reforms that Vichy used to repress political threats. See Alain Bancaud, "La magistrature et la répression politique de Vichy ou l'histoire d'un demi-échec," *Droit et Société* 34 (1996): 557–574.

55. Algerians make up nearly 30 percent of the names on the list, while they represented closer to 3 percent of the population of Marseille at the time. ADBR. 4 M 3281.

56. ADBR. 76 W 205. SAA. "Note." April 21, 1941.

57. For example, the list that cited 30 percent Algerian names includes no details about why these men were arrested on anti-French charges.

58. This is likely the same Djerdi discussed earlier. ADBR. 76 W 205. SAA. "A/s de Djerdi D." June 6, 1941.

59. The report makes no specific mention of the behavior considered anti-French by the police.

60. Olivier Le Cour Grandmaison states that administrative internment, rooted in the indigénat code, was briefly permitted in France from 1938–1944. Laroubi was likely detained under this wartime expansion. Le Cour Grandmaison, *De l'indigénat*, 111.

61. ADBR. 76 W 204. Law 474 du April 17, 1942.

62. Today, the French Civil Code allows judges to strip citizenship from naturalized citizens for charges of terrorism, a practice reminiscent of these Vichy-era anti-French laws.

63. ANOM. 1 F 112. Commissaire de Police, Mosconi. January 24, 1941.

64. ANOM. 1 F 112. Commissaire de Police, Mosconi. January 24, 1941.

65. On politics in Algiers in this moment: Rey-Goldzeiguer, *Aux origines de la guerre d'Algérie*; Alfred Salinas, *Les Américains en Algérie, 1942–1945* (L'Harmattan, 2013), 136.

66. ANOM. 1 F 119. Commissaire Gourierec. "Propos séditieux tenus par le nommé Bedoudjhou B." December 1942.

67. ANOM. 9 H 27. RG. "Cris séditieux et rébellion." October 11, 1943.

68. ANOM. 9 H 27. RG. "Cris séditieux et rébellion." October 11, 1943.

69. ANOM. 1 K 212. Le Commissaire Principal des RG à M. le Préfet. "A/s du nommé Mohammed T. (et non Madedet)." March 5, 1945.

70. ANOM. 1 K 212... "A/s du nommé Mohammed T. (et non Madedet)." March 5, 1945.

71. See, for example, Boittin, *Colonial Metropolis*.

72. Algerian Jews did not face deportation, in part because the Allied invasion of Algiers was simultaneous with the ramp-up of deportation. See Kalman, *Law, Order and Empire*, 128. On these brigades: Joly, *L'antisémitisme de bureau*. On North Africa: Boum and Abrevaya Stein, eds., *The Holocaust and North Africa*. On Marseille: Ryan, *The Holocaust and the Jews of Marseille*.

73. The Germans dynamited more than a thousand buildings in Marseille's Le Panier neighborhood in 1943. Although justified as a matter of "public health," the authorities, aided by police from Paris, in fact sought to root out Jews, Communists, and dissidents. ADBR. 76 W 104. See also Kitson, *Police and Politics in Marseille*, chap. 7. Sheila Crane notes that many of those arrested were North African, but I could find no evidence of this. Le Panier was mostly populated by Italians and Corsicans in this period. Sheila Crane, *Mediterranean Crossroads: Marseille and Modern Architecture* (University of Minnesota Press, 2011).

74. On the black market in France: Fabrice Grenard, *La France du marché noir (1940–1949)* (Payot, 2008); Fabrice Grenard, "L'administration du contrôle économique en France, 1940–1950," *Revue d'histoire moderne et contemporaine* 57, no. 2 (2010): 132–158; Kenneth Mouré, "La Capitale de la Faim: Black Market Restaurants in Paris, 1940–1944," *French Historical Studies* 38, no. 2 (2015): 311–341; Kenneth Mouré, *Marché Noir: The Economy of Survival in Second World War France* (Cambridge University Press, 2023); Paul Sanders, *Histoire du marché noir: 1940–1946* (Perrin, 2001). On policing the black market in Algeria: Kalman, *Law, Order and Empire*, 135–141.

75. Shannon Fogg, *The Politics of Everyday Life in Vichy France: Foreigners, Undesirables and Strangers* (Cambridge University Press, 2009). On Jews and the black market: Grenard, *La France du marché noir*, 54.

76. Grenard, *La France du marché noir*, 98, 185; Grenard, "L'administration du contrôle économique en France," 143.

77. See Mouré, *Marché Noir*, chap. 1; Kenneth Mouré, "'Economic Tyranny' and Public Anger in France, 1945–1947," *Contemporary European History* (2022): 1–14.

78. Grenard makes this argument based on an analysis of Paris records and files from other departments. Grenard, *La France du marché noir*, chap. 6.

79. Grenard, *La France du marché noir*, 178; Grenard, "L'administration du contrôle économique en France," 152.

80. Mouré points out that the Contrôle Economique measured its efficacy through the number of fines issued. Fining vulnerable North Africans might have been one strategy for increasing numbers without incurring public backlash. Mouré, *Marché Noir*, chap. 3; Mouré, "Economic Tyranny," 4.

81. ADBR. 76 W 205. SAA. Wender. "A/s Aperçu de la vie indigène à Marseille." February 13, 1942.

82. ADBR. 76 W 144.

83. ADBR. 76 W 205. SAA. "A.S. Louaib Sghrir." May 10, 1941.

84. ADBR. 76 W 206. CIE de Constantine. "A/S des indigènes et du marche noir en France." March 14, 1942.

85. ADBR. 76 W 205. SAA. Wender. "A/s indigènes de la rue des Chapeliers." November 3, 1942.

86. ADBR. 76 W 205. SAA. Wender. "A/s indigènes . . ." November 3, 1942.

87. ADBR. 76 W 205. SAA. "Situation des nord-africains immobilisé dans la Métropole." January 30, 1943.

88. ADBR. 76 W 205. SAA. "Situation des nord-africains . . ." January 30, 1943.

89. The "month of fasting" is a reference to Ramadan. ADBR. 5 W 366. Commissaire de Police à M. le Commissaire Principal de la Sûreté. March 3, 1942.

90. ADBR. 5 W 366. Commissaire de Police . . . March 3, 1942. The police found all the accusations to be false.

91. ADBR. 63 W 1057. Résident 40 Rue des Petites Maries à M. le Procureur. February 4, 1942.

92. Hada, one of the rare Algerian women to appear in police archives in Marseille, is an anomaly in that she appears to have migrated to Marseille alone. Her first name, Hada, could be either Arabic or Hebrew in origin, indicating that she might have been an Algerian Jew. If so, the letter makes no reference to it. ADBR. 63 W 1057. Résident 40 Rue des Petites Maries . . . February 4, 1942.

93. See Ryan, *The Holocaust and the Jews of Marseille*.

94. ADBR. 63 W 1057. Procès-Verbal. "Affaire c/ D. Perle." January 9, 1942.

95. Samuel Kalman argues that Vichy focused on policing European profiteers in Algeria, but after the Allied invasion, police attention shifted to Algerian traffickers. In Algiers, however, I saw a consistent focus on Algerians, regardless of the government in power. Kalman, *Law, Order and Empire*, 137.

96. ANOM. 1 F 120. Commissaire Central. "Activité de la brigade économique." February 28, 1943.

97. ANOM. 1 F 124. Commissaire Corria. "Opérations de police." August 20, 1945.

98. ADBR. 76 W 206. SAA. "A.S. Mesures spéciales aux indigènes." January 13, 1942.

99. Salinas cites a population growth of nearly two hundred thousand, based on American military sources. Salinas, *Les Américains en Algérie*, 189. Mahfoud Kaddache, however, argues that there are no reliable statistics on Algiers's wartime populations. Kaddache, *La Casbah*, 35–36.

100. The Economic Brigades were created during the war to police the new rationing system. See Mouré, *Marché Noir*. ANOM. 1 F 121. Chef de la Brigade Économique, Friand à M. le Commissaire Central. July 19, 1944.

101. ANOM. 1 F 121. Chef de la Brigade Économique . . . July 19, 1944.

102. ANOM. 1 F 121. Chef de la Brigade Économique . . . July 19, 1944.

103. ANOM. 1 F 125. "Au sujet du Secrétaire H. Cl Friand René et du G.P. auxiliaire Bobin André . . ." November 2, 1944.

104. ANOM. 1 F 125. "Au sujet du Secrétaire H. Cl Friand René . . ." November 2, 1944.

105. ANOM. 7 CAB 12. "Quel revenu mensuel un indigène peut-il tirer du trafic de ses tickets d'alimentation?" May 20, 1942.

106. When such reports do occur, it was typically for overcharging in stores, especially butcher shops. For example: AWA. 4 H 89.

107. On land expropriation in Algeria, see Sessions, *By Sword and Plow*; Guignard, *1871: L'Algérie Sous Séquestre*.

108. ANOM. 1 K 631. "Rapports journaliers de la brigade économique d'Alger." December 5, 1942.
109. ANOM. 1 F 439. Commissaire Central Adjoint, Lafond à M. Le Commissaire Central. September 13, 1944.
110. ANOM. 1 F 439. Préfet d'Alger à M. le Gouverneur Général. "Réquisition de la main d'œuvre agricole." October 20, 1944.
111. ANOM. 1 F 439... "Réquisition de la main d'œuvre agricole." October 20, 1944.
112. ANOM. 1 K 130. RG. March 4, 1943.
113. ANOM. 1 F 439. *Dossier Dépôts des Travailleurs à Kouba.*
114. On immigration to Algiers during the war: Kaddache, *La Casbah*, 36; Descloitres, Reverdy, and Descloitres, *L'Algérie des bidonville*, 79.
115. ANOM. 1 F 439. Directeur de l'Office Régional du Travail à M. Le Préfet. "A/s des délinquants du marché noir en résidence surveillée à la section disciplinaire agricole de Kouba." September 29, 1944.
116. ANOM. 1 F 439... "A/s des délinquants du marché noir..." September 29, 1944.
117. ANOM. 1 F 439. *Dossier Dépôts des Travailleurs à Kouba.*
118. The idea of the internal enemy has been theorized by Mathieu Rigouste to describe the treatment of postcolonial immigrants as "internal enemies," an extension of Cold War attitudes about Communism and decolonization. My research demonstrates that this process was already underway during World War II. Mathieu Rigouste, "L'ennemi intérieur: De la guerre coloniale au contrôle sécuritaire," *Cultures et Conflits* 67 (automne 2007): 157–174.

5. A NEW POLICE FOR A NEW REPUBLIC

1. The title *J'accuse* is a reference to Emile Zola's work of the same name. AN. F 60 871. Ferhat Abbas. "J'accuse l'Europe." *Cahiers des Amis du Manifeste et de la Liberté*. Undated, likely 1946, 5.
2. AN. F 60 871. Ferhat Abbas. "J'accuse l'Europe."... Undated, likely 1946, 5.
3. Herrick Chapman, *France's Long Reconstruction: In Search of the Modern Republic* (Harvard University Press, 2018), chap. 1.
4. See Eric Jennings, *Free French Africa in World War II: The African Resistance* (Cambridge University Press, 2015).
5. The new constitution was approved in October 1946. Chapman, *France's Long Reconstruction*, chap. 1.
6. See, for example, Nicolas Bancel, Pascal Blanchard, and Françoise Vergès, *La République coloniale* (Albin Michel, 2003); Jennifer Boittin, "Black in France: The Language and Politics of Race in the Late Third Republic," *French Politics, Culture and Society* 27, no. 2 (2009): 23–46; Emily Marker, *Black France, White Europe: Youth, Race, and Belonging in the Postwar Era* (Cornell University Press, 2022).
7. AN. F 1a 5012. Ministre de L'Intérieur, Tixier à M. le Ministre des Finances. "Projet de décret portant suppression de services dont relèvent les travailleurs nord-africains résidant en France métropolitaine." Undated.
8. ADBR. 148 W 193. "Le statut des originaires de l'Algérie." Undated.
9. Jean-Jacques Jordi, "L'inconscience ou le péril," in *Alger 1940–1962: Une ville en guerres*, ed. Jean-Jacques Jordi and Guy Pervillé (Autrement, 1999), 89. Although I cite this book for a timeline of events and decrees, I approach other claims within it with caution.
10. On the new electoral system: Stora, *Histoire de l'Algérie coloniale*, 110; James McDougall, *A History of Algeria* (Cambridge University Press, 2017), 184–185.
11. McDougall, *A History of Algeria*, 184. Other colonized women also could not vote, but most European French women, in metropole and colony, could. See Pascale Barthélémy, *Sororité et colonialisme: Françaises et Africaines au temps de la guerre froide (1944–1962)* (Éditions de la Sorbonne, 2022).

12. McDougall, *A History of Algeria*, 184.
13. AN. F 1a 3297. "Législation répressive susceptible de s'appliquer en Algérie." May 14, 1945.
14. BNA. *La Liberté*. July 12, 1945.
15. ANOM. 1 K 81. *La Voix Indigène*. November 9, 1943.
16. AN. F 1a 3297. Ministre de l'Intérieur au Gouverneur Général de l'Algérie. October 10, 1945.
17. The CAI carried out political surveillance of West African, Indochinese, and Malagasy populations in France. See Bollenot, "Maintenir l'ordre impérial."
18. ADBR. 150 W 171. Gouvernement Provisoire. "Suppression du service dont relèvent les travailleurs nord-africains résidant en France métropolitaine." Décret of November 17, 1945. The CAI was also closed after World War II.
19. On the dissolution of the BNA: Blanchard, *La police parisienne et les Algériens*, chap. 2.
20. AN. F 1a 5012. Le Ministre de l'Intérieur, Tixier à M. Le Ministre du Travail. "Suppression des services d'exception dont relèvent les Musulmans qui résident en France." May 29, 1945.
21. ADBR. 150 W 170. Préfet des Bouches-du-Rhône à Divers Maires. "Cartes d'identité des Français Musulmans d'Algérie." March 25, 1946.
22. ADBR. 150 W 170. Chef de la Ière Division à M. le Chef de Cabinet du Préfet. "Cartes d'identité des Musulmans Nord-Africains." November 19, 1945.
23. See Chapman, *France's Long Reconstruction*.
24. AWA. 1 Z 155. *Dossier Association des Polices Résistants Républicains du 8 Novembre*.
25. Samuel Kalman paints a different picture of collaboration and epuration in Constantine, arguing that police there tried to undermine epuration. Kalman, *Law, Order, and Empire*, 145.
26. Kitson, *Police and Politics in Marseille*, 284.
27. ADBR. 76 W 204. Commissaire de la Sûreté, Mattei. "A/S du nommé Poussardin Louis." February 17, 1943.
28. ADBR. 76 W 204. . . "A/S du nommé Poussardin Louis." February 17, 1943.
29. Poussardin spent the rest of the war in jail. The police suggested that he was a member of COMBAT, a resistance network in Marseille. A later note from Vichy, however, oddly accused Poussardin of working for Germany, distributing ID cards only to infiltrate and betray Gaullist networks. Commandant Wender of the SAA was also sent to a German prison in 1942 for his political views. See Aliénor Cadiot, "Agir seul ou en réseau? La 'résistance' du commandant Robert Wender et le Service des Affaires Algériennes (1941–1943)" (presentation, French Colonial Historical Society, Martinique, 2023).
30. ADBR. 148 W 269. Police des RG. "Affiche apposée à Marseille par le syndicat des inspecteurs de la police d'état." June 2, 1948.
31. BNA. "A quand l'épuration dans les polices d'état?" *La Liberté*. November 23, 1944.
32. BNA. "La police et le complot fasciste." *La Liberté*. May 31, 1945.
33. BNA. "La police et le complot fasciste." *La Liberté*. May 31, 1945; "Dockers matraqués, marins licenciés, protestent contre les provocations hitlériennes." *La Liberté*. August 16, 1945; "Méthodes hitlériennes." *La République Algérienne*. May 30, 1947.
34. On this sympathy, see Cadiot, "Vichy et les Algériens," 119.
35. AN. F 1a 3297. Général d'Armée, Catroux à M. le Général de Gaulle. October 30, 1944.
36. AN. F 1a 3297. Le Préfet d'Alger, Périllier à M. le Gouverneur Général de l'Algérie. August 31, 1945.
37. Although called "Senegalese," these soldiers came from throughout French West Africa.

38. BWA. Bulletin Municipal Officiel de la Ville d'Alger. Séances du May 12 and June 9, 1939. On colonial prostitution: Elisa Camiscioli, *Selling French Sex: Prostitution, Trafficking, and Global Migrations* (Cambridge University Press, 2024); Christina Firpo, *Black Market Business: Selling Sex in Northern Vietnam, 1920–1945* (Cornell University Press, 2021); Taraud, *La prostitution coloniale*; Caroline Séquin, *Desiring Whiteness: A Racial History of Prostitution in France and Colonial Senegal, 1848–1950* (Cornell University Press, 2024).

39. AN. F 60 733.

40. For example: ANOM. 1 F 118. Commandant de la Section de Gendarmerie d'Alger, Soymie. "Incident survenu le 24 Octobre 1941 à Alger entre tirailleurs sénégalais et civils indigènes." October 25, 1941.

41. The lowercase "noir" here is a reflection of the orthography in the quote. ANOM. 1F 126. Commissaire Divisionnaire Laperriere. August 21, 1944.

42. For one evaluation of the stakes of this claim to whiteness: Cheryl Harris, "Whiteness as Property," *Harvard Law Review* 106, no. 8 (1993): 1707–1791.

43. ANOM. 1 F 124. Commandant la Section de Gendarmerie d'Alger, Broise. "Sur un incident entre tirailleurs sénégalais et population indigène à Alger." June 12, 1945.

44. ANOM. 1 F 124... "Sur un incident entre tirailleurs sénégalais..." June 12, 1945.

45. ANOM. 1 F 124. Rapport. Commissaire Principal Magne. "Incident entre tirailleurs sénégalais et civils musulmans." July 2, 1945.

46. ANOM 1 F 149. Commissaire Dumas. "Propagande nationaliste musulmane." August 2, 1948; ANOM 1 F 176. "Incidents entres militaires sénégalais et Musulmans." August 10, 1949.

47. Some sociologists refer to the area between Gare St. Charles and Cours Belsunce as Marseille's "Petit Harlem," although usually in reference to the influx of African migrants in the 1950s. See Brigette Bertoncello et Sylvie Bredeloup, "A la recherche du docker noir," in *Dockers de la Méditerranée à la Mer du Nord: Des quais et des hommes dans l'histoire*, ed. Jean Domenichino, Jean-Marie Guillon, and Robert Mencherini (Édisud, 1999), 144–146; Pattieu, "Souteneurs noirs à Marseille."

48. ADBR. 149 W 171. Secrétaire Général pour la Police à M. le Commissaire Régional. "Rixe entre indigènes dans la rue des Chapeliers." June 7, 1945.

49. ADBR. 149 W 171... "Rixe entre indigènes dans la rue des Chapeliers." June 7, 1945.

50. ADBR. 149 W 171... "Rixe entre indigènes dans la rue des Chapeliers." June 7, 1945.

51. ADBR. 149 W 172. Secrétaire Général pour la Police à M. Le Commissaire Régional. "Rixe entre indigènes à Marseille." June 8, 1945.

52. ADBR. 149 W 171... "Rixe entre indigènes dans la rue des Chapeliers." June 7, 1945.

53. ADBR. 149 W 171... "Rixe entre indigènes dans la rue des Chapeliers." June 7, 1945.

54. For example: ANOM. 1 F 121. M. Laurens-Berge. "Bagarre entre indigènes et tirailleurs sénégalais à la Campagne Mahieddine." July 27, 1944.

55. For example: A report on the "manque de sécurité" in the Casbah notes an incident in which Allied soldiers broke into the house of an "indigène" and raped his wife. ANOM. 1 K 130. Police des RG. December 8, 1942. On conflict with Allied soldiers in Algeria: Kalman, *Law, Order, and Empire*, 142. On the sexual violence of Allied soldiers in France, see Mary Louise Roberts, *What Soldiers Do: Sex and the American GI in World War II France* (University of Chicago Press, 2013).

56. On "undesirable" mobility: Boittin, *Undesirable*.

57. Europeans from North Africa in Marseille were housed in Camp de la Blancarde and were also given financial assistance to return to Algeria. ADBR. 149 W 137. Compte Rendu. October 24, 1944.

58. ADBR. 149 W 137. Compte Rendu. October 24, 1944.
59. ADBR. 149 W 137. M. Le Commissaire Guyomarc à M. Le Commissaire Principal des RG. "Comportement des Musulmans Nord-Africains durant la semaine écoulée." July 1945.
60. ADBR. 149 W 137. Service Départemental des RG. "A/s de la réunion tenue par l'Association des Musulmans Algériens de Marseille." July 25, 1945.
61. ADBR. 149 W 201. "Mlle Caunignac." September 21, 1945.
62. Administrators did not seem overly concerned with this possibility, however, as I found no records of officials in Marseille or Algiers commenting on stowaways returning to Algeria.
63. ADBR. 7 W 61. Ministre des Prisonniers de Guerre, Déportés et Réfugiés aux Commissaires Régionaux et les Préfets. "Instructions sur le rapatriement des réfugiés civils nord-africains." August 29, 1945.
64. ADBR. 150 W 170. Préfet d'Alger à M. le Préfet des Bouches-du-Rhône. March 5, 1946.
65. MacMaster, *Colonial Migrants and Racism*, 19. See also Sayad, *La double absence*; Jacques Simon, *L'immigration algérienne en France: Des origines à l'indépendance* (Paris-Méditerrané, 2000).
66. Simon, *L'immigration algérienne en France*, 187.
67. For example: Blanchard, *Histoire de l'immigration algérienne en France*; MacMaster, *Colonial Migrants and Racism*; Sayad, *La double absence*; Stora, *Ils venaient d'Algérie*. Muriel Cohen focuses, in contrast, on family immigration. Cohen, *Des familles invisibles*.
68. ADBR. 148 W 193. Service Départmental des RG. April 17, 1952.
69. ADBR. 148 W 193. Service Départmental des RG. April 17, 1952.
70. ADBR. 148 W 273. Service des RG. "Rivalités entre Algériens et Marocains de Marseille." December 14, 1949.
71. ADBR. 148 W 273... "Rivalités entre Algériens et Marocains..." December 14, 1949.
72. ANOM. 1 F 128. Police d'état d'Alger. Commissaire de Police, Mercadal. May 17, 1947.
73. A large collection of these reports and articles can be found in ANOM. 9 X 58.
74. ADBR. 150 W 170. Ministre de l'Intérieur, Service des Affaires Musulmanes Nord-Africaines. September 1, 1945.
75. Multiple examples can be found in: ADBR. 148 W 215; 148 W 216; 148 W 217.
76. On the failed efforts to control Algerian immigration post-1945 see Malek Ath-Messaoud and Alain Gillette, *L'immigration algérienne en France* (Entente, 1976), 40; Blanchard, *Histoire de l'immigration algérienne*, 76; MacMaster, *Colonial Migrants and Racism*, 180.
77. Descloitres, Reverdy, and Descloitres, *L'Algérie des bidonvilles*, 79.
78. Descloitres, Reverdy, and Descloitres, *L'Algérie des bidonvilles*, 80. Benjamin Stora, however, says French citizens still made up 60 percent of Algiers in 1950. Stora, *Histoire de l'Algérie coloniale*, 56.
79. Descloitres, Reverdy, and Descloitres, *L'Algérie des bidonvilles*, 83–84.
80. On the policing of bidonvilles: Jim House, "Colonial Containment? Repression of Pro-Independence Street Demonstrations in Algiers, Casablanca and Paris, 1945–1962," *War in History* 25, no. 2 (2018): 172–201; Crane, "Housing as Battleground."
81. On continuities post-Vichy, see Berlière, *Le monde des polices en France*.
82. ADBR. 150 W 165. Le Secrétaire Général pour la Police à M. Le Préfet. April 20, 1946.
83. In Marseille, officials even requested that agents from other regions of France be sent to Marseille to fill a severe shortage of officers. ADBR. 150 W 165. Commissaire Central à M. le Préfet. "Personnel." April 9, 1946.

84. The 1949 report evoked the "return" of a targeted police brigade, as had existed in the "big cities of France," but it made no specific mention of the history of such a brigade in Marseille.

85. ADBR. 148 W 271. Service des RG. "Brigade Nord Africaine." April 20, 1949.

86. ADBR. 148 W 271. Service des RG. "Brigade Nord Africaine." April 20, 1949.

87. The CAI, for example, did carry out targeted political surveillance of colonial populations but did not limit itself to one racial or ethnic group. See Bollenot, "Maintenir l'ordre impérial."

88. ADBR. 148 W 271. Service des RG. "Brigade Nord Africaine." April 20, 1949.

89. In Paris, the Brigade Nord-Africaine closed, only for a "brigade des aggressions et violences" designed to police Algerians to open a few years later. See Blanchard, *La police parisienne et les Algériens*, chap. 5; Prakash, "Colonial Techniques in the Imperial Capital."

90. ADBR. 148 W 271. Chef de la Brigade du Quartier de la Bourse à M. le Commissaire Central. "Activité de la brigade. " May 10, 1949.

91. The note mentions only Arabic, although later letters suggest a knowledge of Amazigh, too. ADBR. 148 W 219. Directeur Départemental des Services de Police à M. le Préfet. February 23, 1949.

92. ADBR. 148 W 271. Service des RG. "Brigade Nord Africaine." April 20, 1949.

93. ADBR. 148 W 271. Service des RG. "Brigade Nord Africaine." April 20, 1949.

94. ADBR. 148 W 191. Chef de la Brigade du Quartier de la Bourse à M. le Commissaire Central. "Population Musulmane." June 13, 1949.

95. ADBR. 148 W 191. . . "Population Musulmane." June 13, 1949.

96. ADBR. 148 W 219. Directeur Départemental des Services de Police à M. le Préfet. February 23, 1949.

97. For example: ADBR. 148 W 272. Commissaire de Police du Quartier de la Bourse à M. le Commissaire Central. "Décès du sieur Cipoletta Gilberto." September 7, 1949. The brigade also sometimes handled cases in the Bourse neighborhood that did not involve North Africans.

98. ADBR. 148 W 272. Chef du Service des Recherches de la Sécurité Publique à M. le Commissaire Central. September 28, 1949.

99. For example: ADBR. 148 W 220. Commissaire de Police Principal à M. Le Commissaire Divisionnaire. "Vol par effraction et complicité de linge et tapis divers . . ." January 13, 1950; ADBR. 148 W 191. Commissaire Central à M. le Directeur Départemental des Services de Police. "Mouvement éventuel chez les nord-africains." November 29, 1951.

100. ADBR. 148 W 271. Service des RG. "Doléances des travailleurs musulmans nord-africains au président de l'association des musulmans algériens." June 1, 1949. Talmoudi was a prominent figure in North African life in Marseille and was associated with the ʿUlamā.

101. ADBR. 148 W 219. Directeur des Services de Police à M. le Préfet. "Quartier Saint-Charles." July 27, 1949.

102. ADBR. 148 W 219. Commissaire Divisionnaire à M. le Directeur Départemental de Police. "Surveillance et répression des délits de toute nature dans les rues . . ." July 15, 1949.

103. ANOM. 1 F 77. Rapport Mensuel. June 20, 1946.

104. In monthly reports from 1949, the police of Algiers repeatedly make this claim. ANOM. 1 F 133.

105. May 1 is a holiday with ties to the Communist Party. Protests had also occurred in several other Algerian cities. See Rey-Goldzeiguer, *Aux origines de la guerre d'Algérie 1940–1945*.

106. AN. F 60 872. Comité de l'Afrique du Nord. "Note au sujet de la lettre . . . relative aux incidents de Reibell le 18 Avril 1945." May 3, 1945.

107. AN. F 60 872. Gouverneur Général de l'Algérie à M. le Ministre de l'Intérieur. May 4, 1945.

108. The reasons for violence in each city were different, but in both cases clashes between protestors and police led to horrific bloodshed. See Jean-Pierre Peyroulou, *Guelma, 1945: Une subversion française dans l'Algérie coloniale* (La Découverte, 2009); Marcel Reggui, *Les massacres de Guelma, Algérie, Mai 1945: Une enquête inédite sur la furie des milices coloniales* (La Découverte, 2006). See also Kalman, *Law, Order and Empire*, 149.

109. Algerian nationalist sources cite fatalities as high as forty-five thousand in the days following the protests (e.g., *Horizons*, May 6, 1989). More modest estimates suggest twenty thousand deaths. Official French sources in 1945 cited 7,500 casualties, almost certainly too low. See Boucif Mekhaled, Jean-Charles Jauffret, and Mehdi Lallaoui, *Chroniques d'un massacre: 8 mai 1945, Sétif, Guelma, Kherrata* (Syros, 1995), 209.

110. For example: ANOM 4I 181. "عن الوطنييد الدفاع و الخارجية . . . ؟." Undated.

111. Mekhaled, Jauffret, and Lallaoui, *Chroniques d'un massacre*, 146.

112. AN. F 1a 3297. Secrétaire Général de la Fédération des Syndicat de Police d'État d'Algérie, Sentier à M. le Ministre de l'Intérieur. June 26, 1945.

113. ANOM. 40 G 55. Bulletin Mensuel d'Information et de Documentation sur la Situation Politique et les Faits Intéressant l'Ordre Social en Algérie. February 1945.

114. For example: ANOM. 40 G 55. Bulletin Mensuel d'Information et de Documentation sur la Situation Politique et les Faits Intéressant l'Ordre Social en Algérie. March 1945.

115. For example. ANOM. 4 I 32. CIE. "État d'esprit des populations à Alger." May 22, 1945.

116. Interestingly, the police here refer to European "coreligionnaires," a term typically used to refer to Algerians. ANOM. 1 F 125. Commissaire Divisionnaire des RG à M. le Préfet. "A/s renouvellement des domiciliations chez les commerçants." October 7, 1946.

117. ANOM. 1 F 433. Lettre. President du Syndicat de Défense & d'Initiative du Quartier "Clos Salembier." Havaux à M. Le Préfet. September 7, 1944.

118. ANOM. 1 F 433. Lettre. . . Havaux à M. Le Préfet. September 7, 1944.

119. On Muslim housing in Clos Salembier: Çelik, *Urban Forms and Colonial Confrontations*, 131. On the bidonvilles: Crane, "On the Edge"; Descloitres, Reverdy, and Descloitres, *L'Algérie des bidonvilles*; Jim House, "Intervening on 'Problem' Areas and Their Inhabitants: The Socio-political and Security Logics Behind Censuses in the Algiers Shantytowns, 1941–1962," *Histoire and Mesure* 34, no. 1 (2019): 121–150; Jim House, "Shantytowns and Rehousing in Late Colonial Algiers and Casablanca," in *France's Modernising Mission: Citizenship, Welfare and the Ends of Empire*, ed. Ed Naylor (Palgrave Macmillan, 2018).

120. ANOM. 1 F 125. Rapport. Brigadier Marquillanes "Etat d'esprit de la population musulmane." October 3, 1945.

121. BNA. "Climat d'insécurité pour les Musulmans." *La République Algérienne*. February 27, 1947.

122. Stora, *Histoire de l'Algérie coloniale*, 110.

123. See Danielle Beaujon, "The Algerian Enemy Within: Policing the Black Market in Marseille and Algiers, 1939–1950," *French Historical Studies* 47, no. 2 (2024): 289–318.

124. AWA. 4 H 89. November 6, 1944.

125. ANOM. 1 F 435. Directeur du Contrôle Économique d'Alger à M. le Préfet. "Trafic délictueux, dit à la sauvette." January 28, 1947.

126. ANOM. 1 F 435. Inspecteur Godard à M. le Directeur Départemental. "Article de presse." January 25, 1947.

127. ANOM. 1 F 435. . . "Article de Presse." January 25, 1947.

128. For example: ANOM. 1 K 631. Rapport Journalier. Services des Fraudes et Brigade Économique. December 27, 1947.

129. ANOM. 1 K 631. 1947.

130. ANOM. 1 F 435. Gardiens de la Paix Ferrer & Pecheur à M. Le Chef de la 3ème Compagnie. August 30, 1946.

131. Mouré, "Economic Tyranny," 7–8.
132. ADBR. 149 W 171. Secrétaire General pour la Police à M. le Commissaire de la République. "Incidents se produisant dans le quartier de la rue des Chapeliers." March 30, 1945.
133. ADBR. 149 W 171. Secrétaire Général pour la Police à M. le Commissaire de la République. "Rapport bi-mensuel sur la situation générale dans le département des Bouches-du-Rhône." June 14, 1945.
134. ADBR. 150 W 161. Chef de la Section de la Voie Publique à M. le Commissaire Central. "Marché noir du tabac." June 19, 1947.
135. ADBR. 150 W 160. Commissaire de Police, Chef de la Section de la Voie Publique à M. le Commissaire Divisionnaire. June 5, 1947.
136. ADBR. 149 W 171. Secrétaire Général pour la Police à M. le Général, Commandant d'Armes de la Place de Marseille. March 23, 1945.
137. ADBR. 149 W 171. Secrétaire Général pour la Police... March 23, 1945.
138. ADBR. 148 W 216. Chef de la Section de Voie Publique à M. le Commissaire Divisionnaire. "Opération de Police." March 24, 1948.
139. ADBR. 148 W 271. Chef du Service des Recherches de la Sécurité Publique à M. le Commissaire Central. "Opérations de Police." May 5, 1949.
140. ADBR. 148 W 221. Directeur Départemental des Services de Police à M le Préfet. "A/s du tapage occasionné par des Nord-Africains, rue Poids de la Farine." November 14, 1951.
141. ADBR. 148 W 221... "A/s du tapage occasionné par des Nord-Africains..." November 14, 1951.
142. Talmoudi à M. le Préfet des Bouches-du-Rhône. 1948. Cited in Témime, *Marseille transit*, 72.
143. This conflict between national rhetoric and local practice was also true in immigration. See Patrick Weil, "Racisme et discrimination dans la politique française de l'immigration 1938–1945/1974–1995," *Vingtième Siècle Revue d'histoire*, no. 47 (1995): 77–102.
144. ADBR. 148 W 271. Service des RG. "Critiques de L'UDMA Parti du Manifeste Algérien de Ferhat-Abbas contre la Police des Renseignements Généraux." January 15, 1949.

6. POLICING POLITICS AT THE END OF EMPIRE

1. ANOM. 4I 106. *Dossier ABABSA Abdelmadjid*. Chef du SLNA. "Objet: Théâtre Arabe—Troupe Ababsa." November 24, 1952.
2. A North African instrument similar to a bagpipe.
3. This is my translation of the French (mis)translation, which does not exactly match the Arabic lyrics. ANOM. 4I 106. *Dossier ABABSA Abdelmadjid*. Chef du SLNA. "Objet: Troupe Ababsa." January 30, 1953.
4. ANOM 4I 32.
5. On Algerian nationalism, see Kaddache, *La vie politique à Alger*; Kaddache, *Histoire du nationalisme algérien*; McDougall, *History and the Culture of Nationalism in Algeria*.
6. On the policing of anarchists, see Merriman, *Ballad of the Anarchist Bandits*.
7. On policing Communism, see Charpier, *Les RG et le Parti Communiste*.
8. See Rosenberg, *Policing Paris*; Blanchard, *La police parisienne et les Algériens*; Prakash, "Colonial Techniques in the Imperial Capital."
9. On Messali Hadj: Benjamin Stora, *Messali Hadj: Pionnier du nationalisme Algérien, 1898–1974* (L'Harmattan, 1986); Renaud de Rochebrune, ed., *Les mémoires de Messali Hadj* (Jean-Claude Lattès, 1982). On migration and national identity, see Rabah Aissaoui, *Immigration and National Identity: North African Political Movements in Colonial and Postcolonial France* (I. B. Tauris, 2009).
10. Hadj was released from jail in March 1943 but kept under house arrest for much of the war. Jacques Simon, *Messali Hadj, 1898–1974: Chronologie commentée* (L'Harmattan, 2002), 109.

11. ADBR. 148 W 273. Service des RG. "État d'esprit des milieux PPA de Marseille . . ." November 29, 1949. On the political exclusion of Busquant, see Marie-Victoire Louis, "Émilie Busquant, Madame Messali," *Parcours*, nos. 13–14 (1990): 103–112. This tension is also discussed in the fictionalized biography of Émilie Busquant: Mohamed Benchicou, *La parfumeuse: La vie occultée de Madame Messali Hadj* (Riveneuve, 2021).

12. Neil MacMaster discusses the FLN's ambivalent attitude toward French wives and girlfriends and highlights the pressure put on Messali to divorce Busquant. Neil MacMaster, "The Role of European Women and the Question of Mixed Couples in the Algerian Nationalist Movement in France, circa 1918–1962," *French Historical Studies* 34, no. 2 (Spring 2011): 357–386. See also Michael Goebel, "Spokesmen, Spies, and Spouses: Anticolonialism, Surveillance, and Intimacy in Interwar France," *Journal of Modern History* 91 (2019): 380–414.

13. ANOM. 1 F 147. Renseignements. May 5, 1948.

14. ANOM. 3 F 134. Rapport. Inspecteur des RG, Bernardie à Chef de Poste de Bouzaréah. May 27, 1948.

15. ANOM. 3 F 134. Rapport. Inspecteur des RG . . . May 27, 1948.

16. The couple eventually informally separated and Busquant returned to France, where she died in 1953. In his eulogy, Hadj praised her as a symbol of the "good French" who joined Algeria's liberation struggle. See Louis, "Émilie Busquant, Madame Messali"; Marie-Victoire Louis, "Madame Messali," *Cahiers du Gremamo* no. 7 (1990): 146–159; de Rochebrune, ed., *Les mémoires de Messali Hadj*.

17. The claim of fifteen times higher criminality was repeated frequently in government documents, but no dataset is ever cited. AN. F 60 865. Ministère de l'Information. "L'immigration étrangère en France." August 30, 1945.

18. He explicitly noted that Moroccan and Tunisian workers should not be considered part of the problem. AN. F 1a 5061. Directeur de la Police Judiciaire à M. le Préfet de Police. November 22, 1951.

19. AN. F 1a 5061. Directeur de la Police Judiciaire . . . November 22, 1951.

20. AN. F 1a 5061. Directeur de la Police Judiciaire . . . November 22, 1951.

21. In 1948, for example, Parisian police authorities advanced statistics in a public hearing claiming that North Africans committed half of all aggressions but privately admitted that this assertion was false. Blanchard, *La police parisienne et les Algériens*, 269–270.

22. AN. F 1a 5061. "Chronique de la pègre nord-africaine." *L'Aurore*. August 23, 1949; "La criminalité nord-africaine soulève un problème national." *Le Monde*. September 10, 1949.

23. ANOM. 9 X 58. Jean-Marie Garraud. "230,00 nord-africains en France." *Cahiers du Monde Nouveau* 6, no. 43 (1950).

24. For example: ANOM. 9 X 58. Yves Mazellier. "La migration nord-africaine." 1955.

25. ADBR. 148 W 273. Service des RG. "Réaction des milieux travailleurs NA de Marseille . . ." October 12, 1949.

26. ADBR. 148 W 273. . . "Réaction des milieux travailleurs . . ." October 12, 1949.

27. ADBR. 148 W 190. Commissaire de Police, 2ème Arrondissement à M. le Commissaire Central. "Réunion de l'association des Musulmans." Febraury 20, 1949.

28. ADBR. 148 W 193. Chef de la Section de Voie Publique à M. le Commissaire Principal. "Délinquance nord-africaine et délinquance d'ensemble comparée." January 2, 1953.

29. The police counted North Africans at around thirty thousand, compared with a total population of about eight hundred thousand in Marseille.

30. In contrast to the bloody faits divers stories of the local press, however, murders committed by North Africans were essentially nonexistent in 1950–1952.

31. ADBR. 148 W 193. . . "Délinquance nord-africaine . . ." January 2, 1953.

32. On race and statistics in the United States, see Muhammad, *The Condemnation of Blackness*.

33. A *bousaadi* is a knife traditionally fabricated in the town of Bou-Saada in Algeria, famed for its metalworkers. BWA. "Un chevalier du bousaadi." *Journal d'Alger*. February 1, 1947.

34. For example: ANOM. 1 F 132. Statistique. October 31, 1948.

35. For example, in February 1950, more than a hundred Algerians received permission for a gun and seventy-nine petitions were rejected. Meanwhile, fewer Europeans filed requests for guns, but "rejection" was not even a category in the paperwork. ANOM. 1 F 80. Rapport Mensuel. Commissaire Central de Police d'Alger, Laperriere. February 20, 1950.

36. ADBR. 150 W 161. "Les Renseignements Généraux communiquent." September 5, 1947.

37. ADBR. 148 W 193. Service Départemental des RG. "Trafic d'armes à Marseille entre militaires américains et Nord-Africains." July 11, 1952.

38. ADBR. 148 W 272. Service des RG. "Réaction des milieux Nord Africains de Marseille au sujet de rentrées massives en Afrique du Nord de travailleurs musulmans." September 27, 1949.

39. ADBR. 148 W 272... "Réaction des milieux Nord Africains..." September 27, 1949.

40. ADBR. 148 W 193. Commissaire Divisionnaire du C.E. Marseille à M. l'Inspecteur Général de l'Administration. "Examen de situation du nommé C. Saïd." April 28, 1953.

41. ADBR. 148 W 193... "Examen de situation du nommé C. Saïd." April 28, 1953.

42. For example: ANOM. 1 F 80. Rapport Mensuel. Commissaire Central Laperriere. March 20, 1950.

43. ANOM. 1 F 133. Bulletin Mensuel de Renseignements. Xe Région Militaire. March 31, 1949.

44. ANOM. 1 K 212. Commissaire de Police du Port, Mercadal. "Port d'arme prohibée et importation d'arme et de munitions sans autorisation." March 10, 1949.

45. ANOM. 1 K 212. Commissaire de Police du Port, Mercadal. "Importation d'arme sans autorisation." March 11, 1949.

46. ANOM. 1 K 212. Commissaire de Police du Port, Mercadal. "Porte d'arme prohibée." June 7, 1949.

47. Customs and border patrol officers are members of the Sûreté.

48. ANOM. 1 K 812. Commissaire Divisionnaire de la Police à M. le Directeur Général de la Sécurité Générale. "A/s du nommé Bengrine et non Belgrine..." October 24, 1950.

49. ANOM. 1 K 812... "A/s du nommé Bengrine et non Belgrine..." October 24, 1950.

50. On police as enforcers of colonial-capitalist interests: Thomas, *Violence and Colonial Order*.

51. For example: Algiers principal police commissioner, Paul Giannontoni, went to Marseille in 1953 to track down a ring of gun traffickers and collaborated with two Marseille officers in his investigation. ANOM. 1 K 812. Commissaire Principal, Giannantoni à M. le Commissaire Divisionnaire. "A/s trafic d'armes sur l'Afrique du Nord." April 2, 1953.

52. ANOM. 1 F 147. Commissaire de Police, LaJeunesse. "Propagande anti-française." April 14, 1947.

53. ANOM. 1 F 147. Commissaire de Police, LaJeunesse. "A/s quêtes faites au profit du PPA." April 21, 1948.

54. On Islam and resistance to French Imperialism, see Clancy-Smith, *Rebel and Saint*. On religion in interwar Algerian politics: Kaddache, *La vie politique à Alger*.

55. ANOM. 1 F 128. "Pèlerinage de 1946 aux lieux saints de l'Islam." December 9, 1946.

56. ANOM. 1 F 149. Gouverneur Général de l'Algérie à MM. Les Préfets. "Demandes de subventions, de secours, etc...." June 21, 1948.

57. On the Scouts: Nicolas Bancel, Daniel Denis, and Youssef Fates, eds., *De l'Indochine à l'Algérie: La jeunesse en mouvements des deux cotés du miroir colonial, 1940–1962* (La Découverte, 2003). On soccer: Kalman, *Law, Order, and Empire*, Ch. 3.

58. ANOM. 1 F 149. Commissaire Divisionnaire des RG, Costes à M. le Préfet. "A.S. Scouts musulmans Algériens—Propagande politique." June 22, 1948.

59. ANOM. 1 F 149. . . "A.S. Scouts musulmans Algériens . . ." June 22, 1948.

60. This strategy of withholding funds to discourage nationalist sympathy was later deployed against the Scouts Musulmans Algériens. ANOM. 1 F 169. SLNA. "A/s des Boy Scouts Musulmans Algériens." June 9, 1952. See Raphaelle Branche, "Min Djibalina: Une 'signature impériale'?" in *Une histoire sociale et culturelle du politique en Algérie et au Maghreb: Etudes offertes à Omar Carlier*, ed. Morgan Corriou and M'hamed Oualdi (Éditions de la Sorbonne, 2018).

61. On the development of Arabic theater in Algeria, see Arlette Roth, *Le théâtre algérien de langue dialectale, 1926–1954* (F. Maspero, 1967); Hadj Dahmane, *Le théâtre algérien: De l'engagement à la contestation* (Orizons, 2011); Julie Champrenault, "Cultures et empire: Une société théâtrale en situation coloniale? Algérie 1946–1962" (PhD diss., École doctorale de Sciences Po, 2015).

62. This was true, for example, in the case of Mahieddine. See Danielle Beaujon, "'Purely Artistic': Police Power and Popular Culture in Colonial Algerian Theater," *Historical Reflections/Réflexions Historiques* 46, no. 2 (2020): 89–109.

63. ANOM. 1 F 139. *Dossier de M. AIZEL Méziane*. Aug 8, 1947.

64. ANOM. 1 F 139. *Dossier de M. AIZEL Méziane*. "Notice de rensignements on M. Aizel Méziane." May 10, 1948.

65. ANOM. 1 F 141. *Dossier Hillal el Djezairi*. 1948.

66. ANOM. 1 F 149. Gouverneur Général à M. le Préfet d'Alger. "Propagande PPA." August 21, 1948.

67. ANOM. 1 F 149. . . "Propagande PPA." August 21, 1948.

68. ANOM. 1 F 149. Rapport. "Objet: Arrestation de deux indigènes . . ." September 29, 1948.

69. On the criminalization of nationalist party politics in postwar Algeria: Kalman, *Law, Order, and Empire*, chap. 5. Kalman examines police repression of political organizing and party politics in depth, while I address how this political policing spilled over into other aspects of Algerian life.

70. Omar Carlier, *Entre nation et jihad: Histoire sociale des radicalismes algériens* (Presses de la FNSP, 1995).

71. For example: Samuel Kalman, "Unlawful Acts or Strategies of Resistance? Crime and the Disruption of Colonial Order in Interwar French Algeria," *French Historical Studies* 43, no. 1 (February 2020): 85–110; Kalman, *Law, Order, and Empire*, chap. 3.

72. On the role of women: Natalya Vince, *Our Fighting Sisters: Nation, Memory and Gender in Algeria, 1954–2012* (Manchester University Press, 2015).

73. On the "citoyen diminué" status of North Africans in Paris: Blanchard, *La police parisienne et les Algériens*, 203.

74. ADBR. 148 W 191. Inspecteur de la Brigade de la Bourse à M. le Commissaire de Police. May 13, 1950.

75. ADBR. 148 W 193. Service Départemental des RG. "Rapport bi-mensuel sur les milieux musulmans des B.D.R." June 19, 1952.

76. The transimperial focus of the protestors' slogans might indicate that the French Communist Party played a role in organizing this march. On Communism in Algeria and the tense relationship with the FLN: Allison Drew, *We Are No Longer in France: Communists in Colonial Algeria* (Manchester University Press, 2014); de Rochebrune, ed., *Les mémoires de Messali Hadj*, 161.

77. ADBR. 148 W 191. Police des RG à M. le Préfet. September 17, 1950.
78. ADBR. 148 W 191. Commissaire du Quartier St-Lazare à M. le Commissaire Central. "Affichage la nuit." September 4, 1950.
79. ADBR. 148 W 191. Chef de la Section de Voie Publique, Gilous. September 11, 1950.
80. ADBR. 148 W 193. Secrétaire de Police O.P.J Semidei à M. le Commissaire de Police, Chef de la Section de Voie Publique. January 5, 1952.
81. On Moroccan nationalism, see John Halstead, *Rebirth of a Nation: The Origins and Rise of Moroccan Nationalism, 1912–1944* (Harvard University Press, 1967); Daniel Zisenwine, *The Emergence of Nationalist Politics in Morocco: The Rise of the Independence Party and the Struggle Against Colonialism after World War II* (I. B. Tauris, 2010).
82. ADBR. 148 W 143. Commissaire Principal Chef de la Sûreté à M. le Commissaire Divisionnaire. "Voyage à Marseille de sa Majesté Impériale le Sultan du Maroc les 4 et 5 Novembre 1950." November 7, 1950.
83. The "quartiers nord" of Marseille would become quintessential spaces of North African immigrant life in the postcolonial period.
84. ADBR. 148 W 143. . . "Voyage à Marseille de sa Majesté Impériale . . ." November 7, 1950.
85. Historians document that the majority of Algerians in France were from Kabylia. It is possible that the police associated Kabyles with "elites," suggesting a familiar discourse that nationalism only had elite appeal. However, it is an interesting contrast with the traditional French favoritism of the Kabyle populations over "Arabs."
86. ADBR. 148 W 272. Service des RG. "Activité du PPA à Marseille." July 11, 1949.
87. For example, one report had to outline the basics of Ramadan because police officers had been raiding cafés granted permission to stay open late for North Africans to break their fast. ADBR. 148 W 272. Service des RG. "Carême musulman." July 2, 1949.
88. On Morocco: Clancy-Smith, *Rebel and Saint*. On Egypt: Israel Gershoni and James Jankowski, *Egypt, Islam, and the Arabs: The Search for Egyptian Nationhood 1900–1930* (Oxford University Press, 1987). On Senegal: Douglas Thomas, *Sufism, Mahdism and Nationalism: Limamou Laye and the Layennes of Senegal* (Continuum International, 2011).
89. On policing Mahieddine, see Beaujon, "Purely Artistic."
90. ADBR. 148 W 193. Préfet des Bouches-du-Rhône à M. Le Ministre de l'Intérieur. "Tournées théâtrales arabes en France." October 8, 1952.
91. ADBR. 148 W 193. M. le Directeur Départemental des Services de Police. "Représentations théâtrales organisées par la troupe algérienne 'Les Artistes Associés.'" 1952.
92. Censorship had ended in France in 1906 with the defunding of the censor's bureau, and laws on censorship were formally abrogated in 1945. Although French theater troupes did need to ask prefectural permission to rent large halls, these permissions were perfunctory and not connected to the content of the shows. On censorship: Robert Goldstein, *The Frightful Stage: Political Censorship of the Theater in Nineteenth-Century Europe* (Berghahn Books, 2009).
93. On police violence as social control: Mars, *Deadly Force, Colonialism, and the Rule of Law*; Cazenave, *Killing African Americans*.
94. The police monopoly on state violence is not unique to colonial situations. Rather, it is a defining feature of all police. See Egon Bittner, *Aspects of Police Work* (Northeastern University Press, 1990); Seigel, *Violence Work*.
95. For example: ADBR. 4 M 2306. Commissaire Spécial à M. Directeur de la Sûreté Générale. "Arrestation du sujet tunisien Hali B." December 20, 1919.
96. "Legitimate defense" would continue to be used as an excuse for violence against racialized populations in France, both by police officers and civilians. See Rachida Brahim, *La race tue deux fois: Une histoire des crimes racistes en France (1970–2000)* (Syllepse, 2020), 193.

97. ADBR. 148 W 219. M. le Procureur de la République. June 27, 1949.
98. ADBR. 148 W 223.
99. ADBR. 148 W 249. Procès-Verbal. René Bardin. April 17, 1954.
100. Bardin noted that the North African willingly gave him the ID. Perhaps Mohamed cooperated because a "verification of papers" was routine for Algerians in Marseille, constantly stopped and questioned. ADBR. 148 W 249... René Bardin. April 17, 1954.
101. ADBR. 148 W 249... René Bardin. April 17, 1954.
102. ADBR. 148 W 249... René Bardin. April 17, 1954.
103. ADBR. 148 W 249. Procès-Verbal. Mohamed S. April 17, 1954.
104. ADBR. 148 W 249... René Bardin. April 17, 1954.
105. ADBR. 148 W 249. *Dossier Blessure d'un Nord-Africain par un Gardien CRS*.
106. ADBR. 148 W 249... Mohamed S. April 17, 1954.
107. ADBR. 148 W 249. Commissaire de CRS, Fontry, à M. le Directeur Général de la Sûreté Nationale. "Blessure par arme à feu occasionnée par Bardin René, gardien à la CRS." April 21, 1954.
108. ADBR. 148 W 249... "Blessure par arme à feu occasionnée par Bardin René..." April 21, 1954.
109. Benchebana was likely an Algerian Jew. ANOM. 1 K 212. Commissaire du 3ème, Cruz, "Homicide (légitime défense) et coups et blessures." June 23, 1948.
110. ANOM. 1 K 212... "Homicide (légitime défense)..." June 23, 1948.
111. ANOM. 1 K 212. Commissaire du 7ème, Ballay, "Incidents entre 2 gardiens de la paix en tenue bourgeoise et des musulmans." July 23, 1948.
112. ANOM. 1 K 212... "Incidents entre 2 gardiens de la paix..." July 23, 1948.
113. ANOM. 1 K 212... "Incidents entre 2 gardiens de la paix..." July 23, 1948.
114. Dazard's reaction is reminiscent of the citizen complaint letter about these same stairs from World War II, which highlighted "jeune indigène" as a threat to European safety. See chap. 3.
115. BWA. "Les scandaleux abus de la police d'Alger." *La Liberté*. January 18, 1951.
116. BWA. "Tueur en uniforme." *La Liberté*. November 12, 1953; "Une question écrite sur les tortures de la police." *La Liberté*. May 10, 1951.
117. BNA. "البوليس الفرنسي يقتحم ادارة جريدة المغرب العربي". *El Maghreb el Arabi*. September 9, 1948.
118. On the distinction between police and military, see Bittner, *Aspects of Police Work*; David Bayley, *Patterns of Policing: A Comparative International Analysis* (Rutgers University Press, 1985). On the police/military overlap in colonial situations: Anthony Cayton and David Killingray, *Khaki and Blue: Military and Police in British Colonial Africa* (Ohio University Center for International Studies, 1989).
119. On police operations against the FLN in Marseille, see, for example, ADBR. 148 W 194. "Affaires algériennes: Renseignements sur des Nord Africains suspects, 1954–1956." Emmanuel Blanchard shows this militarization in Paris. Blanchard, *La police parisienne et les Algériens*, 330–331.

EPILOGUE

1. ANOM. 1 K 881. "Le Comité de Défense de la Casbah s'élève contre la démolition de 462 maisons mauresques du 'Djebel.'" *La Dépêche Quotidienne d'Alger*. December 11–12, 1949.
2. On bidonvilles, see Crane, "Housing as Battleground"; House, "Intervening on 'Problem' Areas and Their Inhabitants"; Descloitres, Reverdy, and Descloitres, *L'Algérie des bidonvilles*.
3. ADBR. 148 W 193. Ministère de la Justice à M. le Préfet des Bouches-du-Rhône. "La démolition des quartiers arabes." June 19, 1952. Place Jules Guesde is where the Porte d'Aix stands. This "slum-clearing" project occurred while Marseille faced a housing crisis and mirrored other government initiatives to relocate squatters. See Minayo Nasiali,

Native to the Republic: Empire, Social Citizenship, and Everyday Life in Marseille Since 1945 (Cornell University Press, 2016), chap. 1.

4. Emile Témime, for example, notes that the *souks* and meublés of Rue des Chapeliers were "erased" in the mid-1950s. Témime, *Marseille transit*, 122.

5. On these neighborhoods, see Nasiali, *Native to the Republic*.

6. On this protest: Blanchard, *La police parisienne et les Algériens*, 129–142; Daniel Kupferstein, *Les balles du 14 juillet 1953: Le massacre policier oublié de nationalistes algériens à Paris* (La Découverte, 2017); Maurice Rajfus, *1953, un 14 juillet sanglant* (Agnès Viénot, 2003).

7. Blanchard, *La police parisienne et les Algériens*, 138.

8. Kupferstein, *Les balles du 14 juillet 1953*, 106–108.

9. Evans, *Algeria: France's Undeclared War*, 113.

10. On the state of emergency: Sylvie Thénault, "L'état d'urgence (1955–2005), De l'Algérie coloniale à la France contemporaine: Destin d'une loi," *Le Movement Social*, no. 218 (2007): 63–78. On changes to Algerian policing in this period: Kalman, *Law, Order, and Empire*, 185.

11. BNF. Récits de vie de policiers, PC.

12. Frantz Fanon, *Damnés de la terre* (F. Maspero, 1968).

13. BNF. Récits de vie de policiers, JS.

14. Blanchard, *La police parisienne et les Algériens*, chap. 11.

15. Blanchard, *La police parisienne et les Algériens*, chap. 11. Emmanuel Blanchard argues that in addition to taking on military functions, the judicial police in Paris also took on political functions, a similar "blending" of politics and policing to what I explore in chap. 6. Emmanuel Blanchard, "Police judiciaire et pratiques d'exception pendant la guerre de l'Algérie," *Vingtième Siècle: Revue d'Histoire* no. 90 (2006): 61–72.

16. See, for example, Joshua Cole, "Entering History: The Memory of Police Violence in Paris, October 1961," in *Algeria and France: Identity, Memory, and Nostalgia, 1800–2000*, ed. Patricia Lorcin (Syracuse University Press, 2006); Jean-Luc Einaudi, *Octobre 1961: Un massacre à Paris* (Fayard, 2001); Jim House and Neil MacMaster, *Paris 1961: Algerians, State Terror, and Memory* (Oxford University Press, 2006).

17. Blanchard, *La police parisienne et les Algériens*, 178.

18. See, for example: Fatima Besnaci-Lancou, Benoît Falaize, and Gilles Manceron, *Les harkis, histoire, mémoire et transmission* (Ouvrières, 2010); Isabel Boussard, "Les rapatriés dans le monde rural métropolitain," in *La Guerre d'Algérie et les français: Colloque de l'institut d'histoire du temps présent*, ed. Jean-Pierre Rioux (Fayard, 1990); Claire Eldridge, *From Empire to Exile: History and Memory Within the Pied-Noir and Harki Communities, 1962–2012* (Manchester University Press, 2016); Jean-Jacques Jordi, *De L'exode à l'éxil: Rapatriés et pieds-noirs en France; l'exemple marseillaise, 1954–1992* (L'Harmattan, 1993).

19. For example: BNF. Récit de vie de policiers, RC.

20. This periodization was proposed by Sayad but is generally reproduced in literature on Algerian immigration. See Sayad, *La double absence*.

21. By 1975, French reports note the presence of 35,000 Algerians in Marseille, as well as more than 6,000 Tunisians and 2,500 Moroccans. Jean-Jacques Jordi, Abdelmalek Sayad, and Émile Témime, *Histoire des migrations à Marseille: La choc de la décolonisation (1945–1990)* (Edisud, 1989), 121.

22. On negative French attitudes toward Algerians during this period: Yvan Gastaut, *L'immigration et l'opinion en France sous la Ve République* (Seuil, 2000).

23. For discussion of this violence: Brahim, *La race tue deux fois*, chap. 1; Yvan Gastaut, "Marseille, 1973" in *Les batailles de Marseille: Immigration, violences et conflits, XIXe-XXe siècles*, ed. Stéphane Mourlane and Céline Regnard-Drouot (Presses Universitaires de Provence, 2013); Nasiali, *Native to the Republic*, 83–85.

24. The CRS is a police unit used to control crowds or protests. The gardes mobiles are a mobile criminal investigation unit. *Le Méridional*, August 26, 1973. Quoted in Nasiali, *Native to the Republic*, 84.

25. Brahim, *La race tue deux fois*, 127.

26. For example: Assa Traoré and Elsa Vigoureux, *Lettre à Adama* (Seuil, 2017).

27. For example: Fabien Jobard, "Police, justice et discriminations raciales," in *De la question sociale à la question raciale: Représenter la société française*, ed. Didier Fassin, Eric Fassin, and Stéphane Beaud (La Découverte, 2009); Fabien Jobard and Sophie Névanen, "La couleur du jugement: Discriminations dans les décisions judiciaires en matière d'infractions à agents de la force publique (1965–2005)," *Revue française de sociologie* 48, no. 1 (2007): 243–272; Omar Slaouti and Fabien Jobard, "Police, justice, état: Discrimination raciales," in *Racismes de France*, ed. Omar Slaouti and Olivier Le Cour Grandmaison (La Découverte, 2020).

28. Didier Fassin, *Enforcing Order: An Ethnography of Urban Policing* (Polity, 2013).

29. This literature is vast in the US context, but among the seminal works are: Alexander, *The New Jim Crow*; Muhammad, *The Condemnation of Blackness*; Beth E. Richie, *Arrested Justice: Black Women, Violence, and America's Prison Nation* (New York University Press, 2012); Keeanga-Yamahtta Taylor, *From #BlackLivesMatter to Black Liberation* (Haymarket Books, 2016).

30. ANOM 1F 390. Letter. Houria B à M. Le Préfet d'Alger. February 19, 1946.

Bibliography

ARCHIVE ABBREVIATIONS

ADBR	Archives Départementales des Bouches-du-Rhône
AMM	Archives Municipales de la Ville de Marseille
ANOM	Archives Nationales d'Outre-Mer
AN	Archives Nationales de France
APP	Archives de la Préfecture de Police
AWA	Archives de la Wilaya d'Alger
BNF	Bibliothèque Nationale de France
BNA	Bibliothèque Nationale d'Algérie
BWA	Bibliothèque de la Wilaya d'Alger

NEWSPAPERS

Alger Républicain.
Cahiers du Monde Nouveau.
De la France Outre-Mer.
El Maghreb el Arabi.
Journal d'Alger.
L'Aurore.
L'Écho d'Alger.
La Défense.
La Dépêche.
La Justice.
La Liberté.
La Lutte Sociale.
La République Algérienne.
La Voix du Peuple.
La Voix Indigène.
Le Petit Provençal.
Le Petit Marseillais.
Le Provençal.
La Marseillaise.
Le Quotidien.
Le Radical.

PUBLISHED PRIMARY SOURCES

Crouse, Elizabeth. *Algiers*. James Pott, 1906.
Favre, Lucienne. *Dans la Casbah*. Collette d'Halluin, 1949.
Favre, Lucienne. *Tout l'inconnu de la Casbah d'Alger*. Baconnier, 1933.
Krull, Germaine, and André Suarès. *Marseille*. Éditions d'Histoire et d'Art, 1935.
Londres, Albert. *Marseille, Port du Sud*. Editions de France, 1927.

SECONDARY SOURCES

Ageron, Charles-Robert. "Les populations du Maghreb face à la propagande allemande." *Revue d'histoire de la Deuxième Guerre mondiale* 29, no. 114 (April 1979): 1–39.
Aissaoui, Rabah. *Immigration and National Identity: North African Political Movements in Colonial and Postcolonial France*. I. B. Tauris, 2009.
Alexander, Michelle. *The New Jim Crow: Mass Incarceration in the Age of Colorblindness*. New Press, 2010.
Ambroise-Rendu, Anne-Claude. *Petits récits des désordres ordinaires: Les faits divers dans la presse française des débuts de la IIIe République à la Grande Guerre*. Seli Arslan, 2004.
Anderson, David. *Histories of the Hanged: Britain's Dirty War in Kenya and the End of Empire*. Phoenix, 2006.
Anderson, Malcolm. *In Thrall to Political Change: Police and Gendarmerie in France*. Oxford University Press, 2011.
Anderson, Melissa. "For 'the Love of Order': Race, Violence, and the French Colonial Police in Vietnam, 1860s–1920s." PhD diss., University of Wisconsin–Madison, 2015.
Arnaud, Patrice. *Les STO: Histoire des Français requis en Allemagne nazie, 1942–1945*. CNRS, 2010.
Arnold, David. *Police Power and Colonial Rule: Madras 1859–1947*. Oxford University Press, 1986.
Ath-Messaoud, Malek, and Alain Gillette. *L'immigration algérienne en France*. Entente, 1976.
Babou, Cheikh Anta Mbaké. *Fighting the Greater Jihad: Amadu Bamba and the Founding of the Muridiyya of Senegal, 1853–1913*. Ohio University Press, 2007.
Balto, Simon. *Occupied Territory: Policing Black Chicago from the Red Summer to Black Power*. University of North Carolina Press, 2019.
Bancaud, Alain. "La magistrature et la répression politique de Vichy ou l'histoire d'un demi-échec." *Droit et Société* 34 (1996): 557–574.
Bancel, Nicolas, Pascal Blanchard, and Françoise Vergès. *La République coloniale*. Albin Michel, 2003.
Bancel, Nicolas, Daniel Denis, and Youssef Fates, eds. *De l'Indochine à l'Algérie: La jeunesse en mouvements des deux cotés du miroir colonial, 1940–1962*. La Découverte, 2003.
Barthélémy, Pascale. *Sororité et colonialisme: Françaises et Africaines au temps de la guerre froide (1944–1962)*. Éditions de la Sorbonne, 2022.
Bayley, David. *Patterns of Policing: A Comparative International Analysis*. Rutgers University Press, 1985.
Beaud, Stéphane, and Michel Pialoux. *Violences urbaines, violence sociale: Genèse des nouvelles classes dangereuses*. Fayard, 2003.
Beaujon, Danielle. "The Algerian Enemy Within: Policing the Black Market in Marseille and Algiers, 1939–1950." *French Historical Studies* 47, no. 2 (2024): 289–318.
Beaujon, Danielle. "The Chaouch of Marseille: Metropolitan Intermediaries and Colonial Control, 1928–1945." *French Politics, Culture, and Society* 41, no. 1 (2023): 1–21.
Beaujon, Danielle. "Policing Colonial Migrants: The Brigade Nord-Africaine in Paris, 1923–1944." *French Historical Studies* 42, no. 4 (2019): 655–680.
Beaujon, Danielle. "'Purely Artistic': Police Power and Popular Culture in Colonial Algerian Theater." *Historical Reflections/Réflexions Historiques* 46, no. 2 (2020): 89–109.
Begag, Azouz. *Place du Pont, ou la médina de Lyon*. Autrement, 1997.
Bella, Sihem. "Le voyage à Alger dans les guides touristiques français au XXe siècle." *Diacronie* 36, no. 4 (2018). https://doi.org/10.4000/diacronie.10531.

Bellance, Hurard. *La police des Noirs en Amérique (Martinique, Guadeloupe, Guyane, Saint-Domingue) et en France aux XVIIe et XVIIIe siècles*. Ibis Rouge, 2011.
Benatia, Farouk. *Alger: Agrégat ou cité; L'intégration citadine de 1919 à 1979*. SNED, 1980.
Benchicou, Mohamed. *La parfumeuse: La vie occultée de Madame Messali Hadj*. Riveneuve, 2021.
Berceot, Florence. "Renouvellement sociodémographique des juifs de Marseille, 1901–1937." *Provence historiques* 44, no. 175 (1994).
Berlière, Jean-Marc. *Le monde des polices en France: XIXe–XXe siècles*. Complexe, 1996.
Berlière, Jean-Marc, and Laurent Chabrun. *Les policiers français sous l'Occupation: D'après les archives inédites de l'épuration*. Perrin, 2001.
Berlière, Jean-Marc, and René Lévy. *Histoire des polices de France: De l'Ancien Régime à nos jours*. Nouveau Monde, 2011.
Berthelier, Robert. *L'homme maghrébin dans la littérature psychiatrique*. L'Harmattan, 1994.
Bertoncello, Brigette, and Sylvie Bredeloup. "A la recherche du docker noir." In *Dockers de la Méditerranée à la Mer du Nord: Des quais et des hommes dans l'histoire*, edited by Jean Domenichino, Jean-Marie Guillon, and Robert Mencherini. Edisud, 1999.
Besnaci-Lancou, Fatima, Benoît Falaize, and Gilles Manceron. *Les harkis, histoire, mémoire et transmission*. Ouvrières, 2010.
Bittner, Egon. *Aspects of Police Work*. Northeastern University Press, 1990.
Bittner, Egon. *The Functions of the Police in Modern Society: A Review of Background Factors, Current Practices, and Possible Role Models*. Oelgeschlager, Gunn & Hain, 1979.
Blanchard, Emmanuel, *Des colonisés ingouvernables: Adresses d'Algériens aux autorités françaises (Akbou, Paris, 1919–1940)*. Presses De Sciences Po, 2024.
Blanchard, Emmanuel. "Des contrôles migratoires aux conséquences funestes: Le 'drame du Sidi Ferruch,' avril 1926." *Encyclopédie d'histoire numérique de l'Europe*.
Blanchard, Emmanuel. "Des Kabyles 'perdus' en région parisienne: Les 'recherches dans l'intérêt des familles' du Service des affaires indigènes nord-africaines (années 1930)." *Revue du Monde Musulman et de la Méditerranée* 144 (2018): 29–44.
Blanchard, Emmanuel. *Histoire de l'immigration algérienne en France*. La Découverte, 2018.
Blanchard, Emmanuel. *La police parisienne et les Algériens, 1944–1962*. Nouveau Monde, 2011.
Blanchard, Emmanuel. "Le mauvais genre des Algériens: Des hommes sans femme face au virilisme policier dans le Paris d'après-guerre." *Clio: Histoire, femmes et sociétés* 27, no. 1 (2008): 209–224.
Blanchard, Emmanuel. "Police judiciaire et pratiques d'exception pendant la guerre de l'Algérie." *Vingtième Siècle: Revue d'Histoire* 90 (2006): 61–72.
Blanchard, Emmanuel, and Sylvie Thénault. "Quel 'monde du contact'? Pour une histoire sociale de l'Algérie pendant la période coloniale." *Le Mouvement social* 236, Juillet–Septembre (2011): 3–7.
Blévis, Laure, Hélène Lafont-Couturier, Nanette Jacomijn Snoep, and Claire Zalc. *1931: Les étrangers au temps de l'exposition coloniale*. Gallimard, 2008.
Boittin, Jennifer. "Black in France: The Language and Politics of Race in the Late Third Republic." *French Politics, Culture and Society* 27, no. 2 (2009): 23–46.
Boittin, Jennifer. *Colonial Metropolis: The Urban Grounds of Anti-Imperialism and Feminism in Interwar Paris*. University of Nebraska Press, 2010.
Boittin, Jennifer. "The Militant Black Men of Marseille and Paris, 1927–1937." In *Black France/France Noire: The History and Politics of Blackness*, edited by Tricia Keaton, T. Denean Sharpley-Whiting, and Tyler Stovall. Duke University Press, 2012.
Boittin, Jennifer. *Undesirable: Passionate Mobility and Women's Defiance of French Colonial Policing, 1919–1952*. University of Chicago Press, 2022.

Bollenot, Vincent. "Maintenir l'ordre impérial en métropole: Le Service de Contrôle et d'Assistance en France des Indigènes des Colonies (1915–1945)." PhD diss., Université de Paris I Panthéon Sorbonne, 2022.
Boum, Aomar, and Sarah Abrevaya Stein, eds. *The Holocaust and North Africa*. Stanford University Press, 2019.
Boussard, Isabel. "Les rapatriés dans le monde rural métropolitain." In *La Guerre d'Algérie et les français: Colloque de l'institut d'histoire du temps present*, edited by Jean-Pierre Rioux. Fayard, 1990.
Brahim, Rachida. *La race tue deux fois: Une histoire des crimes racistes en France (1970–2000)*. Syllepse, 2020.
Branche, Raphaëlle. "Min Djibalina: Une 'signature impériale'?" In *Une histoire sociale et culturelle du politique en Algérie et au Maghreb: Etudes offertes à Omar Carlier*, edited by Morgan Corriou and M'hamed Oualdi. Éditions de la Sorbonne, 2018.
Brunet, Jean-Paul. *Police contre FLN: Le drame d'octobre 1961*. Flammarion, 1999.
Cadiot, Aliénor. "Agir seul ou en réseau? La 'résistance' du commandant Robert Wender et le Service des Affaires algériennes (1941–1943)." Presentation to the French Colonial Historical Society, Martinique, 2023.
Cadiot, Aliénor. "Vichy et les Algériens: Indigènes civils musulmans algériens en France métropolitaine (1939–1944)." PhD diss., École des hautes études en sciences sociales, 2020.
Camiscioli, Elisa. *Reproducing the French Race: Immigration, Intimacy, and Embodiment in the Early Twentieth Century*. Duke University Press, 2009.
Camiscioli, Elisa. *Selling French Sex: Prostitution, Trafficking, and Global Migrations*. Cambridge University Press, 2024.
Cantier, Jacques. *L'Algérie sous le régime de Vichy*. Odile Jacob, 2002.
Cantier, Jacques, and Eric Jennings, eds. *L'Empire colonial sous Vichy*. Odile Jacob, 2004.
Carlier, Omar. *Entre nation et jihad: Histoire sociale des radicalismes algériens*. Presses de la FNSP, 1995.
Carlier, Omar. "Le café maure: Sociabilité masculine et effervescence citoyenne (Algérie XVIIe-XXe siècles)." *Annales: Histoire, Sciences Sociales* 45, no. 4 (1990): 975–1003.
Carlier, Omar. "Medina and Modernity: The Emergence of Muslim Civil Society in Algiers Between the Two World Wars." In *Walls of Algiers: Narratives of the City Through Text and Image*, edited by Zeynep Çelik, Julia Clancy-Smith, and Frances Terpak. Getty Research Institute, 2009.
Cazenave, Noel A. *Killing African Americans: Police and Vigilante Violence as a Racial Control Mechanism*. Routledge, 2018.
Çelik, Zeynep. "Historic Intersections: The Center of Algiers." In *Walls of Algiers: Narratives of the City through Text and Image*, edited by Zeynep Çelik, Julia Clancy-Smith, and Frances Terpak. Getty Research Institute, 2009.
Çelik, Zeynep. *Urban Forms and Colonial Confrontations: Algiers under French Rule*. University of California Press, 1997.
Champrenault, Julie. "Cultures et empire: Une société théâtrale en situation coloniale? Algérie 1946–1962." PhD diss., École doctorale de Sciences Po, 2015.
Chapman, Herrick. *France's Long Reconstruction: In Search of the Modern Republic*. Harvard University Press, 2018.
Charpier, Frédéric. *Les RG et le Parti Communiste: Un combat sans merci dans la guerre froide*. Plon, 2000.
Childers, Kristen Stromberg. *Fathers, Families, and the State in France, 1914–1945*. Cornell University Press, 2003.
Clancy-Smith, Julia. *Rebel and Saint: Muslim Notables, Populist Protest, Colonial Encounters (Algeria and Tunisia, 1800–1904)*. University of California Press, 1994.

Clayton, Anthony, and David Killingray. *Khaki and Blue: Military and Police in British Colonial Africa*. Ohio University Press, 1989.
Cohen, Muriel. *Des familles invisibles: Les Algériens de France entre intégrations et discriminations 1945–1985*. Editions de la Sorbonne, 2020.
Cole, Joshua. "Entering History: The Memory of Police Violence in Paris, October 1961." In *Algeria and France: Identity, Memory, and Nostalgia, 1800–2000*, edited by Patricia Lorcin. Syracuse University Press, 2006.
Cole, Joshua. *Lethal Provocation: The Constantine Murders and the Politics of French Algeria*. Cornell University Press, 2020.
Colonna, Fanny. *Instituteur algériens, 1883–1939*. Presses de la Fondation nationale des sciences politiques, 1975.
Conklin, Alice. *A Mission to Civilize: The Republican Idea of Empire in France and West Africa, 1895–1930*. Stanford University Press, 1997.
Conklin, Alice, Sarah Fishman, and Robert Zaretsky, eds. *France and Its Empire Since 1870*. Oxford University Press, 2015.
Cragin, Thomas. *Murder in Parisian Streets: Manufacturing Crime and Justice in the Popular Press, 1830–1900*. Bucknell University Press, 2006.
Crane, Sheila. "Housing as Battleground: Targeting the City in the Battles of Algiers." *City and Society* 29, no. 1 (2017): 187–212.
Crane, Sheila. *Mediterranean Crossroads: Marseille and Modern Architecture*. University of Minnesota Press, 2011.
Crane, Sheila. "On the Edge: The Internal Frontiers of Architecture in Algiers/Marseille." *Journal of Architecture* 16, no. 6 (2011): 941–973.
Crews, Robert. *For Prophet and Tsar: Islam and Empire in Russia and Central Asia*. Harvard University Press, 2006.
Dahmane, Hadj. *Le théâtre algérien: De l'engagement à la contestation*. Orizons, 2011.
Darmon, Pierre. *L'Algérie de Pétain*. Perrin, 2014.
Daughton, J. P. *An Empire Divided: Religion, Republicanism, and the Making of French Colonialism, 1880–1914*. Oxford University Press, 2006.
De Rochebrune, Renaud, ed. *Les mémoires de Messali Hadj*. Jean-Claude Lattès, 1982.
Descloitres, Robert, Jean-Claude Reverdy, and Claudine Descloitres. *L'Algérie des bidonvilles: Le tiers monde dans la cité*. Mouton, 1961.
Dewitte, Philippe. *Les mouvements nègres en France, 1919–1939*. L'Harmattan, 1985.
Drew, Allison. *We Are No Longer in France: Communists in Colonial Algeria*. Manchester University Press, 2014.
Einaudi, Jean-Luc. *Octobre 1961: Un massacre à Paris*. Fayard, 2001.
Eldridge, Claire. *From Empire to Exile: History and Memory within the Pied-Noir and Harki Communities, 1962–2012*. Manchester University Press, 2016.
Elkins, Caroline. *Imperial Reckoning: The Untold Story of Britain's Gulag in Kenya*. Henry Holt, 2006.
Evans, Martin. *Algeria: France's Undeclared War*. Oxford University Press, 2012.
Fanon, Frantz. *Damnés de la terre*. F. Maspero, 1968.
Fanon, Frantz. *Pour la révolution africaine. Écrits politiques*. F. Maspero, 1969.
Farge, Arlette. *Le goût de l'archive*. Seuil, 1989.
Fassin, Didier. *Enforcing Order: An Ethnography of Urban Policing*. Polity, 2013.
Feldman, Ilana. *Police Encounters: Security and Surveillance in Gaza under Egyptian Rule*. Stanford University Press, 2015.
Fenton, Paul, and David Littman. *L'exil au Maghreb: La condition juive sous l'islam, 1148–1912*. Presse de la Université de Paris-Sorbonne, 2010.
Firpo, Christina. *Black Market Business: Selling Sex in Northern Vietnam, 1920–1945*. Cornell University Press, 2021.

Fletcher, Yaël Simpson. "'Capital of the Colonies': Real and Imagined Boundaries between Metropole and Empire in 1920s Marseilles." In *Imperial Cities: Landscape, Display and Identity*, edited by Felix Driver and David Gilbert. Manchester University Press, 1999.

Fogg, Shannon. *The Politics of Everyday Life in Vichy France: Foreigners, Undesirables and Strangers*. Cambridge University Press, 2009.

Frank, Sarah Ann. *Hostages of Empire: Colonial Prisoners of War in Vichy France*. University of Nebraska Press, 2021.

Fuentes, Marisa. *Dispossessed Lives: Enslaved Women, Violence, and the Archive*. University of Pennsylvania Press, 2016.

Gastaut, Yvan. *L'immigration et l'opinion en France sous la Ve République*. Seuil, 2000.

Gastaut, Yvan. "Marseille, 1973." In *Les batailles de Marseille: Immigration, violences et conflits, XIXe-XXe siècles*, edited by Stéphane Mourlane and Céline Regnard-Drouot. Presses Universitaires de Provence, 2013.

Gershoni, Israel, and James Jankowski. *Egypt, Islam, and the Arabs: The Search for Egyptian Nationhood 1900-1930*. Oxford University Press, 1987.

Ghettas, Aïcha, and Fatima Zohia Guechi. "La communauté juive dans les relations rive nord–rive sud." In *Parlez-moi d'Alger: Marseille-Alger au miroir des mémoires*, edited by Abderrahmane Moussaoui and Florence Pizzorni. Réunion des musées nationaux, 2003.

Ginio, Ruth. *The French Army and Its African Soldiers: The Years of Decolonization*. University of Nebraska Press, 2017.

Ginio, Ruth. "The Implementation of Anti-Jewish Laws in French West Africa." In *The Holocaust and North Africa*, edited by Aomar Boum and Sarah Abrevaya Stein. Stanford University Press, 2019.

Ginio, Ruth. "La propagande impériale de Vichy." In *L'Empire colonial sous Vichy*, edited by Jacques Cantier and Eric Jennings. Odile Jacob, 2004.

Go, Julian. *Policing Empires: Militarization, Race, and the Imperial Boomerang in Britain and the US*. Oxford University Press, 2023.

Goebel, Michael. "Spokesmen, Spies, and Spouses: Anticolonialism, Surveillance, and Intimacy in Interwar France." *Journal of Modern History* 91 (2019): 380–414.

Goldstein, Robert. *The Frightful Stage: Political Censorship of the Theater in Nineteenth-Century Europe*. Berghahn Books, 2009.

Gonon, Laetitia. *Le fait divers criminel dans la presse quotidienne française du XIXe siècle*. Presses Sorbonne Nouvelle, 2012.

Gouriou, Fabien. "Le sexe des indigènes. Adolphe Kocher et la médecine légale en Algérie." *Droit et cultures* (2010): 59–72

Grenard, Fabrice. "L'administration du contrôle économique en France, 1940–1950." *Revue d'histoire moderne et contemporaine* 57, no. 2 (2010): 132–158.

Grenard, Fabrice. *La France du marché noir (1940-1949)*. Payot, 2008.

Guignard, Didier. *1871: L'Algérie sous séquestre*. CNRS, 2023.

Halstead, John. *Rebirth of a Nation: The Origins and Rise of Moroccan Nationalism, 1912-1944*. Harvard University Press, 1967.

Harris, Cheryl. "Whiteness as Property." *Harvard Law Review* 106, no. 8 (1993) 1707–1791.

Hartman, Saidiya. *Lose Your Mother: A Journey along the Atlantic Slave Route*. Farrar, Straus & Giroux, 2007.

Hattery, Angela, and Earl Smith. *Policing Black Bodies: How Black Lives Are Surveilled and How to Work for Change*. Rowman & Littlefield, 2017.

Herf, Jeffrey. *Nazi Propaganda for the Arab World*. Yale University Press, 2009.

Hoisington, William, Jr. "The Mediterranean Committee and French North Africa, 1935–1940." *Historian* 53, no. 2 (1991): 255–266.

House, Jim. "Colonial Containment? Repression of Pro-Independence Street Demonstrations in Algiers, Casablanca and Paris, 1945-1962." *War in History* 25, no 2 (2018): 172-201.
House, Jim. "Intervening on 'Problem' Areas and Their Inhabitants: The Socio-Political and Security Logics Behind Censuses in the Algiers Shantytowns, 1941-1962." *Histoire et Mesure* 34, no. 1 (2019): 121-150.
House, Jim. "Shantytowns and Rehousing in Late Colonial Algiers and Casablanca." In *France's Modernising Mission: Citizenship, Welfare and the Ends of Empire*, edited by Ed Naylor. Palgrave Macmillan, 2018.
House, Jim, and Neil MacMaster. *Paris 1961: Algerians, State Terror, and Memory*. Oxford University Press, 2006.
Icheboudene, Larbi. *Alger: Histoire et capitale de destin national*. Casbah Editions, 1997.
Jennings, Eric. *Free French Africa in World War II: The African Resistance*. Cambridge University Press, 2015.
Jobard, Fabien. "Police, Justice et Discriminations Raciales." In *De la question sociale à la question raciale: Représenter la société française*, edited by Didier Fassin, Eric Fassin, and Stéphane Beaud. La Découverte, 2009.
Jobard, Fabien, and Sophie Névanen. "La couleur du jugement: Discriminations dans les décisions judiciaires en matière d'infractions à agents de la force publique (1965-2005)." *Revue française de sociologie* 48, no. 1 (2007): 243-272.
Joly, Laurent. *L'antisèmitisme de bureau: Enquête au cœur de la préfecture de police de Paris et du commissariat général aux questions juives (1940-1944)*. Grasset, 2011.
Jordi, Jean-Jacques. *De L'exode à l'exil: Rapatriés et pieds-noirs en France*. L'Harmattan, 1993.
Jordi, Jean-Jacques. "L'inconscience ou le péril." In *Alger 1940-1962: Une ville en guerres*, edited by Jean-Jacques Jordi and Guy Pervillé. Autrement, 1999.
Jordi, Jean-Jacques, Abdelmalek Sayad, and Émile Témime. *Histoire des migrations à Marseille: La choc de la décolonisation (1945-1990)*. Edisud, 1989.
Kaddache, Mahfoud. *Histoire du nationalisme algérien: Question nationale et politique algérienne, 1919-1951*. EDIF, 2000.
Kaddache, Mahfoud. *La Casbah*. Unpublished manuscript, Les Glycines, Le centre d'études diocésain, 1950.
Kaddache, Mahfoud. *La vie politique à Alger de 1919 à 1939*. SNED, 1970.
Kalifa, Dominique. *L'encre et le sang: Récit de crimes et société à la Belle Époque*. Fayard, 1995.
Kalman, Samuel. "Criminalizing Dissent: Policing Banditry in the Constantinois, 1914-1918." In *Algeria Revisited: Contested Identities in the Colonial and Postcolonial Periods*, edited by Rabah Aissoui and Claire Eldridge. Bloomsbury, 2016.
Kalman, Samuel. *French Colonial Fascism: The Extreme Right in Algeria, 1919-1939*. Palgrave Macmillan, 2013.
Kalman, Samuel. *Law, Order, and Empire: Policing and Crime in Colonial Algeria, 1870-1954*. Cornell University Press, 2024.
Kalman, Samuel. "Unlawful Acts or Strategies of Resistance? Crime and the Disruption of Colonial Order in Interwar French Algeria." *French Historical Studies* 43, no. 1 (2020): 85-110.
Kateb, Kamel. *Européens, "Indigènes" et Juifs en Algérie (1830-1962): Représentations et réalités des populations*. Editions de l'INED, 2001.
Katz, Ethan. *The Burdens of Brotherhood: Jews and Muslims from North Africa to France*. Harvard University Press, 2015.
Keller, Kathleen. *Colonial Suspects: Suspicion, Imperial Rule, and Colonial Society in Interwar French West Africa*. University of Nebraska Press, 2018.
Keller, Richard. *Colonial Madness: Psychiatry in French North Africa*. University of Chicago Press, 2007.

Kitson, Simon. *Police and Politics in Marseille, 1936–1945*. Brill, 2014.
Kocher, Adolphe. *De la criminalité chez les Arabes*. J. B. Baillière, 1884.
Kupferstein, Daniel. *Les balles du 14 juillet 1953: Le massacre policier oublié de nationalistes algériens à Paris*. La Découverte, 2017.
Laskier, Michael. *North African Jewry in the Twentieth Century: The Jews of Morocco, Tunisia, and Algeria*. New York University Press, 1994.
Lawrence, Benjamin, Emily Osborn, and Richard Roberts, eds. *Intermediaries, Interpreters, and Clerks: African Employees in the Making of Colonial Africa*. Madison: University of Wisconsin Press, 2006.
Lebourg, Nicolas, and Abderahmen Moumen. *Rivesaltes, le camp de la France: 1939 à nos jours*. Trabucaire, 2015.
Le Cour Grandmaison, Olivier. *De l'indigénat: Anatomie d'un monstre juridique; Le droit colonial en Algérie et dans l'empire français*. Zones, 2010.
Lefebvre, Henri. *The Production of Space*. Blackwell, 1991.
Le Gaoziou, Véronique, and Laurent Mucchielli. *Quand les banlieues brûlent: Retour sur les émeutes de novembre 2005*. La Découverte, 2006.
Legg, Charlotte. *The New White Race: Settler Colonialism and the Press in French Algeria, 1860–1914*. University of Nebraska Press, 2021.
Lespès, René. *Alger: Étude de géographie et d'histoire urbaines*. Félix Alcan, 1930.
Lewis, Mary. *The Boundaries of the Republic: Migrant Rights and the Limits of Universalism in France, 1918–1940*. Stanford University Press, 2007.
Lipsitz, George. "The Racialization of Space and the Spatialization of Race." *Landscape Architecture* 26 (2007): 10–23.
Lorcin, Patricia. *Imperial Identities: Stereotyping, Prejudice and Race in Colonial Algeria*. I. B. Tauris, 1999.
Louis, Marie-Victoire. "Émilie Busquant, Madame Messali." *Parcours* nos. 12–14 (1990): 103–112.
Louis, Marie-Victoire. "Madame Messali." *Cahiers du Gremamo* no. 7 (1990): 146–159.
Lyons, Amelia. *The Civilizing Mission in the Metropole: Algerian Families and the French Welfare State During Decolonization*. Stanford University Press, 2013.
MacMaster, Neil. "The Algerian Café-Hotel: Hub of the Nationalist Underground, Paris, 1926–1962." *French Politics, Culture and Society* 3, no. 2 (2016): 72.
MacMaster, Neil. *Colonial Migrants and Racism: Algerians in France, 1900–62*. Palgrave Macmillan, 1997.
MacMaster, Neil. "Patterns of Emigration, 1905–1954: 'Kabyles' and 'Arabs.'" In *French and Algerian Identities from Colonial Times to the Present: A Century of Interaction*, edited by Alec Hargreaves and Michael Heffernan. E. Mellen, 1993.
MacMaster, Neil. "The Role of European Women and the Question of Mixed Couples in the Algerian Nationalist Movement in France, circa 1918–1962." *French Historical Studies* 34, no. 2 (2011): 357–386.
Malka, Adam. *The Men of Mobtown: Policing Baltimore in the Age of Slavery and Emancipation*. University of North Carolina Press, 2018.
Mann, Gregory. *Native Sons: West African Veterans and France in the Twentieth Century*. Duke University Press, 2006.
Mann, Gregory. "What Was the Indigénat? The 'Empire of Law' in French West Africa." *Journal of African History* 50, no. 3 (2009): 331–353.
Marker, Emily. *Black France, White Europe: Youth, Race, and Belonging in the Postwar Era*. Cornell University Press, 2022.
Mars, Joan. *Deadly Force, Colonialism, and the Rule of Law: Police Violence in Guyana*. Greenwood, 2002.

Massard-Guilbaud, Geneviève. *Des Algériens à Lyon: De la Grande Guerre au Front Populaire*. L'Harmattan, 1995.
Matsunuma, Miho. "La politique du gouvernement de Vichy vis-à-vis des militaires coloniaux rapatriables." *Outre-Mers: Revue d'histoire* 362 (2009): 227–240.
McDougall, James. *A History of Algeria*. Cambridge University Press, 2017.
McDougall, James. *History and the Culture of Nationalism in Algeria*. Cambridge University Press, 2008.
McKittrick, Katherine. *Demonic Grounds: Black Women and Cartographies of Struggle*. Minneapolis: University of Minnesota Press, 2006.
McKittrick, Katherine, and Clyde Woods, eds. *Black Geographies and the Politics of Place*. South End, 2007.
Mekhaled, Boucif. *Chroniques d'un massacre: 8 mai 1945, Sétif, Guelma, Kherrata*. Syros, 1995.
Mendoza, Victor Román. *Metroimperial Intimacies: Fantasy, Racial-Sexual Governance, and the Philippines in U.S. Imperialism, 1899–1913*. Duke University Press, 2015.
Merriman, John. *Ballad of the Anarchist Bandits: The Crime Spree That Gripped Belle Époque Paris*. Nation Books, 2017.
Milliot, Vincent, Emmanuel Blanchard, Vincent Denis, and Arnaud-Dominique Houte, eds. *Histoire des polices en France: Des guerres de religion à nos jours*. Belin, 2020.
Montel, Laurence. "Espace urbain et criminalité organisée: Le cas marseillais dans le premier XXe siècle." In *Villes en crise? Les politiques municipales face aux pathologies urbaines (fin XVIIIe–fin XXe siècle)*, edited by Yannick Marec. Créaphis, 2005.
Mouré, Kenneth. "'Economic Tyranny' and Public Anger in France, 1945–1947." *Contemporary European History* (2022): 1–14.
Mouré, Kenneth. "La Capitale de la Faim: Black Market Restaurants in Paris, 1940–1944." *French Historical Studies* 38, no. 2 (April 2015): 311–341.
Mouré, Kenneth. *Marché Noir: The Economy of Survival in Second World War France*. Cambridge University Press, 2023.
Mucchielli, Laurent. "Criminology, Hygenism, and Eugenics in France, 1870–1914: The Medical Debates on the Elimination of 'Incorrigible' Criminals." In *Criminals and Their Scientists: The History of Criminology in International Perspective*, edited by Peter Becker and Richard Wetzell. Cambridge University Press, 2006.
Mucchielli, Laurent, ed. *Histoire de la criminologie française*. L'Harmattan, 2004.
Muhammad, Khalil Gibran. *The Condemnation of Blackness: Race, Crime, and the Making of Modern Urban America*. Harvard University Press, 2010.
Nasiali, Minayo. *Native to the Republic: Empire, Social Citizenship, and Everyday Life in Marseille Since 1945*. Cornell University Press, 2016.
Nightingale, Carl. *Segregation: A Global History of Divided Cities*. University of Chicago Press, 2012.
Noiriel, Gérard. *Les origines républicaines de Vichy*. Hachette, 1999.
Ochonu, Moses. *Colonialism by Proxy: Hausa Imperial Agents and Middle Belt Consciousness in Nigeria*. Indiana University Press, 2014.
Ogle, Gene. *Policing Saint Domingue: Race, Violence, and Honor in an Old Regime Colony*. University of Pennsylvania, 2003.
Pattieu, Sylvain. "Souteneurs noirs à Marseille, 1918–1921: Contribution à l'histoire de la minorité noire en France." *Annales: Histoire, Sciences Sociales* 64, no. 6 (2009): 1361–1386.
Paxton, Robert. *Vichy France: Old Guard and New Order, 1940–1944*. Columbia University Press, 1972.

Peabody, Sue. *There Are No Slaves in France: The Political Culture of Race and Slavery in the Ancien Régime*. Oxford University Press, 2002.
Perrier, E.G. *La police municipale, spéciale et mobile: Historique & organisation*. M. Giard & É. Brière, 1920.
Peyroulou, Jean-Pierre. *Guelma, 1945: Une subversion française dans l'Algérie coloniale*. La Découverte, 2009.
Phéline, Christian. *La terre, l'étoile, le couteau: Le 2 août 1936 à Alger*. Editions du croquant, 2021.
Pick, Daniel. *Faces of Degeneration: A European Disorder*. Cambridge University Press, 1989.
Pierce, Steven, and Anupama Rao, eds. *Discipline and the Other Body: Correction, Corporeality, Colonialism*. Duke University Press, 2006.
Planche, Jean-Louis. "Violences et nationalismes en Algérie, 1942–1945." *Les Temps modernes* no. 590 (1996): 112–134.
Pollard, Miranda. *Reign of Virtue: Mobilizing Gender in Vichy France*. University of Chicago Press, 1998.
Prakash, Amit. "Colonial Techniques in the Imperial Capital: The Prefecture of Police and the Surveillance of North Africans in Paris, 1925–circa 1970." *French Historical Studies* 36, no. 3 (2013): 479–510.
Prakash, Amit. *Empire on the Seine: The Policing of North Africans in Paris, 1925–1975*. Oxford University Press, 2022.
Prochaska, David. *Making Algeria French: Colonialism in Bône, 1870–1920*. Cambridge University Press, 1990.
Rajsfus, Maurice. *1953, un 14 juillet sanglant*. Agnès Viénot, 2003.
Reggui, Marcel. *Les massacres de Guelma, Algérie, Mai 1945: Une enquête inédite sur la furie des milices coloniales*. La Découverte, 2006.
Regnard, Céline. *En transit: Les Syriens à Beyrouth, Marseille, Le Havre, New York, 1880–1914*. Anamosa, 2022.
Regnard-Drouot, Céline. *Marseille la violente: Criminalité, industrialisation et société, 1851–1914*. Presses Universitaires de Rennes, 2009.
Rettig, Tobias. "From Subaltern to Free Worker: Exit, Voice, and Loyalty among Indochina's Subaltern Imperial Labor Camp Diaspora in Metropolitan France, 1939–1944." *Journal of Vietnamese Studies* 7, no. 3 (2012): 7–54.
Rey-Goldzeiguer, Annie. *Aux origines de la guerre d'Algérie 1940–1945: De Mers-el-Kébir aux massacres du Nord-Constantinois*. La Découverte, 2002.
Richie, Beth E. *Arrested Justice: Black Women, Violence, and America's Prison Nation*. New York University Press, 2012.
Rigouste, Mathieu. "L'ennemi intérieur: De la guerre coloniale au contrôle sécuritaire." *Cultures et Conflits* 67 (automne 2007): 157–174.
Rios, Jodi. *Black Lives and Spatial Matters: Policing Blackness and Practicing Freedom in Suburban St. Louis*. Cornell University Press, 2020.
Roberts, Mary Louise. *What Soldiers Do: Sex and the American GI in World War II France*. University of Chicago Press, 2013.
Roché, Sebastian. *Le frisson de l'émeute: Violences urbaines et banlieues*. Seuil, 2006.
Rosenberg, Clifford. *Policing Paris: The Origins of Modern Immigration Control Between the Wars*. Cornell University Press, 2018.
Roth, Arlette. *Le théâtre algérien de langue dialectale, 1926–1954*. F. Maspero, 1967.
Roubaud, Louis. *Pays de Marseille*. Gallimard, 1933.
Rougelet, Patrick. *RG: La machine à scandales*. Albin Michel, 1997.
Ryan, Donna. *The Holocaust and the Jews of Marseille: The Enforcement of Anti-Semitic Policies in Vichy France*. University of Illinois Press, 1996.

Saada, Emmanuelle. "La loi, le droit et l'indigène." *Droits* 43 (2006): 165–190.
Saada, Emmanuelle. *Les enfants de la colonie: Les métis de l'empire français entre sujétion et citoyenneté*. La Découverte, 2007.
Sachs, Miranda. "'But the Child Is Flighty, Playful, Curious': Working-Class Boyhood and the Policing of Play in Belle Époque Paris." *Historical Reflections/Réflexions Historiques* 45, no. 2 (2019): 7–27.
Salinas, Alfred. *Les Américains en Algérie, 1942–1945*. L'Harmattan, 2013.
Sanders, Paul. *Histoire du marché noir: 1940–1946*. Perrin, 2001.
Sayad, Abdelmalek. *La double absence: Des illusions de l'émigré aux souffrances de l'immigré*. Seuil, 1999.
Scheck, Raffael. "Nazi Propaganda Towards French Muslim Prisoners of War." *Holocaust and Genocide Studies* 26, no. 3 (2012): 447–477.
Schwartz, Paula. *Today Sardines Are Not for Sale: A Street Protest in Occupied Paris*. Oxford University Press, 2020.
Scott, James C. *Seeing Like a State: How Certain Schemes to Improve the Human Condition Have Failed*. Yale University Press, 1998.
Seigel, Micol. *Violence Work: State Power and the Limits of Police*. Duke University Press, 2018.
Séquin, Caroline. *Desiring Whiteness: A Racial History of Prostitution in France and Colonial Senegal, 1848–1950*. Cornell University Press, 2024.
Sessions, Jennifer. *By Sword and Plow: France and the Conquest of Algeria*. Cornell University Press, 2015.
Shabazz, Rashad. *Spatializing Blackness: Architectures of Confinement and Black Masculinity in Chicago*. University of Illinois Press, 2015.
Shepard, Todd. *Sex, France and Arab Men, 1962–1979*. University of Chicago Press, 2018.
Simon, Jacques. *L'immigration algérienne en France: Des origines à l'indépendance*. Paris-Méditerranée, 2000.
Simon, Jacques. *Messali Hadj, 1898–1974: Chronologie commentée*. L'Harmattan, 2002.
Sinclair, Georgina, and Chris A. Williams. "'Home and Away': The Cross-Fertilisation between 'Colonial' and 'British' Policing, 1921–85." *Journal of Imperial and Commonwealth History* 35, no. 2 (2007): 221–238.
Slaouti, Omar, and Fabien Jobard. "Police, Justice, Etat: Discrimination raciales." In *Racismes de France*, edited by Omar Slaouti and Olivier Le Cour Grandmaison. La Découverte, 2020.
Spire, Alexis. *Etrangers à la carte: L'administration de l'immigration en France, 1945–1975*. Grasset, 2005.
Stoler, Ann Laura. *Along the Archival Grain: Epistemic Anxieties and Colonial Common Sense*. Princeton University Press, 2009.
Stoler, Ann Laura. *Carnal Knowledge and Imperial Power: Race and the Intimate in Colonial Rule*. University of California Press, 2002.
Stoler, Ann Laura, ed. *Haunted by Empire: Geographies of Intimacy in North American History*. Duke University Press, 2006.
Stora, Benjamin. *Histoire de l'Algérie coloniale (1830–1954)*. La Découverte, 1991.
Stora, Benjamin. *Ils venaient d'Algérie: L'immigration algérienne en France (1912–1992)*. Fayard, 1992.
Stora, Benjamin. *Messali Hadj: Pionnier du nationalisme Algérien, 1898–1974*. L'Harmattan, 1986.
Storm, Eric, and Ali Al Tuma, eds. *Colonial Soldiers in Europe, 1914–1945: "Aliens in Uniform" in Wartime Societies*. Routledge, 2015.
Surkis, Judith. *Sex, Law, and Sovereignty in French Algeria, 1830–1930*. Cornell University Press, 2019.

Taieb-Carlen, Sarah. *The Jews of North Africa: From Dido to de Gaulle.* University Press of America, 2010.

Takabvirwa, Kathryn. "Citizens in Uniform: Roadblocks and the Policing of Everyday Life in Zimbabwe." *American Ethnologist* 50, no. 2 (2023): 236–246.

Tal, Yuval. "The 'Latin' Melting Pot: Ethnorepublican Thinking and Immigrant Assimilation in and Through Colonial Algeria." *French Historical Studies* 44, no. 1 (2021): 85–118.

Taraud, Christelle. *La prostitution coloniale: Algérie, Tunisie, Maroc (1830–1962).* Payot, 2003.

Taraud, Christelle. "Les *yaouleds*: Entre marginalisation sociale et sédition politique." *Revue d'histoire de l'enfance "irrégulière"* 10 (2008): 59–74.

Taylor, Keeanga-Yamahtta. *From #BlackLivesMatter to Black Liberation.* Haymarket Books, 2016.

Témime, Emile. *Marseille transit: Les passagers de Belsunce.* Autrement, 1997.

Témime, Emile, Marie-Françoise Attard-Maraninchi, and Jean-Jacques Jordi, eds. *Migrance: Histoire des migrations à Marseille; Vol. 3, Le cosmopolitisme de l'entre-deux-guerres, 1919–1945.* Edisud, 1990.

Thénault, Sylvie. "L'état d'urgence (1955–2005): De l'Algérie coloniale à la France contemporaine; destin d'une loi." *Le Movement Social,* no. 218 (2007): 63–78.

Thomas, Douglas. *Sufism, Mahdism and Nationalism: Limamou Laye and the Layennes of Senegal.* Continuum, 2011.

Thomas, Martin. *Violence and Colonial Order: Police, Workers and Protest in the European Colonial Empires, 1918–1940.* Cambridge University Press, 2012.

Traoré, Assa, and Elsa Vigoureux. *Lettre à Adama.* Seuil, 2017.

Vince, Natalya. *Our Fighting Sisters: Nation, Memory and Gender in Algeria, 1954–2012.* Manchester University Press, 2015.

Vitale, Alex S. *The End of Policing.* Verso, 2021.

Weil, Patrick. "Racisme et discrimination dans la politique française de l'immigration 1938–1945/1974–1995." *Vingtième Siècle Revue d'histoire* no. 47 (1995): 77–102.

Wilder, Gary. *The French Imperial Nation-State: Negritude and Colonial Humanism between the Two World Wars.* University of Chicago Press, 2005.

Zimmerman, Sarah. *Militarizing Marriage: West African Soldiers' Conjugal Traditions in the Modern French Empire.* Ohio University Press, 2020.

Zisenwine, Daniel. *The Emergence of Nationalist Politics in Morocco: The Rise of the Independence Party and the Struggle against Colonialism after World War II.* I. B. Tauris, 2010.

Index

Ababsa, Abdelhamid, 155
Abbas, Ferhat, 32, 50, 128–129, 153, 157
Aix-En-Provence, 139
Akli, Mohamed, 55–57, 108, 116–117
alcohol, 37, 134–135
   use by North Africans, 39–40, 56, 96–97, 115–117, 151, 174
   use by police officers, 29, 177
Algerian citizenship, 4, 93, 115, 141–142, 152–154
   reforms to, 60, 129–130
Algerian nationalism, 14, 109–110, 114–117, 132–133, 145–148, 154
   arms trafficking, 162–165
   history of, 50, 109, 157
   nationalist cultural production, 155–156, 165–169, 172–173
   policing of, 106–107, 157–159, 169–173, 178–179, 182
Algerian police officers
   in Algiers, 26, 28, 55–57, 108–109, 116–117, 158, 183
   in Marseille, 79–81, 184
   See also individual officers
Algerian theater, 167–168
Algerian War of Independence, 178–179, 182–184
L'Algérie Libre (newspaper), 170–171
Algiers School of Psychology, 33
Allied Forces (WWII), 101–102, 112–113, 126–129, 131, 153
   African American GIs, 163
   conflict with soldiers, 116, 137
   Operation Torch, 99–102, 109, 112, 116, 131–132
Amazigh, 2n4, 19, 106, 140
   police competency in, 27, 30–33, 60, 62, 158
   See also Kabyle
anti-Blackness, 9, 12, 134
anti-French, 54, 102, 113–118, 127, 147, 173
   black market, 120–122, 124, 152
anti-national, 113–118, 126, 133
   See also anti-French
antisemitism, 121
   in Algiers, 50, 112

history in North Africa, 111
   Vichy policy, 78–79, 111, 127
apaches, 35
apolitical organizations, 166–167
Arab Bureaus, 130
Arabic (language), 69, 78, 116, 140
   Arabic-language theater, 167
   German propaganda, 111, 113
   police competency in Algiers, 27, 30–33, 106, 108–109, 158, 165–166, 168
   police competency in Marseille, 30–33, 106, 143
   SAINA competency in, 58–60, 63
   See also translation
archives, 13–14, 40–41, 104, 107, 124–125, 159, 175
arms trafficking, 162–165
assault, 108, 147–148, 150–151, 186
   sexual assault, 41–43, 137n55
   by soldiers, 55, 134–136
   See also police violence
Association des Amis du Manifeste et de la Liberté, 133, 157
Association des Musulmans Algériens de Marseille (AMA), 139, 144, 152, 160, 172
Association of Republican Police Resistors, 132
Atlantic Charter, 128
Aziel, Méziane, 167

Bab El Oued, 90, 149–150
baptism, 32, 166
Bardin, René, 174–176
Beaux-Arts Museum (Algiers), 93–94
Behind the Bourse, 66, 68, 86–87, 89, 143–144, 152
   urban history of, 21–23, 180
Ben Abdallah, M'haer, 107
Ben Badis, Abdelhamid, 50, 70
Ben Chaouch, Mahmoud ben Omar, 79–81
Benchebana, Edouard, 176
Ben Hadj, Mohamed, 61–62, 86–87
Benichou, Salomon, 29
Bernardie, Lucien, 158–159
bidonvilles, 141–142, 147, 180
Black Lives Matter, 185

black market, 90, 108, 162, 165
  cigarette trafficking, 119, 150–153
  European participation in, 118–119, 123, 149
  policing of, 118–126, 149–153
Blanchard, Emmanuel, 10, 57n44, 160, 179n119, 183n15
Blum, Léon, 60
Blum-Viollette Law, 60
Boittin, Jennifer, 10n53
Bollenot, Vincent, 11n57, 58n55, 107n23
Boufedji affair, 68–69
Boukerdenna, Abderrahmane, 53–54, 91–92, 97–98
Boukroufa, Messaoud, 53
Boulevard Cervantes, 92, 177
Bourgeois, Jules, 141
Bouzaréah, 158
Bretin, Marius, 29
Brigade de la Bourse, 143–145
Brigade Nord-Africaine (BNA)
  of Marseille, 57, 59, 64, 142–144
  of Paris, 57, 59, 79–80, 142, 157
Bultel, Gabriel, 176–177
Bureau des Affaires Musulmanes Nord-Africaines (BAMNA), 82, 104, 132
  creation of, 78
  dissolution of, 131, 142
Busquant, Émilie, 158–159

café maures, 2, 62, 67–69, 72, 107, 124, 169
caïd, 44, 64
Canebière, 170
Camp Lyautey, 83–86, 99, 103–104, 138
Carlier, Omar, 72n135, 169
Casbah, 67, 134–135, 137
  black market in, 122–124, 150
  policing of, 52–57, 96–97, 116, 145–146, 165–166, 181–182
  prostitution in, 21, 36–37, 53, 116, 134
  urban history, 2, 18–21, 141, 180
Catroux, Georges, 133–134
Centre d'Information et d'Études (CIE), 50, 78n29
Cercle du Progrès, 70
chaouch, 58, 61, 86
circulaire, 43, 52n19, 77
  Circulaire Michel, 70–71
circumcision ceremony, 32, 166
citizen complaint letters, 65,149
  from Europeans, 38–40, 68, 84–85, 91–93, 120–121, 144–145, 147, 152
  from North Africans, 64–66, 92–93, 95–96, 117, 152, 164, 174, 186
Clos Salembier, 147
Cole, Joshua, 50
colonial racial hierarchies, 5, 9, 134–138, 151–152
colonization of Algeria, 4, 123, 178
colons, 4, 91–93, 98–99, 115–116, 139
color-blind republicanism, 3
  contradictions of, 135, 138, 144–145, 161, 168, 179
  legal reforms, 129–130, 148–149, 153–154
commune de plein exercise, 4
commune mixte, 58
Communist Party
  influence on North Africans, 69, 71, 109, 169
  police targeting of, 7, 77, 95, 106–107, 114, 132, 157, 165
  publications, 51–52, 178
concubinage, 38, 108
Congrès Musulman, 72
Constantine
  Constantine Riots (1934), 50, 53–54
  department of, 119, 146, 153–154, 175
coreligionnaires, 66, 116, 119, 135, 143, 147, 177
corruption, 2, 29, 45, 64–65, 80, 91, 132
Corsican immigrants, 28, 117n73, 142, 152
Costes, Georges, 167
Cours Belsunce, 23, 42, 151, 170
Crémieux Decree, 4–5, 78–79
criminology, 33
Crouse, Elizabeth, 19
customs (police service), 1, 44, 141, 162–165

darija, 30–31, 54, 56, 63, 93, 108, 143
Darlan law, 77
Dazard, Julien, 176–178
Defense of the Casbah Committee, 180
De Gaulle, Charles, 99, 114, 126, 129, 133, 183
Direction of Muslim Affairs, 130
Du Chastaignier, Jean-Baptiste Joseph Lallé, 69–70

economic brigade, 122, 149–150
El Biar, 134, 185
El Hamma, 92–93, 141, 164, 176–177
El Okbi, Tayeb, 32, 70–71
epuration, 131–133
Er-Rachid, 110
Étoile Nord-Africaine (ENA), 50, 109, 157
Evian Accords, 184

fait divers, 34–35, 52, 160–161
Fanon, Frantz, 34n80, 183
fascism, 49, 73, 75–76, 132
Favre, Lucienne, 36–37, 54–56
Feldman, Ilana, 11
foyer, 69–70, 85
Français Musulman, 95, 129–131, 168
Francisi affair, 45
Franco-Algerian couples, 36–40, 85–86, 87n78, 136–137, 158–159
Free French Army, 99, 99n126, 101, 114, 116, 128–129
French Resistance, 114, 116, 118, 129
  police participation in, 131–132
French West Africans, 11, 23, 57, 77, 133–138, 142
  See also tirailleurs sénégalais
Friand, René, 122–123
Front de Libération Nationale (FLN), 28n47, 158n12, 179, 182–183, 185

garde champêtre, 27n45, 32, 74n1
gardes mobiles, 185
Gare St. Charles, 2, 21, 144–145, 171
Garraud, Jean-Marie, 160
Gaubert (police commissioner), 77, 85–86, 107
Gauthier (police commissioner), 90
Gelibert (police officer), 65
gendarmerie, 6, 86, 88, 104, 141, 185
Gianotti, Alice, 85
Giraud, Henri, 116
Godard (police inspector), 149–150
Godin, Pierre, 57
groupes mobiles de réserve, 77
guardian of the peace
  in Algiers, 27, 56, 76, 96–97, 176–177
  in Marseille, 59–61, 105, 151, 170, 174–176
Guelma, 146, 148, 157

Hadj, Messali, 50, 145, 157–158
  marriage to Émilie Busquant, 158–159
  See also ENA, MTLD, PPA
Halle Puget, 24, 65
Hartman, Saidiya, 13
Haut Comité Méditerranéen (HCM), 60
Hebert (police commissionner), 28
Hillal el Djezairi (theater troupe), 168
Hitler, Adolf, 73, 76, 109–113, 132, 145
Hussein Dey, 28, 142, 164

ID cards
  creation of, 43, 95–96, 131
  North African services, 62–63, 78–79, 132, 141

  policing of, 42, 86–87, 89, 120, 144–145, 152, 174–176
îlotier, 53–55, 65, 108, 116
indigénat code, xiii, 4–5, 50, 53, 130–131, 181
Indochinese migrants, 11, 57, 77, 142, 173
informants, 69, 78, 83–84, 106–107, 119, 140, 161
intermediaries, 27, 64, 70
  corruption, 80–81
  North African bureaus, 62, 84
  police, 30, 45, 49, 57, 90–91, 104–105, 137–138
intimacy, 10–11, 27–28, 117–118, 126, 179
  daily life, 66–72, 83, 126, 152–154, 156, 164–169, 172–173
  relationships, 36–43, 102–105, 136–137, 139–140, 158–159
  spatial, 49, 62, 92
Islam, 5, 79, 120–121, 130, 135
  hadj (pilgrimage), 71, 166
  Marseille mosque, 72
  Paris mosque, 71–72
  policing of, 31–32, 70–72, 116, 166–167, 172
  politics, 50, 113, 157–158
Italian immigration, 7, 27–28, 30–31, 68, 93, 115–116, 159
  policing of, 41–43, 45, 114, 117, 142

Janon, René, 48, 64
Jardin d'essais, 93
judicial police, 159–160, 183n15

Kabyle, 2n4, 58, 62–63, 119, 172
  migration to Casbah, 19–20
  migration to Marseille, 21
  See also Amazigh
Kalman, Samuel, 7n31, 8n40, 27n41, 27n44, 121n95, 132n25, 169n69
Kasderli, Mostefa, 167–168
Kitson, Simon, 6n24, 77n23
Kocher, Adolphe, 33–34, 36, 41
Kouba, 19, 41n113, 124–125
Klein (guardian of the peace), 96–98

labor, 75, 77, 82–83, 99, 138, 178
  requis labor, 81–89, 124–125
Lafond, Georges, 123–124
Lainyech (police commissioner), 90–91
LaJeunesse (police commissionner), 166
Lamoudi, Lamine, 113
Le Beau, Georges, 50
Lefebvre, Henri, 12
legitimate defense, 56, 173–178

Little Casbah, 92–94, 141, 176–177
Londres, Albert, 23
Luhaka, Théo, 185

Macron, Emmanuel, 186
Mahieddine, Bachetarzi, 172–173
Mamane, Salomon, 78
mapping race, 11–13, 35–36, 99, 126, 153, 162, 181
   in Algiers, 121–122
   in Marseille, 86–89, 114, 143–145, 170
Marabuto (police commissionner), 101
marketplace, 89–92, 122–123
Marquillanes, Pierre, 147–148
masculinity, 29, 36–43, 105, 136–138, 140, 159
matraque, 52–53, 56, 176
mauresque, 91, 140
   architecture, 180
   See also North African women
Mehdi, Ahmed Saïd, 35
Mercadal, François, 140
Merzouk, Nahel, 16, 185–186
Mezergues, Georges, 32
Ministry of Labor, 83
Ministry of the Interior, 51, 58–59, 78, 84, 111, 130
   correspondence with, 115, 146, 172
Ministry of Youth and Education, 167
Mohamed V, Sultan of Morocco, 170–172
Moroccan immigrants, 44–45, 58, 82, 85, 103, 140, 160n18
Morocco, 11, 21, 23, 44, 84, 170, 172
Mouré, Kenneth, 119n80
Mouvement pour le Triomphe des Libertés Démocratiques (MTLD), 157–159, 167
Municipal Council of Algiers, 6, 27–28, 44, 134, 180
   Algerian councilors, 27, 32, 37, 53–54, 67, 91–92, 97–98, 150
music, 68, 108, 155–156, 165–169, 172
Muslim Scouts, 167

Napoleon III, 19
Nasiali, Minayo, 180n3
National Ministry of Information, 159–160
Nazi Germany, 128–129, 145
   antisemitism, 79, 117, 121
   military, 73, 76
   propaganda among North Africans, 80, 82, 109–116, 126, 132
North African criminality, 8, 94, 184–186
   colonial ethnography, 33–34
   in *fait divers*, 34–35, 160–161

   police conceptions of, 11–13, 35–36, 58, 119–121, 142–143, 151–153, 181–182
   politics, 178
   statistics, 7, 143, 156, 159–162
North African immigration, 3–5, 31, 43, 57, 144, 184–185
   to Algiers, 20–21, 122n99, 141–142
   family migration, 37, 138–140
   fear of, 140–141, 160
   illegal immigration, 44–46, 138, 141, 171
   to Marseille, 5, 21–23, 61, 103, 139, 161n29, 184n21
   regulation of, 37, 43–44, 46, 120, 130, 138–139, 144
North African Jews, 4–5, 111
   in Algiers, 54, 168
   in Marseille, 21, 29, 45, 60, 79n37, 119n92
   under Vichy, 74–75, 77–79, 95, 99, 121, 132
North African merchants, 23–24, 65–66, 87–88, 91–92, 122, 136, 150
North African sexuality, 43, 85
   homosexuality, 36, 40–43
   relationships with European women, 37–40
North African women, 104–105, 130, 159, 169
   in Algiers, 36–37, 68–69, 90–92, 169
   in Marseille, 37, 84–85, 121, 139–140
   See also mauresque

Office de la Main-d'œuvre Indigène (MOI), 82, 85
Oran, 99n126, 121, 153, 155
Oulid, Aïssa, 67

Papon, Maurice, 183
Paris, 36, 76, 106, 109–111, 129, 170, 183
   Algerian nationalism in, 50, 182–183
   Brigade Nord-Africaine, 57, 59, 79–80
   North African migration to, 119, 139, 163
   policing of North Africans in, 10n51, 16, 160, 183
   SAINA, 57–58, 71–72, 130
Parti du Peuple Algérien (PPA)
   history of, 50, 157
   policing of, 116–117, 133, 155–156, 163, 165–166, 168, 172
   See also Hadj, Messali
Parti Populaire Français, 76
peddler, 32, 122
   See also street vendor
Pétain, Philippe, 75–76, 96, 108, 112, 126
Place Jules Guesde, 180
police demographics, 26–29, 31, 109
police d'état, 27, 106, 109, 123, 132, 142, 146

nationalization, 6, 26, 77
police violence, 7, 9–11, 16, 30, 148, 185–186
  critiques of, 132, 178
  against North Africans, 28, 32, 56, 65–66, 87, 96–99, 122–123, 173–178
  October 17th massacre (Paris), 183
  passage à tabac, 51–52
  protests, 146–147, 170, 182
polygamy, 36, 105
Popular Front, 60–61
port, 11, 84
  blockage, 102–103
  North African connection to, 21, 23, 83, 119
  policing of, 31, 42–45, 139–141, 163–164
Porte d'Aix, 41, 107, 136, 172
Poussardin, Louis, 60, 62–64, 66, 86–87, 132
Prakash, Amit, 12n64, 49n5
prisoners of war, 77n18, 111–112, 138
prostitution, 6, 38, 107–108, 134–137, 144, 167
  in the Casbah, 21, 36–37, 43

quartiers nord (Marseille), 69, 171, 180

racial profiling, 36, 75, 88–89, 142, 152, 170–173, 185
rationing, 90–91, 107–108, 118, 122, 126, 149
Régnier Decree, 51–52
Régnier, Marcel, 51
Renseignements Généraux (RG), 106–109
  of Algiers, 74, 112–113, 117, 124, 157, 167
  of Marseille, 80–81, 139–140, 142, 144, 160, 163, 172
  Service for North African Affairs, 38, 59, 80, 108
repatriation, 44, 77, 88, 105, 111–112, 138–139, 140–141
  by SAINA, 7, 60–62
  World War II, 84–85, 102–103, 111–112, 138–139
requis, 81–89, 99, 124–125, 145
Rigouste, Mathieu, 126n118
Rios, Jodi, 13n66, 99n127
Rozis, Augustin, 67
Rue des Chapeliers, 2, 104, 136–137
  arms trafficking, 162–165
  black market on, 120, 150–152
  criminality in, 35, 45, 65, 126, 153, 160, 181–182
  policing of, 68, 72, 86, 107, 153
  raids on, 86–89, 120, 170–171
  urban history, 23–24, 37, 48, 135, 144, 180
Rue Marengo, 20–21, 54, 56, 72
Rue Randon, 19–20, 48, 54

policing of, 55, 91–92, 116–117, 122, 150, 165–166

Safrana, Albert, 168–169
Saint-Eugène, 19
Sallet (police commissionner), 31, 44
Saurat, Auguste, 66
Secretary General for Indigène Affairs and Police, 130
segregation, 12–13, 19, 23–24, 37, 116, 133–138, 146–147
Seigel, Micol, 9
Service de Contrôle et d'Assistance en France des Indigènes des Colonies (CAI), 11n57, 57, 58n48, 130nn17–18, 142n87
Service des Affaires Algériennes (SAA), 78–80, 87–88, 103, 108, 111, 114–115, 119–120
  surveillance of requis, 82–84
  See also Wender, Robert
Service des Affaires Indigènes Nord-Africaines (SAINA), 66, 68–69, 71–72, 86–87, 130–131, 144
  creation, 58–60
  duties, 61–65
  of Paris, 57, 59, 71
  reorganization of, 78
Service des Liaison Nord-Africains (SLNA), 155–156
Sétif, 146, 148, 157, 168
special police, 45–46, 77, 82, 85, 105–109, 157
state of emergency, 183
statistics, 7, 33, 61, 143, 156, 159–162
stereotypes
  black market, 119, 124, 152
  criminality, 23, 33–36, 48–49, 52–53, 142–143, 159–162, 181
  gendered, 36–43, 137, 139–140
street vendor, 32, 91–92, 123
  See also peddler
Sûreté, 6, 59, 78, 86–87, 185
Susini (police commissionner), 89–90

Takabvirwa, Kathryn, 11n54
Talmoudi, Hamouda, 144, 152, 160, 174
theater, 108, 155–156, 167–169, 172–173
theft, 41, 64, 74, 89–90, 134–135, 144, 147
  as "Algerian" crime, 33–35, 49, 119, 123–124, 161–162, 181, 184
tirailleurs algériens, 133, 163
  WWI, 5, 15, 114
  WWII, 76–77, 129, 110–112, 138–139
tirailleurs sénégalais, 11, 55, 71, 129, 133–138
Tixier, Adrien, 130–131

Tizi Ouzou, 19
Todt, 82
torture, 55, 172–173, 178–179, 183–184
Tournée Mahieddine, 172–173
translation, 27–33, 45, 54–55, 61–63, 83,
    106–108, 168
Trans-Mediterranean world, 3–6, 17–18,
    43–46, 102–105, 138–142, 162–165, 181
Traoré, Adama, 185
Tunisia, 21, 23, 44, 82, 103, 156, 160n18

'Ulamā, 50, 70–71, 157, 113n52, 144n100
Umm Kulthum, 156
Union Démocratique du Manifeste Algérien
    (UDMA), 157

vagrancy, 23, 39, 88, 120, 140–141
Vichy, 75–77, 101–103, 110, 113–118,
    126–127, 129, 131–133
  police reforms, 77–78
  policing of Jews, 78–79, 95, 99, 111, 117,
    121, 132
  policing of North Africans, 87–89, 95–98
  policy towards Algerians, 78–82
Viel (guardian of the peace), 96–98

vigilante violence, 174–177
  Constantine (1934), 50
  Constantine (1945), 146
  Marseille (1973), 184–185
Ville d'Alger (boat), 182
Vieux-Port, 2, 21
Vrolyk, Frenand, 60–61

Wender, Robert, 78–79, 87–88, 111–112,
    114–115, 119–120, 132n29
World War I, 26, 37, 45, 105, 114
  mobilization, 5, 27, 71
  postwar migration, 21, 34, 43, 57
World War II, 73, 75, 94–95, 101, 118,
    141, 168
  demobilization, 77, 110–112, 133, 135,
    138–139
  liberation, 127–129
  mobilization, 76
  See also Nazi Germany, rationing, Vichy

yaouleds, 93–94, 134–135, 147, 168, 176–177

Zannettacci, Stéphanopoli Jean, 58–60
Zeralda affair, 74–75, 95, 98–99

www.ingramcontent.com/pod-product-compliance
Lightning Source LLC
Chambersburg PA
CBHW030535230426
43665CB00010B/907